Patterns of Poverty in the Third World

Charles Elliott
assisted by
Francoise de Morsier

Published in cooperation with
the World Council of Churches

The Praeger Special Studies program—
utilizing the most modern and efficient book
production techniques and a selective
worldwide distribution network—makes
available to the academic, government, and
business communities significant, timely
research in U.S. and international economic, social, and political development.

Patterns of Poverty in the Third World

A Study of Social and Economic Stratification

Praeger Publishers   New York   Washington   London

PRAEGER SPECIAL STUDIES IN INTERNATIONAL ECONOMICS AND DEVELOPMENT

Library of Congress Cataloging in Publication Data

Elliott, Charles, 1939-
    Patterns of poverty in the Third World.

    (Praeger special studies in international economics
and development)
    Includes bibliographical references and indexes.
    1. Africa—Economic conditions.   2. Asia—Economic
conditions.   3. Income—Africa.   4. Income—Asia.
5. Poverty.   6. Underdeveloped areas—Social conditions.   I. De Morsier, Francoise, joint author.
II. Title.
HC505.P6E44   1975   330.9'172'4   75-1223
ISBN 0-275-09920-2
ISBN 0-275-89300-6 (pbk.)

PRAEGER PUBLISHERS
111 Fourth Avenue, New York, N.Y. 10003, U.S.A.

Published in the United States of America in 1975
by Praeger Publishers, Inc.

Printed in the United States of America

This report was commissioned in April 1972 by the World Council of Churches and financed by a consortium that included the Council, Sodepax (a joint committee of the Council and the Pontifical Commission Justice and Peace), the Canadian International Development Agency, the Canadian Catholic Organization for Development and Peace, and the Primate's World Relief and Development Fund. Subsequently, the Overseas Development Ministry, London, gave a grant towards travel in Asia. The study was undertaken at the University of East Anglia under the direction of the principal author, a member of the Overseas Development Group.

A small number of special studies were either directly commissioned or partially financed. These are acknowledged in the text, where major findings are presented. Those used in this volume are:

M. Abdel-Fadil, University of Cairo/Department of Applied Economics, Cambridge: *Employment and Income Distribution in Egypt, 1952-1970.*

D.G.R. Belshaw, Overseas Development Group, University of East Anglia: *Equity Trends in Kenya: A Case Study in an Agrarian Economy.*

R.B. Charlick, Centre Ivoirien de recherches economiques et sociales, Abidjan, Ivory Coast: *The Socio-Economic and Regional Origins of Ivorien Students at the University of Abidjan.*

Sam Nii Dodoo, University of Ghana: *The Distributive Effects of the Taxation of Cocoa Farmers 1947-1966.*

J. Ofori-Atta, University of Ghana: *The Political and Economic Issues on the Growth and Pattern of Government Expenditures in Ghana, 1957-1969.*

A. Shorter, Gaba Pastoral Institute, Uganda: *Concepts of Social Justice in Traditional Africa.*

Ellen Sondermeijer, University of Leiden, The Netherlands: *A Socio-Medical Study of Villages in Volta Region, Ghana.*

Additionally, the following post-graduate students of the School of Development Studies worked on a number of specific problems: Michael Grainger, Jeremy Lester, Nigel Rayner, and Sumit Roy.

Linda Platten-Jarvis undertook much of the statistical work. Helen Kenyon and Anne Maw successively oversaw the detailed administration and secretarial servicing of the project. Michael Jones drew the diagrams. We are most grateful to all four for their industry, good humour, and horse-sense.

Drafts at various stages of incompletion were read by Athole Mackintosh, Richard Jolly, Chris Edwards, Tony Barnett, Leon de Rosen, Julio de Santa Ana, Diogo de Gaspar, and Paul Streeten. Chris Edwards was generous in sharing with us his own continuing work on industrialization in Malaysia. We benefitted hugely from the comments of these colleagues. The many remaining imperfections are our responsibility alone.

Charles Elliott
Francoise de Morsier

CONTENTS

vii

LIST OF TABLES AND FIGURES

xi

Patterns of Poverty in the Third World

1

ENRICHMENT AND IMPOVERISHMENT

THE THEME

The basic configuration of world poverty is well known. Although the detailed statistics are unreliable, the services of a statistician are not required to establish that the majority of mankind is ill-fed, ill-clothed, ill-housed, under-educated, and prey to preventable disease.

This book asks why.

Is it inevitable? Are there really so many people and such scarce resources that all cannot have enough? Or is it merely a temporary phenomenon which time and the application of more productive techniques will cure?

Or is world poverty the result of a causal chain that runs from the rich to the poor at both the international and the national levels?

On the answer to these questions depends not only the designs of programmes to eradicate poverty in the so-called Third World, but, more critical for most of the readers of this book, the specification of the strategy towards the kind of society that has a long-term future in the rich world.

If we believe that world poverty is the result of too many people and too few goods, as those who lay great emphasis on "the population explosion" or the "finitude of space-ship Earth" would have us believe, then a basic strategy must be to reduce the growth of population and increase the supply of goods. If we believe that over time the laws of supply and demand will establish an optimal equilibrium in the national and the international markets, as we are told by those who put great faith in market mechanisms, then we must be careful not to interfere with the operation of those laws. If we believe that the fundamental cause of world poverty is the ability of the privileged to protect and extend their privileges, then we, the rich, need to look very carefully at the structure of our own society as a necessary *precondition* of the eradication of world poverty.

But how do we decide between these contending viewpoints? In a field where such facts as are available have been specified to answer quite different questions, and where even the most purblind economist recognizes the need to take account of non-economic (and often unquantifiable) factors, the inevitable temptation is to choose one cosmology, one world view, one ideological position and then select data, with greater or less intellectual discipline, to illustrate the relevance of that chosen frame of reference. We impugn neither the motives nor the scholarship of authors who have done this, but we believe that the result has at best a very partial resemblance to reality.

The neo-classical economist, who with Harry Johnson believes that "the remedies for the main fault which can be found with the use of the market mechanism, its undesirable social effects, are luxuries which under-developed countries cannot afford to indulge in if they are really serious about attaining a high rate of development," may duck the issue entirely.[1] At best, he will look to a minimum of government intervention to relieve the most obvious absolute poverty, and to time and the market to remove the most threatening relative poverty. It would be mistaken to imagine that such an approach is wholly discredited. Rather more recent neo-classical writers have emphasized less the conflict between growth and equity than the part prices can play in reconciling that conflict. One major international mission, publishing its report in 1974, has laid very great emphasis on market mechanisms, on "getting the prices right," on "not pricing oneself out of the export market," on resisting attempts to protect unskilled labourers in the towns by the aggressive application of minimum wages.[2]

To the structuralist, this emphasis on markets flies in the face of the fact that the most cursory examination of any developing country reveals the imperfection of the market mechanism. Interest groups, institutions, and structures of all sorts—political, administrative, legal, tenurial, and industrial—combine to ensure that markets work imperfectly, if at all. That imperfection may arise from quite "neutral" technical factors, or from the fact that markets are manipulated, biased, and influenced to work in ways that do not conflict with the perceived interests of those in power. The structuralist therefore would lay emphasis upon the institutional forces that bias the nature and distribution of the social product against the poorest. One particular quasiinstitution that he would investigate is technology. Laying emphasis on international transfers of technology, he would trace their influence not only on the nature of the productive process but also on the specification of the product and the generation of administrative and political relationships.

In this he would be approaching a neo-Marxist analysis. At the margin, these two cosmologies become almost indistinguishable, but the neo-Marxist would start from an analysis of the distribution of political power and seek to explain it in terms of the distribution of the ownership of productive assets.[3] He would argue that the distribution of the product follows directly from the distribution of power. He would therefore expect to see the most powerful groups gradually (or perhaps rather quickly) specifying the nature, and assuming the major part, of the social product.

Each of these approaches has its attractions, each its pitfalls. Neo-classical analysis can too easily obscure the multifaceted nature of reality. Interdisciplinary research on a foundation of neo-classical economics is not usually convincing. The structuralist analyst can explain too much in terms of structure and too little in terms of the pressure of the market and the ways in which institutions can adapt to those pressures, and also too little in terms of the political determinants of the speed of that adaptation. Neo-Marxists tend to be long on theory, much of it illuminating, but short on empirical demonstrations of that theory. There are good reasons for this, two being, first, that the exercise of political power can often only be observed indirectly though its effects and, second, that in sub-Saharan Africa (and arguably in Asia) *classes* based on the ownership of productive assets and limited by a common realization of self-interest, have hardly emerged. The first point tends to commit the Marxist to assuming that the effect relates to an assumed cause. He finds it difficult to disentangle what is usually a very complex web of causality, made the more complex by his attempt to fit that complexity to an analytical framework that may be premature.

It is still far too early in our view to look for a theoretical synthesis that brings these three very different approaches into a genuine methodological unity. Gunnar Myrdal and his collaborators have perhaps come nearer than anyone to achieving that. Certainly it is intended as no criticism of *The Asian Drama* to say its major contribution is still destructive, sweeping away much irrelevant and inappropriate theory, rather than erecting a convincing theoretical unity. Our own efforts, as presented in this study, can certainly make no claim to that grand design. Here we present no synthesis; rather, we offer an eclectic approach. (In this we differ from more ambitious writers, notably G. Lensky, who have tried to produce a new synthesis tested against empirical investigation. That Lensky's work is important and constructive is not in dispute, but his historical sweep—and often rather limited historical analysis—offers a dimension of differentiation that is not attempted here. Most of our empirical material has been drawn from post-independence experience, although we have tried to relate that back to the colonial period.[4])

Drawing from each of the three approaches we have outlined, and trying to combine with them elements of British empiricism, we offer an explanatory frame that seems to be consistent with the data. But it is not a predictive model. Nor is it an attempt to present a new theoretical structure based either on an existing corpus of well-tried theory or on a huge body of statistically tested data. It is no more than one logical frame that seems to us to make sense of most of the data we have examined. Those data comprise a rather complex and wide-ranging set of facts, observations, and impressions, drawn from a number of countries with very different cultures, histories, and styles of government. It is precisely this wealth of material that demands an ideological openness, a methodological eclecticism, and simultaneously an analytical model that is sufficiently complex to handle the data but sufficiently clear to be intelligible.

THE FRAME

To emphasize the inevitable provisional nature of this framework and its logical bastardy, we present it first by mildly whimsical analogy. Those who prefer to take their theory neat and those who are determined that their economics shall be not only dismal but dull will, we hope, stay with the argument, assured that we shall soon resume a proper academic sobriety.*

The first illustration shows the major outline of the system: It comprises a set of goldfish bowls, set one on top of another. Each is smaller than the one beneath it, but the fish it contains are larger, although less numerous. Now these bowls are connected by means of access cones, so that a determined or lucky fish can pass from a lower bowl to a higher one. These cones vary in shape, diameter, and position within the bowl. At the simplest, the cone is little more than a cylinder set in the bottom of the bowl. The fish can see clearly the size of the further orifice, the length of the cone, and the feasibility of passing up it. But some cones are set on the convex side of the bowl and may thus give an *illusion* with respect to the real nature of the cone—its size, its length, and the difficulty involved in getting up it.

For reasons that will become clear later, most fish in fact wish to pass into a higher bowl; competition on these access cones is therefore intense. Dozens of fish hurl themselves at the cones, but only relatively few get through.

---

*Those whose sense of the dignity of man exceeds their sense of humour will please note that the analogy is *not* to be taken as in any sense pejorative or derogatory of poor countries in general or of particular groups in those countries. The analogy is indeed not confined to low-income countries, although its application to rich countries is not pursued in this study.

(i) The Access System

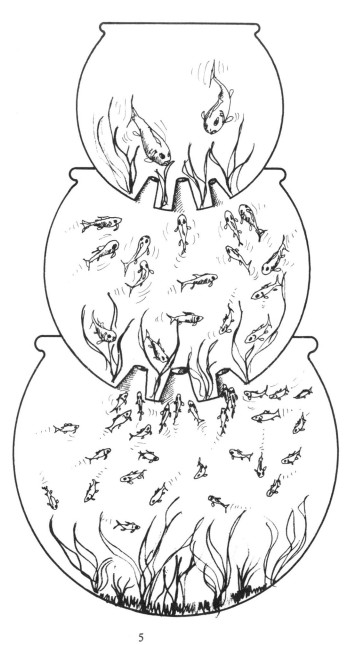

There is a further feature of these cones: They change over time. They may change as a direct result of the pressure on them from below, expanding to meet at least some of the excessive demand for access. Or they may change, in any dimension and in either direction, as a result of the intervention of the fish in the higher bowls. For instance, if the topmost fish think the middle bowls are becoming too full, they may seek to reduce the diameter of one or more of the access cones. In an extreme case, one cone may be closed altogether. Conversely, if the biggest fish want to see more fish in the middle bowls (or even in the top bowl), they can expand (or shorten) the cones.

The *conical* character of these access routes deserves some emphasis. For it implies that it is unusual for a fish to make the reverse passage *down* the system. This is not ruled out. But it is significant, for instance, that most fish in the top bowl have grown too big to make the downward passage—at least through the cones as they currently exist. Once a fish has attained a certain size, then, it is unlikely to go down the system.

So much for access to the different bowls. Let us now turn to the supply of nutrients. These are produced "naturally" in the water without specific location, and constitute the main source of supply for each bowl. But there is a circulatory system that, at the initiative of the topmost fish, can affect the distribution of nutrients as between bowls. It can, for instance, remove nutrients from the bottom bowl and deposit them in higher bowls or vice versa. But as the fish in the higher bowls are larger—and therefore require more nutrition—the *net* flow tends to be from the lower bowl(s) to the higher(est).

However, observation of the behaviour of the system suggests that it is more complicated than this. It is not unknown for fish, especially in the middle bowls, to perceive that the net upward flow of nutrients is large and that access to the higher bowls is exceedingly difficult. When these two phenomena occur together, small groups of the deprived "captive" fish may seek, usually ineffectively, to wreck the system. They may do so by trying to sabotage the circulatory system; by boycotting the access cones; by acts of aggression against individual fish in the higher bowls; or, in an extreme case, by madly hurling themselves at the sides of the bowl in an attempt to knock over the whole structure. As few of them join in these activities, they are usually ineffective.

But since they are at the top of a rather delicately balanced structure, this last activity is particularly decried by the largest fish, and they are in general careful to ensure that the lower fish are not in fact driven to these lengths, and that those that do behave in this way are quickly isolated and eaten. More generally the fish in the top bowl, with the concurrence of those in the next-to-top, try to manage the system through the manipulation of access cones and the distribution of nutrients in such a way that the vast majority of fish regard the system as competitive but acceptable. They have to compete with each other for food and access to a higher bowl. They have to compete with those in

(ii) The Circulation of Nutrients

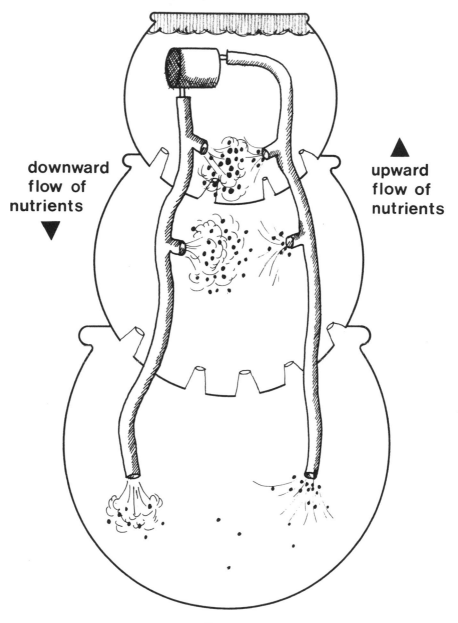

downward
flow of
nutrients
▼

▲
upward
flow of
nutrients

(iii) The Relations with the Outside World

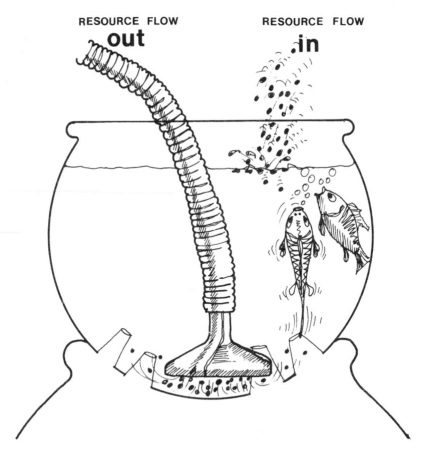

RESOURCE FLOW **out**

RESOURCE FLOW **in**

higher bowls for a greater share in the distribution of nutrients—e.g., by sucking more at the circulation pipe or by more aggressive "shows" of threats to one or more parts of the system. But as long as they can observe *some* of their number rising through the cones and/or *some* nutrients coming from the circulation pipes (although they may not realize that there is still a net loss), they tend to accept this competition as inevitable, or even as appropriate. (Interestingly, attempts by the larger fish to make the access cones larger, or even to increase the net flow of nutrients, are sometimes treated with great suspicion. This suggests that the lower fish held the status quo ante as imperfect but acceptable.

It is important to emphasize that the three-bowl system is not closed. It is open to the "outside" both in terms of access and in terms of the flow of nutrients. The largest fish can be promoted to another set of bowls altogether, inhabited by much larger creatures and characterized by a much more nutritious environment. Some of the antics of the largest fish are thought to be explained by the desire to secure such promotion. Further, nutrients can be sucked out of the system or replaced in it. Evidently, the co-operation of the topmost fish is required for the former (since they control the circulation pump). As regards replacement of nutrients from outside, these are usually scattered on the topmost bowl, where they tend to be eaten by the topmost fish. There are mechanisms by which the largest fish can ensure that these "external" nutrients pass through the circulation system to the bottom bowl; they are, however, not very efficient, principally because the middle-level fish tend to suck them out en route.

There is a final point of considerable importance that a cursory glance at the system may not reveal. Although the fish are segregated in their bowls, roughly according to size, observation shows that there are *vertical* channels of communication between individual fish. This is exhibited in a number of ways—from passing a bolus of food from one bowl to another to a large fish helping a smaller one through an access cone. Although the outward appearance of the system is one of horizontal divisions, vertical mobility, and a net upward movement of nutrients, this vertical relationship must never be lost sight of—its existence may well explain the acceptability of the competitive system.

We suggest that the explanation for inequities between and within countries lies in a fuller understanding of access from one "bowl" to another, the competition within any one "bowl" for resources, and the competition between "bowls" for the resources available.

It is the analysis of these three sets of issues that this book is all about. Accordingly, we do not deal thematically with some of the classical issues currently in vogue among economists and aid strategists. We do not give a thematic treatment to population (although we do discuss the distributional effect of population pressure in terms of differentiation in the rural areas and the relationship between family size and the incidence of poverty). Nor do we explicitly discuss the equity growth trade-off (although much of what we have to say is directly relevant to a dynamic understanding of that trade-off). We fail to include more material on the international aspects of access and competition only because of the lack of adequate data and case studies. We have tried to indicate the ways in which the international dimension fits in; we are conscious of the fact that often we have been unable to do more than that.

That having been said, let us now relate the major themes of the succeeding chapters to the system of goldfish bowls. We take the view that poverty, impoverishment, is the result of a causal process of which enrichment is a major but not exclusive component. We are therefore interested in the three different processes of enrichment and impoverishment: the process of selection, which determines socio-economic status; the intra-group competition, which determines which individuals within the group acquire control over resources; and inter-group competition, which determines how resources are divided between groups with obviously different interests. With regard to selection, we are no less interested in the inverse process by which some are excluded from upward mobility as a result of changes in their economic, social, or family circumstances. It is central to our arguments that both exclusion and downward mobility, which are no more than the processes of relative and absolute impoverishment, are most frequently the reverse image of the enrichment of another group. This may result from direct personal confrontation between individuals with differing bargaining skills and power (as, for instance, in village monopoly/monopsony situations) or it may result from structural biases that are introduced and maintained in order to serve a particular common interest of a specific group that has the power to impose its own sets of preferences upon that structure. Examples of this latter would be the education system, the distribution of credit, wage policy, and many aspects of economic policy.

The interest groups that we identify as crucial in this process are, in very broad terms, fairly clear. Although their size, political leverage, organization, and inter-relationships obviously vary from country to country, they include the political elite, the bureaucratic elite, the owners and/or managers of large businesses, organized ethnic associations (usually incorporating elements from all of the foregoing), the military, landowners and/or large farmers, the representatives of foreign trading and manufacturing interests, and (less frequently) organized urban labour.

These interest groups manipulate processes of selection in order to limit the risk of downward mobility for themselves and to ensure that the structures that benefit them are adequately served with appropriately trained manpower. The avenues of upward mobility or access cones are highly competitive entry points that are biased in favour of selected groups (or the succeeding generations of selected groups). In some cases, when seen from the "bottom," they appear more open (or more "fair") than in fact they are. But the feature that gives them both their own legitimacy and the function of legitimization of those who successfully pass through them is precisely that, despite the biases, some do pass through them. It is important to emphasize that even the most biased processes of selection are not entirely closed. Indeed, if they were so, they would the sooner be revealed for what they are, with the result that they would forfeit both confidence and legitimacy. To survive at all, the structure must allow sufficient genuine upward mobility to preserve that confidence and that legitimacy.

These are key characteristics of processes of differentiation:
1. Individual enrichment
2. Intra-group competition for that enrichment
3. Selective biases within that competition
4. Selective biases that are not obvious to those who compete
5. A system sufficiently "open" to retain competitors' confidence and/or bestow legitimacy on those who compete successfully
6. Acquisition of direct and/or indirect benefit to those who control the mechanism

These traits are so common that we shall call any process of differentiation manifesting them a confidence-mechanism, or con-mech for short. They are confidence-mechanisms because (see 4 and 5 above) they depend for their long-run survival on their ability to retain the belief among competitors that they have a chance—not necessarily an "even" or "fair" chance, but an acceptable (or acceptably unfair) change of winning the competition. That acceptability can be raised by clever propaganda or political diversions of one kind and another; it will not be our purpose to analyse that dynamic here, important as it may be. But one observation is in order: The more obviously and overtly competitive the mechanism, the more the individual is likely to attribute failure to his own shortcomings (e.g., low intelligence) rather than to either biases within the system or the nature of the system itself.

The contrast between characteristics 1 and 6 above is a field of investigation that needs much closer study than it can be afforded here. Analytically one could distinguish between a "strong" and "weak" form of con-mech. In the former, the economic benefits, net of direct costs, under point 6 would exceed those under point 1; in the "weak" case, the sum of individual net benefits of the target group under 1 would exceed the net benefits under 6. We have not attempted to apply that distinction in the analysis; we have had to be content to point out the ways in which economic benefits accrue to ruling interest groups through mechanisms that are supposed to benefit other groups. We have usually referred very briefly to some of the major non-economic benefits—political patronage, propaganda, or the advancement of party interest. This, too, is a field in which much more work might be usefully undertaken in the future.

We shall use the concept of the con-mech extensively. It is therefore important to understand that the concept is not limited to means of access. For example, the process of fiscal redistribution within the system may itself be a con-mech. The classical way of analysing this is in terms of tax burden/benefit ratios. This has made such little progress in the countries in which we are concerned, particularly in terms of the social groups in which we are interested, that we are not able to present classical burden/benefit ratios. What we try to do is to examine the incidence of taxation for the excluded groups, and ask whether structural obstacles to access and take-up bias benefits in favour of or against those groups. We shall argue that the bulk of benefits are annexed by the privileged groups as a result of both political and technical factors. But the confidence of most of the population is maintained, sometimes by tangible benefits, perhaps more often by glamour projects. In that way, the legitimacy of the system is not called into question.

This is an example of a con-mech operating within the arena of inter-group competition. It is a concept, then, that we shall apply to access or mobility, and to inter-group competition. Note that it does not imply that the competition is a zero-sum game in which winners' gains and losers' losses cancel out. That would be an extreme form of con-mech; it is not a defining characteristic. The definition does imply that a considerable (perhaps major) beneficiary group is not involved in the competition—whether for access or resources.

It goes without saying that the con-mechs operate in different ways in the urban and rural areas. Obviously education is a much more powerful access point in the urban areas than it is in the rural. But the similarities are no less striking than the differences. The distribution of credit, of agricultural extension, of access to markets, of the benefits of agricultural research and of land reform—all, we shall argue, are heavily biased against the excluded. The bulk of the benefits are appropriated by those who are already privileged. But none of these systems is closed. They do offer access (or income) to limited numbers of the excluded and therefore maintain both their legitimizing role and the confidence of those who are the victims of biases.

We shall examine (in Chapter 13) one con-mech that operates between the rural and the urban areas, namely, the pricing of foodstuffs. This is fairly familiar ground to economists, who have examined the income and barter terms of trade of farmers for signs that food pricing has an "urban bias."

Let us now turn to intra-group rather than inter-group competition for resources. We have first to deal with the methodological problems. It could be said that the process of competition defines social groups and that intra-group competition is of minimal importance by comparison with inter-group competition. In theory, we agree. In practice, we lack the sociological data to define sufficiently closely the formation and operation of competitive groups in the arenas we highlight. Marxist categories are helpful, but not exclusively so. For we are obliged to define groups very broadly—e.g., progressive farmers, small farmers, wage earners in the formal sector, landless labourers—and therefore have to analyse conflicts for resources within these broadly defined groups. If we could have used a finer definition of interest groups, we could indeed have analysed all competition as inter-group and none as intra-group.

One kind of intra-group competition comes from mutually conflicting objectives within the group. For instance, among unskilled urban workers there are two principal objectives. The first is to increase real wages; the second is to increase the probability of finding employment. As a result of a larger con-mech to which we shall return, the two objectives are regarded as mutually inconsistent by the elite. Since the unemployed have even less political leverage than the unskilled employed, the solution of the conflict tends to favour the latter. It is not true that the solution may favour the unemployed only when they start to threaten the system as a whole. It may well be in the interests of the elite to hold down real wages and perhaps thereby hold down the wage bill of both the private and the public sector and allow employment to expand.* Furthermore, since the time scales of the unemployed, the employed, and the employers are not necessarily identical or congruent, the solution of this kind of intra-group competition may not be readily predictable.

Let us turn now to the total structure. The main feature of this is that a relatively small group (the topmost fish) control much of the production and all the fiscal redistribution in such a way that their interests and their level of living are not seriously threatened. They are sufficiently sophisticated to realize that there are conflicts between the short term and the long term: Short-term costs have to be paid for long-term stability. They make make errors in the assessment of those costs and of the long-run benefits that they accrue from them. As a group, they may be ignorant of those benefits,† or a significant minority (or even a majority) may believe, *or want to believe*, that they cannot change the system in such a way as will enduringly alter the distribution of benefits.

Further, we do not discount completely the altruism or humanitarian interest in the poor, particularly the visible and non-threatening poor. Nonetheless, the elites maintain a system in which function, as hierarchically ordered by

---

*Assuming the elasticity of substitution between labour and other factors is less than one and output remains constant—probably more defensible assumptions in the public than in the private sector.

†But this does not imply that no one understands the benefits. That is unlikely (although not necessarily self-contradictory). We are merely arguing that the "theory of the general plot" is unnecessary until one has examined the "theory of general (but not universal) ignorance and apathy."

them, is differentially rewarded. Despite the huge weight of evidence that suggests that the incentives for progress up this hierarchy are grossly exaggerated or, to put it into more neo-classical terms, that income differentials work in the wrong direction (with the result, for instance, that Sri Lanka has a high level of "A" level unemployment but a shortage of toddy tappers), the system is kept in being. In this sense, the system as a whole is a con-mech. It is, to repeat, a mechanism that depends upon the confidence of the deprived that it is roughly fair and legitimate while delivering to a small group a disproportionate share of privileges. Even though the effective socialization of consumption has nowhere been perfected (and even where it has been tried, as in Cuba, has been abandoned), we cannot wholly ignore the fact that the arbitrary ordering of function and the no less arbitrary connection between function and reward in themselves constitute a con-mech. Any approach to the eradication of poverty that ignores this paradigm of the con-mech is unlikely to prove very helpful.

We put this strongly now because in the chapters that follow we shall be in danger of losing sight of this. We shall present much evidence on changes in differentials, changes in real incomes, differential bargaining power, differential access to productive resources, and all the paraphernalia of the analysis of impoverishment and enrichment.

But every now and again we must stand back from this detailed analysis, important though it is, to ask whether there is any evidence that the structure as a whole can adapt and is adapting to this major con-mech. We shall argue in the final chapter that, whereas the material of the intrastructural con-mechs and inter-group conflicts is remarkably plastic, there is very little evidence that the system as a whole (in the sense of hierarchy of functions and the relationship between function and reward) shares this plasticity.

Details of the system are remarkably adaptable. The essence of the system is wholly unadaptable.

THE METHOD

Our method has been to look at thirteen countries, ten in Africa, three in Asia, chosen on a basis of the relative availability of relevant data to represent a spectrum of alleged political commitment to the eradication of poverty. Thus we have countries—Egypt, Tanzania, and Sri Lanka—that have used, with varying degrees of constancy, a rhetoric of equity and redistribution. On the other wing we have countries—the Philippines, Malaysia, Kenya, and Ivory Coast—that have shown much less, if any, regard for the problems of equity but have rather given economic growth a pre-eminent position in their economic and social strategy. If, slightly unfairly, one likes to put it that way, the latter have taken Harry Johnson's advice, the former have ignored it. We have included in the African countries one extremely poor Sahelian country, Upper Volta, and two very much richer: one, Zambia, with its riches based on an industrial raw material, exploited at independence exclusively by multinational corporations; the other, Ghana, dependent very largely upon an agricultural raw material produced by peasant-farmers. Of the three countries in the ideological middle, one, Cameroon, is nearer to Ivory Coast than to the opposite wing, but it is less dominated by expatriates in general and Frenchmen in particular. Tunisia is nearer the opposite wing, and is particularly interesting because it seems to have solved some problems of educational inequity. Lastly, Uganda flirted with a Tanzanian-type of experiment—and failed.

Clearly we do not regard this group as representative of the Third World as a whole. It is not a sample in any but the most lay sense. Although we sometimes use that word as a synonym for "the countries which we have studied," we should not be taken to be attributing to this group any representative character. There are, for instance, no Latin American countries included in the study. Nor are there any centrally planned economies. Such conclusions as we reach, then, should not be regarded as universal generalizations, however watertight their demonstration seems to be—itself a fairly rare occurrence. At best, patterns that seem applicable to all thirteen countries can form no more than hypotheses to be tested elsewhere.

This raises another more heuristic problem. Is the analysis presented here an attempt to describe a universal law, or hypotheses about a universal law? Or does the main interest lie in the contrasts between the "equity" group and the "growth" group? There is no sound theoretical reason why these two questions should be mutually exclusive, and in the best of all Panglossian worlds we obviously would want to try to formulate a general law based on thirteen observations, and then inspect in close detail the cases that do not conform to that general law. But this research has not been carried out in a Panglossian world. We often have had to draw data and case material from very different countries in order to produce even the main outlines of a feature or phenomenon that we want to analyse. If you can only get five observations, it is surely premature to produce a long disquisition upon why the sixth case does not seem to fit the trend suggested by the five observations. If, on the contrary, one has thirteen observations, and twelve are mutually consistent but one is not, then there obviously is a point in trying to explain the deviance. That, in general, has been our approach.

As a sub-theme throughout the volume, we try to draw attention to significant differences between the two groups of countries. But, as is clear from a quick glance at the chapter headings, our main concern has been to try to produce a synthetic account of the processes of impoverishment and enrichment. As more work is done in this field, so the more analytically interesting identification and explanation of deviance will become possible.

NOTES

1. H.G. Johnson, "Planning and the Market in Economic Development," *Pakistan Economic Journal* 8, no. 2 (1958); republished in *Money, Trade and Economic Growth,* ed. H.G. Johnson (London: Allen and Unwin, 1962).

2. International Labour Organization, *Sharing in Development: Programme of Employment, Equity and Growth for the Philippines* (Geneva: ILO, 1974).

3. For a particularly fine summary of neo-Marxism that does justice to its diversity as well as its intellectual unity, see Aidan Foster-Carter, "Neo-Marxist Approaches to Development and Underdevelopment," in *Sociology and Development,* eds. Ed. de Kadt and G. Williams (London: Tavistock, 1974), pp. 67-108.

4. See G. Lensky, *Power and Privilege: A Theory of Social Stratification* (New York: McGraw-Hill, 1968).

2

RURAL
DIFFERENTIATION
IN EAST AFRICA

In this chapter we shall identify the major con-mechs and inter-group conflicts in the processes of rural differentiation in the four countries of Eastern Africa that we have studied: Kenya, Uganda, Tanzania, and Zambia. The major emphasis will be on the post-independence period, but as the momentum of differentiation began to gather pace during the colonial regime, some of the more significant features of that period will be highlighted. We conclude the chapter by presenting such data as are available on the distribution of rural incomes in an attempt to put the necessarily rather abstract discussion of differentiation into a more quantitative setting.

Differences of enrichment and impoverishment in the rural areas of Africa are not new. Although the extent of differentiation in and, indeed, before colonial times varied greatly, it is a romantic error to imagine that traditional African society was egalitarian in the sense of a perfectly equal distribution of wealth and income. Some tribes were highly hierarchical, and if it was true that no man starved or was unemployed, it also was true that concentrations of wealth and power were at least as great as in much of the modern sector. The Asantehene of Ashanti in West Africa, the King of Buganda in East Africa, and the Paramount Chief of the Lozi in Central Africa are adequate testimony of the economic differentiation of these tribes. Admittedly drawn from West Africa, the following description of the Asantehene's procession gives some idea of the traditional wealth of one of the richest tribes of sub-Saharan Africa:

From early dawn the thousands of people from all parts of Ashanti stream to Manhyia, precinct of the Palace of the Kings of Ashanti. The Chiefs will be seen in their magnificent festive attire of locally woven, stamped, embroidered and appliqued cloths and imported fabrics of silk, velvet, brocade and damask; bedecked with glittering jewelry of silver and gold and

17

precious beads; canopied under large state umbrellas of brilliant colours; stalking to the rhythm of traditional processional music and having carried before and after them several items of their regalia.

The principal figure is the Asantehene who appears in all the traditional splendour and majesty which occupants of the Golden Stool have built up over the centuries. The Golden Stool, which has been described as the "palladium" of the ancient Kingdom of Ashanti, with its own special regalia and those of the Asantehene, will be gracefully carried in the Asantehene's procession by their custodians, clad in their ceremonial robes. Among these are silver and gold plated stools and chairs; ceremonial swords and guns; treasury objects, such as leather wallets with embroidered designs and silver and gold padlocks; a variety of ornamented musical instruments and objects of personal or domestic use, for example, gold-studded sandals, silver and gold plated tobacco pipes, and horse and elephant-tail fly whisks with gilt handles.[1]

It is true that many other tribes were less hierarchical in structure and less economically differentiated. The Masai, Chewa, Benba, and even the Kikuyu, though not wholly egalitarian, had none of the great concentrations of cattle and other assets in the hands of the chief or ruler.

Differentiation was then deeply rooted in traditional society, but to widely differing degrees. But it was differentiation of obligations as well as assets. In theory, if not always in practice, the chief or ruler had concentrations of wealth in order to enable him to meet his social, economic, and cultic obligations. In theory he held them on behalf of all the people, to be used for all the people. The hospitality he gave to strangers, to travellers, to supplicants, to cultic officials, and to military leaders was part of the fulfilment of his own social function. Although the practice sometimes differed from the theory, there were always within traditional society checks on the usurpation of power and of communal wealth, and in an extreme case a consistent usurper would lose his position and his life.

The differentiation was not that of individual wealth achieved by individual effort amassed by the process of appropriating part of the community's surplus for one's sole benefit. At this point, modern urban differentiation and traditional rural differentiation are wholly unlike: Modern rural differentiation comes somewhere between the two, precisely where depending upon the social structure and economic opportunities of the relevant group. The rich farmer of Iringa in Tanzania or Mumbwa in Zambia does not expect his social obligations to increase in parallel with his assets *outside his own kin group or beer circle*. He amasses his wealth by his own energy, foresight, and cunning, and expects to share it within the nuclear family and the kin group. The point needs no labouring. It lies at the heart of critiques of the individualistic ethic and its impact on traditional African society. But it does mean that great caution is necessary in interpreting the historical continuity of rural differentiation in areas that are the tribal homes of highly hierarchical and therefore highly differentiated societies.

CON-MECHS AND COMPETITION IN THE COLONIAL PERIOD

At a first glance one might think that the nature of British rule in Eastern Africa was such that the deliberate construction and introduction of con-mechs was not necessary. The colonial regime did not need a legitimizing process of upward mobility: indeed, given the racial barriers, the whole concept of upward mobility was meaningless. By contrast, we might very well expect to find vigorous inter-group conflict in the rural areas precisely because upward mobility (e.g., from peasant farmer to large-scale producer or even plantation owner) was impossible.

Such a distinction is valid in only the broadest terms. If the main interest of the colonial period is the creation of pressures of *downward* mobility of Africans (e.g., from peasant farmer to landless labourer) as a precondition of the enrichment of European farmers, it should not be too readily assumed that the colonialists had no interest in the structural transformation of at least parts of African agriculture. We shall see that they had a mixture of motives—economic and political—for encouraging a limited degree of upward mobility, which itself generated additional forces for the impoverishment of the excluded.

We need not delay long on the first process—that of the creation of a rural proletariat to service the farms and plantations of the settlers in Zambia, Kenya, and Tanzania (but not Uganda). The creation of this rural proletariat was achieved in a number of ways: the sale of consumer goods, the introduction of poll and capitation taxes, direct forced labour, the prohibition of the cultivation of competitive cash crops by Africans, and the destruction of traditional fallow systems of agriculture (by the creation of overcrowded "reserves") and thereby the generation of a new class of landless labourer or their equivalent. (By the equivalent of landless labourers we mean those who held rights to such small parcels of land, often exhausted land, that they had a strong inducement to leave the land and enter cash employment to ensure their subsistence.)

The emergence of this rural proletariat is obviously a matter of fundamental importance. But as a social group it was and remains inconstant, impermanent, and wholly unstructured. For one of its features is that an individual may take cash employment, working on an estate or a large farm, while maintaining links with—and even his own subsistence plot in—his native or adopted village. Thus at any moment the rural proletariat is itself divided between those who have literally no other form of subsistence except perhaps the small plot allowed them for that purpose by the employer, and those who are, in a very diluted sense of the term, "target workers"—working for a limited period in order to amass savings for a predetermined objective. In colonial days the need to earn money to pay tax, school fees, a fine, or bride price was a common motive for undertaking temporary work.

By contrast with some Asian countries, the pure landless labourer, who has no possibility of providing a subsistence for himself and his family from land that he either owns or enjoys in usufruct, was and remains a relative rarity, except in areas of extreme population pressure.* Some may be temporarily landless because a father is unwilling to give his son land or oxen, or, as it were, voluntarily landless because of tribal disputes or reluctance to return to the native village after an unsuccessful period in town. Some of the involuntarily and permanently landless may accept rural cash employment precisely in order to establish a claim by residence and friendship bonds on the land of their "adopted" clan or tribe. Others will move to less densely settled areas to open up new land. There is evidence of this happening on a huge but unrecorded scale in all four countries of Eastern Africa.[2] But socially it can be a very costly solution.

If this type of differentiation was imposed in the immediate interests of the colonialists, a second (and no less important) type was almost a by-product of their activities. For the colonial era established a demand for labour in the urban as well as the rural areas. This had two major effects. The first was to reduce the labour available in peasant agriculture. Since family income was highly sensitive to labour supply, reduction in labour supply was likely to reduce family consumption. Even in societies where the women did the directly productive work of sowing, weeding, and harvesting, the labour of men was required to clear new land and thus maintain fertility of land under cultivation. Hence derives the great importance of contemporary discussions of stability of the work force. Once men began to settle in town over periods of more than two years, the rate of decline of fertility, especially in shifting cultivation systems, was likely to increase. From the employers' point of view, this stability meant a rise in skill and productivity of the labour force. From the farm families' point of view, it could, in the absence of offsetting technical change and continued remittances from town, bring great hardship (see below, p. 99).

For our purposes, the second effect of this migration is more important, for it was a major motor of inter-group conflict for scarce resources, particularly

---

*Or where, as among the Chagga, the laws of inheritance dispossess some of the sons. Where new land is available, these sons would start new shambas; where it is not, they are obliged to work as labourers.

land. Those who took jobs in the modern sector—on estates or farms, in local government or in town—and worked their way up to less menial (and more highly paid) jobs, were able to amass sufficient savings to buy or develop larger farms in their native areas.

We have a good example of this from Kikuyuland. M.P. Cowen has documented with great care that the athomi (rich farmers) were themselves successful wage-earners or traders in the modern sector or else sons or sons-in-law of such. (He also emphasizes that a poor Kikuyu could inherit land by marrying into the family of a muthomi.[3]) Surveying two areas of Kikuyuland recently, he found that in earlier urban employment, the mean incomes of present-day labourers (or their fathers) had been much lower than those of present-day farmers (or their fathers). In this way occupational differentiation in the urban areas is directly related to economic differentiation in the rural areas. For, of course, the larger farmers required wage labour. By 1948 this was already well established:

The rich man is the progressive farmer in Kikuyu country. He may make his money at trading, but when he has made it he generally converts it into land and goes in for improved methods of cultivation. Though, it may be truly said that a landless class is springing up, it is not really to be regretted as it is the poor and ignorant who ruin the lands and are the least amenable to instruction. Better that these people should seek a living elsewhere or learn to work for the bigger land owner for wages.[4]

And the people did so learn, less because they were ruining their own land than because of population pressure in the Kikuyu Reserve. With no possibility of extending their acreage and with declining fertility, average income per head on the smallest farms inevitably fell. When a secure wage exceeded an insecure subsistence income, wage employment for a large farmer became the lesser of two evils—for men *and* women. This point was approached more rapidly if the family was growing fast, since consumption would then be growing but output would be constant or falling;* or if voluntary or involuntary charges—school fees, fines, taxes—raised the need for income. Only with the occurrence of technological changes—e.g., new crops that could be adopted at the appropriate (i.e., very small) scale—could this extra income be earned from within the farm.

---

*We assume that the possibilities of increasing output through increasing labour input *alone* are very limited. Certainly they are not infinite; thus, even if falling real income per head does not set in immediately, we are safe in assuming that, on small farms, it did so. Contemporary reports of declining fertility are good indirect evidence to this effect.

The scale point is crucial but often overlooked since attention usually is focussed on credit and extension. Take the cases of grade dairy cattle and tea in Kenya, both innovations that raised the potential (and actual) labour productivity of small farms in the Kikuyu areas. The minimum satisfactory size for a grade dairy cattle enterprise is a "flying herd" (i.e., without followers) of two milking cows. This would require, even under good management, a grazing area of approximately one hectare. Tea plantings, although in theory infinitely divisible, are planned on a minimum area of 0.4 hectares, to minimize supervision, leaf collection costs, etc. In 1969-70 it was estimated that 36 percent of holdings in Nyeri District were below one hectare in size.[5]

It is perhaps true that this type of inter-group competition occurred most vigorously in native reserves where the possibilities of extending acreage under cultivation were gradually exhausted. But it should not be assumed that it was confined to the reserves, or that it suddenly ceased with the abolition of the reserves and the gradual return of settlers' lands to African occupation. One development that ensured that the demand for agricultural labour on African lands spread was the attempt, mounted at different periods and with differing degrees of success through Eastern Africa, to introduce African production of export crops.

The effects of this were many. First and most obvious, it made the standard of living of those who were encouraged to grow the crops dependent upon the vagaries of national and international trade cycles and the operations of international commodity cartels (see below, p. 107-09). Second, it gave to the colonial powers and to their national successors an easy way of taxing the rural sector through cesses or levies on export crops (see below, pp. 351 - 54). Third, and from our point of view most relevant, it inevitably accelerated the process of rural differentiation.

It did so in two main ways. First, by introducing a major source of cash income into some areas, it increased income disparities between geographical regions. We shall examine some of the effects of this process in Chapters 5 and 12. Second, it increased the demand for wage labour. For the labour-intensive crops, such as cotton, coffee, and tea, could after a period be grown on a scale that was beyond the labour resources of a single family. (This scale was reached at quite a small total production if the labour peak of the export crop coincided with that of a subsistence crop.[6]) Labour then had to be hired in by the larger growers (or by absentee growers). Since the colonial regimes wished to encourage these crops for their own purposes,* there was a powerful coincidence of

---

*Except when settlers were already growing the crop and thought demand inelastic. There is thus a major distinction between cotton in Uganda and coffee in Kenya, at least up to the Lancaster House Conference.

interests between the colonial authorities and the native growers to ensure that an adequate supply of labour was forthcoming.

Since European farmers were in competition for labour, it might be expected that wages would rise. The evidence suggests that rural wages were, in fact, extremely inflexible; indeed, since it was argued that less labour would be forthcoming if wages were raised, a rational response to a labour shortage was not to raise them. Rather than raise the wage, African farmers seem to have preferred to forgo hired labour.[7] Rural wages were thus kept below any other recorded wage, and cash wages were not infrequently half the legislated minimum wage in the rural areas.* It should therefore not be inferred that inter-group competition—in this case for labour—will necessarily work through the price system to re-establish a situation in which demand is met by supply, much less a new "equilibrium" in which the sum of individual welfare is increased. We shall have to return to a more detailed examination of rural wages in Chapter 5. For the moment, it is important to emphasize that inter-group conflict is not automatically reconciled by the operation of the market.

Let us now turn to one example of "upward mobility": the creation of "yeoman farmers." Despite nervous reactions from European farmers who saw their markets and labour supply threatened by the low costs of successful African peasant farmers, the colonial administration expected members of this class to fulfill several functions. First, they would supply a marginal quantity of food to the towns and to wage labourers in the rural areas; second, they would increase export earnings (e.g., coffee and tea in Kenya); third, they would act as agents of technical change in their own environment and thus raise the standard of "native agriculture"; and fourth, they would act politically as (in one interpretation) yeoman farmers in European history have always acted, namely, as a conservative and stabilizing force in times of political change. By attempting to select the most progressive farmers and concentrate an array of inputs—credit, marketing facilities, extension services—on them, the colonial administration sought to raise their income to levels that would compare with, and possibly exceed, those of even skilled blue-collar workers in the urban areas. The significance of this approach will become clear later; for the moment

---

*In most cases the farmer would supply board and lodging, which an employer covered by a minimum wages order would usually not. He might also allow a labourer a small patch of land on which to grow at least some of his food. Discrepancy in wage costs is not therefore as great as the text implies, although the marginal costs of board and lodging to a farmer would be small. The difference in the real value of wages is less than wage costs, although obviously much would depend upon how much cash a minimum wage labourer had to spend on board and lodging. If he held land locally, this would be negligible.

we emphasize only that the notion that relative wealth could be secured on a scaled-down version of a European farm, usually with hired-in labour, had taken hold in many areas of Eastern Africa before independence.

The Swynnerton Plan for the development of parts of Kikuyuland is a classic example of this approach. Technically brilliant in the context of its time, it had a political effect that sparked off opposition and distrust among those whom it was supposed to benefit. One source of that political opposition was precisely the observation that the Plan created a new "class" in Kikuyu society. By bene-fiting relatively few, it differentiated them from the many. It gave them a status, security, and income denied to others. Further, it made inevitable the gradual deterioration in the status of those excluded into a semi-proletariat.

While it was true that the emergence of a group of landless labourers had been occurring for at least 30 years before the implementation of the Plan, con-temporary European comments shows a complete inability to grasp the signifi-cance of this. For instance, it was expected that village industries would absorb the landless and that rich farmers would invest their savings in the rapid devel-opment of such industries. Naive transfer of a half-baked understanding of the European agricultural revolution to the Kenya situation was very common—with disastrous results.[8] The fact that many of the landless Kikuyu were subse-quently settled on farms purchased from departing Europeans is relevant only in that it shows both the political influence of the Kikuyu (or even landless Kikuyu) after independence and the sensitivity of government, politicians, and administrators (among whom the Kikuyu were disproportionately represented) to the emergence of a large group of landless.

POST-INDEPENDENCE

As implied in the last section, the independent governments of Eastern Afri-ca faced a very different task in relation to rural development. In every case, the political and paramilitary pressure for independence had come mainly from the rural areas. Even in Zambia, with its unusual concentration of unionized la-bour on the Copperbelt, it had been the Bemba in the north who had chal-lenged Sir Roy Welensky most effectively. This rural support created obligations upon the new political leadership, obligations made statistically stronger by the fact that no politician could expect to survive on the strength of urban popu-larity alone. Although the rural population often lacked the means of expressing its disfavour and disgruntlement by comparison with urban workers, party con-ferences provided a forum for lonely political figures from the rural areas to air their grievances.

It is thus inaccurate to assume that rural dwellers have no political kick. They have much less than more elite groups in the towns, and those who claim to represent them are sometimes, as in Buganda, themselves feudal relics rather than democratically elected representatives. But they have sufficient kick to ensure for most of the time that governments must at least *appear* to give rural development a high, even the highest, priority.

That is a political problem. The technical problem is the design of rural development strategies to meet criteria that are either inconsistent or vague. It is almost certainly wrong to blame politicians for the widespread adoption of the efficiency algorithm—the maximization of output per unit input. This neo-classical algorithm, which fails to ask anything about the nature and distribution of the output, is more convincingly explained as a fall-back device adopted by conscientious but anxious planners (usually expatriate, nearly always Western-trained) as a defensible strategy that politicians can change if they wish. Except in Tanzania, no group of politicians has *consistently* challenged it, although the history of rural development since independence is full of minor special pleas to put a project here, build a road there, and create employment for this troublesome group.

We identify this algorithm as a major con-mech. To revert to the language of the fish bowls, it is seen as an access cone in the sense that credit, extension, marketing, and physical inputs are allegedly provided to the rural areas in general, but are actually provided to a very limited group. For those who can make effective use of these inputs are limited in three senses. First, the resources themselves are scarce and are simply not available on request to everyone who thinks he might like to try them out. Second, their management is demanding and they often bring with them a much higher level of risk than many families are ready to accept; thus, some "adopters" drop out and revert to traditional styles of farming. Third, since the local agricultural officers have been taught the importance of output for output's sake ("Ask not for whom . . . "), they rightly concentrate their attention on the farmers whom past experience has shown are most likely to increase production. We shall return to this theme below.

The second feature of the con-mech is that it maintains the confidence of those who are trying to use it. In this the "reinforcement of success" efficiency algorithm is perfect. Although there have been major errors of research, development, and extension in all four countries, and although the rate of failure (as measured by "disadopters" or "droppers" as a proportion of "adopters") is sometimes very high, there are few programmes indeed that are so bad that no farmer increases his income. Those who fail to do so, it is easily explained, either did not do what they were told, or did not do it for long enough, or, having done it, had extraordinarily bad luck in the shape of a drought, or the failure of a piece of machinery, or a visit from a herd of elephants.

The last feature of the con-mech is that it profits, either directly or indirectly, the ruling groups who control it. In what sense does the efficiency algorithm do that? We have already seen that it has an obvious political benefit. Ministers and MPs can show how government expenditures in the rural areas have risen. Occasional difficulties, as in Zambia in 1969 when a deflationary budget hit rural development harder than any other sector, may need to be side-stepped, but the general point can be maintained. More centrally, the value of the efficiency algorithm is:

1. It produces the "maximum" rate of growth of output.
2. It gives resources to those who are in at least some senses "progressive."

Value 1 is important for a number of reasons. Most obviously, the output thus created serves the modern urban sector either directly as food or raw materials, or indirectly as foreign exchange. (That the "reinforcement of success" was an *efficient* strategy is not denied; it seems to have achieved rates of return competitive with, and perhaps much in excess of, those achieved by public sector investment in non-agricultural projects.[9]) Second, a rapid rate of growth of output is important for its own sake, both politically and internationally. Third, there may well be important economic linkages with the progressive rural sector that the politicians, bureaucrats, and business interests are anxious to exploit. Coffee trading in Uganda and Kenya would be good examples.

Value 2 has political significance because those who are likely to compete effectively for resources dispensed under this algorithm are those who are more likely to be politically well connected and personally influential at the village or district level. The abandonment of the efficiency algorithm would entail refusing resources to at least some farmers who have or could acquire local political leverage. This is not to argue that there is a perfect correlation between agricultural progressiveness and political aggression. It is to argue that an alternative algorithm—e.g., a need-based algorithm—is likely to pose much greater political problems. The opposition Tanzania African National Union (TANU) has encountered in Iringa and Lake provinces is a telling example.

The argument is, then, that the efficiency algorithm, which has had a profound but not exclusive effect on the distribution of agricultural resources at both the national and district levels, exemplifies the leading features of the con-mech. Let us examine how it has worked in practice.

Arguably, the algorithm has a short-run effect of concentrating income distribution in the rural areas, but in the long run it raises all rural incomes and reduces the concentration. But this is a gross over-simplification, for it ignores the fact that modern technology involves a *package* of new imputs and new technologies. To adopt one part of a package without adopting the other—e.g., to use improved seed without using fertiliser—is to lower the productivity of that one technique to a point at which there is a major risk that it becomes uneconomic. Thus an intensive study in Zambia revealed that "individual agronomic practices, apart possibly from the use of nitrogenous fertilisers on maize, could not be systematically associated with trends in yields of either maize or groundnuts." But when those practices were grouped in packages, yield per labour hour rose from 1.49 pounds of maize for the crudest set of techniques to 10.77 pounds for the most sophisticated. This increase was, however, achieved by using labour more efficiently on a larger acreage rather than by intensification.[10]

But to adopt the whole package requires two characteristics that are by definition scarce in most rural populations. The first is a high level of managerial skill to organize the supply of inputs and to apply them in the right order in the right combination at the right time. Second, it requires finances adequate to pay for the input before the output is sold. This second condition can be met if agricultural credit is available widely, cheaply, and without risk. In all four countries attempts have been made to make credit more widely available, but the credit programmes seldom insure the farmer against risk of failure. If the crop fails, the farmer is obliged either to default or to use cash he has saved for quite different purposes for the repayment of the debt. If he defaults (and this is a general phenomenon), then the credit programme will not last long. If he is obliged to use earmarked cash for the discharge of his debt, he is unlikely to take the risk again (or indeed be able to). Thus crop failure provides a filter element in even the best credit programme.

The fact that the technology is comprised of indivisible components therefore means that it is successfully adopted only by those who combine a high degree of managerial efficiency, a positive response to risk-taking, and adequate unearmarked cash resources to discharge debts in bad years. That those who meet these criteria are not the poorest is self-evident. They are more likely to be either returning urban workers or the most able and aggressive of the rural population. A limited number of farmers can be helped over these hurdles by an intensive extension campaign or a high level of supervision. But by definition that level of supervision cannot be maintained over a long period or extended to the entire population. The paradoxical result is that the less able are left to adopt the new technology by imitation, with no official support and no supervision. Almost inevitably, then, when the technology is new, lumpy, and risky, it spreads slowly—and differentially.

We get a good glimpse of this process from resent research in Kenya. A study of 354 of the 12,000 registered farmers in the Tetu Division of Nyeri District, Kenya, divided the farmers into four groups (most progressive, upper middle, lower middle, and least progressive) on the basis of their adoption of improved methods of farming. The most progressive had twice as much group contact with the extension service and three times as many visits from extension personnel. They were six times more likely to get a loan from an official source. They had more than three times as much land, and their median income was at least seven times more than that of the least progressive.[11]

So far we have assumed that the nature of the technology is fixed, or determined exogenously. This is not correct. The demands of the con-mech determine the technology. If the con-mech is an output-maximizing algorithm, the technology is likely to aim to maximize output per farmer and will be much less concerned with asking which particular farmers are to benefit. The distribution of research resources on export crops, cattle and maize, to the almost total neglect of traditional vegetables and the complete lack of interest in manioc is a broad example.

More illuminating are two specific examples. For one, very little research has been done in inter-cropping systems, although for small farmers this can be agronomically and economically highly efficient. This efficiency is likely to increase as nitrogenous fertilisers become more expensive. But inter-cropping is not an efficient system for the larger and particularly the mechanized farmer, especially if he has ample resources (owned or borrowed) to finance his cash flow.

The second specific example is the neglect of synthetic as opposed to hybrid maize.* The virtues of the former are that the new (expensive) seed does not have to be bought each year, and it performs better when interplanted with legumes than does hybrid maize. Its vice is that its maximum yields are lower than those of the hybrids. But the smaller farmer seldom (perhaps never) realizes the maximum potential of the hybrid. To that extent the strain on his cash flow and the reduction in his net income that comes from buying and fertilising expensive hybrids is pure loss if the synthetic (whose seed he can produce himself) will give the same yield.† Socially, the wider loss is that small farmers find the hybrid varieties too demanding an innovation, and either do not try them or become disillusioned and return to open-pollinated varieties.[13] Agricultural researchers in Kenya recognized these problems[14] but abandoned research on synthetics following the outstanding success of hybrids among larger farmers. (But despite the enthusiasm for hybrids, after four years of extension work only 5 percent of Central Province was under hybrid in 1969/70.)

But we should not be too ready to conclude that the algorithm only benefits the groups identified as a target by the efficiency algorithm. The extension

---

*A hybrid variety results from the controlled crossing of a limited number of inbred parent lines. The hybrid's characteristics are fixed for only the one generation. A synthetic variety, on the other hand, is derived from a wide reservoir of breeding material, using random pollination within the parent populations. Its selected characteristics are more stable over time than the hybrid's.[12]

†If the synthetic gives a lower yield than the achieved hybrid yield, it is still more attractive to the point at which the loss in yield offsets the extra cost of the hybrid, including the value of consumption and/or investment forgone between seed purchase and harvest-sale.

strategy based on the algorithm has long been justified on the grounds that there are major spillovers to other groups that may not be able to use the whole package of inputs or use them with optimal technical efficiency, but can, nonetheless, use them to derive some benefit.

Research in Kenya in an area adjacent to that in which Joseph Ascroft and his collaborators worked enables us to examine this contention. Drawing on detailed data for the period 1964-71, a period characterized by extensive adoption of tea and improved dairy cattle by peasant small-holders the study reveals rapid rises in average income. More revealing, the data indicate a significant reduction in income inequality, essentially through the entry of large numbers of previously poor non-adopters into the middle-income range, coupled with a *relative* worsening of the position of both the richer and poorer tails of the distribution. This striking conclusion is summarized by the decline of the Gini coefficient of concentration of income over the period studied in Table 2.1.

Commenting on these results, M.P. Cowen states:

Gatei, the sublocation characterized by a higher man/land ratio, a lower mean size of holding, a lower proportion of holdings more than twice the mean size of holding shows not only a slightly higher average annual rate of growth in total income than Gaikuyu but a far higher average annual decrease in measured inequality. Moreover, the decrease in the measured inequality is more pronounced in Gatei for the households occupying the middle range of deciles than in Gaikuyu. Indeed, the relative position of the poorest group of households has worsened in both centres [and] whereas the rise of inequality at the *bottom* end of the distribution embraces 20 percent of the producers in Gatei, 30 percent of the producers in Gaikuyu are so affected. Correspondingly at the *top* end of the distribution, the group occupying the highest decile has not been able to maintain its relative position to the same extent in Gatei as in Gaikuyu.[15]

As Cowen goes on to point out, dairy and tea production had accelerated as a result of resources made available by the national government and international donor agencies in response to demands from the (relatively) politically well-connected progressive farmers. But these resources were deflected to the "middle peasantry" because the larger farmers were unable to maintain the pace of their early growth. They were encountering constraints on their own ability to manage larger and more complex farms, but more particularly they could no longer buy land and hire labour from the "middle peasants," who wished to develop these activities on their own account. But this break-in was confined to the middle peasants; it was not shared by the poorest peasants.

TABLE 2.1

Kenya: Total Income from Milk and Tea, Two Sub-Locations of Nyeri District, 1965-70

Sub-location	Mean-Sized Holding (1970) (acres)	Population Density (persons/ km^2)	Gini Coefficient 1965	Gini Coefficient 1970	Average Annual Change in Gini Coefficient (percent)	Average Annual Rate of Growth in Total Income (percent)
Gatei	3.8	420	0.62	0.50	-4.4	19.7
Gaikuyu	6.5	370	0.62	0.56	-2.0	18.5

Source: M.P. Cowen, "Concentration of Sales and Assets: Dairy Cattle and Tea in Magutu, 1964-1971," mimeo. (Institute for Development Studies, University of Nairobi, 1974); correction to fourth column by the author.

They found it impossible to develop these new activities, and their only "bene-fit" was a slowly rising money wage-rate as the demand for casual labour for tea picking increased.

A more marked example of this con-mech is the attempt to create not so much a class of yeoman farmers as African equivalents of large-scale European farmers, particularly those specializing in the production of high-value export crops. The motivation for such experiments is obvious. Given the economies of scale associated with the production of these crops and the fact that existing technology (and in some cases existing capital equipment) has been developed by and for European farmers, it is a "rational" use of resources to try to replace anachronistic settlers with a new breed of African successors. While this proc-ess has perhaps gone furthest in Kenya (with very substantial investment in ex-European farms and plantations by urban elites), it has received most direct official support in Zambia. There the tenant farmer scheme in tobacco is a good example. Under this scheme the government buys existing tobacco farms from Europeans and installs in them African tobacco farmers trained through a gov-ernment-financed apprenticeship scheme. The newly installed African farmers initially grow 20 acres of tobacco but then expand production to 60 acres. Since Virginia tobacco prices are heavily subsidized, this scale of production implies a gross revenue of about K40,000.

Although the number of farmers involved in this scheme is still small and perhaps will always remain so, it is nonetheless a good example of government deliberately subsidizing the emergence of a group of rural capitalists cast in the mould of their European forerunners. For tobacco is a highly labour-intensive crop; a 60-acre farm would employ perhaps 120 labourers at the peak period in the production cycle. Equivalent schemes in dairying and beef production in Zambia are less labour-intensive but have the same essential features—heavy government subsidy for the creation of a small number of opportunities for beneficiaries to become, by the standards of even urban Zambia, exceedingly wealthy. Production depends upon the use of unskilled or semi-skilled rural labourers—a group that has some protection in law with respect to both wages and housing, but whose protection is seldom enforced.

We do not imply that all rural enrichment is the result of the efficiency con-mech. By no means is that the case. The second fundamental mechanism at work is intra-group competition for existing resources. Before we turn to that question, we must mention one other process of differentiation: that of inter-group competition by which assets are "sucked up" into the top bowl.

We have already mentioned the tendency in Kenya for urban savings to be invested in rural assets. That is, of course, a continuing process, sometimes reinforced by the ability of a limited number of commercial barons to buy European-owned assets at a substantial discount by offering payment in ster-ling. We may draw another, less extreme, example from Uganda. "Mailo" estate holders in Buganda were a group of the Kabaka's political retainers, some of whom have become remarkably successful coffee and mixed arable farmers. In a small survey of 64 Buganda farmers in the middle 1960s, A. Mafaje found 10 farmers with *farm* incomes of over Shs.8,500 per annum and 13 with *total* incomes of over Shs.17,000 per annum.[16] Mixing large-scale farming with trad ing, particularly in coffee, haulage contracting, and political jobbery, these "big men," as they are colloquially called, included some "nouveaux riches" who have been able to buy Mailo estate land from the original grantees. Traders who make money buy land in this way, invest their wealth in making it productive, and then slowly withdraw from their other interests.

These wealthy landed coffee growers-cum-graders are, of course, a small proportion of the rural population of Buganda and a tiny minority in rural Uganda as a whole. They are a continuous reminder of the hierarchical basis of Buganda society and of the fortunes that have been and can still be made by effective farming. They received little encouragement from Obote's government and even less from its successor. They had emerged by an auto-generative proc-ess of which competent large-scale farming is an essential element. The feature of this group, which is common to all four countries but least frequent in Tan-zania, is that large-scale urban savings are invested in the rural areas to maintain or produce a capitalist style of agriculture. The number of capitalists involved is small, even tiny. But the long-run social and economic effect may be considerable.

INTRA-GROUP COMPETITION

The large farmers we described at the end of the last section may be considered inter-group competitors since they compete for resources (most notably high-quality or strategically placed land) with peasant farmers. Quantitatively much more important is the intra-group competition for resources of all sorts, most especially land and access to markets. We illustrate this with respect to the provision of rural services. In all four countries it is the larger, more progressive farmers who tend to dominate the trading and retail activities in the rural areas. The flow of funds can be in either direction: surpluses earned in trade invested in land, or surpluses earned in farming invested in trade.

Much more important is the fact that the attractive investment opportunities in the self-employment sector in the rural areas, most notably transport contracting, tend to be exploited not by the poor or even by the not-so-poor but by those who can bring entrepreneurial skills, a certain amount of capital, and influential contacts to bear upon a wide range of investment opportunities in agriculture and rural economy at large. Although we have no concrete data that prove the point, our impression, based on observation in three countries, is that the investment opportunities created by the withdrawal of Asian traders from the rural areas have not been seized by the rural poor (in whose name the Asians were often driven out) but by the rising rural elites, which tend to offer poorer service at a higher mark-up than did the Asians whom they so vociferously condemned as exploiters.

A special case of this is the hire of tractor service. In extensive arable systems the main constraint on production is the amount of land that can be ploughed and weeded during the early part of the growing season. This gives the tractor owner a great advantage, particularly if he owns not only a plough but also a cultivator. If he is well organized and can perform the operations at the optimal time, he can achieve high yields on his own farm. But he has a further advantage. He can hire out his tractor services at sub-optimal times to those without motive power. He can do so, as is more frequent in Zambia, for a straight cash payment per acre ploughed or, as is reported in Iringa, Tanzania, on a share-crop basis. Further, in the dry season he can make a considerable income by carting grain to the buying depot or even by using his tractor as a rural taxi service. The careful management of a productive asset (one, furthermore, often bought on credit supplied by a public agency) certainly increases the total wealth of the community (by increasing acreage and probably yields) but also tends to concentrate that wealth in relatively few hands.*

An extreme example of this process has been described by Adhu Awiti in a study of Ismani in the Iringa region of Tanzania. According to Awiti, the farmers with less than 15 acres (comprising 68 percent of the households in his sample area) were obliged to hire tractors as only they could cultivate sufficiently deeply and quickly for the prevailing physical conditions.† But as the poorer farmers could not afford manure or fertiliser, land fertility and yield were declining yearly. The charge for tractor hire therefore took a rising proportion of gross income. For farmers with less than 6 acres under cultivation, tractor hire could take up to 50 percent of gross income. In order to reduce this strain on their cash incomes, some farmers were obliged to rent land to tractor owners in return for tractor services. Thus a remarkable concentration of land use has developed in the short period (since the early 1950s) in which this community has been settled. In 20 years this area has changed from one in which there was almost perfectly equal usage of land to one in which 9 percent of households farmed 53 percent of the land.[17]

The significance of these examples of intra-group competition is that those who lose in the competition are made dependent upon those who gain. An extreme example of this may be taken from the case of the very poorest farmers who work for larger farmers during periods of peak labour demand. This is a pattern that reinforces the poverty of the poorest. Because the rural poor tend to be small family units and sometimes single individuals, they are unable to manage a sufficiently large area of maize to assure themselves of food throughout the year. They therefore seek to earn cash in order to buy food in the lean months, and also a minimum of non farm products throughout the year. But because the demand for labour is at a peak during the critical weeks in the season, their own crops suffer neglect and yields are correspondingly low. They are thus made the more dependent upon their own cash earnings. This pattern is illustrated in Table 2.2 based on data from a sample survey of farmers near Katete in Zambia's Eastern Province.

---

*Formally, the degree of concentration depends upon the extent to which the tractor owner uses his tractor to extend his own acreage rather than that of his contractees; the extent to which he uses it to increase productivity on his own farm by performing tasks at the optimal time; and the extent to which the price he charges for services reflects the true increase in total output achieved by using his services. This last is unlikely to be fulfilled (but see below). The first two conditions certainly seemed to be approximated in Zambia.

†It seems highly improbable that they were *obliged* to cultivate by tractor, in the sense that hoe cultivation was impossible. More likely they had a strong preference for hiring a tractor because of the consequent increase in acreage and reduction in the sheer physical labour of hoeing their plots.

TABLE 2.2

Zambia: Sources of Cash Income, Eastern Province, 1968
(percentage distributions)

Source of Income	Total Annual Income							
	0-10	11-50	51-100	101-200	201-300	301-400	401-500	501-750
Crops	13.6	21.5	31.3	21.8	34.3	28.6	50.9	37.0
Livestock	20.1	6.5	15.3	3.8	5.4	1.9	—	0.5
Agricultural wages	8.9	8.4	1.1	1.3	0.2	2.1	0.6	—
Non-agricultural wages	5.2	7.4	8.4	34.4	18.1	28.9	17.3	0.1
Self-employment	7.5	5.8	14.6	5.9	1.4	3.4	10.4	6.5
Sale of beer	20.2	30.1	15.5	9.6	4.9	1.7	1.4	1.2
Gifts	24.2	17.0	12.3	13.2	2.1	2.9	0.2	6.0
Loans	—	2.0	0.7	7.5	28.4	19.0	19.2	48.3
Capital items	—	—	0.3	—	4.8	1.0	—	—
Other	0.3	1.3	0.5	2.5	0.4	10.5	—	0.4
Total number of farmers	8	53	14	13	8	5	1	1
Average income	7	26	66	142	241	314	487	603

Source: C. Elliott (ed.), J. Bessell, R. Roberts, and N. Vanzetti, "Universities of Nottingham and Zambia Labour Productivity Investigation (UNIZALPI), mimeo., Report to the Government of Zambia no. 3 (1971).

If we look at the structure of earnings of the low-income group (income less than K50), there are a number of points of great interest. The first is that the proportion of income earned from agricultural wages is much higher for this group than it is for the higher-income groups. Second, agricultural wages are a more important source of cash than non-agricultural wages (in sharp contrast to the wealthier groups or self-employed). Note, too, the much greater proportionate importance of gifts. Those in the tiny but very poor group of eight farmers with cash incomes of less than K10 receive nearly a quarter of their meagre incomes from gifts—evidence, perhaps, of some social redistribution.

Because much of the income of the poorest group is derived from the sale of beer, the dependence upon peak labour demand employment is reinforced. For a minimum cash income is required in order to purchase the inputs, of which sugar (which cannot be produced locally) is the most important. Thus for this group an assured cash income from paid employment (whether in agriculture or not) is essential, for without it the brewing season cannot start and the main source of cash income will be forfeit. (While it is true that gifts yield as much income as earnings, they are almost certainly a less reliable form of income.)

One way of escaping this poverty and this dependence is to become a full-time labourer. As we shall see, this is a very risky and demanding decision that those who can survive, even in the hazardous circumstances we have described, are unlikely to take willingly. Where that decision is made, *and where land is not in short supply,* the effect is likely to be a reduction in per capita consumption in the family.

Many studies of Eastern African agriculture have emphasized the effect of labour supply, particularly family labour supply, on acreage and therefore on family income.[18] Certainly if one corrected the income distribution figures presented in this chapter for size of family, one would find a much less skewed income distribution than appears in Tables 2.2 and 2.3. But even on a per capita basis and at a given level of managerial expertise, a large family is likely to be better off than a small family. The technical conditions of production tend to ensure that, *so long as land is not in short supply,* the marginal product of labour is positive and high. A Zambian study, for instance, found that for large farmers the value of the extra production of one hour of hired labour was K29; for smaller family farms it was K6 per hour.[19] Thus larger family units tend to have higher per capita incomes—and therefore the ability to save more rapidly to invest in modern productive assets.

Why, then, it will be asked, do people leave the family to look for jobs? This is readily explained when land is in short supply, for then marginal productivity may be lower than consumption. But how can it be explained when there is plenty of land and marginal product is high? This kind of question reveals the limitations of a neo-classical approach. The migration, especially of younger, better-educated men, is not readily explained by realistic differences between marginal productivity and consumption. The value of the Harris-Todaro model is that it focusses on expectations, even if it does so within a basically neo-classical frame.[20] For whether or not there is land for the tilling, the young migrant expects his urban wage to exceed his consumption level in the village. His ignorance of urban prices, his over-optimistic assessment of his earnings in town, and his ability to find a job at all, tend to raise his expectations above the certainties of village life—extremely hard, boring work for a fraction of the family output.

This is a theme to which we shall return in a later chapter. For the moment we have to emphasize that one of the sources of rural poverty is lack of labour on the peasant farm. That lack results directly from intra-group competition for for resources and markets. Although that poverty may be somewhat offset by gifts from the migrants to their dependents in the rural areas, the processes of differentiation in the rural areas tend to exacerbate that poverty both absolutely and relatively. For the rural poor become dependent upon the rural rich, both for services such as transport and motive power, and for income in terms of sales of beer and labour.

TABLE 2.3

Uganda: Total Annual Income of Sample Rural Households, 1969/70

Income (Shs.)	Households	
	Number	Percent
Less than 200	373	22
201-300	232	14
301-500	314	19
501-1,000	371	23
1,000-1,500	146	9
1,501-2,000	78	5
2,001-2,500	29	2
2,501-3,000	29	2
Over 3,000	58	3
No answer	11	1
Total	1,641	100

Note: The data presented refer to total household income. No allowance has been made for farming expenses (which for about a quarter of the farmers seem to have been significant), and it is impossible to subtract non-farming incomes. More important, no allowance has been made for subsistence income from own produce consumed on the farm. This makes these figures consistent with those first quoted from the Buganda coffee survey, but they should not be compared with figures for urban incomes.

Source: "Baseline Survey of Uganda Agriculture," mimeo. (Washington, D.C.: U.S. Agency for International Development, April 1970).

RURAL DIFFERENTIATION AND INCOME DISTRIBUTION

The last two sections should not be taken to imply that either the workings of the con-mech of the efficiency algorithm or of intra-group competition have yet produced a deeply differentiated rural society marked by a host of non-reciprocal relationships. Although regional differences in income have almost certainly increased greatly, in Kenya perhaps above all, the relatively small numbers of beneficiaries and their enduringly modest income levels mean that one does not find greatly concentrated patterns of income distribution. The major changes are most probably confined to the "tails," with a smallish number of very rich farmers emerging together with a rising number of labourers increasingly dependent upon wages. But the "tails" in this sense are small: Concentration upon them should not blind us to the much greater volume of the slowly rising income of the "middle peasantry." To put the rich farmers into perspective, we shall first present some data from Uganda to show how atypical are the Buganda coffee growers, and then we shall examine national data from Tanzania to put in perspective the current concern about rural inequalities in that country.

First a methodological point must be emphasized. The collection, analysis, and interpretation of rural income figures are unusually difficult. Even if correctly reported, there are serious problems about the treatment of subsistence income, of non-monetary farm costs (e.g., "borrowed" labour that has to be paid back later), of loans, and of barter trade. The most important of these is subsistence income. The large-scale farmer, for instance, may produce very little of his own food while a small peasant farmer will produce virtually all of his. A comparison of cash incomes, then, gives a quite misleading representation of the differences in income and welfare between them. In the figures that follow, allowance has been made for this difference, but the means by which that is done varies. None is perfect.

A survey of coffee growers in Buganda in 1963 showed that farm income varied from an average of Shs.290 for a group of farmers in one area growing less than 1.5 acres each to Shs.2,810 for a group of farmers in a slightly more prosperous area growing 8 acres or more each. This big differential of roughly one to ten was modified when the value of shamba produce and gifts in kind was taken into account, but even then the farmers with the larger area under coffee had an average total income of more than four times that of the group with the smaller acreage. It is interesting that average receipts from paid employment were nearly ten times as high among farmers with larger acreages as among farmers with small acreages. This suggests the presence of a significant number of part-time farmers in the richer group, relying more heavily on paid labour under occasional supervision.* By comparison, hired labour was paid a shilling a day. (Data on *earnings* of hired labour are scarce and unsatisfactory, but a labourer would be lucky to work more than 200 days a year. Family size for the two groups of farmers was very nearly the same.) The picture that emerges is consistent with that of another study of large-scale farmers in Buganda (see above, p. 31). Conducted in the mid-1960s, this study found that a third of the farmers surveyed had total incomes of over Shs.8,500 a year; less than half that number had incomes of less than Shs.1,700 a year. The great

---

*The group with the lowest incidence of paid employment came from the same area but had a smaller acreage than the richest group. This lends some support to the suggestion that the large coffee growers were mostly absentees.

majority of these were uneducated peasants (Bakopi) who had made sufficient money during the coffee boom of the 1950s to buy their land or increase their acreage and thus establish themselves in the top income stratum of Buganda rural society. With the collapse of coffee prices in the early 1960s, they had seen their real income halved. Some had gone out of coffee production altogether and either returned to trading or developed other crops.

Just what a rural elite these coffee growers and large-scale farmers are is revealed in Table 2.3, the results of a sample survey conducted in 1970 by a team from Makerere University. The survey was conducted in 26 parishes throughout Uganda, chosen to represent seven different agricultural systems. The great majority of holdings were small: 67 percent less than 5 acres, only 3 percent more than 15 acres. Accepting all the methodological shortcomings of Table 2.3, it is nonetheless significant that only 13 percent of the sample had incomes over Shs.1,500 in 1970 prices, whereas the average income of each group in the Buganda coffee survey was above (or only very fractionally below) this figure in 1963 prices. In real terms, then, even the poorest of the coffee growers was in the richest eighth of the rural population. By contrast, over half the Uganda-wide sample had incomes (farm and non-farm) of less than Shs.500 per household—which suggests an average total cash income of less than Shs.100 per head.*

The same general picture—a tiny rural elite superimposed on a vast mass of low-income farmers—comes from the recent Household Budget Survey of Tanzania. This survey showed much exchange and payment in kind for labour (payment in kind accounted for 3 percent of total output) but relatively little permanent employment and few employers permanently dependent upon hired labour. Although 222,000 workers were reported to be in employment at

---

*Again, it is important to remember that these figures include no allowance for subsistence incomes. This is, of course, a serious omission. One interesting sidelight of the Buganda coffee study is that the average value of shamba produce and gifts was Shs.1,026 a year—i.e., significantly more than the majority of paid employees were earning. If we gross that to 1970 values, it adds Shs.1,539 to the incomes presented here. Such a procedure is extremely questionable, however, given the wide local variations in diet as well as the well-known problems of the valuation of auto-consumption. But it does suggest that, even on a minimal estimation of shamba produce, the urban/rural gap is not as great as is sometimes alleged. For example, a conservative allowance of Shs.1,000 per household would put the income of 78 percent of rural households at a level reached by 82 percent of urban paid employees. Further, if farm gate prices increased faster than unskilled wage rates (which is not very likely but, in the light of a 50 percent increase in the food component of the low-income price index, cannot be ruled out), the gap could, in fact, have narrowed.

some time during the year, only 2,600 households reported employment of 11 or more labourers at any one time. Also, 45 percent of labourers were hired on farms using three or fewer labourers, and the great majority of these would not be permanent labourers. We have corroborative evidence from the census, which revealed only 14,000 regular employers of labour and only 140,000 employees in agriculture, out of a total active agricultural work force of 5.4 million.*

If this suggests a very small rural elite and a small *permanent* agricultural proletariat, we would expect income distribution to be relatively equal, with a small high-income group contrasting with a large mass of poor farmers. Table 2.4, based on expenditure data, shows this to be the case.

Only 2 percent of rural households spent more than Shs.6,000; slightly over half of these were large families with more than six members.† Further, there was the high correlation that we have already noticed between high-income farm families and non-farm employment of at least one member of the farm household. To that extent, the table overstates inequality resulting from purely agricultural activities.

If, then, the process of differentiation is at work in Eastern Africa, but has not yet produced many of the common forms of exploitation resulting from antagonistic relationships in rural society—rack-renting, usury, insecurity of tenure, monopsony—is there a problem at all? If the real situation is that all are poor but some are poorer than others, is not concern about social relationships among the poor akin to concern about an ingrowing toenail on a terminal case of cancer?

To some it appears so.[21] And perhaps that is a view encouraged by much of the analytical paraphernalia of agricultural economists and, no less, by the need of local and national politicians to show signs of success in very concrete terms— e.g., production targets met, projects successfully implemented, agricultural techniques modernized, and visible symbols of "rural improvement," i.e., by precisely those forces that maintain the basic con-mech of efficiency. The real question—and one to which we shall have to return in the last chapter—is whether, in the long run, rural development in any sense but the most quantitatively banal is possible, if differentiation and inequality are allowed to develop

---

*But it is very possible that the census underestimates both regular employers and regular employees, partly because of the timing of the census in relation to the Arusha Declaration and partly because employees may have been reluctant to identify themselves as such.

†Because of the difficulties of measurement, especially of trading income, it is possible that the numbers and incomes of some of the richer farmers have been under-recorded. But the scale of such under-recording is highly unlikely to affect these conclusions.

TABLE 2.4

Tanzania: Rural Households by Size and Total Expenditure, 1969

Total Expenditure Per Year (thousands of Shs.)	Household Size (thousands of households in each category)			
	All	1-2 Members	3-6 Members	7 or More Members
0-0.99	658	226	329	103
1-1.99	1,048	116	616	316
2-3.99	499	32	241	226
4-5.99	111	1.5	48.5	61
6-7.99	32	1.2	15.8	15
8-9.99	8.5		5.5	3
10 or more	11	0.8	1.2	9
Total	2,368	378	1,257	733

Source: Unpublished data from the Household Budget Survey as quoted in M. Gottlieb, "The Extent and Character of Differentiation in Tanzanian Agricultural and Rural Society 1967-8," mimeo., East African Universities Social Science Council, Eighth Annual Conference Proceedings, 1972.

along a spectrum, say, from Tanzania through Kenya and Ghana to Egypt and ultimately the Philippines. To neo-Marxists, the development of a kulak* class is inconsistent with a type of rural development that it still possible for at least some parts of Africa—a type that depends on co-operation, not competition; on community, not isolation; on sharing, not owning. This may or may not be a romantic dream. But the fact that the dream exists, at least among some political leaders, explains why it is scientifically naive to dismiss rural differentiation as unimportant. For to Presidents Nyerere and Kaunda and at least some influential figures in Kenya,[22] that dream has been spelled out as a high political priority. And it cannot be realised if differentiation becomes firmly established and brings with it the cementing of dependent relationships and the associated intensification of intra-group competition.

It is precisely to counter these tendencies that Tanzania has begun to experiment with an alternative form of rural development. (We put it in this somewhat

---

*It is worth remembering that the meaning of the Russian "kulak" is literally "fist."

tentative form because the theory and practice of Ujamaa is still in a rather
early stage—a point sometimes forgotten by both its critics and its admirers.)

The intention of the policy of Ujamaa is to remove economic differentiation
and the possibility of exploitative relationships from rural (and ultimately the
whole of) Tanzania. By encouraging peasants to pool their resources and their
skills and to find an equitable way of sharing the produce and investing the
surplus, the intention is to provide both a more efficient productive environment and a less antagonistic social environment. The theory of Ujamaa, then,
rests on the assumption that individual peasant agriculture is inefficient particularly with respect to scale, and as such is likely to lead to the creation of dependent and dominant relationships between the various groups of farmers.
Ujamaa therefore requires as a necessary precondition a technical solution to
the peasant's farming problems that presents him with the opportunity to increase his family welfare as a result of co-operative farming. Whether or not
this is possible in every ecological and economic environment is perhaps an
open question. What is quite clear is that, for this pre-condition to be met, there
has to be a very high level of technical research and planning in every village. It
is the difficulty of providing such initial support that goes a long way to explaining why in very many, and perhaps the majority of, Ujamaa villages in
Tanzania the level of co-operation (and socialization) still remains more cos-
metic than fundamental.*

In this context it is significant that the major thrust of the Ujamaa programme has been in new settlement schemes (what at one point was called
"villagization"). The generalizability of this approach is obviously limited and
can itself lead to a new kind of dependence upon the local representatives of
central government.

If problems with Ujamaa abound at both the theoretical and practical
level,[23] it does nonetheless represent the only major attempt in Eastern Africa
to overcome the processes of differentiation that we have sketched in this
chapter. Much has been learnt, much is being learnt, and many fundamental
political and administrative realignments have taken place since the launching
of the Ujamaa policy. Tanzania has still doubtless much to learn about Ujamaa,

---

*If differentiation has gone far, it is highly improbable that there will be any
village production plan that makes possible a net increase in the welfare of all
villagers and a fair distribution of the product. For this reason, among others,
Ujamaa has been most successful in the poorer areas of Tanzania. Even there
it has been necessary to exclude from the village any of the wealthier, more successful entrepreneurial farmers. There is thus the added dimension of differentiation—of Ujamaa villages often well served with public services but with a
low per capita income and more prosperous individual peasants with substantial
cash incomes but little access to public services.

and it would be not only unsympathetic but unscholarly to write off the whole policy of Ujamaa on the basis of five years' hard experimentation. However, the question has to be faced: In a society already as differentiated as Tanzania (and much more Kenya, Uganda, and Zambia), can a socialist approach to rural development survive?

Even in Tanzania the continuous re-emergence of forces that tend to subvert the essence of Ujamaa into a set of administrative procedures suggests that it is going to be a hard struggle; just how hard was dramatized by the shooting of the Commissioner in Iringa in 1972, motivated by fear that the prosperous farmers there were to be forced into Ujamaa villages. No one can predict the outcome with any certainty. But the evidence suggests that at the moment it would be wrong to conclude that Tanzania, with its well-defined ideology, its strong political leadership, the discipline and articulation of its party, and its relative independence from the grosser forms of neo-colonialism, represents even a minimum condition for the successful transmogrification of individualistic differentiation into a non-antagonistic form of rural development. And if that is the case, one begins to grasp the full enormity of the problem presented by the drift towards a fully capitalist pattern of rural development. At least it is being faced in Tanzania, and to a lesser extent in Zambia. Elsewhere in Eastern Africa it has hardly been identified as a problem by the ruling elites.

NOTES

1. A.A.Y. Kyerematen, *Regalia for an Ashanti Durbar* (Kumasi: Ghana National Cultural Centre, 1971), p. 1.

2. See, for instance, P.M. Mbithi and Carolyn Barnes, "Spontaneous Settlement Problems in the Context of Rural Development in Kenya," mimeo., Institute for Development Studies, University of Nairobi, 1974.

3. M.P. Cowen, "Differentiation in a Kenya Location," mimeo. (East African Universities Social Science Council, Eighth Annual Conference, Nairobi, December 1972); and with Frederick Murage, "Notes on Agricultural Labour in a Kenya Location," in "Developmental Trends in Kenya," mimeo., proceedings of a seminar held at the Centre of African Studies, University of Edinburgh, April 1972.

4. Quoted in Cowen, "Differentiation" op. cit., from District Commissioner's Half-Yearly Report, June 1948, Central Province, Kenya National Archives.

5. International Labour Organization, *Employment, Incomes and Equality: A Strategy for Increasing Productive Employment in Kenya,* report of an interagency team financed by the United Nations Development Programme and organized by the ILO (Geneva: ILO, 1972), p. 33.

6. For a detailed analysis of this point with respect to cotton, see C.C. Wrigley, *Crops and Wealth in Uganda: A Short Agrarian History* (Kampala: Oxford University Press for Makerere Institute of Social Research, 1970).

7. Cowen with Murage, "Notes," op. cit; W.J. Berber, *The Economy of British Central Africa* (London: Oxford University Press, 1961).

8. See M.P.K. Sorrenson, *Land Reform in the Kikuyu Country* (Nairobi: Oxford University Press for the East African Institute of Social Research, University College of Makerere, 1967), pp. 22 ff.

9. See R.G. Saylor, "A Social Cost/Benefit Analysis of Agricultural Extension and Research Services among Smallholder Coffee Producers in Kilimanjaro District," in *Agricultural Policy Issues in East Africa,* ed. V.F. Amann (Kampala: Makerere University Press, 1973).

10. C. Elliott (ed.), J. Bessell, R. Roberts, and N. Vanzetti, "Universities of Nottingham and Zambia Labour Productivity Investigation (UNZALPI)," mimeo., Report to the Government of Zambia, no. 3, 1971, p. 54.

11. J. Ascroft, N. Roling, J. Karinki, and Fred Chege, *Extension and the Forgotten Farmer* (Nairobi: Institute for Development Studies, 1973); N. Roling, "Problem Solving Research: A Strategy for Change," mimeo., Organization for Economic Cooperation and Development, Seminar on Development Projects Designed to Reach the Lowest Income Groups, Paris, 1974. The data are *not* standardized for family size; this could explain some of the differences in income and acreage if, as is not improbable, both increase with the size of family.

12. For a detailed discussion in a standard plant genetics text, see G.F. Sprague, *Corn Breeding: Corn and Corn Improvement* (New York: Academic Press, 1955).

13. J.J. Gichuki, "Some of the Problems of Growing Hybrid Maize by Peasant Farmers of Nueri District, Kenya," *Agricole* 1 (1968): 28-33.

14. M.N. Harrison, "Maize Improvement in East Africa," in *Crop Improvement in East Africa,* ed. C.L.A. Leakey (Farnham Royal: Commonwealth Agricultural Bureau, 1970).

15. M.P. Cowen, "Concentration of Sales and Assets: Dairy Cattle and Tea in Magutu, 1964-1970," mimeo. (Institute for Development Studies, Nairobi, 1974).

16. A. Mafaje, "The Farmers: Economic and Social Differentiation," in *Subsistence to Commercial Farming in Present-day Buganda: An Economic and Anthropological Survey,* eds. A.I. Richards, Fred Sturrock, and Jean Fortt (Cambridge:Cambridge University Press, 1974).

17. Adhu Awiti, "Economic Differentiation in Ismani, Iringa Region: A Critical Assessment of Peasants' Response to the Ujamaa Vijijini Programme," seminar paper (Economic Research Bureau, Dar es Salaam, 1972).

18. Norman Long, *Social Change and the Individual: A Study of the Social and Religious Responses to Innovation in a Zambian Rural Community*

(Manchester University Press for the Institute of Social Research, University of Zambia, 1968); Arne Larsen, "Variation in Income among Farming Areas in Sri Sukumaland," mimeo., paper presented at the East Africa Agricultural Economics Society Conference, Dar es Salaam, April 1970; E.M. Ruigu, "Some Aspects of Employment on Smallholder Farms in Selected Areas of Kenya," in *Agricultural Policy Issues in East Africa,* ed. V.F. Amann, Proceedings of the East African Agricultural Economics Society Conference, 1971 (Kampala: Makerere University Press, 1973).

19. "UNIZALPI," op. cit.

20. J.R. Harris and M.P. Todaro, "Migration, Unemployment and Development: A Two-Sector Analysis," *American Economic Review,* March 1970, pp. 126-42.

21. Manuel Gottleib, "The Extent and Character of Differentiation in Tanzanian Agricultural and Rural Society, 1967-68," mimeo. (East African Universities Social Science Council, Eighth Annual Conference Proceedings, 1972).

22. For Nyerere and Kaunda, see their many writings on Ujamaa and on Zambian humanism, respectively; for Kenya, see C. Leys, *Politics in Kenya,* forthcoming.

23. See L.R. Cliffe, "Planning Rural Development," in *Towards Socialist Planning,* Uchumi Editorial Board (Dar es Salaam: Tanzania Publishing House, 1972); "The Policy of Ujamaa Vijijini and the Class Struggle in Tanzania," in *Socialism in Tanzania,* vol. II, eds. L. Cliffe and J. Saul (Nairobi: East African Publishing House, 1973).

In this chapter we first consider Ivory Coast, Ghana, and the Sahelian countries as one socio-agricultural system in which the rich littoral states (and especially the coffee and cocoa forest areas) feed upon the poverty of the Sahel. We argue that, taken as one, this system is a good example of an international con-mech. Second, we look at some more, rather different intra-group conflicts in the littoral states; these form a point of contrast with conflicts we shall examine in the next two chapters.

A preliminary point must be made about the geography of West Africa. Most of our material will be drawn from Ivory Coast, Ghana, and Upper Volta, and we shall usually be obliged to couch the analysis in those gross national terms. This is, of course, very misleading, for geographically and to a lesser extent economically, the norther reaches of both the littoral states have much more in common with Upper Volta, especially Western Upper Volta, than with the forest belts to the south. The real contrasts lie between the coastal plains, the forest zone and the savannah—and the dry savannah of the extreme north and east as a logical extreme. This crude typology of agronomic systems should be borne in mind throughout this chapter. For it is the stuff out of which present patterns of enrichment and impoverishment have been woven.

WEST AFRICAN AGRICULTURAL SYSTEMS AS A CON-MECH

The essence of the argument is very simple. We shall sketch in broadest outline in this paragraph and then substantiate it so far as the data allow at somewhat greater length. To repeat the three basic characteristics of a con-mech: (1) it is a mechanism of enrichment whereby many feel they can benefit but few do; (2) it survives because the few who do benefit give it a legitimacy in the eyes of those who do not; (3) it enriches not only those who successfully use the mechanism to achieve upward mobility but also those who control it or keep it in being.

Put at its crudest, our argument is that, given the huge differentials in agricultural potential between the dry savannah and the forest, migrants from the north are attracted to work in the south by the prospect of work either in the urban areas or at least on the estates in Ivory Coast at the legislated minimum wage. In fact, very few actually find work in town or on the estates; most work on smallholdings where they are relatively poorly paid and where it is unusual for them to become share-croppers or outright "owners" of land. But the existence of a large pool of rural migrant workers enriches those who have access to land; indeed, it has become very nearly a necessary pre-condition for capital accumulation in the rural areas, especially in Ivory Coast.

Let us now review the evidence. Table 3.1 presents estimates of cash incomes in rural and urban regions of Ivory Coast and Ghana as multiples of the best available guesstimate of agricultural cash income in Upper Volta. This latter is not only uncertain; it is a composite of a range of cash incomes varying widely over the country. In the East, there are scattered communities that are— or were until the last four or five years—almost entirely self-sufficient. There cash income is very near to zero, and the need for cash is modest. By contrast, in the favoured Organisme regional de developpement of Volta Noire, where cotton production is expanding rapidly and a wide range of rural services is concentrated, average cash incomes are comparable with those in the non-littoral regions of Ivory Coast. (Even in the overcrowded and infertile Mossi Plateau, there is a high degree of income concentration. According to one survey, 3.5 percent of households accounted for 46.7 percent of total expenditure in the region.[1]) But this is exceptional. Particularly in the very heavily populated regions of Yatenga, Koudougou, and Ouagadougou, holdings are small (up to one hectare per able-bodied adult), the soil is weak, erosion is widespread, and rainfall is uncertain. For the 5.5 million people living here, it is no exaggeration to say that remittances from the South—an aggregate of 5 billion (thousand million) F CFA annually—are an essential element in the struggle to survive.

Now it could be argued that rural development in at least parts of Upper Volta (e.g., Volta Noire) has already made these comparisons irrelevant. Serious drought apart, so it might be said, the effect of the rapid spread of cash crops has begun to raise incomes and close the gap between the favoured areas of Upper Volta and the richer zones to the south. Output of groundnuts rose 50 percent during the period 1962-70, of cotton by nearly 600 percent. Between 1963 and 1970 the value of total sales through official agencies increased

TABLE 3.1

Ivory Coast and Ghana: Multiples of Average Rural Cash Incomes in Upper Volta, 1968-70

Ivory Coast		Ghana	
Average consumption per head including consumption of food produced on the farm, by region		Wages in Northern Ghana	3.2
		Wages in food-growing forest area, permanent labourer	3.9
Bouake	3.1	Wages in cocoa belt, permanent	
Daloa	3.5	labourer	5.2
Southeast	3.5	Minimum wages in Accra	7.1
South	5.0		
Minimum wages			
Plantations	5.6/8.2[a]		
Industrial	14.9/18.6[b]		

[a] Depending on type of plantation.
[b] 1968/1970.

Sources: Ivory Coast—Ministere du plan, "Dossiers pour l'exploration du long terme—consommation et mode de vie" (Societe d'etudes techniques et financieres, 1970). Ghana—B.E. Rourke, *Wages and Incomes of Agricultural Workers in Ghana,* Technical Publication Series no. 13 (Legon: Institute of Statistical, Social and Economic Research, University of Ghana, 1971); A.S. Appiah, "The Organization of Labour in the Production of Cocoa Beans: A Survey of Tepa District" (Legon: Department of Agriculture and Economics and Farm Management, University of Ghana, May 1970); B.E. Rourke and A.S. Appiah, "The Organization of Labour for the Production of Cocoa Beans in Ghana," CMB *Newsletter* no. 44 (April 1970); N.O. Addo, *Migration and Economic Change in Ghana,* vol. 1: *Social and Demographic Characteristics of the Cocoa Farming Population in Brong-Ahafo Region* (Legon: Demographic Unit, University of Ghana, 1971).

by more than two and a half times.[2] In part this is true. But three crucial points have to be considered.

The first point is that this rapid expansion of commercial crops has been achieved in the densely populated areas by the simultaneous adoption of high-yielding sorghums that release land for alternative uses. These "new" sorghums are less drought-resistant than their traditional cousins, and therefore expose the cultivators to a greater risk when the rains are inadequate. For the wealthy (or fortunate) few who can irrigate their crops or who can afford to take the risk, this technical deficiency is acceptable. For the much greater number who can do neither, but who nonetheless want to increase their income, the risks are huge. For if the rains fail, the cash crop and the subsistence crop are both forfeit.* Thus rural development in this sense has raised incomes (in some areas) but has also greatly raised the uncertainty of those incomes.

Second, when the rains do fail, farmers (especially in the more developed areas) are obliged to borrow from Ivorien merchants who thereby acquire a lien on subsequent crops, usually at pre-determined "distress" prices. This implies that, in the good years, net incomes to the producer are much lower than official figures suggest.

Third, the average figure that we have been obliged to use in Table 3.1 as the denominator obscures the concentration of income even in a country as poor as Upper Volta. Even on the overcrowded and infertile Mossi Plateau, where one might expect income concentration to be low, we have already quoted admittedly rather old data that show a high degree of concentration of *expenditure*.[3] Even if this is more marked than in the less poor areas—and there is no reason to assume that—it does suggest that average figures must be viewed with even greater caution.

These three points together suggest that the orders of magnitude in Table 3.1 probably underestimate the real differences in income for most Voltaiques. They certainly take no account of the greater security of income available in the south, especially in the formal urban sector. But the great majority of migrants do not get jobs in the urban sector at all. In Ivory Coast some, a small minority, work on plantations; many more end up working on coffee and cocoa smallholdings as permanent labourers. There, it is true, their wages are more than their likely incomes in Upper Volta, but one half to one third of what they would earn as a minimum wage on the plantations. Further, they have there no security of employment—and indeed no certainty of payment. It is this latter features that sometimes enables them to acquire land. A Voltaique who has a sharecrop agreement that the landowner consistently fails to honour may eventually be given a piece of land in lieu of his wages.

In the case of Ghana, the same basic mechanisms were at work, with the same basic result: Namely, that most of the Voltaique migrants were to be found in the forest zones working on cocoa or food farms as labourers. Very few became sharecroppers, and even fewer cocoa farmers in their own right.[4] The Aliens Compliance Order of 1969, by which the unemployed (or rather, those whose employers were unwilling or unable to secure work permits for them) were expelled, arose primarily from urban-based political pressure, because the migrants presented competition to urban job-seekers lacking

---

*For this reason it will be very surprising if, after the recent series of droughts, high-yielding sorghums retain their popularity.

education and qualification to improve their competitive position. But the large-scale withdrawal of labour from the rural areas left the Ghana cocoa industry seriously short of labour.[5] The semi-official Cocoa Marketing Board *Newsletter* put it this way:

> The "compliance order" has brought into true perspective the extent (and it is frightfully large) to which our cocoa farmer depends on the "sweat" of aliens.
>
> It is not that we detest the idea of having aliens working in our midst . . . but that we fear the relegation of the cocoa industry which is inextricably interwoven with our economic life to aliens exclusively is anomalous and pregnant with many risks.
>
> That is why we join the clarion call of the many voices which have been appealing to Ghanaians, especially the youth to take interest in the cocoa industry and for that matter, farming.[6]

The first two conditions of the con-mech therefore apply. But note that the con-mech is not a zero-sum game. The Voltaiques do benefit to the extent that the wages they actually earn exceed their wages or net farm incomes in their area of origin. The point is that the actual returns are much less than the anticipated returns; entry to a higher status (sharecropper or landowner) is a great deal more difficult and competition for employment of any kind more intense than they may have expected. But what of the third condition, the enrichment of those who control the mechanism? We shall examine three groups: the Ivorien plantations, the Ghanaian cocoa farmers of the forest belt, and the much less well known (and more recent) rice farmers of northern Ghana.

Since independence, foreign-owned plantations in Ivory Coast have concentrated on non-traditional crops. For government has encouraged their development partly as a means by which agricultural production can be diversified and partly as a means of earning foreign exchange. They earned 21 percent of visible export revenue in 1960 and 31 percent in 1971. (Samir Amin has shown that, in terms of both foreign exchange and income generated, during the period 1950-65 the absolute and relative importance of foreign-owned agricultural enterprises increased.[7]) This increasing dependence on foreign-controlled plantations is paralleled by the increasing financial outflows from Ivory Coast. For in 1970 Europeans appropriated over 60 percent of the total income of the plantation sector: About 14 percent went on European salaries (spent largely on luxury imports or saved to be repatriated later) and the rest was repatriated to Europe (principally to France) as profits.

This pattern of mutual but vicious interdependence—of governments for foreign exchange, and investors (and expatriates) for high returns—is typical of the estate sector and we shall have more to say of it in a rather different context in Chapter 5. For the present we emphasize the increasing dependence of Ivory Coast on foreign plantations—and the plantations' increasing dependence on foreign labour.

For one of the characteristics of the plantation economy is a heavy reliance upon unskilled labour and a small number of highly paid European supervisors. As Table 3.2 shows, the great bulk of unskilled labour is non-Ivorien, migrant workers from Upper Volta and Mali. The much smaller number of Ivorien citizens who work on the plantations have a slightly higher level of education and/or technical qualification, but in general the supervision is European. As may by expected, this hierarchy is reflected in wage levels. The average earnings of Ivorien workers on the plantations were 1.4 times the average earnings of non-Ivoriens. By contrast, Europeans earned 25 times as much as non-Ivoriens.

This illustrates one of the fundamental paradoxes of rural development in both Ivory Coast and Ghana. In Ivory Coast, despite a relatively high rate of economic growth compared to other West African countries, and a worsening of urban unemployment and rural under-employment among nations, there is a chronic shortage of unskilled labour in the agricultural sector and an increased need for foreign manpower (for evidence from Ghana, see below, p. 113). Nationals with access to land are reluctant to accept work as hired labourers at the same wage rate as migrants from the Sahel. Those without the necessary (and increasingly high) qualifications to secure full-time employment in the formal sector have two possibilities: They can go to town in the hope of getting an unskilled job and gradually working their way up the skill pyramid, or they can start farming on their own account, a prospect made the more attractive by the relative ease with which they can either hire migrant workers themselves or, at least in their own region, secure help in establishing a farm through communal work sharing. Except in those few areas where population pressure has reduced access to land, there is little incentive for an Ivorien national to work in the plantation sector. For the minimum agricultural wage paid on the estates is less than half the *cash* income earned by smallholders growing export crops. Only if each household has at least two full-time employees on the estates is family income likely to be as high as that of the average of smallholders. Even then the family may suffer loss of production on family food plots.

When there is so little incentive to work as a hired labourer in agriculture in general and on the plantations in particular, a shortage of local labour is inevitable. But this is not confined to the plantations or even smallholder export crops. It is most acute in the lower-paying, food-growing savannah areas in the north. A study by Louis Roussel suggests that in the later 1970s this region will face an acute shortage of labour.[8] On admittedly very rough workings, he expects the available labour force in the savannah areas of Ivory Coast in 1980 to be only half that required to meet production targets for food and export crops.

TABLE 3.2

Ivory Coast: Distribution of Employees on Plantations by Ethnic Origin and Occupational Level, 1965 (percentages)

Ethnic Origin	Professional Category*				Total	
	1	2	3	4	Percentage	Number
Africans						
Ivoriens	16.0	1.8	0.1	0.1	18.0	4,500
Non-Ivoriens	79.4	1.1	0.1	—	80.6	20,150
Non-Africans						
Expatriates	0.1	0.1	0.3	0.7	1.2	300
Non-expatriates	—	—	0.1	0.1	0.2	50
Total	95.5	3.0	0.6	0.9	100.0	25,000

*Category 1: Unskilled labourers, semi-skilled and specialist workers
      2: Skilled employees and qualified workers
      3: Technicians and managerial staff
      4: Upper-class professionals
Source: Cote d'Ivoire, 1965, Emploi (Abidjan: Ministere du plan, 1965).

There are two possible solutions. The omens, from the limited experience in both Ghana and Ivory Coast, are not good for the first—to increase labour-substitutive mechanization in the savannah areas.[9] This would imply the introduction of a full package of mechanization, improved seeds, and fertilisers. The second solution would be a huge increase in the number of migrant workers in the savannah areas. For the Sahelian countries, this would have obvious attractions. But the effect of both solutions would be to increase the dependence of the Ivory Coast on non-national resources—on foreign technology and capital in the case of mechanization, and on foreign labour in the case of the second solution.

More important for our perspective, both strategies reinforce existing patterns of and pressures towards differentiation. If mechanization is achieved through the expansion of individual family farms, it tends to increase income disparities—in the short run by the immediate effect of raising the incomes of those who can mechanize, and in the long run by making possible the emergence of a limited number of very large holdings. If mechanization is organized through the extension of state farms, the supervisory cadres, probably Europeans in the early days, introduce the same pattern of social and economic differentiation we have already observed in the plantation sector.

If the labour shortage is made good by increased migration from northern countries, the immediate differentiation may be less sharp. For, great as it may be, the income gap between the smallholder and the migrant worker is less than

that between the large-scale farmer and his labourers. But the long-run effect is
to introduce an ethnic hierarchy whereby the labour of one ethnic group creates wealth and income for another ethnic group. With neither market nor legal
mechanisms to protect them or to ensure that they share in the wealth thus
created, those in the labour group thus become permanently locked into their
own servitude. The analogy with the labour races on Asian estates is not perfect, but it is too close for comfort (for a description of Asian estates, see below, pp. 134-40). Indeed, the evidence is that such a rigid hierarchy is already
established.

In that respect present-day Ivory Coast differs from the historical experience
of Ghana. There the emergence of agricultural capitalism in cocoa growing did
not depend heavily *in the first instance* on hired labour, either local or migrant.
Indeed, as we shall emphasize in Chapter 5, one of the institutional arrangements that made possible the accumulation of large areas of cocoa also made
possible a high degree of economic mobility whereby labourers could learn the
techniques of growing cocoa and eventually become cocoa farmers in their own
right.

But the development of the cocoa industry in Ghana has certainly been associated with an increasing concentration of income. That has been possible only
because the larger farmers are heavily reliant upon sharecroppers (abusamen)
and labourers, many of whom were from the Sahelian countries until they were
driven out in 1969.* A survey of 3,700 farmers found that, as size and development of the farm (or farms) increased, so the dependence on hired labour rose.
Two out of five farmers managed entirely on family labour; these were predominantly small farms, owned by farmers with few other cocoa farms. But
more significant, the majority of farms in this group had not yet come into
bearing and so the labour requirement was still comparatively low. By contrast,
those employing permanent labour had larger farms with higher yields and they
owned as many as nine individual farms.[10]

This latter point is important, for the concentration of income in the cocoa-
growing areas of Ghana has arisen from the ability of some farmers to go on
starting new farms (or expanding their original holding), leaving their existing
farms in the care of sharecroppers and labourers. This process of accumulating
acreage has been much accelerated by the reinvestment of proceeds from established farms to buy additional land and to hire labour to clear and plant it.
Farmers who are in the course of this expansion are thus doubly dependent
upon labour—to service their existing investment and to accelerate their accumulation.[11]

---

*By the Aliens Compliance Order. But many of the better organized cocoa
farmers managed to get work permits for their labourers.

That this process will result in a highly unequal distribution of wealth and income is clear. It is only now becoming possible to see just how unequal that distribution is. From Table 3.3 it seems that 5 percent of farmers produce 31 percent of all cocoa; 15 percent of farmers produce 54 percent. In fact these are underestimates of concentration, as the note to Table 3.3 indicates; it could well be that the richest 15 percent of farmers produce nearly two-thirds of all cocoa.

Less surely we can convert this distribution of gross revenue from cocoa into gross income from all sources, including subsistence food production. This shows, on the assumptions made in Table 3.4, that 38 percent of cocoa farmers receive total gross incomes of under N¢200 per annum. Five percent receive seven times as much—a distribution of income that is considerably more unequal than among recorded employees in the formal sector (respective Gini coefficients are 0.54 and 0.39).

We know very little about the stability of this small number of wealthy cocoa farmers. On their death, their farms are split up and distributed to a rather wide group of kinsmen, custom varying from group to group.[12] But the ability of the richer farmers to finance expansion had, until the Aliens Compliance Order of 1969, ensured that there was within the cocoa belt a dynamic of differentiation that would constantly tend to concentrate income in the hands of those who chose to exercise this ability. How far the reported shortage of labour, already much more acute for the larger farmers than the smaller, will impede this dynamic is not clear; as we show in Chapter 5, there is no sign of larger farmers bidding up the wages of Ghanaian labourers in an attempt to maintain the rate of expansion. (But the relevant survey was conducted at a time of weak cocoa prices, when there was little incentive to expand.)

If cocoa incomes are highly concentrated and if wealthy cocoa farmers co-exist in the forest belt with other farmers who, much less integrated into modern markets or modern production methods, have incomes even lower than the poorest cocoa farmers, it is wrong to imagine that this pattern is limited to the fertile forest areas. It can be found, perhaps to an even greater degree, in the north. For the development of rice farming has produced a capitalist style of farming, heavily dependent upon hired labour. Large-scale farmers have more than one fifth of all rice land in Ghana, nearly all of it in the Northern and Upper Regions. As with cocoa, most of the large-scale rice farmers (those with more than 50 acres) started with quite modest plots but expanded rapidly, with government encouragement and assistance (although some of the largest rice farmers were never even contacted by the estension staff[13]). In a rather typical case, a farm grew from 4 to 60 acres in six years. All of these larger rice farmers employ permanent and casual labour: 70 percent of all farm costs are wages. But as the farms are mechanized, the level of permanent employment is

TABLE 3.3

Ghana: Distribution of Gross Income from Cocoa, 1963/64
(Percentages)

Percentages of farmers accounting for percentages of production, by size distribution of production, measured in loads of 60 lbs.

Region	Average Output (loads)	Median Output (loads)	10		10-20		20-40		40-100		100-200		200		Share in Output of Top 10 Percent
			Farmer	Output	Farmer	Output	Farmer	Output	Farmer	Output	Farmer	Output	Farmer	Output	
Ashanti	71	38	13	1	18	4	21	8	27	25	14	27	7	35	42
Brong-Ahafo	66	32	19	1	18	5	19	8	26	25	11	23	7	38	45
Central	52	27	23	2	19	6	21	12	23	28	10	25	4	27	45
Eastern	54	31	14	1	20	6	27	15	27	32	8	20	4	26	42
Volta	38	20	26	3	25	10	24	19	18	29	5	16	2	23	47
Western	41	22	26	3	21	8	23	16	21	31	6	22	3	20	44
National	57	30	18	2	20	5	22	11	25	28	10	23	5	31	45

Note: There are two flaws in the important study on which Table 3.3 is based. First, it underestimates the concentration of cocoa income, since it proved impossible to combine the sales of the same farmer from different districts. Thus a large farmer with two farms in different districts will appear in the study as two separate farmers. Further, it did not always credit sales to farmers rather than sharecroppers. Second, the figures relate to gross revenue rather than net income; that is, costs are ignored.

Source: Bjorn Beckman, "The Distribution of Cocoa Income," mimeo., Staff Seminar Paper no. 13 (Department of Economics, University of Ghana, 1969-70).

TABLE 3.4

Ghana: Total Income of Cocoa Farmers Including Subsistence Food Production: Percentage of Farmers in Each Income Group, 1963/64

N₵	0-108	108-200	200-370	370-790	790-1,420	1,420 & above
Percent	18	20	22	25	10	5

Note: The most important assumptions made in this table are:

1. That the ratio of total cash income to income from cocoa varies between 1.1 and 1.3 from the highest to the lowest income groups, in accordance with the 1961 survey finding that the average ratio is 1.17.

2. That home-produced food is a constant proportion of total food consumed.

3. That the distribution of consumption in the Eastern Region Household Budget Survey can be generalized for the other cocoa-growing areas.

The figures in Table 3.4 are still gross of costs.

Source: Calculated from Bjorn Beckman, "The Distribution of Cocoa Income," mimeo., Staff Seminar Paper no. 13 (Department of Economics, University of Ghana, 1969-70).

quite low, although a large number of casual workers may be brought in to weed the padi or harvest the crop.

With a profit of between N₵34 and N₵77 per acre,[14] it is clear that these large rice farmers are earning high incomes by comparison with even the wealthiest cocoa farmers. By contrast their labourers, on an optimistic calculation, receive N₵90 per annum—enough to buy no more than one and a half pounds of rice per day for the whole family.* With free land in plentiful supply, tractors readily available for purchase from the Ministry of Agriculture or on hire with a 50 percent subsidy, a guaranteed (and rising) price for padi, plentiful subsidized credit from the Agricultural Development Bank (ADB), and a wage rate that does not nearly reflect the marginal productivity of labour, the rapid growth of this band of rice growers is a classic example of the development of rural capitalism. (However, as to credit, the ADB normally demands collateral from farmers who are not members of a co-operative. As even large farmers may be only leaseholders and have little faith in the co-operatives, this can limit the flow of credit.[15])

---

*But this does not represent the whole food supply of the family, as land is readily available for family food farms.

A final example is much less well attested and can be put only in hypotheti-cal form until more work follows Polly Hill's important research.[16] In her study of herdsmen on the Accra plains, she found, as has long been known, that the great majority of herdsmen are immigrants from the Sahel or northern Nigeria. Indeed, *all* herdsmen are called Fulani. She also found, more interest-ingly, that at least some of the Fulani build up their own herds and even aspire to become kraal-owners, employing their own herdsmen and taking other owners' cattle into their care. Thus, while the traditional picture of the Fulani has been of an exploited group, paid only in milk with no prospect of accumu-lating capital from a miserable wage, Polly Hill stresses the extent to which up-ward mobility does in fact occur.

Now we still know too little about this group to be able to show that it ful-fils all the conditions of the con-mech. What is it that brings the Fulani south? How many come? What proportion find employment? How many actually be-gin to build up their own herds? Under what conditions? How has the Aliens Compliance Order changed the system? We do not know with any certainty, and it would be unjust to force Polly Hill's evidence into this mould.

INTER-GROUP COMPETITION

We shall examine briefly only one form of inter-group competition here. We shall ignore a number of obvious areas such as the competition for land in the forest zone, the competition for subsidized inputs and markets, and competi-tion in supply of services to the rural sector, either because the volume of re-cent research makes generalization even more hazardous than in the case of Eastern Africa or because the basic mechanisms, so far as they can be under-stood from the evidence available, do not differ substantially from those of Eastern Africa. For instance, there is no shortage of evidence that urban savings are reinvested in cocoa and coffee farms in Ivory Coast and Ghana, thus tend-ing to increase the concentration of landholdings.[17] Similarly, many rural services—e.g., transport contracting—tend to be in the hands of the wealthier peasants/rural capitalists. Despite intensive efforts to promote marketing co-operatives, especially in Ghana, these remain weak, with a low expectation of effective life. It is, however, in the field of marketing that we shall examine inter-group competition in Ivory Coast, Ghana, and Cameroon. Is it the case that small and inefficient market operators exploit producers through village monopolies, thus reducing the impact of incentive prices, or that large oli-gopolies appropriate a major share of the value of farmers' produce?*

---

*In our terms the former case, village monopoly, might legitimately be regarded as intra-group conflict: the latter is clearly inter-group conflict.

We must hold over a consideration of the latter possibility to Chapter 13, where we shall show that in all three littoral countries the activities of the state marketing boards have the effect of transferring very large proportions of producers' incomes to other, usually more privileged, groups. We shall argue there that this process has some of the features of the con-mech in the sense that the reality is not fully appreciated by the victims of the con-mech and that it enriches those who control it.

Here we address only the village monopoly question. Is this an important part of enrichment and impoverishment at the village level in West Africa? Without claiming that produce markets are perfect in any sense at all, the balance of the evidence suggests that non-reciprocal relationships at the village level are not a feature of most areas of West Africa, as they are in much of Asia and parts of Eastern Africa.

The commercial ability of Ghanaian and Bamileke (in Cameroon) traders usually results in rather fierce competition for the farmer's product. For example, rice growers consistently get a higher price from traders than from the state-owned mills. This is not to say that traders' gross margins are tight: The price to the final Southern consumer is often double the price received by the farmer. We have no information on traders' net margins.[18]Cattle owners either auction their beasts to the highest bidder or bargain with a number of traders individually. The reported reluctance of cattle owners to sell consistently to one buyer or to allow themselves to be drawn into any kind of obligation relationship with prospective buyers shows how well aware they are of the potential for market manipulation. But Polly Hill has suggested that the Northern cattle trade may be becoming increasingly concentrated in a few hands.[19]

That apart, the only exception to the pattern of fairly competitive product markets seems to be Cameroon. Despite the official policy of guaranteeing a fixed price to the farmer, the marketing of export crops is controlled by a small number of merchants, dominated by Greeks and Levantines. Some of these merchants employ travelling buyers who act in collusion (through geographical market sharing) in the village to force the price down. The cocoa and coffee is then sold to the Caisse de Stabilisation at fixed prices. Only if the grower can transport his produce to Douala can he sell direct to the Caisse. But as transport is controlled by the oligopoly and as the Caisse will buy only in minimum lots that exceed the produce of most small farmers, this defence is available only to the larger growers. It was this system of marketing agents that was a source of bitter resentment in Ghana and ultimately obliged the Cocoa Marketing Board to establish a network of buying depots to which the individual seller has access. In Ivory Coast, export houses, all French-owned, operate as buying (and selling) agents for the Caisse de Stabilisation; we have no evidence of widespread malpractice as in Cameroon, possibly because the Caisse polices the activities of the agents more effectively.

At the village level, then, the relatively sophisticated networks of traditional traders and the intra-group competition within those networks may limit the gross margins of traders, to the benefit of producers and consumers. But the balance is fine. Once a farmer's independence is jeopardized—e.g., through indebtedness to the trader—he is likely to find prices moving against him. The long-term danger is that the institutionalization of the supply of credit, the rising demand for credit (particularly for consumption), and the concentration of trading activities will have exactly that effect.

NOTES

1. Ministere du developpement et direction de la statistique, *Enquete budget de consommation, 1963-64* (Upper Volta, 1966).

2. Unpublished data from the Direction de Commerce, Ouagadougou.

3. *Enquete budget,* op. cit.

4. N.O. Addo, "Some Employment and Labour Conditions on Ghana's Cocoa Farms," paper presented to Cocoa Economics Research Council, Institute of Statistical, Social and Economic Research, Legon, 1973 (mimeo.)

5. Ibid.

6. Editorial, CMB *Newsletter,* April 1970, p. 5.

7. S. Amin, *Le developpement du capitalisme en Cote d'Ivoire* (Paris: Presses Universitaires de France, 1967).

8. L. Roussel, "Problemes et politiques de l'emploi en Cote d'Ivoire," *International Labour Review* 104, no. 6 (1971).

9. See, for instance, B.E. Rourke and H.S. Hiadzi, "The Use of Tractors in the Accra Agricultural District," Report of the Second Meeting of the National Advisory Committee on Agricultural Mechanisation in Ghana (Accra, January 1970).

10. Addo, op. cit.

11. Cf. C. Okali, M. Owusuansah, and Blair Rourke, "The Development Pattern of Large Cocoa Holdings in Ghana: Some Case Studies," mimeo., paper presented to Cocoa Economics Research Council, Institute of Statistical, Social and Economic Research, Legon, 1973.

12. Polly Hill, *Migrant Cocoa Farmers of Southern Ghana* (Cambridge: Cambridge University Press, 1963), pp. 109-37.

13. J.Th. Van Logehem, "The Focus and Concentrate Programme in the Bolgatanga District: Evaluation of an Extension Programme," mimeo., Research Report Series no. 7, Social Studies Project (Cape Coast, 1972).

14. E. Amonoo, "The Production, Distribution, and Marketing of Rice in the Bolgatanga District," mimeo., Research Report Series no. 8, Social Studies Project (Cape Coast, 1972).

15. Ibid., pp. 11-15.

16. Polly Hill, *Studies in Rural Capitalism in West Africa* (Cambridge: Cambridge University Press, 1970).

17. Okali et al., op. cit.

18. Amonoo, op. cit.

19. Hill, *Rural Capitalism,* op. cit.

4

RURAL
DIFFERENTIATION
IN RICE-GROWING
COUNTRIES

Access to land is the primary axis of rural differentiation in any society and supremely in those countries where man/land ratios are high in relation to the carrying capacity of the land. Although there are considerable cultural variations in the symbolic and psychological value attached to land—e.g., Malays are more land-oriented than the Chinese, the Kandyans of Sri Lanka more than the Karavas or Goyigamas—in each of the four countries we discuss here, access to and ownership of land is the touchstone of economic success and social status. Traditionally, this was reflected in feudal and caste divisions of function: To-day, the security, independence, and potential income deriving from the owner-ship of land make it one of the most highly valued of assets at levels of the eco-nomic and social hierarchy.

In this chapter we shall be concerned exclusively with patterns of land own-ership and tenancy, and with the processes by which those patterns have been changed and are today undergoing change. Our main concern will be to show that the enrichment of some sections of the rural community has been at the cost of the absolute or relative impoverishment of those who have been ex-cluded from access to land. We shall postpone until the next chapter the de-tailed consideration of the levels of living of the excluded—both small farmers and hired labourers. Nor shall we consider in this chapter all the non-reciprocal relationships that account substantially for the impoverishment of the excluded. Rather, we shall confine the discussion entirely to the means by which land is acquired, transferred, and used. For that is the essence of rural differentiation.

In this chapter we adopt the same basic approach as in Chapters 2 and 3; that is, we analyse agricultural change in terms of con-mechs and inter- and intra-group conflicts. But as a necessary prelude to modern processes of rural differentiation, we begin with a short and highly schematized account of the genesis of the dualism of agricultural structure in all four countries. For it is an important part of our argument that the processes we describe later depend in whole or in part upon this dualism. In Asia, this took the form of the imposition of a large-scale, high-productivity, export-based plantation sector upon a basically peasant agriculture. In Sri Lanka and Malaysia, the plantation sector is largely, but not exclusively, foreign-owned; in the Philippines, it is heavily dependent upon overseas interests for its inputs, especially suppliers' credits for machinery, and of course its markets. We shall argue that it is the infiltration of nationals into this structure that goes far to explain both its endurance and its relatively generous treatment at the hands of governments of a variety of ideological hues.

THE ORIGINS OF DUALISM

The dualistic nature of agrarian structure in all four countries hardly needs emphasis, although there are great differences in the institutional and ownership characteristics of that dualism. In Egypt and the Philippines, foreign ownership is unimportant, although in the latter, dependence upon foreign markets and foreign capital is such as greatly to qualify the technical independence of large-scale agriculture, especially in sugar. In Egypt, even after nine years of land reform, the larger holdings, tiny in number but significant in acreage, were predominant in the use of hired labour, tractors, and irrigation.* This raises important questions to which we shall return in Chapter 5. For the present we confine the discussion to the effect of the establishment of the dualistic agricultural economy in the three Asian countries.

There the export-oriented estates—with their large scale of operation, relatively high levels of management, dependence upon large numbers of hired labourers, and their full integration into the international economy—are in obvious contrast to the traditional padi farmers with smallholdings, relying almost exclusively on family labour and, until very recently, using techniques that have changed only slowly over the last hundred years. It is wrong to interpret this

---

*According to the 1961 Agricultural Census, holdings in excess of 20 feddans (approximately 21 acres) accounted for 2 percent of all holdings, but 32 percent of cultivated area. Two thirds of total labour input was hired, and those owning these holdings used three quarters of all tractors and nearly half of "fixed tools of irrigation."

dualism as static and devoid of mutual interaction. Although the details naturally vary between countries and over time, the interaction is in fact pervasive,
continuous, and fundamental.

It is most clearly seen, of course, in the process of the establishment of
the estates themselves. The earliest, and in some ways the most clear-
cut, example was the establishment of the rice haciendas in Luzon and
the sugar haciendas in Negros in the Philippines. Until after the end of the
Napoleonic war, Spanish colonial policy disregarded the agricultural potential
of the colonies. The Philippines, for example, were little more than an entrepot,
handling the Chinese silk and Mexican silver trade. As a result of Spain's increasing impoverishment, and economic conditions in the colonies themselves, the
second quarter of the nineteenth century saw an agricultural boom in the Philippines. Whereas the major landowners in Luzon in the eighteenth century, for
instance, had been the religious orders, by 1840s colonists, mestizos, and a
small band of Filipino notables had begun to put together very substantial land
holdings in the rice-growing areas of Luzon and in the rich plains of Negros Island. In both cases, but more particularly in Luzon where the density of population was much greater, the establishment of these haciendas led not only to
the breakdown of the barangay land tenure system but also to a change in the
status of the cultivators from usufruct owner/tenants to paid labourers on the
haciendas. But note that the degree to which the barangay system of usufruct
had begun to be replaced by individual ownership in pre-Hispanic times is the
subject of much academic debate. But it is probably a mistake to assume that
evidence of payment is evidence of a substitution of ownership for usufruct. It
is not uncommon in either East or West Africa for both phenomena to exist
side by side for prolonged periods.[1]

Particularly significant in the case of the Negros sugar estates is that this
process of change in land tenure from a communal or semi-communal system
of small subsistence producers to a plantation-type of tenure and organization
is still continuing. With access to the profitable American market for sugar and,
as we shall see in Chapter 5, profit margins of over 100 percent of direct costs,
the sugar estates continue to expand. Output has doubled in the last decade
and, with yield falling sharply, acreage under sugar more than doubled as unsuitable and marginal land was brought into production. The way in which land
is acquired does not differ substantially from some of the ways that the early
nineteenth century hacienderos used. In both Mindanao and Negros, it is only
necessary to convince the local land tribunal that one has had the use of un-
registered land for two years to be given title. Alternatively, unalienated land
can be bought direct from the state. In theory, an officer of the tribunal is supposed to visit the site and ensure that it is unoccupied. In fact, this is seldom
done and the semi-feudal system of political relationships is able to ensure that
unfavourable reports are not passed through to the land tribunal. If the evicted

farmers protest, the local administration is too weak to secure a detailed investigation and, in most cases, is too much under the power of the large landowners to press the case further. It is not insignificant that the army commander of Mindanao estimates that three quarters of law-and-order cases in the rural areas result from disputes over land.

The Philippine case is revealing in that the sugar and rice haciendas were not established exclusively by Spaniards. A number of leading Filipino families were as quick as the colonists to exploit the new possibilities. Indeed the early land deeds reveal a mixture of Tagalog and Spanish names, with a small sprinkling of French and even British interlopers. In much the same way, in Sri Lanka the early coffee boom (before the introduction of tea) was not confined to British and Dutch colonists. By 1835 Geronis de Soysa had become the first Sri Lankan coffee grower; thirty years later half of the coffee exported was grown on estates owned by Sri Lankans, the vast majority of them by Karavas. (The Karavas originally were a fishing community and came into contact with Europeans much earlier than, for instance, the Kandyans. They were early adherents to Christianity and therefore became better educated and better integrated with the British colonists. As a result, they became wealthy and soon dominated the indigenous commercial life of the colony. One writer reckoned that in the mid-1950s some 90 percent of the richest families in Colombo were Karava.[2])

Thus developed a group of rich Sri Lankans who, unlike their Filipino haciendero counterparts, combined the functions of estate owner, trader, transport contractor, and exporter. In this they followed some of the more enterprising foreign planters who realized that the uncertain fluctuations of the crop could be much mitigated by forward integration into handling, transport, insuring, shipping, and, much later, processing and distributing in the consumer countries. It was these better integrated concerns that most easily survived the destruction of coffee by disease and most quickly diversified into tea. Although, apart from a number of Karavas, few Sri Lankans planted high-grown tea, much of the middle and lower land was bought and planted by Sri Lankans, the great majority of them from the low country rather than from Kandy itself.

In Sri Lanka the effect on the economy of the Wet and Dry Zones of this rapid expansion of tea and, to a much lesser extent, rubber was little short of disastrous. For after the imposition of Pax Britannica in the highlands and the eradication of malaria, the population grew rapidly and the traditional agricultural systems of both zones came under great pressure. That pressure was reinforced by two results of the colonial administration. The first was the technical regression resulting from the neglect and, in some cases, wilful destruction of the tanks or reservoirs used for storing irrigation water. The second was the failure of the estates to absorb local labour. The expectation had been that, after the abolition of feudal bond service, many in the local population, both Kandyans and lowlanders, would work on the estates. But such an occupation was unacceptable to those of higher caste; and those of lower caste were not highly motivated to work ancestral land for those who had usurped it.

By the outbreak of World War I, then, official concern was being expressed at the mounting population pressure in the Wet Zone, characterized by familiar problems of illicit clearing of forest land, cultivation of hill slopes, under-employment, and a declining level of living. A piecemeal approach, which involved breaking up redundant estates or settling farmers on small plots in state reserves, may have had some small local effect, but in the aggregate it did little to solve the basic problem. The Dry Zone colonization schemes were more dramatic attempts at a solution: They involved shifting population out of the Wet Zone into the Dry Zone. In this way the initial disturbance created by the estates was transferred into the Dry Zone, in some cases to the great benefit of the purana villages there. For these villages profited not only from the substantial expenditures on social infrastructure associated with the settlement schemes but also from the opportunity to act as middlemen, traders, moneylenders, and suppliers of miscellaneous services to the colonists. Many of the colonists found the agronomic demands of the schemes overtaxing and were soon heavily in debt—a condition made the more permanent by the lack of off-farm employment, so customary in the colonists' area of origin.

In Malaysia the same feature of local entrepreneurial participation in export crop production is complicated by racial patterns. In so far as non-Europeans participated in estates at all, it was the immigrant Chinese who adopted this style of production. The Chinese participation in estates has never equalled in scale that of the Sri Lankans in tea or Filipinos in sugar; the racial pattern is more noticeable in smallholdings. Although Malays and non-Malays (Chinese and Indians) share roughly equally in the ownership of 2 million acreas of rubber smallholdings, the average size of Malay holdings is only one third of non-Malay holdings. The great majority of these larger smallholdings, like the majority of small estates, are owned by Chinese. (The official boundary between a smallholding and an estate is 100 acres. At independence, the sale of European-owned estates allowed Chinese to acquire more land, break it up into smallholdings, and let it to Malays, thereby securing maximum replanting subsidies.)

During the colonial period, then, in all three countries an entirely new system, scale, and style of land ownership was superimposed upon the traditional agricultural system of small family holdings of padi land usually held under some kind of collective tenure. But as land acquired a scarcity value as a result of the interaction of population pressure and cash crop production, so ownership became less collective and more individual. We have already illustrated this with the breakdown of the barangay system in the Philippines and the substitution for it of individual freehold (or tenancy), already widespread by the end of the nineteenth century. But the best example is the spate of litigation that followed the increase of population pressure in the Wet Zone in Sri Lanka. Aggravated by caste and ethnic differences, litigation over land had reached formidable proportions by the 1930s. Indeed, as we shall emphasize later, the ability to finance litigation became one of the touchstones of economic and social security in the Wet Zone. In other words, the tenant/sharecropper/land-owner relationship, so fundamental to an understanding of distribution of agricultural income today, is the direct result of the pincer movement of land alienation and population growth begun in the colonial era. The scarcity value of land is so acute in Lower Egypt, Luzon, the Wet Zone of Sri Lanka,* and the West Coast of Malaysia that it gives the landowner an overwhelming leverage in relation to the tenant. The result is that this inter-group competition for the product is heavily biased in the landowner's favour. It is to this that we now turn, before resuming the theme of the dualistic nature of land use and its effects.

LANDLORD AND TENANT: INTER-GROUP COMPETITION

We are fortunate in being able to examine the relationship between land-owner and tenant at a time of unprecedented technical change in the traditional sector. For the impact of the introduction of new varieties of seed and associated technological changes in padi production has meant that the institutionalized and, in important senses, socialized relationships between landowner and tenant have come under severe strain. By analysing, as closely as the scattered data allow, changes in those relationships, we are able to ask how the patterns of ownership and tenancy have changed under the impact of the style of rural development defined by technical changes in production. More particularly, we are able to ask whether these technical changes have led to a deterioration in the relative and absolute positions of tenant and labourer. (We shall return to a consideration of the position of hired labourers in Chapter 5; in this chapter we shall be concerned exclusively with the relationship between landowner and tenant.)

A tenant may be made worse off in four ways: The rent may rise; it may have to be paid earlier or in cash; it may buy fewer services along with the land;

---

*And parts of the Dry Zone. The dichotomy between land-surplus Dry Zone and land-scarce Wet Zone is an over-simplification that ignores areas of great population pressure in the Dry Zone, especially in the Jaffna area. But, as B.H. Farmer pointed out in his celebrated work, *Pioneer Peasant Colonization in Ceylon,* many Dry Zone areas at least had the possibility of shifting cultivation in the jungle as an additional source of food.

and, finally (and perhaps most important), the chances of the tenant improving his status to that of owner-occupier (or perhaps a full member of some kind of collective unit) may be reduced. Let us review each of these in turn.

There is scattered evidence that, with the diffusion of new technologies, the landowner has increased his provision of inputs (seed, fertiliser) and simultaneously—and disproportionately—raised his share of the crop. Table 4.1 shows that in a longitudinal study of 42 farms in Laguna, Philippines, the landowner was found to have secured nearly half of the increase in income (38 percent plus 11 percent). That this is not an isolated case is suggested by a United Nations Research Institute for Social Development (UNRISD) study of farms in three different provinces. In every case, the landlord's share had increased—in some cases dramatically.[3] In a very different setting, in Trengganu in West Malaysia, researchers found a significant correlation between the demand for land (as reflected in land prices) and the ability of the landowners to make tenants pay for fertiliser.[4]

It is dangerous to generalize from three local studies. But there are sound theoretical reasons for expecting the landowner's share to rise in areas where there is an acute shortage of land and where customary or institutional price-fixing is beginning to collapse. Apart from the obvious pressures of supply and demand, the landlord is able to bargain with the tenant about the disposal of the extra income accruing from the introduction of the new technology. For, from the tenant's point of view, it is preferable to have a slightly smaller share of a much higher income than a larger share of a much lower income. Since he is unable to secure credit and supplies easily himself, the co-operation of the landowner is an essential precondition of an increase in the tenant's income. The tenant cannot go it alone, so he is ready to cede to the landowner a higher proportion of farm income.

Second, there is some evidence that the *form* of rent payment is changing, especially in areas where new technologies have greatly increased yields. In the northern states of Malaysia, landlords are increasingly insisting on cash payment of rents. For the tenant this involves two major changes. First, cash payments are usually made at the beginning of the season, thus placing on the tenant a much greater demand for cash at a time when traditionally his cash reserves are at nearly their lowest ebb. He is therefore obliged to borrow at high rates of interest, and his total disposable income is reduced. Second, the risk is shifted from the landlord and tenant jointly to the tenant alone. If the crop fails, he still has to pay the same fixed cash rent.* If he fails to raise money from his

---

*It is also true that, if the crop is super-abundant, he gets the full surplus rather than only half of it. But the "downside" risk is much greater than the "upside," especially if the cash rent is fixed in relation to the "normal maximum" production.

TABLE 4.1

Philippines: Distribution of Rice Output, Laguna, 1966/69

Output Share	1966[a]		1969[b]		Increase, 1966-69 (Percent)	Share of Increased Income (Percent)
	₱	Percent	₱	Percent		
Operating capital	69	7	147	9	113	11
Hired labour	183	18	341	20	87	23
Tenant	348	35	540	32	55	28
Landowner	393	40	648	39	65	38
Total	993	100	1,676	100		100

Note: Data based on records of 42 farms changing from local varieties in 1966 to high-yielding varieties in 1969 (wet season).

[a]Local varieties.

[b]High-yielding varieties.

Source: Annual Report of the International Rice Research Institute (IRRI), Los Banos, 1970, p. 181.

creditors for the next payment of rent, he can quickly be evicted and replaced by one of the large number of landless labourers.

Third, we have already seen that the services of the landlord—e.g., supply of inputs— can be shifted back to the tenant. How far this is a general phenomenon outside Tregganu is more difficult to say. Certainly one of the features of the early diffusion of improved seeds in the Philippines was the readiness, and even eagerness, of landowners to enable their tenants (especially sharecrop tenants) to use them. But whether there has been a *subsequent* shift of the financial burden is unclear. The UNRISD study of South Cotabato, Iloilo, and Camarines Sur, shows considerable regional variation. In Iloilo and Camarines Sur there is fairly clear evidence that the proportion of expenditure on seeds and fertiliser borne by the share-tenant is rising sharply; there is no such evidence for South Cotabato, perhaps reflecting the less vigorous competition for land there.[5]

Finally, is it true that tenants now find it more difficult to change their status to owners? Are patterns of differentiation becoming hardened? As Table 4.2 shows, the increase in the productivity of land has been reflected in rising land prices, giving to landowners very substantial windfall profits. The question is whether the tenants' net income has risen faster than the value of land. Land is valued by reference to the actual and potential income of the landowner. Since landowners' incomes have risen faster than tenants' incomes, it is probable

TABLE 4.2

Philippines: Land Values in San Bartolome, Tarlac

Year	Mean Price of Land (₽/hectare)
1936-40	600
1950-56	2,000
1957-59[a]	3,200
1967-69[b]	7,500

[a]Camiling River irrigation system completed.

[b]IRRI varieties introduced.

Source: Annual Report of the International Rice Research Institute (IRRI), Los Banos, 1970, p. 181.

that the value of land has increased faster than tenants' incomes. The tenant finds it more difficult to buy land.

It is also probable that the value of land in relation to the income associated with it has risen (i.e., the price/earnings ratio has risen). In the Philippines and Malaysia, the long tradition of landowning by urban capitalists (albeit sometimes quite small capitalists) has been much boosted since the adoption of new techniques and the wide publication of their potential. How far threats of land reform in the Philippines and the re-enactment of the Control of Rent Act in 1967 in Malaysia have deterred urban investors is questionable. The maximum permitted holding under the former is high, and the latter is widely known to be a dead letter. Under these conditions, urban (or quasi-urban) capital is likely to bid up the price of land in relation to its yield—making it even more difficult for the tenant to buy.

In so far as land is reverting to the operator, it is the owner-tenant—i.e., the farmer who owns most of his farm and rents an additional plot—who is able to use the much higher income from his owned land to buy the tenanted portion of his farm. This suggests a gradual polarization in the agrarian structure, with owners able to earn high incomes (in relation to the rest of the rural population) while the incomes of tenants rise much more slowly (for wages of labourers, see below, pp. 126-36).

In the light of this evidence, it is difficult to escape the conclusion that, although the incomes of both landlords and tenants have risen in areas affected by the new technology, the non-reciprocal relationships that are the essence of differentiation have become strengthened thereby. In other words, technological change has strengthened even further the leverage of the landowners in this kind of inter-group competition. This is not to say that they have appropriated all the gains; they clearly have not done that. But it is to argue that the delineations of differentiation, of which income is an important but not exclusive part, are becoming more firmly drawn and less easily erased than hitherto.*

This raises a most important point. If the result of technological change is to ossify socio-economic relationships (even as the ways in which those relationships are expressed change quickly) so that two of the most fundamental status changes for the poor—from labourer to tenant, and from tenant to owner—become more difficult, then it is clear that mobility in this sense is reduced (for the condition of labourers, see Chapter 5). Further, in the long run the twin forces of land concentration and market saturation reduce the rate of growth of owner-operators. The access cone becomes both longer and narrower. But there can be no certainty that the numbers trying to get through that cone will fall simultaneously as a result of the expansion of industrial employment. To believe in so simple an automaticity would require a trust in a neo-classical growth model of breathtaking naivete.

Are we therefore justified in seeing technological change, so vigorously promoted by aid organizations and national elites, as a con-mech? It certainly enriches those who are able to adopt it efficiently. It is accompanied by intra-group competition for scarce resources. That competition is selective and favours primarily those who have access to credit, physical resources, and, perhaps, better "farm-gate" prices. The competition for resources is probably sufficiently open to retain confidence, particularly where sources of credit are diverse and continually changing (e.g., as new official or quasi-official bodies are created). Benefits are not limited to farmers who apply the new technology—they accrue (perhaps to a larger degree than to the farmers themselves), to land-owners, to merchants, and to commercial suppliers of inputs and processors of output. In so far as these "control" the technological parameters of small-scale farming, they certainly share richly in the benefits of the new technology—a point to which we shall return.

In terms of inter-group competition, then, the basic conditions are satisfied. But what of access? Is technological change also a con-mech in terms of access to a change of status from tenant to owner? It may prove to be so ex post, since, the price of land may rise faster than a tenant's disposable income. In that sense, a tenant may consistently misjudge the size of the access cone. But we have to be careful not to apportion to the tenant a motivation that he may not in fact have. He adopts a new technology less to change his status than to increase his income. It would be legitimate to see technological change as an

---

*The major exception to this, already mentioned, is the sharecrop tenant/ owner, who may now be better able to buy in the rest of his land and thus establish himself as a full owner-operator. This is not necessarily an insignificant group, but it is a group that was already privileged.

access con-mech only if it were clear that a major reason for adopting (or seeking to adopt) such change was, ex ante, to buy land. The high proportion of extra income that is consumed is (fragile) evidence that this is not usually the case.

All we can say, then, is that if status change *is* a major motive, it is likely to be frustrated by the enrichment of those who presently own land that is appreciating in value. Certainly there is no evidence of structural change whereby tenants do in fact become landowners: Such limited evidence as there is points the other way.[6]

INTER-GROUP CONFLICT AND INSTITUTIONAL CHANGE

In the last section we were concerned with the effect of technical change— more specifically, the introduction of high-yielding varieties—on patterns of ownership and the rewards of tenancy. As we shall emphasize in the next chapter, the number of farm families that have benefitted from this new technology is limited to those who meet a fairly rigorous set of conditions—ability to acquire the inputs, skill to apply them reasonably efficiently, access to a market that can handle the increased output without dropping the price, access to additional peak-period labour, and to adequate irrigation and drainage. Large groups of farmers are thus by-passed, a fact that has over the last few years raised in much sharper form a fundamental question of the nature of rural development. While it would be putting it too strongly to say that it has brought the efficiency algorithm into disrepute, it has made planners and politicians face yet again the issue of who are to be the beneficiaries of rural development. Let us illustrate this in the case of Malaysia.

The division of authority at independence left the Chinese with the great weight of urban economic power, and the Malays with political power. Long before the 1969 riots, therefore, rural development aimed primarily at the Malays was seen as a viable political goal that the Chinese would not find econominically threatening. But that development was conceived in terms of providing infrastructure and inputs rather than as tackling the roots of poverty creation in the rural areas. This conception did not stem from a naive diagnosis of the sources of Malay poverty, though such naivete is no stranger to official documents. Rather, it stems directly from the structure of Malaysian government and the political difficulties and dangers attaching to any attempt to adjust relationships at the grass roots. For there is no tradition of independent and democratic local government in Malaysia. Feudal authority is enshrined in the constitution at state level. Even after the introduction of the New Economic Policy (NEP)—with its more clearly defined target groups of poor Malays—the regulation of rents, reform of land tenure, limitation on rates of interest, and particularly the smashing of the power of merchants and middlemen would have released economic and political forces that national or state politicians would have been unable to control. The history of rent control is a good example, to which we shall return.

The alternative approach, then, was to provide a thick "ground cover" of administrative units, directed from Kuala Lumpur and aimed exclusively at solving the *technical* problems of small-scale agriculture.[7] (An incomplete count of government agencies operating services available to padi farmers and/or rubber smallholders in early 1974 revealed 15 organizations.) Credit extension, co-operation, irrigation—all these parts of a total package were supplied by a bewildering, overlapping, and sometimes conflicting set of institutions at federal, state, and mukim level. Rural *marketing* was much less thoroughly institutionalized, with the result that the guaranteed price of padi was not always paid to the farmer (see below, pp. 95-97).* Co-operatives were not very efficient at remedying this situation, particularly because the richer farmers tended to join farmers' associations that were not necessarily sensitive to the needs of the smaller farmers. Government's reaction was to create a Farmers' Organization Authority in 1973 to end the conflict between farmers' associations and co-operatives. But it is significant that the Authority's powers in marketing are limited to providing technical assistance to local farmers' organizations. It will be surprising indeed if this proves an effective means of challenging the power of the small trader over the small farmer.

The Malaysian experience is not unique. The charade of land reform in the Philippines and the failure of successive Sri Lankan governments to solve the problems created on the resettlement schemes in the Dry Zone by the activities of traders and moneylenders are further examples of the same phenomenon—a definition of rural development that stops short at the solving of (some selective) technical problems without seeking to provide a legal and administrative frame within which the rights and interests of the economically weak may be safeguarded.

But this is not accidental.

It results directly from the perception of the political risks involved in challenging those in the rural areas who benefit from the fact of non-reciprocity—e.g., the large landowners, the rural banks and traders. We would classify the ameliorative reforms that result as pure con-mechs. They are sold

---

*The Federal Agricultural Marketing Authority was established in 1972. So far its major activities have been the provision of marketing channels for newly introduced crops. How far it will be an effective competitor with traditional traders dealing with traditional crops remains to be seen.

to the rural poor as a means by which their status and/or income levels can be fundamentally, even radically, improved. In fact, as we shall show, the effect in most cases has been very modest. Apart from the political benefits accruing to the ruling elites from appearing to take action on behalf of the rural poor, the major benefits arise from turning attention away from more relevant and basic issues, such as the remaining dualistic structure of agriculture and landholding, the continued foreign dominance and ownership of scarce resources (especially land), and the infiltration by, and co-option of, the elite into the plantation sector. Let us illustrate this with some examples of ameliorative reform, before turning in conclusion to structural reform.

We begin with the ameliorative approach in Malaysia. Popular disturbances (and suspected affiliation to the Communist guerrillas) in Kedah in northern Malaysia prompted serious concern about the plight of tenants in the early 1950s. After some delay, the colonial administration issued the Padi Cultivators (Control of Rent and Security of Tenure) Ordinance in 1955. This provided for written agreements of one year's duration and laid down maximum rents according to the type of soil and potential yields. But neither the ordinance nor subsequent activity by the administration provided adequate means of enforcement, with the result that, except for a short period in Kedah itself, the ordinance was simply ignored.

Following a federal investigation of the level of rents throughout the country, the federal government passed an act with the same title in 1967. The structure and terms of that act did not differ much from those of the earlier ordinance, except that it laid down in greater detail the mechanics of enforcement. However, under the independence constitution, land legislation is the prerogative of the state rather than the federal government: Although the federal government can legislate on land matters, that legislation is not effective until it has been adopted by the individual state governments. Given the feudal nature of state government, it is no surprise to find that by late 1972 only two states had adopted the act, and in them implementation was slow. In Province Wellesley, for instance, 40 percent of farmers pay rents in excess of the level stipulated in the 1967 act, and the average rent for all farmers is more than 25 percent above the stipulated level.[8] (Excessive rents in this sense are not universal. In Kelantan, where both holdings and yields are lower than in Province Wellesley, rents are generally within the stipulated limits.[9])

Another good example of the ameliorative approach in Malaysia is given by the attempts to relieve population pressure, particularly along the West coast, by making available to the landless unalienated land. The Fringe Alienation and group settlement schemes by which uncleared land was made available to nearby villagers were piecemeal attempts to relieve population pressure near existing settlements. They were only partially successful. Because of a rather low level of ancillary services, the Chinese beneficiaries of the schemes, with their better access to credit and markets and their greater readiness to grow cash crops until tree crops matured, tended to survive much better than the Malay settlers. Indeed, political interference in the choice of settlers tended to ensure that the neediest families were never given the chance to benefit from the schemes. For they were not clients of local politicians.[10]

As an altogether more radical way of tackling the problem, the Federal Land Development Authority (FLDA) was set up as an instrument whereby the poorest rural dwellers could be lifted out of the traditional environment of which they were captive and put into a supervised environment that would give them at least some of the advantages of the modern sector. The criteria of selection for FLDA schemes specify younger married men with some schooling, some agricultural or associated skill, but owning no more than two acres of land. Once selected, the settler is paid a subsistence wage until his trees come into bearing and is kept under close supervision by the scheme managers. As the trees mature, he begins to pay off the cost of his land. At the end of that period, he achieves title and thus ends up with a sufficiently large holding of rubber or oil palm to ensure a very adequate income. (As the operation of oil palm demands large-scale production, groups of farmers co-operatively own blocks of oil palm. Therefore, the individual does not get tenure.)

The significance of FLDA's operations (about half of the new land brought into cultivation during the Second Malaysian Plan is under FLDA's direction) is that it is a very effective way of raising the income of the beneficiaries of the scheme. It is true that for them it can break the circle of indebtedness and exploitation, but it does nothing to break that circle for the much larger number of peasant farmers and smallholders who can never be settled on FLDA land, which was only 7 percent of all smallholdings in 1971.

There is a further point. The improvement in the levels of living of the FLDA settlers is not likely to endure. For the rate of growth of population on the schemes is very high since the selected settlers are in the most fertile age groups. Once rubber or oil palm come into bearing, the amount of work involved falls sharply. This is likely to occur at the same time as the settlers' children reach an employable age. Thus some of the early schemes are plagued by high levels of under-employment, with virtually no opportunity for off-farm work. It is true that with ten acres of rubber the settlers are better off than they would have been with less than two acres, but some kind of formal or informal subdivision is almost inevitable. The reimposition of the non-reciprocal relationships that characterize traditional kampongs cannot then be avoided.

Also, although in general both incomes and provision of social services are higher on FLDA schemes than in the rural areas, one notable exception is the lack of secondary schools. This is one reason why many Malays regard migration to town, even without security of employment, as preferable to settlement on an FLDA scheme.

The second example of ameliorative land reform shows the same concern with raising incomes and the same neglect of the relationships that threaten that income. Land reform in the Philippines has been under active or passive discussion since the beginning of the century. As long as American rule continued, the coincidence of interest between Filipino landlords and American sugar, rice, and timber traders ensured that land reform did not extend beyond the colonization of new lands. The vigorous programme of reform in the 1950s was the victim of administrative weakness: As in Malaya, attempts to fix maximum rents were unsuccessful. (On first-class land, actual rents exceeded stipulated rents by 7.5 percent, and on second-class land by 12.5 percent.[11]) After a closed season during the administration of President Garcia, land reform was again given a high priority by his successor, President Macapagal, who in 1963 forced through a reluctant Congress the Agricultural Land Reform Code. The objectives of this were: (1) to convert sharecroppers to leaseholders, fixing the lease rental at 25 percent of the average net farm income of the preceding three crops, and (2) to convert tenants to purchasing owners.

Perhaps inevitably, progress was slow. The conversion of sharecroppers to leaseholders depended upon the initiative of sharecroppers and the administration of grossly undermanned and badly designed field teams. After five years of operation, fewer than 22,000 sharecroppers had become leaseholders. Thereafter the pace of the reform accelerated, and by the middle of 1971 a quarter of the sharecroppers eligible for leasehold status had achieved it. But the impact of the programme was concentrated in the province of Ecija Nueva as a result of the combined pressure from tenants and foreign aid agencies in that area.

What effect did this rather limited reform have on the income of leaseholders? To answer that question is difficult because it is important to standardize all other variables such as soil, farm size, family size, agricultural skill, and the availability of implements. No existing study does, or perhaps even can, fulfill all those conditions. The two that come nearest to it tell the same story. The effect of the change in tenure has been to decrease output, usually only slightly, but to double income. The reduction in production is almost certainly the result of difficulties that new leaseholders have in securing credit. The institutional substitutes for the landlord have not been successful in reaching the leaseholders, primarily because the leaseholder is unable to offer land as collateral. But as his income has nonetheless doubled, he is unlikely to much regret his inability to farm as intensively as the sharecropper.[12]

Almost inevitably, then, the dependence upon the landlord, at least as a supplier of credit and in some cases other services, has not been much affected by the change in the tenant's status—at least in the short run. This is partly because the tenant himself is reluctant to break the relationship with the landlord for non-economic reasons. Traditionally, the relationship between the landlord and tenant was not purely economic. In Tagalog the relationship was one of "utang-na-loob" or moral indebtedness, almost gratitude. In some cases tenants maintain this relationship for its own sake, but it is interesting that some researchers have found that the readiness of the tenant to preserve the relationship and his concern about his obligation of "utang-na-loob" declines as other forms of credit become more readily available. So it may be that, as and if rural institutions take over the functions of the landlord, this dependency can be broken. So far there is little evidence that such institutions as there are have been successful in reaching the bulk of small farmers. (One authoritative source told us that 60 percent of Agricultural Development Bank loans are made to the sugar hacienderos of Negros.)

The second prong of the Land Reform Code was the conversion of tenants to purchasing landowners. The Land Reform Code provided for the *voluntary* submission of land by large landowners for redistribution; alternatively, it gave the Land Authority power to expropriate land to redistribute it to existing tenants. In practice, no land was expropriated and only intense, and in many cases violent, pressure (particularly in Central Luzon) persuaded landowners to submit their land for redistribution "voluntarily." Therefore, progress was even slower than in the case of sharecroppers. By the end of 1971, less than 5,000 hectares of large farms or haciendas had been submitted; fewer than 2,000 farm families had benefitted, representing less than 3 tenant families per 1,000 in the country as a whole.

The effect of this part of the Land Reform Code has not been studied, but there is no reason to believe that it is different from that of the sharecroppers. But one thing is clear. In so far as the Land Reform Code aimed to eliminate the smallest units and consolidate land ownership in farms that would provide a decent family income, it failed. Very few of the smallest owners were eliminated. Even after the reform and after they had completed payments for the land, it is likely that they would depend upon off-farm income to survive.

A third example may be drawn from Egypt. There land reform was given a very high priority by the army, for it was seen to symbolize at once the distinction of some of the worst abuses of the old order and the shift in the centre of politico-economic gravity that the Revolution embodied. It took the new regime only a month and a half to prepare the first Land Reform Law, evidence of the need for quick, decisive action that would convince the sceptics that the old order had indeed passed away.

But had it? In *structural* terms, the first phase of land reform (1952-61) acted almost exclusively on the "tails" of the landholding distribution. The ceilings were high—200 feddans for a single person with an extra 100 for a dependent child, up to a maximum of 300 feddans (1 feddan = 1.04 acres). But, as large landowners were given time to sell their land privately, much of the cutting edge of the legislation was blunted through intra-familial redistribution and private sales (admittedly often at distress prices) to those whose holding did not quite reach the ceiling. Expropriated land was sold by the state, with priority to the cultivator and then to the non-cultivators with the largest families (on the reasonable expectation that they would have the lowest income per head).[13] But the total area of land involved was less than 9 percent of Egypt's cultivated land; only one million people (including farmers' dependents) changed their status from tenants (pure or mixed) to full owners.

It would be false to expect huge changes in the distribution of ownership. The main effect was to reduce the proportion of land held in farms of over 50 feddans from 34.2 percent to 20.3 percent. The absolute number of farms of less than 5 feddans increased slightly, and the proportion of land in these small farms rose from 35.4 percent to 46.6 percent. We thus find a significant fall in the Gini coefficient (from 0.64 before the reform to 0.49 after it), but a continuation of a structure in which the huge bulk of the population (94 percent) farms holdings of less than five feddans. Abdel Fadil has put it this way: "the lopsided pattern of landownership tended to be preserved under different redistributional mappings. . . . While reducing the overall degree of concentration in landownership, as measured by Gini coefficient, the Egyptian agrarian reforms have failed to produce a major change in the *scale of relativities* in the distribution pattern of landownership."[14]

Now it cannot be argued that this is the simple result of scarce resources and a distribution already heavily concentrated on the small holdings—i.e., the "there is too little for redistribution to make any difference" argument. For even after the more radical reform of 1961 (when the ceiling was reduced to 100 feddans), nearly 30 percent of total area was in holdings exceeding 20 feddans. (And there is reason to believe that official data understate the proportion of land held in larger holdings, since no allowance is made for multiple holdings, although this is known to be quite common.) Thus, despite two major land reforms, the latter taken after the regime's much publicized shift to the left, the distribution of land ownership remained highly skewed. In 1965— the last year for which relatively reliable data are available—the 10,000 largest landowners possessed at least one eighth of all the cultivated land in Egypt. Indeed, 5.2 percent of owners (those with more than 5 feddans) owned at least one third.

If we turn from a consideration of ownership to holdings, we find much the same picture emerges. Between 1950 and 1961, the proportion of holdings under 2 feddans actually increased (from 46 percent to 50 percent of all holdings)—despite an official view that the minimum viable holding for the average rural family was between 4 and 5 feddans.[15] In this sense it is hard to see how the land reform measures achieved much to solve the *structural* problems of the poorest families.

As Doreen Warriner has rightly emphasized, however, the redistribution of land represented a less significant change than the notable "income effect" arising from the rent ceiling.[16] New rents were fixed at a maximum of seven times the land tax. Before the reform, average rant per feddan ranged from £E30 in Lower Egypt to as much as £E70 in Upper Egypt. The ensuing reduction to a country-wide average of £E21 a feddan was thus considerable. Estimates of the aggregate sum thus redistributed from landowners to tenants vary from £E20 million per annum to £E40 million per annum, a particularly difficult source of variance being the area of land actually affected.[17]

B. Hansen and G.A. Marzouk have estimated that the drop in the absentee owners' share in agricultural value added amounted to nearly one half of its previous level prior to the land reform,[18] thus allowing for a rise by about one third in the share going to tenants. But it would be quite misleading to see this as a *permanent* structural change in the distribution of agricultural income. Gabriel Saab, for instance, has documented widespread erosion of the ceilings. A common practice is for a tenant to sign a lease based on the official ceiling, but simultaneously to give an undertaking to pay an additional sum.[19] This "unofficial" rise in actual rents has meant that a proportion, and perhaps a substantial proportion, of the redistributed income has now been lost back to the landowners.

Those who have avoided this "clawback" are, of course, those who have become full owners of redistributed land. In so far as the payment instalments are less than the former rent, there has been a straight financial transfer to this group. Further, in so far as yields have risen faster under ownership than they would have under tenancy (a proposition that is extremely difficult to prove), there has been a further indirect benefit. One estimate is that net *money* incomes increased 137 percent between 1952 and 1965.[20] Lacking reliable budget and price studies, it is impossible to translate these money gains. There is much scrappy evidence of increases in rural consumption of textiles, footwear, tobacco, tea, coffee, and even meat.[21] Particularly marked has been the attempt by small-holders to increase the education of their children; but how far that can legitimately be described as a genuine income effect of land reform is open to doubt.

In general, then, it would be as foolish to write off Egyptian land reform as trivial as it would be to applaud it as a fundamental recasting of rural society. But the scattered evidence of rising, perhaps rather slowly rising, levels of living in the villages is real. We have emphasized that, even after two major attempts at redistribution, the scale of relativities remains remarkably constant. The basic dualism remains inviolate. Further, the rent "ceiling" has proved flexible in the face of strong market forces. Although we cannot measure the extent of "clawback," its reality cannot be denied. Particularly for the 50 percent of farmers on the smallest holdings (less than 2 feddans)—and supremely the 300,000 tenant families among them (accounting for over 2 million people)—it is hard to see how land reform much improved their lot in the long term.

These three examples of ameliorative approaches to land reform are successful in raising the income of some of the poorest in the rural population. That is important, and it is no part of our argument to belittle it. But in two important respects the approach is seriously deficient.

First, it is slow, piecemeal, and selective—with the biases in that selection tending to discriminate against the poorest.

Second, and more important, it leaves nearly intact the circle of dependence and domination that results directly from non-reciprocal relationships at the village level. Even the new institutions perpetuate, if in attenuated form, these relationships. In Malaysia, the FLDA estate manager is substituted in some respects for the landowner. The tenants' economic relationship with him may be different (although on more recent FLDA schemes the tenant is charged a management cess to pay for the services of the management), but their dependence is not much changed. In the case of the Philippines, the former landowner no longer owns the land, but he remains an important source of finance. In that respect the farmer's dependence upon him is not reduced. Even on the much smaller land settlement areas in the Philippines, where one might expect these relationships to be absent,* squatter-settlers are dependent upon monopsonistic traders and moneylenders.

In these ways, then, it seems clear that ameliorative measures are con-mechs. They are offered as a means by which large numbers can improve their status and/or income. In fact, only a small, even tiny, proportion benefits, but the benefits of those few give the con-mech, and the claims made for it, a legitimacy in the eyes of those who do not and cannot benefit. The measures taken leave intact the major structures of inter- and intra-group competition but simultaneously buttress government's credibility. Certainly this credibility is not universally shared—witness the history of rural unrest in Luzon, Mindanao, and, less consistently, north-west Malaysia and the Wet Zone of Sri Lanka. But it is shared sufficiently widely for most of the time to save the elites represented in government from having to run the political risks of a confrontation with the major structures of rural (and sometimes urban) power.

It is only when the con-mech breaks down that such a confrontation becomes inevitable. When the political costs of not challenging at least some of the major power structures in the rural areas exceed the risks of doing so, more fundamental action is taken. The riots of 1971 in Sri Lanka and the continual challenges to the Sri Lankan Freedom Party from both left and right thereafter made sweeping land reform, admittedly with rather generous ceilings, a line of least political resistance. In the Philippines, the same is broadly true. After the declaration of martial law, President Marcos badly needed to convince the

---

*The activities of the land settlement authorities tend to lag behind those of the squatters. Therefore, the operations of the authorities are usually limited to making official the status quo.

electorate, and especially the new race of technocrats with which he had surrounded himself, that this time talk of the New Society was not empty. The following verbatim record of an informal talk by Arturo Tanco, Secretary of Agriculture, is particularly revealing:

> Presidential Decree No. 2, stressing the cornerstone of the New Society, was a decree declaring land reform to be effective throughout the country. Unfortunately, this was issued the second day of Martial Law *and we had no time to confer with the President.* Presidential Decree No. 27 corrected Presidential Decree No. 2 and made it really a fundamental reform of the land because we said to the President: "Sir, what kind of reform is leasehold? It does nothing but reaffirm the Old Society. What we need is to declare farmers owners of the land they till. Let us not pussyfoot around anymore. We have pussyfooted around for 50, 60, 70 years" . . .
>
> I have 4,000 people working night and day, literally, and Sundays, trying to do this, because we feel that this is an impact program. We are convinced that the sincerity of the New Society, its democratic nature, can be proven best in this fashion. We mean it. And for a change, my Bureau of Lands personnel, who used to be one of the slackest—not one of the most corrupt, there are more corrupt people—are up there now working with the single-minded goal of trying to implement this land transfer operation.[22] [Emphasis added.]

In this case, Tanco and his newly drafted colleagues were in a position to insist to a badly shaken regime that the gap between rhetoric and action be at least partly closed.

An interesting question is why more fundamental action did not arise from the same breakdown of existing con-mechs in Malaysia with the riots there. The New Economic Policy (NEP) adopted after the riots is in many ways a highly conservative strategy, particularly in its approach to the rural areas. As we have already argued, the response was to redouble the con-mechs—e.g., substituting farmers' organizations for farmers' associations—rather than to redistribute land or break up foreign-owned estates. The explanation lies in the balance of political and economic power, especially in the urban areas of Malaysia. For the federal government to have instituted a major programme of redistribution of existing assets (i.e., give Chinese assets to Malays) would have run political risks at the federal and state level that no fundamentally conservative group could countenance. Indeed, it was difficult enough to persuade the Chinese to live with the NEP with its emphasis on a preferential distribution of *new* assets. With this constraint, recourse to a new family of con-mechs, with the attendant risks that they will eventually forfeit confidence and collapse, was inevitable.

Let us examine what has happened in the Philippines and Sri Lanka as a result of the breakdown of the con-mechs.

We have already seen that in the Philippines, the imposition of martial law at the end of widespread manifestations of popular resentment at social and economic policy was accompanied not only by a new style of rhetoric but also by a new style of technocratic government that took some elements of the rhetoric seriously. At least some of the technocrats understood that the widespread discontent in the rural areas, symbolized by the organization of guerrilla groups in Northern Luzon, stemmed from and fed upon the perpetuation of these unbalanced relations. For land reform to be effective, it must tackle those relations at their root.

In a very different political context, Mrs. Bandaranaike's Sri Lanka Freedom Party (SLFP) came to power in an alliance with a small Communist party on a platform of radical land reform. Pushed by a fairly uncompromising report from the International Labour Organization, shaken by the insurrection, and goaded by widespread "satiyagarah" by the opposition United National Party, the government had little choice but to take, or *appear* to take, drastic action.* For it was clear that the 1954 Padi Lands Act, which had aimed to regulate the conditions of tenancy and to reduce rents to 25 percent of the crop, had been wholly ineffective—largely because the cultivation committees that were supposed to implement the act had become dominated by landlords.

In both cases, then, there was an unusual but, to repeat, very different concurrence of political interest in tackling the structures of poverty at the village level. In the Philippines, this was done by making the issue of title to all tenants of land conditional upon the farmer becoming a fully paid-up member of a recognized farmers' co-operative. In Sri Lanka, much the same approach has been taken. There a major emphasis of the new land reform is on collective and co-operative developments. Very little land is being made available to individual owner-operators; in nearly every case, an applicant for land has to agree to join a producers' co-operative or to farm a block of land collectively. (This excludes state farms, at least some of which will be organized on collective lines.)

The significance of this is that, for all the well-known failings of co-operatives and other forms of grass-roots farm organizations, and taking due note of all the popular reservations about implementation of legislation in the Philippines, it is clear that both these measures are designed to change completely the economic and social environment in which the farmer lives and works. They are designed to break his dependence upon the moneylender, the merchant, the trader, the landlord, and the shopkeeper. In marked contrast to past attempts in both these countries and continuing attempts in Malaysia, there is a

---

*This may be too negative an account. The SLFP hoped by this legislation to attract some of the radical young who had been sympathetic with and even active in the insurrection.

real political confrontation with the whole web of village monopoly and monopsony.

This is not to say that either experiment will necessarily work. As we emphasized with respect to Ujamaa, of prior importance is the fact that for once the political conditions of effective rural development have been met. They may well be subverted by internal or external political forces. What is relevant for our purposes is that each experiment offers evidence that the pattern of rural differentiation can be changed. Whether it can be changed enduringly remains an open question.

But note how limited this new generation of reform is. It is not a con-mech in the pure sense, because the evidence is that a very significant number of the rural poor will, in fact, benefit, and that there will be a real, net, and lasting redistribution of assets in their favour at the cost of various groups of the privileged. But the ceilings are high in both countries; the foreign-owned estates in Sri Lanka were nearly wholly exempt; the large owner-operator farms and haciendas in the Philippines were not touched; some of the most oppressive forms of land acquisition in Negros and Mindanao continue. The latest reforms are a nice political judgment—to contain popular discontent without undermining the support of the rural outposts of the top elites.

CONCLUSION

We have seen that the dualistic nature of agricultural development in these Asian countries can be properly understood only in the context of a continuing interaction. One effect of that interaction was to trap the traditional sector in a set of exploitative relationships made worse by population pressure and technical change.

In the past, the political reaction to this has been to try to help a small proportion of the worst affected without challenging the root of the problem. Recent developments in Sri Lanka and the Philippines may signal a new approach, but it would be very unwise to accord to either the extravagant and premature praise that Ujamaa received in its early years. For, although both countries may have begun to tackle the nexus of monopoly and monopsony at the village level, the fact remains that foreign estates were excluded from land reform in Sri Lanka. The sugar haciendas in Negros continue to expand. The scale of FLDA's operations remain on a different scale to the problems of rural poverty in Malaysia. In short, dualism is the epitome of differentiation. Impoverishment of the rural areas of Asia is the epitome of poverty.

NOTES

1. See Leslie Bauzon, "Rural History, Land Tenure and the Negros Hacienda Complex: Some Preliminary Notes," *PSSC Social Science Information* 1, no. 3 (1974); Cf. E.H. Blair and J.A. Robertson, eds., *The Philippine Islands 1492-1895,* vol. 7 (Cleveland, 1907); Marshall McLennan, "Land and Tenancy in the Central Luzon Plain," *Philippine Studies* 17 (October 1969).

2. B. Stein, "Development Problems in Ceylon," in *Aspects of Economic Development in Southern Asia* (New York: Praeger Publishers, 1954), p. 87; Cf. G.C. Mendis, *Ceylon under the British* (Colombo, 1944), pp. 55-60.

3. Aida Librero and Mahar Mangahas, as quoted in Ingrid Palmer, "New Rice in Monsoon Asia," part II, mimeo. (Geneva: UNRISD), p. 246.

4. John Drewell and Hj Osman bin Mohd. Noor, "Socio-Economic Survey of Tenancy Patterns in Trengganu Padi Production," mimeo. (Kuala Lumpur, 1971).

5. Palmer, op. cit., Tables 11.5 to 11.7, pp. 239-41.

6. Keith Griffin, *The Green Revolution: An Economic Analysis* (Geneva: UNRISD, 1972).

7. Stephen Chee, "Rural Local Government and Development Administration in Malaysia," South East Asia Development Group (SEADAG) Seminar, Cornell University, Ithaca, N.Y., 1974, mimeo.

8. S. Selvadurai, "Socio-Economic Study of Padi Farms in Province Wellesley, 1968," mimeo. (Kuala Lumpur: Ministry of Agriculture and Co-operatives, March 1969), p. 44.

9. S. Selvadurai, Ani bin Arope, and Nik Hassani bin Mohammad, "Socio-Economic Study of Padi Farms in the Kemubu Area of Kelantan, 1968," mimeo. (Kuala Lumpur: Ministry of Agriculture and Co-operatives, 1969), p. 108.

10. Tunku Shamsul Bahrin, "A Preliminary Study of the Fringe Alienation Schemes in West Malaysia," *Journal of Tropical Geography* 28 (1969), p. 82.

11. Akira Takahashi, *Land and Peasants in Central Luzon* (Honolulu: East-West Centre, 1969), p. 71.

12. P.R. Sandoval and B.V. Gaon, "An Economic Analysis of the Effects of Land Reform in Selected Areas in the Philippines," (University of the Philippines Colege of Agriculture, 1972); Bureau of Agricultural Economics, "Study of Eleven Municipalities in Pampanga and Bulacan," mimeo. (Manila, 1971).

13. Sayed Marei, "The Agrarian Reform in Egypt," *International Labour Review* 69, no. 2 (February 1954): 140-50.

14. M. Abdel-Fadil, *Employment and Income Distribution in Egypt 1952-1970,* Discussion Paper (Norwich: University of East Anglia, 1974). Cf. Rodney Wilson, *Rural Employment and Land Tenure: An Egyptian Case Study* (Cairo: Institute of National Planning (INP), 1973), there quoted.

15. Marei, op. cit., pp. 145-46. Cf. *Rural Employment Problems in the UAR* (Geneva: International Labour Organization, 1969), p. 36.

16. Doreen Warriner, *Land Reform and Development in the Middle East* (London: Oxford University Press, 1962), p. 33.

17. For example, contrast Sayed Marei (a particularly well-informed observer as he was in charge of implementing the 1952 reforms), "UAR Overturning the Pyramid," *Ceres* (Rome, FAO) 2, no. 6 (1969): 50, with U.N. Department of Economic and Social Affairs, *Progress in Land Reform* (New York, 1956), p. 136.

18. B. Hansen and G.A. Marzouk, *Development and Economic Policy in the UAR* (Amsterdam: North Holland, 1965).

19. Gabriel Saab, *The Egyptian Agrarian Reform* (London: Oxford University Press, 1967), p. 145. Cf. Hansen and Marzouk, op. cit., p. 85.

20. E. Eshag and M.A. Kemal, "Agrarian Reform in the UAR," *Bulletin of the Oxford University Institute of Economics and Statistics* 30 (May 1968): 97; but Abdel-Fadil, op. cit.—drawing on material from A. Abdel-Malek, *Military Society* (New York: Random House, 1968)—argues that these estimates much overstate net income since they underestimate the true level of overhead charges, especially irrigation charges and the repayment of earlier debts.

21. Saab, op. cit., pp. 124-25.

22. James Hoyt, ed., *Development in the 1970s,* Fifth Annual Seminar for Student Leaders (Manila, 1973).

5

The purpose of this chapter is primarily descriptive. We have sketched out the processes of competition that exclude some farmers from access to markets and others from access to land. Here we present a picture of those thus excluded, the losers in the competitive process, the victims of the con-mechs we reviewed in Chapters 2 to 4. Where necessary or helpful, we amplify the analysis presented there, especially in terms of the inter- and intra-group competition that affects the rural excluded.

We deal with three very different groups of excluded. The structure of the chapter is straightforward. The first three main sections (pp. 85-101) focus on processes of exclusion and types of the excluded. Motivation, ecological environment, bargaining relationships at the village level, and family structure are the main variables raised in these sections. There then follow four discussions on a regional basis of the conditions surrounding hired labourers. We conclude with a section on one special case of rural labourers, estate workers. This has the useful strategic role of putting the discussion back into an international setting, in preparation for the next chapter in which that setting is fundamental.

Throughout, the basic question, from which the mass of detail and the problems of data collection and interpretation must not be allowed to deflect us, is whether the mechanisms by which others are enriched reinforce or breach that poverty. We shall argue that they have in fact excluded some from access to productive assets and markets. Indeed, we shall show that the sustained poverty of some has been a necessary precondition of the enrichment of others, for it has changed them from self-employed farmers to labourers, dependent to varying degrees on their earnings for their survival.

84

VILLAGERS AND FARMERS

But first we have to make exception of one whole group of rural dwellers—much larger in Africa than in Asia—whose low income is not necessarily evidence of a hostile environment, either ecological or social.

Usually geographically remote and socially self-contained, these families preserve in more or less pure form their traditional culture and economy.* This does not necessarily imply that they have had no contact with the modern economy or modern society, but rather that they have rejected it in favour of a set of values and satisfactions that they find preferable. They may exist side by side with others differently motivated, and indeed they may even be more effective producers than those who seek a higher cash income as a means to a different set of satisfactions.

There are many ways of making this distinction of motivation on the one hand and satisfaction on the other. One study, which used the distinction analytically and therefore is particularly helpful in subjecting the distinction to rigorous testing, put the difference this way:

Villagers have no real interest in making a cash income out of farming. They may have retired to the village after employment elsewhere; or they may still have a paid job outside the village and be concerned more to retain their social position in the village than with making a cash profit; or they may not be sufficiently motivated to try to do more than provide the subsistence needs of their families. They are cultivators because that is a way to live and because it is the way their fathers lived. They are much involved in village affairs and take the social demands of traditional village life seriously. They sell any surplus of production that may occur in a good year, and indeed, as a precaution, they may normally aim to produce slightly more than their subsistence needs, so that in a bad year they will not starve. But they do not view their farming activities as a source of income and are not anxious to expand production. . . .

By contrast, farmers endeavor to produce a surplus to generate income. Whether presently successful or not—and it is important to emphasise that the distinction between villagers and farmers is based on *intention* rather than *achievement* they intend to become more

---

*Cultural minorities—for example, the Orang Asli in Malaysia—are one extreme example. But it much weakens the argument of the following paragraphs to apply it only to such culturally distinct groups.

productive and therefore wealthier through farming. They tend to stand
aside from village affairs—indeed their homesteads are often on the out-
skirts of the village. They regard farming as their principal means of livelihood and although they may derive some cash from petty trading or
even own other enterprises, the greater part of their income comes, or
is intended to come, from their crops.[1]

It obviously would be misleading to apply every detail of that description,
based as it is on a sample survey of only two areas of one country, to the generality of this study. But the main point almost certainly stands generalization.[2]

There are groups that either consciously or unconsciously detach themselves
from pursuit of higher cash incomes. They may wish for some of the modern
forms of social consumption, such as clinics or schools for their children, or
modern forms of private consumption for themselves—bicycles, radios, even
brick houses. To this extent they are not romantic drop-outs calling a plague
on the whole panoply of modernity. Rather, they give a higher priority to their
participation in the community of the village and therefore a high priority to
the preservation of that community.

An interesting example is offered by the Turkana in northern Kenya. Originally a nomadic tribe, the Turkana were left almost completely untouched by
Kenyan development both before and after independence. But when voluntary
agencies and later government first began "development" work in the area, it
became clear that the Turkana were highly selective about what they wanted
and what they did not want. They wanted education, but not the kind of education that led to family disputes, insubordination of children, migration from
the village or tribal home, even though that might bring high material rewards
in town. Nor did they want permanent employment that would impinge upon
the nomadic pattern of their lives and threaten work-sharing in the tribe between the sexes and different age groups. But they did want the opportunity to
earn money to meet discrete expenditures. In other words, they wanted to
maintain their own cultural identity, and they were prepared to use whatever
the modern sector had to offer that, in their view, would enrich that identity.
A study of northern Cameroon has shown clearly how, given the same opportunity, some tribal and ethnic groups have quickly seen education as an instrument of social and economic betterment. Others, however, have shunned it
precisely because it threatens the fabric of their society.[3] There is no reason to
suppose that this a purely African phenomenon; indeed, the very strength of
cultural tradition in Asia makes for a more deeply seated reaction there.

The interesting question about villagers as a group is how far this cultural
identity, almost a cultural chauvinism, is transmitted to the younger generation.
In Zambia, for instance, we would expect the average age of villagers to be

higher than that of farmers.* But the evidence does not support such an expectation. Neither the median nor the average age of each group is significantly different. This is the more surprising given that these two areas are not particularly remote or outside the mainstream of economic and social change in rural Zambia. In that respect they do not bear comparison with the Turkana. Nor is it the case in Zambia that all the villagers are uneducated. The farmers do tend to have a higher level of formal education than the villagers, but the difference is not as striking as one might expect. (The measure reported here refers to family education and therefore includes educated wives and children.) This suggests that the villager phenomenon is not limited to the old uneducated relics of a different culture who have consciously withdrawn from modern life. Rather, the villagers are people who, for whatever reasons (of which fear may be the most important), simply do not want to take part in the competitive struggle to raise cash income. Their exclusion from the processes of enrichment they would regard as a blessing. That is a value judgment that no development expert, of whatever level or nationality, can legitimately challenge.

Poor Farmers on Poor Land

Very different are the unsuccessful farmers, that is, those who do not share the villagers' motivation but who see cash farming as a potentially profitable enterprise. The sources of their lack of success are legion, from the "neutral" fact of a hostile ecological environment to exploitative relationships that make farming success impossible even in a favoured ecological and geographical situation. The Dry Zone farmers of Sri Lanka, the upland farmers of the Philippines, the nomads of central Tanzania or northern Kenya, the dry savannah farmers of northern Ghana, Ivory Coast, or Upper Volta—all of these face an ecological and geographical environment that is hardly conducive to rapidly rising labour productivity. The question is whether the fundamental economic and social relationships, both in rural society and in the nation as a whole, minimize these disadvantages or, at the other extreme, maximize their cost.

We have already argued in Chapter 2 that, as far as governments are concerned, the basic algorithm of maximizing output per unit of input into the

---

*For the villager phenomenon would most easily be explained by the family cycle. As a family grows in numbers, so its need for income rises and its ability to expand its agricultural production increases. But as it contracts, as children come of age and leave the household, so this process is reversed.

agricultural sector inevitably excludes this group of ecologically disfavoured farmers from strategies designed to maximize the growth of output.

In general the efficiency algorithm can be modified only by intense political pressure, and it is no surprise to find more obvious examples of that pressure in the "equity group" than in the "growth group." In some countries, of which Tanzania is the most obvious example, political pressure has been successful in substituting a quite different algorithm—in Tanzania, resources are put at the disposal not of those who will make the most effective use of them but of those who are prepared to live and work in Ujamaa villages. As we have already emphasized, these tend to be in the poorer areas of the country where the productivity of public resources in output terms is probably low.

The Dry Zone colonist schemes in Sri Lanka are a very different case. Here, it is true, there was considerable political pressure to devote public resources to areas of the country that are not ecologically favoured. But the point of these schemes was not primarily to benefit the purana villages in the Dry Zone but rather to provide irrigated land for colonists from the Wet Zone. They owed their existence to political pressure from the relatively rich Wet Zone rather than from the Dry Zone. Although, of course, some purana villages benefitted from the scheme, either directly from gaining access to irrigated land or indirectly by providing services to the colonies, it would be false to see these major schemes as evidence of the modification of the efficiency algorithm through the political pressure of the poor in the hard lands of ecological disadvantage.

If governments have tended to do little to minimize the disadvantages of this group, is there any evidence that, either consciously or unconsciously, they have maximized the costs of the disadvantages? In the intra-group competition of the rural sector, do governments tend to bias success against these farmers? We believe there is evidence that this is so.

Unsuccessful farmers trying to generate a cash income from farming from poor areas are sometimes in competition with farmers from better-favoured areas, especially if they produce the same crop. Then they may use at least some of the same inputs (although they will usually use them less intensively and probably less efficiently) and they sell ultimately in the same market. The successful farmer in an ecologically more favourable area and in close proximity to markets is able to respond more rapidly and more effectively to incentives, such as higher prices, or changes in technology, such as the introduction of new seeds or fertilisers. There comes a point at which domestic self-sufficiency is achieved. Export of surpluses may be practicable, but a fall in the domestic price will be hard to resist. At that point the efficiency algorithm leads inexorably to the exclusion of inefficient producers. This is already a real possibility in the Philippines;[4] a better example is West Malaysia, where rapid expansion of irrigated acreages has combined with the new technology to make national self-sufficiency in rice practically assured.

But what happens to the relatively inefficient producers in the dry land areas? Assuming that they are gradually forced out of rice production, as it is official policy that they should be, there are two possibilities. One adopted by government is diversification.[5] But that runs counter to the technical and infrastructural environment of the great majority of inefficient rice producers. Without major and sustained support while they adjust to a new set of crops, develop new institutions, and adjust land holdings to economic sizes for the new crops,* dry land farmers, especially the poorest of them, will be obliged to revert to subsistence production. This raises the second possibility. Competed out of commercial rice production, they may regard rice as a subsistence crop and seek casual work for their cash income. That may be a less traumatic adjustment than the restructuring of land holdings implied by diversification—provided that off-farm work is available. It is hard to see how that proviso can be met; it is more likely that many will be forced to migrate to find casual work in the rice bowl areas.

If diversification is a bleak prospect for the most vulnerable of the excluded farmers, another approach is to look for technical changes that will greatly increase the productivity of labour in the outlying areas. As is well known, the major research breakthroughs in the recent past have favoured the technically advanced and ecologically advantaged farmer. We have already illustrated this with respect to maize research in Kenya. In terms of rice, the new varieties are designed for adoption by farmers of irrigated land who can utilize their capacity by applying high levels of fertiliser and (in village terms) a sophisticated level of water and cultivation management. There has been no comparable breakthrough applicable to the dry land farmer, although research on this has recently accelerated. In Albay, Philippines, no upland farmer has an income exceeding ₱1,000; and nearly 90 percent have less than ₱500. Over 60 percent of lowland farms achieve a higher income than ₱500, and nearly one in four lowland farms growing only rice earns over ₱1,500 per annum.

This raises two questions. The first is whether there are technical constraints on high-productivity innovations for disadvantaged farmers, e.g., dry land rice farmers or grain and tuber farmers in the weak lateritic soils of Africa. The minute proportion of total agricultural research resources that is committed to research on cassava—potentially an immensely productive source of food energy and indirectly (and possibly directly) of protein—is symptomatic of the neglect of crops that are not relevant to the successful and progressive farmers.

---

*In some of the areas involved, farms are already small: one third are less than 1.75 acres. But some possible alternative crops—e.g., maize, sorphum, vegetables—require an area larger than this to produce an adequate family income. "Consolidation" may therefore be necessary, with the creation of more landless families an inevitable result.

The second question is whether, if such technologies exist—and current work, although exiguous in quantity, suggests that they do—they demand as high a level of management and inputs as the technologies associated with the Green Revolution in rice, wheat, and maize. Can a dry land rice technology, or for that matter a manioc technology, be developed that does not require heavy applications of chemical fertilisers, pesticides, herbicides, deep ploughing, and precisely timed cultivation sequences? We do not know. All that is clear at the moment is that the improved technologies that have been developed are too management- and capital-intensive to be relevant to most of the poorest farmers—and may even have contributed to their continuing impoverishment.

Poor Farmers on Less Poor Land

Unsuccessful and poor farmers are not confined to the ecologically difficult areas. In the less difficult areas, poverty may result from an unwillingness or inability to adopt new technology or, having adopted it, to maintain it. Most relevant to our concern are those who wish to adopt the new technology but find that they are denied access to inputs or adequate markets—i.e., those who are unsuccessful in the intra-group competition. Under what conditions does this occur?

Although we know much about adoption, we know little about non-adoption or disadoption, especially as it is dangerous to infer the determinants of exclusion from those of adoption, on the grounds that one is the inverse of the other. But the need for credit to finance technological change does highlight the vulnerability of those who are excluded from normal (and relatively cheap) credit channels. For example, in Malaysia the institutional spearhead of the new rice technology was provided by the farmers' associations. These have acted as "credit centres," extension bases, and input distributors. Membership in them is therefore useful, although not mandatory. But the smallest farmers, whether tenants or owner-operators, have tended not to join these associations, and the officers of the associations have not thought it desirable to woo the small farmers.* Indeed the associations have come increasingly under the control of local politicians and notables, with the result that at least some of the poorest farmers, often also the least integrated socially, regard membership with great suspicion.

---

*According to a senior official of the Ministry of Agriculture, only 15 to 20 percent of Malay farmers would be eligible for credit through the associations. This would further explain why small farmers have not joined.

How far can this be generalized? Is it universally true that, in any rural group open to the possibilities of rapid technical change, the poorest and least integrated will be excluded from reaping the benefits of that change? Certainly there is much evidence that points in that direction. (for important evidence from Kenya that supports this argument, see above, pp. 27-28). Also, in a 50-village survey in Laguna, researchers found that inability to offer collateral and unwillingness to complete the demanding bureaucratic procedures of the formal credit institutions were the two most important factors driving borrowers into the arms of merchants and moneylenders. These two factors are clearly associated with poverty, under-education, and social insecurity*—features that are unlikely to be relieved by moneylenders who charge 20 percent *per month* and merchants who demand the right to buy the crop at a price below the harvest-time low. This is the classical poverty trap, which has the effect, at times of rapid technological change, of transferring assets (in this case land) from existing owners to those who can make the fullest use of them—a theme which we shall repeat below. (Thirteen percent of all farmers in a Laguna survey borrowed from unofficial sources. One of the advantages offered by those sources is that they are more flexible, at a price, in their repayment demands.[6])

How far social and political pressures act in the same way in Laguna as we have outlined in Malaysia is difficult to say. But there can be no doubt that in the more remote provinces of the Philippines the close association between formal credit institutions and local political bosses acts as a filter to exclude those who challenge the existing power system. Indeed, since the unofficial lenders—merchants and moneylenders—are themselves dependent upon the same local oligarchy, they are loath to bail out known enemies of the oligarchy by lending to them.

A parallel but slightly different example may be cited from Sri Lanka. There the local political pressures are reinforced by racial conflict. In "mixed villages" in which one racial group is in a clear minority, the majority can deny to the minority access to inputs of all kinds in the hope of buying their land and reducing them to landless labourers or even driving them out of the village altogether.[7] This pattern is not confined to the overcrowded areas of the Wet Zone. For example, in a large irrigated settlement in the Dry Zone, a Muslim minority was deprived of water by powerful Tamil "podiyars." Their only recourse was to lease their land to the Tamils and continue to work it as hired labourers.[8]

Now it does not necessarily follow that those thus excluded, the unsuccessful

---

*For intra-family lending/borrowing is the most frequent form of credit in Laguna. Those who have to borrow from merchants and moneylenders are those who cannot mobilize family savings, either because they are isolated or because their kinsmen have no savings to mobilize.

competitors, are always incapable of technical change without access to the normal or privileged sources of inputs. Rhodesian immigrants into Zambia were excluded from the great credit bonanza of 1965-69, as were leading figures in the opposition stronghold in the Southern Province, one of the richest agricultural areas. But these two groups were among the first African farmers in Zambia to make use of hybrid maize, fertilisers, and large-scale tractor operations. The difference, however, is that they had always been economically advanced and thus could survive exclusion. It is those who are already economically deprived who quickly succumb to exclusion.

For exclusion from new technologies is not a static process. As we have already emphasized, the evidence suggests that in the Philippines and Malaysia, the inefficient rice farmers are likely to find themselves competed out of production. The withdrawal of the fertiliser subsidy in the rice bowl areas of Malaysia is a significant straw in the wind, for it suggests the kind of pressure to which the weakest farmers will be increasingly subject, especially if the price of rice begins to fall (in real or money terms).* Tenant farmers are particularly vulnerable. As we have seen (see above, pp. 66) , landlords are already demanding cash instead of a share of the crop† and rents are beginning to rise as land prices reflect the greater potential of double-cropped land. A tenant who cannot or will not raise his productivity is replaced by one who will.

Technical change, then, brings with it an acceleration in the process of differentiation, squeezing out the unadaptable and the unsuccessful, even in areas that are suited to technological change. That process is reinforced by demographic pressure. We have already seen examples of this in Kenya and Sri Lanka, where population pressure led to intense struggles over rights to land. Those who lost in that struggle became labourers dependent upon those who won—a fact that adequately explains the bitterness with which the struggle was fought.

Demographic pressure may accelerate technological change and both combine to deprive the weakest and poorest of access to adequate land. One example of this combination of factors in East Africa is the process of land concentration and domination by a few large landholders of particularly rich pasture land formed from drained swamp. In the area concerned, Kigezi in West Uganda, 78 percent of the land is used by the upper quartile of land users.[9] A new landed elite, drawing a salary from non-agricultural work, has either hired labour to

---

*In the northern areas, the effective price will almost inevitably fall as a result of large-scale smuggling from Thailand induced by higher prices in Malaysia.

†This is symbolic of the change overtaking tenant/landlord relationships. Originally embedded in social, non-monetary relations, they are becoming increasingly commercial.

drain areas of swamp or, once drained, has bought this "new" land and thus excluded from access to it all the poorest households in the area. This is typical of the pressures upon the poorest both to secure additional sources of income to survive and, if possible, to save sufficient funds to buy themselves back into their own homeland.[10]

It might be expected that land concentration would lead to increased employment opportunities in Kigezi and would therefore not by itself cause workers to migrate. This does not seem to be happening because the intensity of farming on the larger holdings remains low. Because the larger landowners are part-time farmers, they are not involved in the labour-intensive farming that has been a feature of agricultural development in Kegezi, such as dairying and vegetable production. They seem more interested in investing their savings in land as a form of security for the future, and possibly as a speculative investment.

This shift in ownership is one example of a more general process. When land becomes short in relation to the demands made upon it, the society can adapt in a number of ways—by finding new technical solutions, by developing ways of sharing land and supplementing income by off-farm work. But there will be some individuals who cannot adapt or for whom the process of adaptation is inoperable. For instance, they may have a weak claim to land and therefore find that their "share" is inadequate and/or be unable to supplement agricultural income from other sources. By a process of economic and social pressure, they are then driven out of the society and obliged to find new ways of maintaining themselves.

A particularly good Asian example of this process is the process of adaptation to rising demographic pressure in the Wet Zone of Sri Lanka. We saw in Chapter 4 that the major attempt to relieve this pressure was through the colonization schemes in the Dry Zone. But who were the settlers? Who was squeezed out of the Wet Zone and obliged to accept the socially and often economically inferior status of a colonist in the Dry Zone? Two factors combined to squeeze out of the Wet Zone villages those who lost in the struggle to maintain a right to high land. (High land rather than padi land gives a right to village membership.)

The first of these was the expense and difficulty of litigation. Even uncontested partition was expensive; contested land cases were very expensive. Those who had jobs outside the village were thus able to pursue litigation with a vigour and determination that those were were constrained by its cost could not. Second, even in padi land some consolidation did take place, either through outright purchase or through rearrangement of holdings, with the result that in some Wet Zone villages land concentration became marked. This did not immediately create a landless class since it is unusual for landowners to operate their own land. A more normal arrangement is one of many variants of sharecropping, but the owners of a small parcel of land might sell it in order to become share-croppers on a larger parcel. If at a later date, in order to oblige kinsmen or other clients, the landowner reduced the size of the parcel, the share accruing to the tenant might be so small that he would be better off working as a labourer or on an estate.

In either case, the vulnerable could best defend themselves by acquiring sources of income outside the village. That way litigation could be pursued and at least sufficient high land kept to protect rights in the village. The likelihood of finding a job outside the village depended upon two features that the most vulnerable in the village were unlikely to possess: education and access to patrons in the formal sector (or even informal sector). Unable to compete in the modern sector and forced out of his own village, the unfortunate ex-villager had no alternative but to sell his labour for whatever he could get for it. Under these conditions, the otherwise unattractive prospect of settlement in the Dry Zone might seem appealing, particularly if he had a sufficiently close relationship with the headman of the village to get nomination as an official colonist with all the advantages in terms of acreage of land, security of tenure, and access to supporting services that that brought. For those who could not secure such nomination, the outlook was grim—they could either work as labourers in the informal sector with no secure residential rights in the village, or take a chance as unauthorized colonists practising shifting cultivation on the fringes of the purana villages in the Dry Zone, in perpetual conflict with the villagers, the colonists, and the government.

INTER-GROUP COMPETITION AT THE VILLAGE LEVEL

So far we have been concerned with intra-group competition between successful and less successful farmers. Now we turn to another kind of competition that could be defined as inter-group, on the grounds that those who provide marketing services are sociologically and economically distinct from the producers we have been considering so far.

It is well known that the marketing arrangements often fail to pass back incentive prices to the farmer; or to put it another way, that middlemen absorb a large (and perhaps rising) share of the retail price. From our point of view, two questions are important: Is the inefficiency of the structure biased against the poorest producers? Are the prices charged by merchants and middlemen for their services excessive?

The first question is less difficult to answer than the second. For the very isolation, indebtedness, and small scale that characterize the poorest farmers are both necessary and sufficient conditions of a monopsonistic market structure in which an individual producer has the choice of selling the crop to a particular buyer—or not selling at all. (But contrast the opposite and important evidence from Ghana; see p. 57.) This has been the situation on settlement schemes in Mindanao and even with relatively advanced crops like pineapples (often interplanted with immature oil palm) in Malaysia.[11]

But this kind of non-reciprocal bargaining situation is not limited to the distant and debt-laden farmer. It may arise from a combination of technical unsophistication and a sheer inability to change a universally accepted system of fraud. The first annual report of the Malaysian Federal Agricultural Marketing Authority (FAMA) had this to say:

> Padi marketing is beset by diverse marketing defects, many of which take the form of widespread malpractices by traders during their purchases of padi. The most common defect stems from excessive deductions traders make from the Government guaranteed minimum price. It is common knowledge that heavy deductions are made for moisture content based on a subjective examination of the grain. Apart from excessive deductions, the manipulation of weighing scales is another malpractice employed by traders. Here, the local "daching" is commonly employed and its reading may be interfered with to the advantage of the buyer. These, combined with the purchase of padi by volume rather than by weight whenever it is more profitable to do so, provide the buyer with more padi than he pays for.
>
> But not every malpractice in padi marketing should be attributed to traders; it is also a frequent complaint that padi offered by farmers is excessively damp and well above the 18 percent moisture level stipulated for rejecting padi. In cases such as these, trading is done at very low prices based on the premise that rejected padi may be bought at whatever price it is worth. There are also complaints that padi is offered for sale with a minimum of winnowing and cleaning and farmers are again the victims of further price deductions.

It is true that FAMA has an axe to grind, but it is over-cynical to assume that the description is exaggerated. And this kind of marketing problem is not limited to padi; the East Coast fishermen have similar problems in their relations with Chinese merchants, especially as Malays cannot usually read Chinese accounts. Since merchants advance more credit in cash or kind during the monsoon, the possibilities of fraud are large.[12]

This raises the second question: Is the profit margin charged by middlemen excessive? Data by which that question may be answered are exceedingly hard to find, as indeed are the criteria by which one judges the level of profits in relation to the services provided. First, however, a general point seems clear. The extreme fragmentation of marketing whereby a cabbage may go through the hands of seven middlemen on its way from the farmer to the consumer is unlikely to be either cheap or efficient even if there is a high degree of competition at each level. But, as we shall see later, this fragmentation is the result of lack of employment in both rural and urban sectors. It is the commercial equivalent of a labour-intensive cottage industry with a high level of underemployment.

But from that it does not follow that competition is keen and margins are cut. To draw that conclusion would be to ignore the force of traditional or institutionalized ideas of "right" prices. In the Philippines the margins of palay and rice wholesalers are fairly standardized at 2.5 percent of the farmgate price. Retailing margins were about equal to the net cost of retail selling in 1966; both have risen rapidly over the last ten years, and it may be significant that net profits have risen less rapidly than net costs. To evaluate this is difficult. Wholesalers add roughly ₱1.00 to ₱1.30 to the value of the product and take a net profit of about ₱0.40—suggesting a generous but not extortionate margin. Both make their largest profits (and losses) from speculating on price movements, but in this they exploit the consumer rather than the producer.

Table 5.1, gleaned from information from the Greater Manila Terminal Food Market, shows the margins at various marketing stages of a number of common vegetables. As is to be expected, perishable or high-risk commodities bear a higher margin than those with good keeping qualities. But given the low risk, low rates of deterioration and shrinkage, and the high value/volume ratios of some of these (e.g., citrus and garlic), the margins look generous to the point of exorbitant. It is hard to see here the forces of market competition reducing costs and prices—nor improving service. (The GMTFM is the only Manila food market where even minimal hygiene regulations are enforced; the older, smaller markets are grim.)

We have no such detailed evidence for African countries, but it would be a mistake to believe that the famed trading skills of Ghanaian mammies or the Bamileke of Cameroon ensure the erosion of excessive margins. Indeed, one aspect of that skill is precisely to preserve margins by establishing patron/client or other dependent relationships with sellers or by limiting entry of new traders into a particular branch of trade. Some producers have been able to resist the establishment of such relationships: Polly Hill reports that Northern cattle owners, for instance, deliberately refuse to sell to any individual buyer on a regular basis (see above, p. 57). But this is evidence of the perception of market distortions by the producers. They adopt such policies because they are well aware of the cost of not doing so. They are fortunate in having a plethora of traders anxious to buy, but they know that as soon as they are committed to one trader, as a result of social or economic obligations, the price will fall.

But producers are not always (and perhaps not often) able to resist either

TABLE 5.1

**Philippines: Vegetable Prices in Manila as Percentage
of Farmers' Selling Prices, 1972**

Commodity	Farmer[a]	Trucker[b]	Wholesaler[c]	Retailer[d]
Ampalaya	100	117	133	200
Cabbage	100	167	200	400
Garlic	100	111-139	153-167	278
Onions	100	100-133	117-150	267
Pechay	100	150	200	600
Potato	100	105	116-126	168-179
Tomato	100	125-167	175-233	300-400
Calamansi	100	—	170	220
Banana	100	—	175	250

[a]Provides containers, compensates for shrinkage.

[b]Bears transport cost, "tong" and pilferage in transit, plus handling fees at source and some spoilage.

[c]Pays market space fees, handling and "protection" fees; may pay storage costs.

[d]Bears any losses through dehydration, trimming, and deterioration.

Source: Economics Unit, Greater Manila Terminal Food Market, 1972.

collusion among buyers or the establishment of an inflexible institutional price. When the government of Uganda, for instance, tried to regulate the activities of coffee and foodcrop traders by announcing minimum prices, the traders simply withdrew until delegations of farmers persuaded government officials not to enforce the prices. In Zambia, maize smuggling from Central Province to Barotse was illegal, but the mouthwatering profits to be made (especially if a trader could bring a bark-load of dried fish from Barotse to Mumbwa or Lusaka) kept the trade alive and indeed expanding—until the people of Barotse developed a taste for roller meal, which individual farmers/traders could not produce.

In short, the small farmer is more likely to be the victim of one or more of the following quite distinct market failings: undetected and/or institutionalized malpractice; an unequal bargaining position against a monopsonistic buyer or set of collusive buyers; and an extended marketing chain that is effective at providing jobs and incomes for traders but inefficient at maximizing incomes for farmers or passing back price incentives.

The orthodox method of protecting the small farmer from these pressures is by the organization of marketing co-operatives and/or state marketing boards.

It is at this point that we detect most clearly the bias against the poorest and most distant producers. For them, organization of and full participation in co-operatives are too demanding of social, organizational, and commercial skills. The very poor may not even be able (or may be very unwilling in the early stages) to buy the requisite number of shares for membership. In neither the Philippines nor Malaysia have co-operatives been effective in solving the marketing problems of the smallest farmers. The attempt to regulate dealers in Malaysia is a sensible approach that, like the Rent Acts, fails in the implementation.

In most African countries, major crops are handled by marketing boards. These may avoid some of the worst abuses of the traders and, in some cases (e.g., Zambia since 1968), may subsidize more distant producers at the expense of central farmers. But, as we shall see at greater length in Chapter 13, these boards have often been subverted into agents by which income is transferred from client-farmers to other sections of the community. In so far as they rely upon them, then, the smallest farmers may find themselves as thoroughly exploited by the official organs of the state as by private traders.

"INEVITABLE LOSERS" AND AGRICULTURAL LABOUR

How far is it always the case that the people who are squeezed out of access to inputs and markets are those who are least competent in both the traditional agricultural economy and in the modern economy? Is there a group of "inevitable losers" in both inter- and intra-group competition who lose out in both sectors and, as it were, inevitably sink to the bottom of the social pyramid?

Empirically, we do not know. Research has not commonly focussed on those who pay the price of agricultural development. We have already seen that the resettlement of Kikuyuland under the Swynnerton Plan is a good illustration of the type of economic thinking that might lead to such a conclusion. For, given the fact that land (and usually complementary factors except labour) is in short supply, an economizing approach is to choose the most effective farmers to use the land. That implies that the less effective are excluded and will become land-less labourers. It is highly improbable that those who are judged unfit to become leasehold farmers, colonists, or approved cultivators will be equipped with the necessary skills and contacts to be successful in the urban areas. Indeed, as we have emphasized with respect to both Kenya and Sri Lanka, the likelihood is that if they were so equipped they would already have left the area under this kind of population pressure.

As a result of deprivation of inputs or markets, then, farmers are obliged to seek alternative ways of making a living. We can think of a range of conditions

under which a poor farmer may find himself. At worst, he may be driven off
the land altogether and become a landless labourer. At best, he will take casual
work during the off-season as a means of earning a little extra (and immediate)
cash. Between these two extremes lies another group, arguably the chief source
of non-casual agricultural labour. If through shortage of land or labour, or as a
result of a poor physical environment, a household is unable to increase its income to meet new cash demands, it has two alternatives: Either it can revert to
a villager level of consumption, expectations, and satisfactions, or it can sell its
only saleable asset—labour. The most common form is for one or more of the
adult males to migrate in search of work, leaving the women and children, with
perhaps some adult males, to secure at least a subsistence from the land. Less
frequently, rural migrants take their families with them;* we shall consider here
the situation of the family left behind by the migrant to survive on the subsistence it can produce and the remittances it may or may not receive from the
migrant.

The fate of the farm family in which the father is absent, and either unemployed or failing to remit regular gifts back to the rural areas, is at best insecure
and at worst disastrous. Under the optimum circumstances—more than one wife
surrounded by supportive kinsmen, with few children, adequate fertile land,
and either reasonable market opportunities or some chance of earning cash income—economic pressures can be moderated in the short run. Providing no
expensive disasters such as drought, litigation over land, fines, or serious illness
occur, the level of consumption of the family need be no worse than that of
the villager with male adults present. But the family is exceedingly vulnerable.
It is vulnerable to withdrawal of support by the kin group. It is vulnerable to
harrassment of all sorts. It is even more vulnerable to natural disasters than
most other families precisely because those who would normally be most adept
at securing assistance, either from official sources or more likely from kin
groups, are not on the spot. And it is vulnerable to even quite small changes in
the economic milieu in which it operates. A rise in school fees, reduction in the
fertility of the land, cessation of demand for casual labour, the unforeseen need
to undertake major improvements on the farm, and perhaps most of all, the
sudden drying up of remittances from town as the migrant either loses his job

---

*This seems to be changing under the impact of a wide range of pressures:
better access to social services in areas of in-migration; breakdown of kin systems in the "home area"; anxiety that the women will be unable to produce
subsistence income. In areas of acute land pressure, the family may be left
behind precisely to protect what rights to land remain—this is especially evident
in the Wet Zone of Sri Lanka. When a migrant has found a good and (hopefully)
permanent job, he may summon his family.

or decides to start a new family in town—any of these can upset the delicate equilibrium of the family and, without substantial support from the kin group, can lead to almost total destitution.

We know very little about the adaptation of kin group support systems to migration and modernization of the rural areas. The data we presented in Chapter 2 suggest that some of the more lyrical descriptions of such systems, even though they are by people who have lived within them, are either out of date or tinged with a certain nostalgic rosiness. For the evidence suggests that, if rural destitution is not common, neither is it unknown. It is typically the old and the single, and especially old and single women, who are most nearly destitute. That alone is evidence that the traditional "mutual welfare society" of rural Africa and Asia is not as mutual as it may once have been.

Nor do we know enough about the flow of remittances from the urban areas to the rural areas to be sure that the rationale of migration from the rural family's point of view is valid. Survey data on remittances are unreliable partly because of the nature of the remittances—e.g., a migrant may bring very substantial gifts when he returns to the village either after a prolonged absence or on a periodic visit—or because respondents are more reluctant to reveal the value of remittances than they are of other cash transactions.* However imperfect the data, it is clear that remittances are not only required for nuclear dependents. They may be shared among a much wider group of kinsmen, among whom the elderly may be particularly relevant. As urban populations become less transient and perhaps as social security systems become more highly developed,† so the need for the migrant to maintain a link with his village, symbolized and kept alive by his remittances and occasional visits, declines. It is significant that in Cameroon, three surveys have shown that in rural areas, remittances rise strongly with income, suggesting that much social redistribution does take place. But in the urban areas there is no such association.[13]

---

*The Consumer Finance Survey of Ceylon, 1963, found that the lowest income group (less than Rs.50 in the two months of the survey) received the lowest level (2 percent) of gifts as a proportion of wage or salary from main occupation or total income. In the Philippines, a Bureau of Census and Statistics survey of 1965 revealed a "U" distribution of "gifts, support, assistance and relief" as a proportion of total income for the rural population. The poorest group received only 2.3 percent of income in this form, and the average for the whole population was only 1.7 percent. The Tanzanian Household Budget Survey of 1969 recorded 4 percent and 3 percent of cash income as gifts and remittances for farm and non-farm rural households, respectively.

†These systems need not necessarily be formal in the sense of actuarially sound state-guaranteed contributory systems; they may be quite informal, based upon the ownership of urban assets.

Once a migrant sees his future, even in old age, purely in terms of an urban environment, the main motive for remittances is removed. Under these circumstances, the elderly, and particularly elderly women, are likely to be at the greatest disadvantage.

Whether dependent upon his remittances or his earnings, the family of a rural labourer is ultimately dependent upon the ability of the household head—or his wife—to find work. To that we turn in the next section.

HIRED LABOURERS IN EAST AFRICA

Structure

In Chapter 2 and in the first sections of this chapter, we examined some of the varieties of inter- and intra-group competition by which unsuccessful farmers are deprived of the use of land and obliged to take work as labourers. In this sub-section we examine the structure of the rural hired labour force; we then turn to consider its rewards.

We saw that "hired labour" covers a spectrum of types—from the permanently landless labourer, wholly dependent upon his earnings for the subsistence of himself and his family, to the self-employed family farmer who takes casual work in the slack season as a way of increasing his cash income (see above, pp. 33, 39). The difference between these two types is so significant that a further examination of this spectrum is necessary.

The first distinction is that between the temporary and the permanent labourer. The temporary labourer is not dependent upon employment for his basic subsistence. But here we have to make a further distinction. For some temporary labourers can take temporary employment only at times that do not conflict with the demands of their own farms. These are labourers who use the slack periods of the agricultural season to increase their cash income, often working on capital-creating activities such as clearing bush or building houses or storage bins or erecting fences.

Quite different are those who are obliged, as a result of either patron/client relationships or economic pressures, to take paid employment during the busy agricultural season, thereby withdrawing labour from their own farms at a time when the returns to their own labour are likely to be at least as high as the wages they receive. This is not necessarily irrational behaviour. They may need cash immediately or before they can realise cash from sale of their crops, or their security of tenure may depend upon their discharging this obligation. This is particularly relevant for immigrants into an area who may have to pay some

kind of labour service to the headman or other tribal authority in recognition
of their status. In this case the labour service usually is unpaid (at least in cash
terms); therefore the real cost to the labourer is high since production on his
own farm—in terms of both area planted and yield—is likely to suffer severely.

Clearly, the most vulnerable in this group are those with small families. For
them, the absence of the head of the household has a greater proportionate
effect on output. For example, in Zambia under simple techniques in maize
growing, withdrawal of one hundred hours of labour at weeding time can reduce yield per acre by over 150 pounds—or 29 percent. Withdrawal of labour
at planting time can be even more disruptive because it reduces acreage sharply.
(The evidence suggests that withdrawal of female labour has a greater effect on
acreage than the withdrawal of male labour. The hiring of female labour at
planting time is, however, unusual.[14])

Contrasting with temporary labourers are permanent labourers. They may
have no access to subsistence production on their own account and therefore
be entirely dependent upon their earnings for survival. Alternatively, they may
come from an area so poor that they can earn more as employees than they can
from their own labour. They thus become migrant workers, perhaps leaving
their families to secure a subsistence income from the farm. We therefore have
to make a further distinction between settled permanent labourers and casual
permanent labourers.* The former, the settled labourers, are those who have
attached themselves to a farm household and who have in at least some respects become part of that household. Indeed, that relationship may be symbolized and further cemented by marriage to a daughter of the household.

In stark contrast to the settled permanent labourer, whose standard of
living may become outwardly indistinguishable from that of the farmer himself, is the permanent casual labourer whose status as a labourer is permanent
but whose employment is casual. This is almost certainly a much larger group
since the number of farmers who are ready to pay permanent labourers is still
small outside the larger, export-crop farms. Some of the larger Buganda coffee
growers, for example, have a permanent labour force of over twenty. Much
more common is the practice of employing a labourer for a given task. Even if
the farmer thinks that he may have difficulty in finding labour for the next
operation, he is unlikely to hoard labour since the need to pay wages represents
a real strain on his own cash resources. If the labour supply is inadequate at
some future date, he will merely postpone the operation until it improves. For
this reason, the number of casual labourers—either temporary or permanent—

---

*This terminology may be inelegant, but it is important to avoid the
classification used by statistics departments of "regular" and "casual"—for
the latter may be permanent employees working on a casual basis, or they
may be temporary employees.

far exceeds the number of permanent settled workers. Precise estimates of the number of either are not available. We have already seen that the number of farmers dependent on permanent settled labour in Tanzania is small. It is probably even smaller in Zambia. Only on the larger, labour-intensive, export-crop holdings in Uganda and Kenya is the number significant: Perhaps as many as 200,000 are permanently employed in Kenya.[15]

Much greater is the number of rural workers taking casual work. Enumeration is plagued by problems of double counting (and of under-enumeration). The Uganda Census of Agriculture of 1963 recorded 726,000 hirings, but an indeterminate number were duplicates. In Kenya some 300,000 (or 7 percent of the adult rural population) may take casual work. In Tanzania, the HBS reported average hirings by all reporting farms of 4 to 6 man-days in a year—hardly a huge volume of total employment. In Zambia, even though employment of hired labour would be extremely profitable on some of the larger, more intensive farms, there is little evidence of rapid growth in its use. (In Mumbwa, while 75 percent of surveyed farms used some hired labour at some point in the agricultural season, only 8 percent of total hours worked on farms was provided by hired labour. The number of farmers permanently employing labour was insignificant.[16])

Wages

It follows from what he have just noted that, in general, wage labour in the rural areas has a weak bargaining position and no legislative protection. In terms of competition with employers, whether permanent or casual, we are unlikely to find institutional or market forces raising the real incomes of rural labourers.

Indeed, the evidence is unambiguous that, except for one important exception to which we shall return, agricultural wages are low and sticky.[17] It is easy to understand why. Employers are reluctant to bid up the price of labour even at times of shortage, and some of the smaller employers believe they cannot afford to pay higher wages. Indeed, for the smaller employer the need to meet a wage bill is a continuous source of embarrassment, and indeed of indebtedness, even when cash wages are paid irregularly and infrequently.[18] Conversely, the labourers themselves are unwilling to see wages reduced. The greater their demand for cash—e.g., to support dependents—the more determined they are likely to be that rates do not fall.

But although there are reports of surprisingly constant money rates over fairly prolonged periods (implying falls in real income of labourers and transfers from them in real terms to their employers), there is equally some evidence of local flexibility. This is particularly the case when employers are wholly dependent upon labourers and when a temporary shortage of labour threatens the successful harvesting of a time-sensitive crop. For the classic defence of the employer is to delay a given operation or do it himself. If his acreage under coffee or tea or cotton is too large for his family, he is unlikely to allow a relatively small adjustment in wage rates to jeopardize his main source of cash income. He may try to negotiate piece rates rather than time rates or add in fringe benefits, but at least he is prepared to negotiate.

Nor is it the case that labourers are always incapable of forcing a rise in wages. M.P. Cowen reports a particularly interesting example from Kenya.

In 1970 the tea growers in the Kikuyu grass zone tried to reduce the rate paid to pluckers by nearly 30 percent. (The occasion was the metrication of weights and measures. The previous rate had been 10 cents per pound in the grass zone but 8 cents in the bracken zone; the new uniform rate offered was 17 cents per kilo.) The pluckers refused to work at the new rates. As one labourer put it, "If you belong to that *Ndini* [literally a religious denomination or sect] you know what to do. You stay at home and refuse to pluck. Those who plucked at 17 cents were those who needed money badly. They who didn't pluck also needed money but they were rich in heart. They weren't rich in the sense that they needed money but they made themselves feel rich." The larger growers broke first because for them an insignificant proportion of the crop could be saved by family labour. That this was not an entirely isolated incident is suggested by a further withdrawal of labour in 1972 when farmers demanded that pluckers exercise greater care to ensure higher quality control over the tea that was plucked.[19]

What is significant about these two events is that they depended upon no formal organization: The word went round and the pluckers stayed home.* This implies that the popular view that the agricultural labourer is entirely without countervailing power against the employing farmers is not strictly true. Doubtless the Kikuyu case was assisted by the fact that a relatively small number of pluckers was involved; that the tea-growing area is fairly compact; that most of the pluckers come from the same tribe; and that the area is densely settled. But the point is that, once farmers become dependent upon labourers, the labourers are thereby given a certain degree of influence, if not of power, over the farmers. At that point, inter-group competition becomes more evenly balanced.

This does not alter the fact that levels of living of permanent agricultural labourers always have been and still are exceedingly low. The terms on which labour is hired vary greatly. At one extreme is the straight cash relationship and

---

*It is also true that the wage was in fact reduced. But that may have been unintentional.

at the other the discharge of kin or village responsibilities in which payment, whether in cash or in kind, forms only a small part of the total transaction. It is almost universal that permanent labourers are given food and shelter, but more rare for them to be given a small parcel of land on which they can grow additional subsistence crops. Permanent settled labourers tend to be paid quarterly or even annually. Casual workers are paid by the piece or task where it can be defined exactly, e.g., so many square yards digging for a shilling. But where precise definition is difficult, payment is usually made by the day.

It is thus extremely difficult to make inter-regional or inter-temporal comparisons of wage rates. Nor is it wholly necessary to do so. For the daily earnings of a labourer who is paid wholly in cash seldom compare with those in any other occupation. In Uganda a general rate of one shilling a day was paid in 1963 and was reported again in 1967 when the minimum legal rate in the rural areas was Shs.2.90 and in the smaller towns Shs.5.20. Even allowing generously for food and lodging provided by the employer (the allowance made locally is 50 cents) it is clear that the difference between the wages of a small-scale farm labourer and, for example, a general labourer employed on an agricultural station,were, given the similarity of their work, substantial. Moreover, over that period the (urban) non-food price index rose over 10 percent.

In Kenya wages rose in the Kiambu district (a relatively high wage area) from Shs.15 a month in 1946 to Shs.65 a month in 1971. No adequate price series is available for that period, but it is highly probable that in real terms wages rose—but very slowly. In 1971 average earnings in large-scale agriculture were Shs.98 per month, and in Nairobi the minimum wage was Shs.175 per month. Even a very generous allowance of Shs.80 per month for subsistence income would mean that in Kiambu labourers were receiving 20 percent less than the urban minimum wage. Elsewhere the difference would be much greater.

For Zambia we have no time series. In Mumbwa in 1967 a rate of between 10 and 20 ngwee a day (say K4 per month) was being paid to casual workers; minimum urban wages were K25.80 per month and in large-scale agriculture (with housing supplied), K11.05 to K12.30.* Thereafter wage rates rose, as did wages throughout the economy, but whether real wages were maintained must remain an open question.

_____

*It is unusual to supply casual workers with food, and therefore it is fair to compare cash incomes. But average "villager" auto-consumption in the area in which these wages were being paid was K1.12 per head per month. This suggests that, even if full allowance is made for subsistence, total monthly incomes of casual workers do not exceed K5.00.

Nor do we have adequate time series for Tanzania. Indeed, even the Household Budget Survey of 1969 revealed very dubious results.* The highest recorded figure for permanent employees by zone puts them in the top decile of rural income earners—a surprising result indeed. No less surprising is the fact that the same group would enjoy approximately the median income of all urban income earners (allowing Shs.700 for subsistence income provided by the employer in the form of food and housing). The average cash income, reportedly an underestimate, plus the average subsistence income, would give a total income of Shs. 1,235—still leaving employees better off than a quarter of urban income earners. But this merely shows how low urban incomes in the informal sector are; for the minimum wage in the formal sector in Dar es Salaam was Shs.2,400—almost exactly double the average total income of rural employees.

If wages are low and in general constant (so that in times of rising prices there is a net transfer from rural labour to farmers), in some other respects the level of living of the permanent labourers, both settled and casual, is hardly distinguishable from that of at least the smaller farmers themselves. They are provided with lodging and eat no worse than the farmer and his family. The privations of rural life on a low income are common to both small employer and employee, and there is no reason to assume that access to other forms of consumption, such as medical care and clean water, is worse for the employee than for the employers.†

But in one crucial respect the permanent labourers are the least privileged of all employees. For except when they can establish an obligation upon the

---

*The average annual income of farm employees is given in the HBS (Household Budget Survey) as Shs.535. But this is admitted to be an underestimate. In the two more developed rural zones (zone 1—Mtara, Rvumu, and Iringa, and zone 2—Arusha, Kilimanjaro, and Tanga), the reported figures were much higher—Shs.1,429 and 1,685, respectively. The low average figure may result from the confusion between settled permanent employees and casual permanent employees. If the latter have long periods of unemployment, the average income of all employees will, of course, be reduced. But in the light of the fact that according to the HBS the average cash income of all farmers in the rural areas is only Shs.777 a year, it would be surprising if on average the earnings of farm employees were very much greater than that. To this extent the figures for the two richer zones quoted above represent an anomalous extreme.

†We specifically exclude education from this discussion since most permanent labourers do not have their families with them. As we shall see in the next section, there is evidence that, where this is not so, access to education is heavily biased against employees.

employer, e.g., through marriage, they have no security of employment. A change in the farmer's circumstances, a fall in the price of an export crop, disease of the plants or sickness of his own body—any of these can deprive him not only of his cash income, but also of his very subsistence. In this respect the permanent labourer engaged in casual work is even more vulnerable than the permanent settled labourer. As soon as one task is finished, he has to look for another. Although the piece rate may be higher than the daily rate (so that his earnings per hour worked may be higher than those of the permanent settled labourer), there is no guarantee that this differential accurately reflects the probability of his finding a job before his meagre savings are exhausted. If he is lucky, he can return to his own village and live on the subsistence production of his family, either nuclear or extended. If he has worked his way further from his home base, or if he simply has no home base, he is then of all men the most vulnerable.

Employment and Export Prices

So far we have couched this discussion in terms of inter-group competition between employers and employees. But there is one other kind of inter-group competition that is worth considering in its effects on rural labour—between export-crop producers on the one hand and competing producers and consumers on the other. The interests of the latter two of course are not identical; in broad terms, competing producers wish to keep their market share and a higher price. The consumers are less concerned about the geographical origins of the crop (unless they are integrated into local processing, as in tea) than about reducing the price.

For our purpose, what is relevant is the relationship between the price received by the farmer for an export crop—i.e., net of marketing costs and taxation*—and the employment of farm labour. The effect of a fall in price on the aggregate demand for labour is subtle. If the farmer believes that the price reduction is short-lived, he is unlikely to switch enterprises, e.g., pull out his coffee trees and go into dairy production. He will merely care for his stock of trees less intensively and harvest the crop less thoroughly. In a study of larger coffee farmers in South Kyagwe in Buganda, David Hougham found that the fall in the price of coffee during the 1960s had reduced the farmers' employment of both permanent and casual labour[20] (for national data there is no statistical relationship between price and yield consistent with this reaction, most

---

*For Taxation, see below, pp.351-54 .

probably because only the larger farmers react in this way, and perhaps only to larger falls in price). Very few farmers were abandoning coffee production altogether, partly because they looked nostalgically back to the years of very high coffee prices in the 1950s and were ready to take a gamble on those prices being achieved again, and partly because they lacked capital or expertise or confidence to diversify.

At the point at which farmers decide that the price outlook is so bleak that it would be more profitable in the long run to switch enterprises, the demand for labour may increase. But that increase is likely to be temporary. For most of the export crops of Eastern Africa—tea, coffee, sisal, cotton—are highly labour-intensive. If the diversification is out of those crops into less labour-intensive crops—dairying, beef, most grains—then the long-run demand for labour will fall.*

The argument can be put in reverse. A rise in prices will lead to greater intensity in production in an effort to increase yield, and if the price rise is thought likely to continue it will lead to new land being put down to the export crop. The likelihood is that that new land will not hitherto have been in a labour-intensive use. Labour demand will be particularly high while land is cleared and planted; less high as the stock matures; and high again as it comes into bearing.

This suggests that the relationship between export prices and labour demand is not simple or direct. But it also suggests that, allowing for the lags and likely alternative uses, they are positively related. Under these circumstances a fall in the growers' price—from whatever cause, national or international—increases the vulnerability of one of the most vulnerable groups in Eastern Africa.

But that should not be taken to imply that farmers cannot adjust to lower prices. The role of relative expectations is critical. Once they believe that a lower price is permanent (i.e., the price will not go lower still), they make quite sophisticated decisions on resource allocation. In this sense, East African coffee supply may be quite inelastic downwards in the longer run, if still lower prices are ruled out. The evidence of low prices reducing labour input is thus not inconsistent with the argument that limitations on acreage—achieved, for instance, by the International Coffee Agreement—reduce the demand for labour. The object of the agreement is to keep prices up for the benefit of the relatively high-cost producers of Latin America. It is highly arguable that it

*The structure of labour demand may change. For instance, coffee and tea growing depend heavily upon casual labour (much of it female), particularly for harvesting, whereas dairying requires the employment of permanent (male) labour. But it is probably true that most arable crops are more labour intensive than coffee or tea being farmed on a "caretaker" level. The contrast then lies between intensive farming of these export crops and food crops.

would be in the interests of the East African countries to accept lower prices for a larger output, providing that farmers were not frightened out of the crop altogether (and that alternative labour-saving crops, such as milk, did not continue to be heavily subsidized and thus competitive for resources). In this sense, the East African producers probably now have the worst of all worlds—a pricing structure that offers little long-term confidence (although sometimes high short-term profits) and a limitation on expansion.

Internationally, then, an increase in the real income of coffee, tea, or cotton consumers and less efficient producers is won at the expense of those deprived of employment thereby. It is naive to assume that their labour can be quickly and easily transferred to other uses. It cannot, unless there is a fortunate (or carefully planned and often expensive) coincidence as new labour-intensive crop crops are developed. Internationally, then, enrichment is a cause of impoverishment. Nothing so well illustrates the fundamental non-reciprocity than the contrast between the bargaining strength of the international oligopolies of coffee producers, processors, and merchants, and the permanent labourers of Uganda and Kenya.

HIRED LABOURERS IN WEST AFRICA

Structure

A characteristic of permanent labourers in East Africa is that productivity on their own farms has fallen so low that they are better off working for an exiguous cash income on farms of others. The reason for that low productivity is usually lack of fertile land and occasionally lack of complementary labour. In West Africa the same pattern is clear, with some important modifications.

The first is that the supply of labourers is the result both of land pressure in the normal sense of high population density and of the infertility of the land that is available. In Chapter 3 we outlined the ecological zones of West Africa and pointed out that, the further north one progresses from the forest belt, the lower the carrying capacity of the land becomes. To recapitulate the argument of that chapter, partly because population densities are sometimes high in relation to that carrying capacity and partly because the range of agricultural technologies to raise incomes in the dry savannah is very limited, incomes in the north are lower (and usually much lower) than in the forest belt.

But the most striking contrast is not between the north of Ghana or the Ivory Coast and the forest belt, but between the cash earnings of farmers in the countries on the Saharan fringe such as Mali, Chad, and Upper Volta, and those of the forest zone farmers. With small average land holdings, an unreliable

climate, poor soil, and minimal infrastructure, cash incomes in the rural areas
of these northern countries are tiny. Furthermore, there are virtually no opportunities for earning income from non-farm employment. The small public
service, concentrated in the more developed regions (particularly the capital),
and a tiny industrial base can absorb very few migrants from the rural areas.
Further, the failure of labour-intensive agriculture to generate even seasonal demand for hired labour means that the peasant farmer from Mali or Upper Volta
has only one possibility for increasing his cash income—migration to the south.

It is this relatively abundant supply of cheap agricultural labour that made
possible the rapid development of export crops in West Africa and that, more
relevant to our argument, has made possible the concentration of assets associated with that expansion.

However, our concern in this chapter is less with processes of accumulation
than with the labour on which that process is dependent. We have already made
a distinction between the permanent settled labourer, the abusaman or sharecropper (and his variants[21]) and the casual labourers required for clearing and
planting. Analytically, the abusaman is not much different from the permanent
settled labourer in East Africa except that his income is usually derived directly
from a share of the crop rather than from an agreed cash wage. Like the permanent settled labourer in East Africa, he may marry into the farmer's family and
use his period as an abusaman as a chance to acquire some cash savings and the
right to buy land, and may indeed begin his own farm while continuing as an
abusaman. To this extent the sharecrop system and the abusa agreement are
(like their less formalized East African counterparts) means of facilitating the
accumulation of capital by favoured poor young farmers who can use them as
means of gaining access to land and labour. In this sense, it is a real access
mechanism although, as we have argued in Chapter 3, it may in part keep in
place the larger con-mech on which West African agricultural development has
depended.

For in Ghana it is unusual for immigrants from other countries to secure
rights to land in this way.* Since the majority of abusamen are from the north
of Ghana, the abusa system is ethnically and tribally limited as a means of economic mobility. (The abusaman usually receives one-third of the gross returns
from the sale of cocoa and the farmer two-thirds. Under the Abunu and
Nkotokuano systems the crop may be shared equally. In rare cases the labourer
who has assisted the establishment of a cocoa farm and who subsequently becomes an abusaman may take all the crop in the early years, before the trees
reach full maturity, when yields are light.[22]) The two-thirds of sharecroppers

---

*But in Ivory Coast immigrant labourers may be paid, over a period of years,
by award of a small piece of land; see above, p. 48.

who come from the north are unlikely to progress from that status—although it is true that a successful abusaman on a large and high-yielding cocoa farm may become prosperous by all but the highest urban standards.[23]

The acreage that an abusaman can manage depends upon the amount of labour he can mobilize. In the first instance he calls upon his family, using wives and children as porters during harvest. In order to extend the acreage under his control, an abusaman will hire labourers directly or organize with others a small, temporary co-operative.

Wages

In the inter-group competition over wages, is there the same general institutional rigidity that we observed in East Africa, and the same collapse of that rigidity when interdependence becomes more mutual?

In the case of abusamen, shares are negotiated according to custom and, apart from occasional bonuses, are not variant. But the progress of a labourer from wages to sharecrop and the proportion of the crop that he acquires are open to negotiation. Polly Hill has described it thus:

On his first employment the labourer might be entitled to "use" all the cocoa he plucked from the young farm on condition that he assisted the farmer in establishing new cocoa-farms—which, later on, he would have a right to harvest. As the yield of this original farm increased, the proportion of the crop to which he was entitled fell to one-third—the traditional "abusa" share. Later on still, perhaps seven to ten years after his first employment, he might (especially if he had not been concerned with the original establishment of the farm in question) be transferred to an "nkotokuano" basis, receiving a certain sum of money for each load of cocoa he plucked, a sum always less than one-third of the value of the cocoa.[24]

We know little about the dynamics of these negotiations. Certainly there is scattered evidence that non-economic relationships are quite as (perhaps more) important as relative scarcity and productivity. One variable is the ease with which an abusaman can develop his own land; another his readiness to mobilize his family and hire labour on his own account. Thus, while it is correct to regard the share of the crop accruing to the labourer/abusaman/nkotokuano man as fixed, the speed and flexibility with which an employee may traverse that spectrum is not fixed.

It is extremely difficult to estimate the income of abusamen since yield

TABLE 5.2

Ghana: Estimated Income of Abusamen Engaged on Cocoa
Farms, 1969/70 (in N¢)

Region	Value of Share	Income from Sources
Volta	60-400	—
Brong-Ahafo	160-1,000	40-100
Ashanti	100-600	25-50
Western	100-500	30-80
Central	150-400	100-150
Eastern	50-330	30-200

Note: Calculated on basis of a price of N¢8 per load of cocoa beans.

Source: B.E. Rourke, Wages and Incomes of Agricultural Workers in Ghana, Technical Publication Series no. 13 (Legon: Institute of Statistical, Social and Economic Research, University of Ghana, 1971).

and acreage vary so much. Inevitably one finds a wide range of incomes and considerable regional variations. Table 5.2 is based on the estimates of agricultural officers at the sub-district level and should therefore be seen as a guide to the orders of magnitude rather than precise estimates. Even though the estimates may be on the high side (since officers may not have deducted enough for the expenses of abusamen), it is clear that, except for Volta and Eastern Regions, abusamen are more highly paid than unskilled workers in larger establishments in the rural areas. For the highest rates recorded for these was 120 cedis a year plus food and medical care.[25]

But if abusamen can earn incomes high by general rural standards, then insecurity and need to use children's labour at periods of peak labour demand together ensure that their children's attendance at school is much below that of farmers' children. Table 5.3 is indicative only, since it was compiled from the opinions of sub-district officers rather than from direct enumeration. Nonetheless, the discrepancies are striking: A farmer's child is twice as likely to be at school as a sharecropper's child. The long-run effect on occupational mobility and earnings will become clear in Chapter 8.

Very different from the relative financial ease of the abusamen is the lot of the annual labourers. Now annual labourers are also permanent settled labourers in so far as they are normally engaged for a year. They may live as part of the household—indeed, A.S. Appiah refers to their employment as "more or less a father/son relationship"—and they are provided with clothing, tools, housing, meals or food money in lieu. Cash incomes for annual labourers in Ghana vary between N¢50 and N¢90 a year, and the most

TABLE 5.3

Ghana: Attendance at School of Landholders' and Sharecroppers' Children, 1970
(in percentages)

Region	Landholders' Children	Sharecroppers' Children
Upper	48	n.a.
Northern	40	n.a.
Volta	70	42
Brong-Ahafo	74	28
Ashanti	90	43
Western	74	48
Central	80	53
Eastern	80	46

Note: n.a.—not applicable.

Source: B.E. Rourke, *Wages and Incomes of Agricultural Workers in Ghana,* Technical Publication Series no. 13 (Legon: Institute of Statistical, Social and Economic Research, University of Ghana, 1971).

commonly reported level is between N₡60 and N₡70. The great majority of year-round labourers are now from northern Ghana rather than from other countries. Very few are from other parts of Ghana. Appiah explains this by the poor conditions of annual labourers: "In view of the higher standards of living people from the south enjoy generally even when unemployed—thanks to the extended family system—they are not prepared to enjoy the unsavoury conditions under which most of the annual labourers are kept."[26]

"Unsavoury conditions" may beg questions of reference. What is clear is that the annual labourer has none of the opportunities for economic mobility the abusaman enjoys. (But abusamen are often recruited from known and trusted annual labourers.) Further, he almost never brings his family with him and can therefore neither share his labour nor increase his earnings by using their labour at peak periods. In Ivory Coast, a national average over the country as a whole is 30,000 F CFA, excluding food and accommodation. This compares with a minimum wage in large-scale agriculture of 60,000 F CFA (assuming 300 days and 8 hours a day).

Unfortunately, we know very little about the market mechanisms that determine the annual labourer's wage. We have some evidence that the same stickiness that we observed with respect to East Africa is characteristic in West Africa, too (if we exclude Volta, Brong Ahafo, and Ashanti regions from Rourke's figures, the most common payment reported is between

N₵60 and N₵70).[27] Given the vigorous inflation in Ghana in the 1960s, this suggests that there has been no effective mechanism for maintaining the real incomes of annual labourers. That might have been expected up to the forcible repatriation of employed aliens who were not given work permits under the Aliens Compliance Order of 1969. Thereafter we would have expected wages to rise quite rapidly, particularly in the light of Addo's finding that many farmers declared that they would be willing to employ more labour if they could recruit it.[28] According to Addo, two thirds of farmers interviewed in his survey maintained that their supply of labour was inadequate. Under these conditions it is surprising that wages, particularly of annual labourers, have not increased more rapidly.

One explanation, offered by cocoa farmers themselves, might be that cocoa farmers lack the finance to pay higher wages. This explanation is unconvincing, not least because the largest deficiency of supply in absolute terms occurs on the largest farms. Thus farms producing between 800 and 950 loads per season are currently employing an average of 6.4 employees but allegedly prefer to employ 9.6.

Alternatively, it may be that farmers think that paying higher wages will not increase the supply of labour. Given the close bond between employer and employee and the way in which labour is recruited, it may be that individual farmers see no advantage in paying higher wages. For higher wages will not increase the supply of labour, nor will they necessarily enable one farmer to recruit a labourer who would otherwise be lost to another farmer. Whatever the explanation, the fact remains that, despite a sudden and sharp fall in the supply of labour, there is no evidence of money wages increasing significantly. The balance of evidence suggests that real wages have in fact fallen over the last 15 years.

It might be thought that the disequilibrium in the labour market produced by the Aliens Compliance Order would be most noticed in the market for casual (rather than annual) labour. As we have already seen, both development of new cocoa farms and the maintenance of existing farms is much dependent upon casual labour, particularly when family labour is deficient. Further, casual labour is common throughout rural areas of Ghana but the work is highly seasonal. This makes inter-temporal comparisons extremely difficult because, although there is evidence of rising money wages between 1953 and 1970 (although falling real wages), we have no means of ascertaining whether regularity of employment has increased over that period. One might expect that improved internal transport would make casual labourers more mobile and therefore able to move round the country with the agricultural seasons. But B.E. Rourke and S.K. Sakyi-Gyinae report somewhat reduced mobility.[29] At the same time the increasing diversification of agricultural production in Ghana has both increased the demand for casual labour and introduced new periods of peak demand.*

Mirgrant casual labourers who are sufficiently well informed of seasonal patterns of demand may be able to secure work more or less the year round. But not all casual workers are migrants or wish to migrate. Rourke and Obeng suggest that in the Tamale area a local casual worker is unlikely to secure more than 160 days' work a year (giving him an annual income of N₵103 a year), and in the Kade area (in the forest but a food growing area) a local man would secure 180 days. In the heart of the cocoa district, however, both local and migrant workers seem to secure more regular work—up to 240 days a year—not much under the theoretical 269 days available.[30] It is thus possible that increasing regularity of employment for casual labourers has offset the slight fall in the real value of wage rates. Further, there is some evidence that the differential between the earnings of casual labourers and minimum wage earners has declined.† Nonetheless, in 1970 the casual agricultural worker earning the highest actual income (that is, including fringe benefits) would receive little more than two thirds of the income of the urban worker on the minimum wage or the rural unskilled employee of government. He would also have less access to health, education, and entertainment facilities.

Employment and Export Prices

We saw that in East Africa the agricultural labourer is vulnerable to the changing economic circumstances of his employer—themselves determined by inter-group competition at the international level. One fact that affects those circumstances is the price of the export crop. Is there evidence that the same is true in Ghana? We have already seen that there is a reported shortage of agricultural labour in the cocoa belt of Ghana and that there is little evidence of rising wages to increase that supply.

----

*For instance, in the Tamale area seasonal migration to work on large rice farms is a relatively recent phenomenon providing work from August to February. In the same way, new sugarcane farmers in the Akuse area require casual labour from November to February.

†Allowing for fringe benefits for casual labourers and assuming that both rates can justifiably be deflated by the Accra cost-of-living index. This is a dangerous procedure since food is heavily weighted in that index and has risen sharply in price. It may therefore understate the increase in real earnings of the casual agricultural labourer.

This suggests, but does not prove, that a high international price for cocoa such as pertained in 1972-74 may increase the demand for labour in the cocoa belt but will not necessarily increase the wage. We simply do not know enough about the reaction of cocoa farmers to high prices in the changed labour conditions since the Aliens Compliance Order.* Against that, Addo reports that many of the farmers in his survey claimed that a higher cocoa price would enable and encourage them to pay higher wages to their labour. This claim almost certainly needs heavy discounting. To many of the larger cocoa farmers, wage costs are a small part of total revenue. But it is possible that the smaller farmers, who currently feel that the employment of permanent labour would take too large a share of gross revenue, would be encouraged to employ permanent labour if gross revenue were substantially higher. If this put a further squeeze on the supply of labour and was seen to accompany rising money incomes of abusamen, it is possible, but not certain, that agricultural wages would rise.

There thus seems to be a less direct relationship than the one we noted with respect to coffee in East Africa. But the price effect might not be symmetrical. There is some evidence that, when prices are very low, farmers not only do not develop new farms but do not cultivate and harvest their existing farms intensively. This certainly reduces the demand for labour—both casual and permanent—and the incomes of abusamen (since yields are likely to decline). There is no evidence that it reduces the money wages of those who are employed, except perhaps through a less open-handed distribution of bonuses. (According to Addo's survey, some farmers pay a bonus or premium to abusamen and permanent labourers for particularly hard or commendable work.[31])

Summary

Agricultural labour in West Africa—or at least in Ghana, whence perforce most of our material has been drawn—seems to have three major features. First, it is a means by which an ambitious young man can become a substantial rural capitalist: It is an access mechanism. Starting as a casual labourer, a man can progress to becoming a settled labourer, to becoming an abusaman, to becoming a cocoa farmer in his own right. There is thus a strong similarity with the

---

*The cocoa farmers have not, of course, benefitted by the full rise in international price since the Cocoa Marketing Board acts as a price stabilizer (see below, pp. 595-96). Further, even if growers' prices rose substantially, it does not necessarily follow that acreage would be rapidly expanded since many farmers will remember with dismay their experience in the 1950s.

process Cowen has documented in Kikuyuland whereby a poor young Kikuyu could become a substantial farmer. The second feature, again directly parallel to East Africa, is that agricultural labour provides migrants and local poor farmers with a chance to increase their family income. To this extent there is a direct complementarity between proto-capitalist agriculture and subsistence agriculture. That complementarity becomes competitive when the labourer's need to earn cash jeopardizes the yield on his own farm. Third, we have again encountered remarkably sticky wage rates. Unlike Kenya, where we quoted evidence of "fine tuning" in the agriculture labour market, in Ghana the evidence at the moment is that farmers prefer to employ fewer men than they would wish, rather than pay a higher wage to attract those extra men. We thus find static or declining real wages and little evidence of dynamic employment growth.

It is no wonder that a significant number of would-be labourers prefer to try their luck in town rather than accept work on the farms under these conditions. Only those who are confident that they can exploit the avenues of mobility in the agricultural labour system or those who, less ambitious, can use the complementarity between employment and subsistence are likely to find agricultural labour a long-run solution to their requirements.

HIRED LABOURERS IN EGYPT

Structure

We consider Egypt separately from the other "rice economies," not only because it is on a different continent but also because the issues that can (just) be addressed in Malaysia, the Philippines, and Sri Lanka have not received adequate study in Egypt as a result of the conflict with Israel. Very limited data are available after 1965; and much of what is available is more than usually unreliable. But the Egyptian case is too important to ignore; with some of the problems, especially landlessness, that are beginning to be major concerns elsewhere already raised in acute form, it calls for at least a brief word on the nature, size, and condition of the rural work force.

According to the 1960 census, about 40 percent of the rural labour force is made up of permanent agricultural labourers. An additional 26 percent are unpaid family workers; most of these are children under the age of fourteen. A major problem lies in the interpretation of the first row of Table 5.4. For it is by no means unusual for farmers on very small holdings to take casual work on larger holdings. There is thus an indeterminate number of those dependent to varying degrees on wage labour in this 34 percent of the permanent rural labour force.

TABLE 5.4

Egypt: Distribution of Rural Labour Force by Employment Status, 1960

Employment Status	Number of Persons (thousands)	Percentage of Total Rural Labour Force
On own farms and self-employed persons	1,713	33.7
Wage agricultural labourers*	1,976	38.9
Unpaid family labourers	1,336	26.3
Unemployed labourers	56	1.1
Total rural labour force	5,081	100

*Should be interpreted as "permanent" wage labourers.

Source: Central Department of Statistics, *1960 Population Census,* vol. 2, General Tables, as quoted in M. Abdel-Fadil, *Employment and Income Distribution in Egypt, 1952-1970,* Discussion Paper (Norwich: University of East Anglia, 1974).

But it does not follow that all permanent labourers work on larger farms, as Table 5.5 shows.

Farms smaller than five feddans employ nearly half of those counted in the census as agricultural wage labourers. But apart from farmers working on their own farms, it is probably the case that the great majority of those hired on the smallest farms (smaller than two feddans) are casual, seasonal, or piecework labourers.

Again we must make the distinction between casual workers who, having their own land, engage in occasional supplementary work, and those who have no land and no permanent job (in so far as insecure employment is never permanent), but who like their sub-Saharan counterparts, must go from one casual or piecework job to another. We thus have the familiar hierarchy:

1. Some (inadequate?) land; occasional work.

2. No land; permanent employment.

3. No land; no permanent employment; succession of casual jobs.

It is with the last category that we shall be concerned here.

Why can't they rent land? Are they permanent losers in a competitive process, either between tenants and would-be tenants considered as a group (intra-group competition) or between landless and either landlords or any other "controlling" group?

First, a simple arithmetic point. At a time when the concentration of government effort has been on consolidation of some of the smallest holdings, usually achieved through variants of co-operative reorganization on the Nawag

TABLE 5.5

Egypt: Distribution of Permanent Labour Force by Size of Farm, 1961

Size of Farm (feddans)	Total Area (feddan)	Labour Force	Percentage of Labour Force	Labour Density/ Feddan	Holdings Employing Outside Hired Labour (percent)
Under 2	716	1,426	37.1	2	24*
2-5	1,638	1,367	35.6	0.8	36
5-20	1,840	782	20.3	0.4	40-60
More than 20	2,003	265	7	0.1	85
Total	6,197	3,840	100	0.6	

*Mainly temporary labourers.

Sources: A. Mohieldine, "Agricultural Investment and Employment in Egypt since 1935," doctoral dissertation, University of London, 1966, and R. Mabro, "Employment and Wages in Dual Agriculture," *Oxford Economic Papers*, November 1971; both as quoted in M. Abdel-Fadil, *Employment and Income Distribution in Egypt, 1952-1970*, Discussion Paper (Norwich: University of East Anglia, 1974).

model,[32] the rapid natural growth of the landless peasants makes it intrinsically improbable that the absolute number of landless *can* fall. Only if there were either technical or structural changes in Egyptian agriculture that raised the effective demand for permanent labour could we expect the number of casual landless workers to fall. We have already seen that land reform has had the effect of much increasing the number of medium-sized holdings, and we would certainly expect that to be associated with a rise in the demand for permanent workers. But we also saw that the total effect was rather small and that even in 1965, the Egyptian agricultural structure continued to be dominated by holdings of fewer than five feddans.

It is thus no surprise to find that the number of casual landless workers has been rising despite land reform and associated technical changes.[33] By 1960, their numbers had reached 1.2 million, of whom about one quarter were females and one half children between 12 and 18. The number of adult males in this group was roughly 500,000 in 1961.

Apart from the structural issues we have touched upon, there are two processes by which they are excluded from land. The first is intra-group competition: They are at a disadvantage because they have limited social leverage and less financial credit to offer the landlord. The first arises from their mobility, their tendency to congregate round the larger holdings where work is more plentiful but small holdings to rent are extremely scarce, and their inability to maintain strong social ties with influential people in the village who will advance their claims when a holding becomes available. They are thus at a natural competitive disadvantage, which is reinforced by their very poverty.

Second and much more important, 60 percent of the adult males are thought to be involved in the notorious tarhila system. By this system, labour is recruited for four to eight weeks for the maintenance of canals and other rural public works. This group of rural labourers—recruited mainly from the highly populated provinces of Upper Egypt and Delta—is freely mobile, willing to enter casual employment not only in the vicinity of their villages but sometimes in distant localities:

> The employers of these casual labourers usually have recourse to special labour contractors (*mokawil anfarr*) who guarantee a regular supply of casual labour for a commission. The *tarahil* labourers suffer the concentration of two modes of exploitation, namely usury and employers' exploitation. The usual practice within the system of *tarhila* is that the contractor has to deduct a commission of not less than 12 percent of wages paid to *tarahil* labourers. Moreover, most of the *tarahil* labourers are under strong pressure from their contractors to work extra *unpaid* days at the end of *tarhila* for the contractor's own account.[34]

In view of the fact that the tarhila system was designed to provide labourers for *public* works at a time when Egypt was moving quite rapidly towards a socialist ideology, one might wonder why the system survived. It was not until seven years after the Revolution that government began to frame policies designed to relieve the tarahil labourer. In the 1960s many attempts were made to set up government-financed substitutes or competitors. These all failed, largely because they took inadequate account of the fact that the labourer is under an obligation to the contractor. He is not a free agent who can choose between a *mokawil anfarr* and a state substitute. He is bound by obligations of kinship, of past relationships, above all of debt and dependence. No state-financed competitor was empowered to lend to the tarahil labourer for the emergencies and rites of passage, which form a major part, not only of his expenditure but also of the fabric of his social relationships. Ignoring this, the government schemes were never effective in breaking the power of the contractors.

But as long as that power endures, the tarahil labourer is caught in a system of perpetual bondage. Heavily in pawn to the contractor, he has no possibility of abandoning the one relationship that gives him a form of security, albeit a very shadowy form, and accepting the risks of tenancy. For the contractor is often either himself the local shopkeeper, produce merchant, landowner, and/or moneylender; or is closely allied with this group of village functionaries. A tarahil labourer who tries to renege on his obligations to the contractor is thus likely to find himself squeezed by the village triumvirate on which he is ultimately wholly dependent. In this competition, he can never win.

Wages

Given the size of the casual labour force and the means by which the major part of it is organized, we would not expect to find money or real wages rising fast in the rural areas. Conversely, given government's need to demonstrate its concern for the rural masses, we might expect at least some action to be taken. We thus find the same kind of political stage management that we shall encounter, perhaps to an even more marked extent, in the estate sector in Asia. This consists of passing seemingly liberal legislation but then failing to enforce it. This enables government to claim that its hand are clean and that the real fault lies with "capitalist farmers" whose perpetual tendency to exploit the weak regrettably cannot be changed by legislation.

The Agrarian Reform Law of 1952 did in fact provide that agricultural labourers should be paid a minimum of 18 piastres a day. But ten years later the average for adult men was only 12 piastres a day.[35] Indeed, between 1950 and 1959 the average rate for men may not have advanced at all in money terms.[36] Bent Hansen has demonstrated very convincingly that the wage rate is highly responsive to local variations in supply and demand,[37] which implies a rather considerable variance around the mean. To that extent, the average figures probably understate the poverty of the poorest.

How far the very modest rise in average money rates (from 9 piastres in 1945 to 18 in 1969) has resulted in rising real incomes is impossible to say. First, we do not know whether regularity of employment of casual workers has increased; we have seen some slight theoretical reasons for assuming it may have diminished. Second, we have no reliable cost-of-living index for rural labourers for the whole of this period. An appropriate index during the 1950-60 period showed a 32 percent rise—consistent with a slight fall in real wages if incidence of employment remained constant. Given the very high rate of growth of prices in the mid-1960s, it is hard to believe that an equivalent index would have risen by less than 40 percent between 1961 and 1969, particularly as some basic necessities—including sugar, tea, tobacco, and paraffin—became much more expensive in this period. Only if regularity of employment was much enhanced, then, is it at all likely that real incomes rose in the 1960s. Without pretending to a certainty the data do not allow, we incline to the view that the great majority of rural casual labourers were no better off in 1969 than they had been when they rejoiced at the overthrow of the old regime.

HIRED LABOURERS IN ASIA

Structure

In this section, we shall consider labour employed in rice production only. The next section is devoted to labour engaged in export crops on large-scale farms or plantations. Here we shall be concerned with the same inter-group competition—that between employers and labourers. But we shall also need to look at intra-group competition as the *structure* of labour demand changes as a result of technological innovation. We know practically nothing about the ways in which this competition is resolved or fought out. But it follows from the nature of the employer/employee bargaining position that the change in structure is imposed with very little room for adjustment on behalf of employees. This is a hypothesis we shall be unable to test further.

In all three countries, the distinction between (1) permanent labourers, settled on one farm; (2) permanent labourers moving from job to job for piece work; and (3) casual workers taking employment to supplement their income from other sources, is valid and important. The permanent labourers are likely to be migrants from poor areas, some of whom may return home at key periods of their home agricultural cycle. But an increasing number of permanent labourers are local, squeezed out of tenancies or ownership by the processes we have already described.

Rice production in Sri Lanka, Malaysia, and the Philippines has grown rapidly over the last 15 years. Much of that increase, especially in Sri Lanka and Malaysia, has resulted from bringing new land under cultivation or increasing the area that can be double-cropped. But a proportion, higher in the Philippines than elsewhere, has come from more intensive cultivation[38]—a feature much emphasized by the seed-fertiliser technology. This implies an increase in the demand for labour only if technological changes have not acted to replace labour with other inputs.

From our point of view, it is extremely important to know whether the demand for labour has increased or diminished. For the new technology has undeniably enriched farmers and landowners. Although there are, of course, very considerable variations between regions and between farms, even within one village, increases in net returns per acre of up to 100 percent are not uncommon.[39] The question that is central to our discussion is how far casual and permanent labour shared in those gains.

The change in the pattern of labour demand implied by the technology of the Green Revolution is well known. Each operation of the growing cycle is more labour-demanding. Ploughing has to be deeper and more thorough; transplanting has to be carried out and is best done in straight rows; weeding is much more demanding, principally because the application of fertiliser increases the growth of weeds as well as of the rice; higher yields involve more work in harvesting and threshing. (There may be a disproportionate increase in the demand for labour at threshing time since some of the improved seeds are short-stemmed, which makes manual threshing more difficult and time-consuming.) Furthermore, the quicker growth and shorter ripening period of the improved varieties, as well as the increased yields, makes double-cropping both more feasible and more attractive. It not only doubles the labour input per hectare but also makes labour peaks more pronounced since operations have to be carried out under a very strict timetable.

Now all this would tend to suggest that the new technology would imply very considerable increases in labour demand. Indeed, there is much evidence that in some areas it has done so. In a survey of 42 farms in Laguna in the Philippines, researchers from the International Rice Research Institute found that the input of *hired* labour increased from 36.3 man-days per hectare in 1966 to 67.2 man-days in 1969.[40] A slightly larger survey over two regions in the Philippines found a modest increase in all labour (including family labour) between 1966 and 1970—a period in which yields increased by 42 percent.[41]

But, at least in some areas, this is not an equilibrium situation. For technical and economic reasons, it may be profitable to the operator to mechanize at least some of the cultivation operations. The technical pressures rise from the need, particularly in double-cropping, to keep to a tight schedule and to speed up certain critical operations such as land preparation and weeding. The economic incentive arises from the fact that cheap machinery is so much more productive than labour that total costs fall.[42] Institutional forces, exerted especially by landlords of sharecrop farmers, may reinforce these pressures * It does not necessarily follow, however, that use of tractors or weedkiller sprays is labour-substitutive. Barker has shown that in Central Luzon and Laguna mechanical and chemical weeding has been accompanied by an *increase* in labour demand for this particular operation.[43] This is probably because little weeding was done before the adoption of the new technology, especially if transplanting was not carried out in straight rows. In this case the new technology has effectively created an obligatory new component of the growing cycle. The fact that it is mechanized does not offset the fact that labour demand has increased.

In this respect, it contrasts sharply with land preparation at harvesting and threshing—operations that are inescapable under all technologies. The evidence suggests that, at least in the Philippines, there is a strong incentive to mechanize

---

*It may be significant that share tenants and owner-cultivators are more inclined to use tractors than are leasehold tenants.

these processes except on the very smallest farms. A survey of farm practices in three Philippine regions showed that in each of them the proportion of farmers using tractors for land preparation and machines for mechanical threshing had increased overall; the former had doubled and the latter nearly quintupled.[44] We thus find that, even in an area like Laguna, which is not characterized by large farms and where soils are too light to support heavy tractors, the rapid spread of small tractors has reduced by almost half the labour requirement for land preparation.[45] In the same way, there is evidence that the use of mechanical threshers has increased. A survey of 76 farms in Central Luzon and Laguna showed that, whereas irrigated one-crop farms tended to give up using threshers, double-cropping farms greatly increased the use of these machines.

The question is whether this mechanization of land preparation and harvesting has led to a net rise or a net fall in the demand for hired labour. In the Philippines, the evidence suggests that the overall effect on hired labour has been relatively small, with some tendency to increase demand. Table 5.6 does not suggest that hired labour has been displaced by mechanization, and in Laguna at least there is evidence of significant increase in hired labour. But at the same time it is clear that, at least in Laguna, the total labour input per hectare has fallen. This implies that farmers are substituting hired labour for their own labour. This could be a change in the tenure structure in Laguna, with more part-time owner-operators displacing tenants and hiring in labour in order to maintain off-farm employment, or, less probable, tenants and owner-operators are seeking off-farm work and replacing their labour with hired hands. We shall return to the former possibility below. Let us first examine intra-group competition as revealed in the structure of labour demand.

Table 5.6 does not adequately reveal the changes in the structure of hired labour that have occurred. The increased demand for labour for the less easily mechanized operations—transplanting and weeding—and the much smaller fall in the demand for hired labour in land preparation has shifted demand from permanent employment to casual employment for these operations. Casual female employment for transplanting and weeding has almost certainly grown substantially, and there is some evidence of rising wages for this activity. Simultaneously, harvesters and threshers who work on a sharecrop basis (and include a significant proportion of migrants) have increased their wages and do not seem to have suffered any reduction in employment. (According to Aida Librero and Maha Mangahas, the harvesters and threshers have increased their gross income by about 50 percent since the introduction of the new technology.[46])

TABLE 5.6

Philippines: Changes in Patterns of Factor Use in Areas of High Rates of Mechanization, Wet Season, 1966-70

	Labour Use				
	1966			1970	
	Man-Days/Hectare		Percent-	Man-Days/Hectare		Percent-
Survey Area	Total	Hired	age Hired	Total	Hired	age Hired
Central Luzon-Laguna						
Land preparation	17	3	18	10	2	23
Pulling and transplanting	15	14	96	17	16	99
Weeding	5	2	36	11	3	31
Other pre-harvest	8	2	19	8	1	15
Harvesting and threshing	18	16	86	21	18	85
Total	64	37	58	67	41	62
Laguna						
Land preparation	20	4	18	11	4	37
Pulling and transplanting	10	9	95	10	10	99
Weeding	16	2	16	18	100	56
Other pre-harvest	8	1	10	10	1	14
Harvesting and threshing	32	32	100	31	31	100
Total	86	48	57	80	57	72

	Technological Development	
	1966	1970
Central Luzon-Laguna		
Tractor users (percent)	14	48
Area planted to high-yielding varieties (percent)	0	67
Yield (metric tons/hectare)	1.9	2.7
Laguna		
Tractor users (percent)	37	76
Area planted to high-yielding varieties (percent)	1	93
Yield (metric tons/hectare)	2.4	3.4

Source: R. Barker, W.H. Meyers, C.M. Crisostomo, B. Duff, "Employment and Technological Change in Philippine Agriculture," *International Labour Review* 106, nos. 2-3 (August/September 1972).

Wages

From this it does not follow that agricultural wages in general have risen. There are doubtless great regional variations, but one study shows that, despite an 85 percent increase in the demand for hired labour, real wages actually fell by 6 percent[47]—ample evidence of an increase in the *supply* of labour from increased migration and/or rising numbers of landless labourers.

What seems to have occurred is that the increase in demand for seasonal labour has led to a rise in money wage rates for that labour—namely casual workers working on a seasonal basis. Table 5.7 shows that, in money terms, wage rates in the Philippines rose quite sharply between 1966 and 1970, except for planting—an exception that is difficult to explain except perhaps in terms of of extreme elasticity of supply of female labour. But note that the rise in money wages is in each case consistent with falls, in two cases very substantial falls, in real incomes, as indicated by the country-wide consumer price index.* Real wages of permanent labour have remained roughly constant or actually declined.

Since the bulk of casual labour for transplanting and weeding is provided by locally resident women, the net effect may well have been to increase family incomes in the rice bowl area but to decrease both the possibilities of employment and the wages of migrants from other areas. Without very much more research on the differential effect of the Green Revolution on hired labour, it is impossible to say more.

In terms of absolute income, we do not have adequate data on the number of days worked per labourer to be able to calculate annual incomes of casual or permanent labourers. Griffin gives a figure of five pesos a day for hired labour in Laguna, but that is an average figure for all kinds of labour over the crop season and almost certainly disguises considerable variation.†

---

*As the wage figures are for conditions of service that do not include provision of food, the relatively high food weights in the consumer price index are less inappropriate than they would otherwise be. But the urban bias of the consumer price index weights is a statistical problem we have not been able to overcome satisfactorily, since we do not know the regional composition of the original Bureau of Agricultural Economics figures.

†For instance, in Calamba the effective wage for harvesting and threshing is P8.20 per man day, whereas in Biñan it is P4.10; on upland palay farms in Nueva Ecija it is only P2.50. Barker et al. show in the *International Labour Review* (1972) that, where harvesting wages are very high, labourers are obliged to weed plots free in order to have the privilege of undertaking the harvest work. To this extent the threshing wages above are overstated. This is good evidence of local adaptation of the labour market to institutional rigidities.

TABLE 5.7

**Philippines: Index of Average Daily Wage Rates (No Meal Provided)
on Palay Farms, 1966-71**

Average of Second and Third Quarters	Ploughing		Planting		Average of Fourth and First Quarters	Harvesting	
	Money	Real	Money	Real		Money	Real
1966	100	100	100	100	1965-66	100	100
1967	108	101	88	83	1966-67	114	108
1968	107	100	92	86	1967-68	102	96
1969	111	105	81	76	1968-69	88	83
1970	119	95	97	77	1969-70	92	73
					1970-71	125	81

Source: Basic data from Bureau of Agricultural Economics.

Even if a labourer is able to secure 200 days work a year, over the year this means an average daily income of P2.74. In fact, this is almost certainly a maximum since, as we have seen, male labour is not usually used for transplanting and the periods of peak demand are relatively short, even in double-cropping farms. (Where mechanization of land preparation is far advanced, many male casual workers will work only at weeding, harvesting, and threshing.)

As Table 5.8 shows, a survey of 50 relatively poor villages in Laguna showed that the median income per day was P4.41; under 30 percent of the surveyed population had incomes as low as P2.74.[8] This suggests that, even on the very generous estimate above, agricultural labourers in the rice bowl area of the Philippines are among the poorest one third of a poor population.*

Much the same pattern emerges from the much smaller volume of research work in Malaysia. There the increasing extent of double-cropping may have increased the demand for permanent labour on some of the larger holdings, and it certainly has led to severe shortages of labour at the periods of peak demand. This has led many farmers to use small tractors for land preparation; these are usually hired from farmers' associations or private contractors. But transplanting

---

*In the surveyed villages, the unemployment rate was 11 percent; only 9 percent had white-collar jobs, 20 percent were farmers, 7 percent were production process workers, and 12 percent were service and communications workers. Farm labourers accounted for 8 percent of the population and 17 percent of the work force.

TABLE 5.8

**Philippines: Income Per Day of Persons Gainfully Employed,
Sample Villages in Laguna, 1972**

Income Per Day (₱)	Percentage
0.01-0.99	9
1.00-2.99	22
3.00-4.99	27
5.00-7.99	22
8.00-15.99	18
16.00 and over	2
Total (2,540 respondents)	100

Median income per day	4.41
Mean income per day	5.51
Standard deviation	4.53

Source: "An Evaluation Research of the Philippine Rural Reconstruction
Movement's Barrio Development Program in Laguna: Baseline Study," a report
from the Asian Social Institute, mimeo. (Manila, January 1973), p. 82.

cannot be mechanized and many farmers on the large irrigation schemes face
critical labour shortages at this time. Harvesting also has not been much
mechanized, despite the attempts of at least one European implement manu-
facturer to introduce it, and at this period labour is in high demand, especially
in double-crop areas where staggering of operations is not feasible. (At Kubang
Sepat, in the Muda Scheme, 78 percent of harvest labour was supplied by migrant workers.)

There is some highly localized evidence that wage rates have risen appreci-
ably in the light of this scarcity.[49] How far that can be generalized is impossible
to say. But in so far as rural development in the poorer areas (especially
Kelantan and Tregganu, from where the seasonal migrants come) creates *local*
demand for labour, the supply may fall and rural wages may then rise throughout Perlis and Kedah. (Although wages in Kelantan are one third the level in
Sungei Manik and one half that of Province Wellesley, which suggests that it
will be some time before the supply of migrant labour from Kelantan to the
West coast is seriously threatened.[50])

But other possibilities cannot be discounted. Sexual divisions of work—e.g.,
women having a near monopoly of transplanting—may break down and family
labour, at present little used in harvesting, may be mobilized for that operation
also. Further, farmers may reduce their own off-farm employment (at present

significant for all except those with the smallest farms) once agricultural wages approach those currently earned by farmers in off-farm work. Where rice farmers are obliged to switch to other crops, demand for labour may fall; it is very likely to fall at the periods of peak demand for rice. Some seasonal migrants from Kelantan are reported to be finding it difficult to secure work in their former areas a result of this diversification.[51] Lastly, farmers may mechanize more widely—especially weeding, harvesting, and threshing. We do not know at what wage rates these reactions would be induced, but there is evidence that initial experimentation is already under way. It would therefore be unwise to infer a rise in wages from well-attested local and seasonal shortages of labour. (In the Philippines, the one has *not* been associated with the other; see above, pp. 126-27.)

Conclusion

In conclusion, it is relevant to draw the parallel between what seems to have been happening in the Philippines and in Africa. In both cases, the group of agricultural workers upon whom there seems to have been most pressure is the most vulnerable group—namely, the migrant workers who depend upon agricultural employment for their subsistence. Unlike local workers, they have no possibility of growing their own subsistence crops; and although they may be given food in addition to a cash wage, once they lose their employment, both cash wage and subsistence food come to an end.

Nor are they at a disadvantage only in terms of income. As we saw in respect to migrant rural labour in Africa, they not only share the general deprivation of the rural areas in terms of all forms of social consumption but even tend to make less use of what social capital is available in the rural areas. Poorly housed, fed at the whim of their employers, and continually on the move from farm to farm, they lack the incentive, time, or energy to exploit the social infrastructure. Unlike most industrial workers in the formal sector and many rural workers on the estates, they have no contract of employment; no formal channels for settling disputes; no insurance against sickness or injury;* no minimum wage; and no redress against an unjust employer. Separated from kin and living on a precarious and insecure income, they are the least enviable of men.

---

*In the Philippines, there is a social security system for all wage earners. But it does not apply to agricultural labour when a "worker . . . is not paid a wage for at least six uninterrupted months a year." This gives employers an incentive to break employment after six months, and then re-engage the worker.

ESTATE WORKERS

We come finally to consideration of a quite different order of inter-group competition, that between plantation owners and their unskilled workers in Asia. We might expect that a relatively leftist country like Sri Lanka would have been more vigorous in ensuring that estate workers are protected than a more conservative country such as Malaysia or the Philippines. In fact, we shall see that no such easy pattern is apparent. Although all estate/plantation workers are without exception poorly paid and ill protected, it is in Malaysia that their grim lot has been most improved.

However inhuman the conditions of estate workers—and objectivity does not disqualify that adjective—one important preliminary point must be made. These conditions tell us by inference much about the conditions of landless labourers who work on larger farms and smallholdings. (In Malaysia, for example, employees on rubber smallholdings earn one half or one third the wage of employees on rubber estates.[52]) For, in all three countries with which we shall be concerned in this section, estate labourers have some legal and institutional support and protection. It may be inadequate. It may not be properly enforced. It may allow the estate worker to be cheated and tricked. But, at the very least, it represents a goal, an optimum towards which recalcitrant employers can, in theory, be goaded. By contrast, the landless labourer working on a smallholding has not even that protection. It is significant that owners and managers of estates often seek to justify the conditions under which their employees live by comparing them with the alternative. That that is worse is often true. In the remaining pages of this chapter, that must always be at the forefront of the reader's mind—not, surely not, to excuse estate owners, but to remain constantly aware of the realities of the poverty of hired labourers outside the estates.

An essential preliminary point, which goes far to explain both the scale of the problem and its differential impact, is the racial composition of the estate labour force. In Sri Lanka, at least 80 percent of the plantation population is Tamil. Originally brought to the island by British tea planters who could not secure co-operation from the local population whose lands had been seized, Tamils have become a racial no man's land. A treaty with India provides for repatriation of some and the granting of Sri Lankan citizenship to the remainder. But that treaty, already over ten years old, is implemented in the symbol more than the substance.

Only 20 percent of the whole population, the Tamils remain concentrated on the estates, the victims of discrimination and exploitation that runs the gamut from the petty to the preposterous. For example, citizen Tamils are given a distinctively coloured ration book, with the result that storekeepers refuse to serve them when free rice runs short. Non-citizen Tamils receive no unemployment benefits, no free rice, and most important, no membership in farmers' co-operatives when estates are affected by land reform. This means that, when land reform is implemented, the most wretched and vulnerable section of the community is deprived of the ill-paid employment it had—and is left with nothing.

In West Malaysia, 56 percent of all estate labour was Indian (mainly Tamil) in 1972-73, and 24 percent Chinese, with only 19 percent Malay.* Generally, the Indians and Chinese are tappers—a job requiring slightly higher skill. But the Chinese are generally employed on contracts, which give them higher wages (by 20 percent in 1971, according to Department of Statistics data) but less security and no fringe benefits. Over the last ten years, the proportion of contract labour has increased, implying a substitution of Chinese and Indians for Malays and a higher rate of unemployment among Malays.

A feature of these racial ghettos is that the labour race tends to become locked in. In Sri Lanka this results directly from government policy; in Malaysia from inadequate education for the children and the need to employ children on the estates at an early age to increase family income. The result is that the estate-based labour force grows naturally at about 2 percent per annum. Unless estate-based jobs grow at the same rate, unemployment on the estates must increase. This seems to have happened in both Sri Lanka and Malaysia. In Sri Lanka, employment grew at less than 0.5 percent per annum from 1947 to 1970. In Malaysia, employment in rubber estates fell by nearly a third from 1963 to 1972. While it is true that employment on oil palm estates increased rapidly, this was inadequate to offset the sharp fall on the rubber estates.† One of the major features of poverty on the estates in these two countries is therefore the high level of unemployment, reportedly 6.8 percent of male estate workers in Sri Lanka in 1968.[53]

The welfare effect of this unemployment would be less damaging if wages and other conditions on the estates were in line with industrial wages.[54] They are not. In Sri Lanka, real minimum wages fell by 12 percent between 1953 and 1969. Further, it is questionable whether workers actually receive the minimum wage, partly because they do not work a full week or month. Hours worked by men fell from 160 per month in 1960 to 140 in 1969. Indeed, underemployment is probably at the same level as open unemployment—about

---

*The 1970 census gives the following distribution to Malaysian population: Indian 10 percent, Chinese 35 percent, and Malay 53 percent.
†The structure of estate employment changed, with a higher proportion of supervisory and clerical workers in 1971 than in 1965. But this is not evidence of upward mobility for the least skilled Malay estate workers, although Malays form a higher proportion of the labour force on oil palm estates.

50,000 man-years each, and both are increasing. (By law, estates are obliged to offer six days' work a week; this law is simply ignored.)

Under these circumstances, monthly earnings for men did not exceed Rs60 (£4) in 1969; for women, Rs52.[55] This can be supplemented by produce of food plots on which employees can work in their spare time, but we do not know how many of the estates give land for this purpose. Some of the larger foreign companies claim to do so. The only examples of food gardens we have personally seen were small, poor, and unproductive; it may be significant that this was one of the major issues in a strike of estate workers in December 1973.

In Malaysia, by contrast, the National Union of Plantation Workers (NUPW) is one of the few unions to have achieved sufficient organization and political leverage to be able to negotiate with some authority. Nonetheless, the minimum wages of tappers declined sharply in 1951-52 and only regained their 1951 level in 1969—as a result of pressure from the NUPW. For field workers, the lowest minimum wage (M$2.3 per day, compared to M$3.8 for tappers in 1951) followed the same general pattern, but rose more strongly in the middle 1960s as the field workers strove for parity with the tappers. In real terms, it is clear that tappers and field workers were worse off in 1968 than they had been in 1951.

But some solid improvements in fringe benefits were achieved in those two decades, including paid holiday, sick leave (agreed in 1962), increased hospitalization pay, housing allowances for those (primarily Chinese and Malay) who do not live on the estates (from 1964), and superannuation schemes (from 1968). Although these still left some major gaps in the welfare provisions for estate workers—most notably compensation for accidents—the contrast with labour hired on rubber and rice smallholdings needs no emphasis. There are, of course, variations among estates, as among any group of employers. It is probable that some of the worst examples are to be found among the smaller, Chinese-owned rather than the internationally owned estates. With a shorter time horizon, a reluctance to invest in the future, and a desire to secure a high return on investment, some of the smaller owners are the least scrupulous.

We have seen that, in Sri Lanka and on the smaller estates in Malaysia, government intervention, inadequate as it may be, is ignored. This problem—of the gap between theory and reality—is raised to a higher power in the Philippine sugar estates. True, the law stipulates a minimum wage of ₱7 or ₱8 per day, according to the region, but 90 percent of estates pay less than the minimum.[56] (Even if the minimum were paid, it would be 28 percent less in real—rice-equivalent—terms than the 1964 minimum.) Union activity (from the rather small but militant National Federation of Sugar Workers) has resulted in pressure on the union of all sorts—from bribing workers not to join to assaults on union organizers—but more revealingly in the deliberate delay of the legal authorities in hearing over 800 cases of lock-outs brought forward by the union.

Under these conditions, workers on the estates are dependent on the goodwill of the estate owner, the haciendero.

There are two categories of workers on the Philippine sugar estates: migrants and permanent workers who live with their families on or near the estate all year. For the latter, the average number of working days is 180 per year, with little chance of finding alternative activities during the off-season. The haciendero does not always allow his workers to grow vegetables on a food plot. The income of the 180 days must, therefore, feed the whole family for 365.

If workers were paid the minimum wage, they would get ₱1,400 for the year, but their actual income seldom exceeds ₱900 a year—allowing only 300 grammes of rice per head per day. In principle, the permanent workers should be paid every two weeks during the milling season. During the off-season, when the workers have no source of income, the landowner "gives" them rice rations—on credit payable during the milling season.*

The other category of workers is the "sacadas," the 30,000 seasonal workers recruited for the milling season from neighboring islands. The majority come from the province of Antiquae on Panay Island. They have even less protection than the permanent workers. Problems start in their home towns, where feudalism and poor soil combine with few work opportunities to oblige them to work in Negros. Hacienderos in Negros sign contracts with local notables in the island of origin. The notables become contractors and commit themselves to bring to the haciendas the agreed number of seasonal workers. With the money he is given by the landowner, the contractor pays for transport, clothes, and tools, and moves with the workers to the hacienda. There he takes charge of the hacienda stores and keeps the accounts of what has been advanced to every sacada.

This labour contract system maximizes the opportunities for deception and exploitation of the migrants. First of all, whereas they should be paid the minimum wage like permanent workers, the common practice is to pay them according to the work they do, by piecework. The rate is about ₱2 per ton of sugarcane cut, and ₱1.50 per ton loaded, which in theory gives them a daily income of ₱4. But because they cannot keep account either of the work they do or of the provisions they buy on credit (and thus are sometimes cheated), they have little money to show for their work at the end of the season. A survey

---

*One of the obstacles to making workers aware of their rights and what they should demand from their landowners is the traditional "debt of gratitude" that employees have for the employer when the latter has done something for them that, while possibly insufficient in the view of the law, in the view of the worker is something to be grateful for. (Cf. the discussion on "utang-na-loob" [the same concept] above, pp. 74-75.)

showed that 35 percent of them end up in debt, 35 percent with less than
₱100, and the rest with an income between ₱100 and ₱400.

Four particular frauds are widespread:

1. The underweighing of the sugarcane cut.

2. The overpricing of goods bought at the canteen (by as much as 100 percent) and of the rice and cooked food advanced to the worker.

3. The usurious "rates of interest" charged by the contractor for the money
"borrowed" by the sacadas (from their wages kept by the contractor).

4. The cut taken on every ton of sugarcane loaded by the contractor—with
the agreement of the landowner.

The sacada can find himself trapped in this system, no less than the Tamil
tea worker in Sri Lanka. For at the end of the season, the contractor persuades
the indebted sacada to sign a contract that commits him to go back to the
hacienda the following season. Failure to honour that commitment will be
reported to the police. A 1970 survey found that, of every five sacadas, two are
the second generation to be so employed; three out of five had been to the
estates at least once before.[57]

In general, then, these estate workers are among the lowest paid of those in
formal employment—a condition that is unlikely to change as long as they are
locked into that employment. It might be argued that much of what they lack
in income is made up in fringe benefits. For example, it is usual for the landowner to supply accommodation on the estate—a form of income supplementa-
tion that brings with it all the problems of tied cottages, especially in an industry in which employment is contracting.

For the quality of housing, much depends on the goodwill of the owner. In
Sri Lanka, 89 percent of the estate population lives in "labour lines" where
each family inhabits one- or two-room units in a long line of identical units.
The law sets a minimum of one room for two adults and two children, but five
or six persons per room is not uncommon. Many units do not have water or
latrines nearby, or the existing drains or latrines are blocked. The chairman of
one foreign company reckoned that at least one third of taps, latrines, and
drains are defective at any one time. The standard of buildings is visually
depressing and hygienically deplorable. On most estates, buildings are not
regularly maintained and few new ones are built, since companies that claim to
be making little profit are reluctant to spend money on housing.

In Malaysia, there is a racial distinction between those who live on estates
and those who live in surrounding villages. Malay and Chinese labour is largely
non-resident, whereas most Indians live on the estate. The former receive a
housing allowance of M$15 a month. Many cultivate food crops near their
homes. On the estates, where most of the Indians live, the problem of over-
crowding is endemic. But facilities compare favourably with the rest of the
rural population—88 percent of the workers' quarters had piped water and 57
percent electricity in 1968.[58]

On the sugar estates of Negros, there is a wide variety of housing; some is clearly below a minimum standard, some is good. The housing of the seasonal labourers is usually in "dormitories"—big one-room shacks where one or two hundred men, women, and children live with the minimum of privacy. The permanent workers are housed in permanent or semi-permanent quarters built of wood or concrete blocks. Unlike workers in the sugar factories (or "centrals"), they are not given any possibility of buying their own housing and thus attaining a modest independence from the haciendero.

The housing conditions, the state of hygiene, the low incomes, and the demanding work all affect the health of the population dependent on the estates. In Negros, life expectancy is 32 years of age; in the Philippines as a whole it is 50. But it is the children whose health is more directly affected. Infant mortality rates are high on estates. In 1972, on the Sri Lanka estates, the infant morality rate was 107 per 1,000 live births. In Negros, the church records of one parish show that 60 percent of deaths in 1972 were of children under three years of age.

These figures suggest that medical facilities, the responsibility of estate owners, are far from adequate. In Sri Lanka, there is a shortage of properly trained and qualified personnel in dispensaries and maternity facilities.* Even on estates with maternity facilities, 22 percent of births are not attended by trained personnel. Six weeks' maternity benefit is legally payable, but only if mothers have worked for 180 days in the previous nine months (that is, 20 days a month—a very high rate for a minimum). For serious illnesses requiring hospitalization, the workers need a note from the Superintendent to gain admission to a state hospital. But, since the estate must pay 50 cents a day for the hospitalization of a worker, estate managers are not easily persuaded to give the requisite notes.

In Malaysia, all workers are theoretically eligible for free medical treatment. In 1968, in fact, 88 percent of rubber estates had a visiting doctor available if necessary; 44 percent had a hospital nearby; and 76 percent were eligible for paid sick leave. How much these services were actually used, we do not know.

In Negros, most hacienderos do not provide medical facilities directly. They contribute to the social security system for each worker, deducting from his wage a proportionate contribution. Again there is a gap between theory and practice that the workers are powerless to close. Unscrupulous hacienderos can pass the full cost of the contribution back to the worker—or, worse, simply fail to register employees, who are thereby excluded from all benefits. Given the high rate of tuberculosis in Negros—and the consequent inability to undertake strenuous work—this can leave a worker wholly destitute.

---

*But there is no *national* shortage of medical manpower. Particularly at the higher levels, there is a surplus, which is relieved by considerable emigration.

We have already presented some evidence that hired labourers are less likely than farmers to send their children to school. Is the same true of estate workers? In Sri Lanka and in West Malaysia, the estate companies are responsible for providing schooling—a responsibility frequently ignored. (In fact, only 19 percent of the rubber plantations in West Malaysia had schools in 1968, which means that the majority of primary school-age children went to outside schools.) In Sri Lanka, schooling in Tamil is not available in the villages around some estates. One of the biggest tea estates in Sri Lanka, Brooke Bond Liebig, provides three years of schooling; the oldest children in its schools are 9 or 10 years of age. Three years of schooling does not offer children in estates a way out of the life they have been born to. They therefore drift into employment on the estate at the age of 12 or 14. This seems to be true in all three countries studied. In Sri Lanka, in 1969-70, only 9 percent of the estate children in the appropriate age groups received secondary education. Only two out of every thousand university students come from estates.

In Malaysia, racial differences appear clearly in attitudes to and achievements in education. The Indians feel that the teaching of tapping to their children is more important than school education, whereas the Chinese and Malays are more positive towards their children's education. At the national level, the primary school drop-out rate is twice as high for Tamils as for Malays.* Even when the plantation provides Tamil schools (and the number dropped by a third from 1956 to 1969), there is no post-primary Tamil education. Aspiring secondary school children must joint "remove classes" to prepare them for English-language secondary schools. These are not in the neighbourhood of the estates, which poses a severe practical problem for the family. As a result, Tamils who have succeeded in entering secondary schools invariably drop out at the third form level.

In Negros, the rate of illiteracy for the whole population is 17 percent. Most children drop out in their second or third grade of primary school, mainly because they are needed to work on the estates and because even "free" primary education imposes costs for books, clothes, and transport. Secondary education is quite out of reach: The annual fee at a government school is between ₱120 and ₱200, or 16 to 25 percent of the yearly income of a permanent worker on the estate. Unless the haciendero will help, even the brightest child will join his father in the cane fields.

A recurrent theme has been the gap between legislative provision and actual practice. It would be possible to represent the legislative provision as a

---

*The drop-out rates in the different mediums of instruction from the first year, in 1964, to the sixth primary year, in 1969, are: Tamil 34 percent, Chinese 18 percent, Malay 16 percent, English 5 percent.

con-mech, in the sense that it maintains the workers' confidence in the system while simultaneously enriching those in power. For that to be wholly convincing, it would be necessary to show that the mass of workers knew what their legal rights were and accepted their own particular inability to secure them. This is almost certainly not the case. The mass of Sacadas, for example, do not know their rights and are often incredulous when told them. Possibly only in Malaysia is the NUPW sufficiently well organized at the local level to have informed the bulk of employees of the legal provisions of employment. Perhaps significantly, there is less evidence there of the gap between theory and practice. Further, there is little evidence that workers do in fact regard labour legislation as legitimizing the plantation system. Some of the most trenchant criticisms of the estate sector in Sri Lanka have come from those who are fully aware of both actual conditions and legal obligations on employers to improve them. If the legislation is intended as a con-mech, then, there is no evidence that it succeeds.

If we ask why more is not done to enforce existing legislation and indeed improve it, this suggests three sets of reasons: (1) the alleged dependence of the country on the export crop; (2) the alleged unprofitability of many estates and therefore the inability of estate owners to pay higher wages; and (3) the nexus between estate owners and political leaders.

As Table 5.9 demonstrates, dependence on export crops—for foreign exchange, employment, and tax revenue—is most marked in Sri Lanka. Note that the table takes account of only the major crop for each country. In Sri Lanka, coconut and rubber; in Malaysia, oil palm; and in the Philippines, coconut would raise the degree of dependence even higher.

In the light of this, policy makers fear that an aggressive defence of the interests of the workers (who are in two cases despised social minorities, and in the third illiterates of no political account whatever) would reduce even further the rate of investment in these crops and thereby reduce the growth of output. As the price of tea, rubber, copra, and coconut oil was weak throughout the 1960s, it was thought imperative to maximize the rate of growth of output in order to increase export earnings—an objective of great political significance to the elites and those dependent upon them. Similarly, at a time when governments were beginning to be frightened by the full dimensions of the employment problem, they were unlikely to take steps that could (and, in Sri Lanka, allegedly did) reduce the number of jobs available in the rural areas.

The most common defence of the living standards of estate workers is that employers cannot afford to pay them more. This has been rigorously disproved in Negros, where the level of profits was not found to be associated with the level of wages.[59] Indeed it is hard to see why it should be, when *net* profits can range between ₱4,000 and ₱5,000 per hectare—and costs average about ₱3,000

TABLE 5.9

Sri Lanka, Malaysia, Philippines: Dependence on Estate Crops

Country	Crop	Percentage of Export Earnings	Percentage of Formal Employment
Sri Lanka	Tea	60 (1972)	14
Malaysia	Rubber	27 (1972)	8
Philippines	Sugar	20 (1970)	8

Sources: On exports—national accounts. On employment—Sri Lanka: *Statistical Abstracts of Ceylon, 1972* (Colombo: Department of Census and Statistics, 1973); Malaysia: *Statistical Handbook, 1972* (Kuala Lumpur: Department of Statistics, 1972); Philippines: *Labor Force, May 1969*, the BCS Survey of Households Bulletin, Series no. 27 (Manila: Bureau of the Census and Statistics).

per hectare. With such high margins, and a highly concentrated pattern of land ownership, the impact of a doubling of wage costs is unlikely to make investment in sugar significantly less attractive. But with low labour productivity (one thirtieth of that in Hawaii), such a change might well have led to more rapid mechanization.

Tea estates in Sri Lanka are a more subtle case. The price of tea has certainly fallen and costs have risen. Thus, Brooke Bond Liebig claims to make no profit from *growing* tea—a claim made less credible by a large item of "head office charges" in the published accounts. It—and the other large foreign-owned companies (but probably not the smaller ones)—certainly do make profits from insurance, shipping, packing, blending, and distributing the tea. Having a stake in growing may be a necessary precondition of profitability in these derivative activities. But that point is secondary to the profitability of the estates themselves. According to the only authoritative published study, profits per acre on high-grown tea fell from Rs959 in 1960 to Rs834 in 1967; they certainly have fallen further and faster since, as the price of tea collapsed at the turn of the decade and costs rose.[60] The national 14 percent rate of return in the middle 1960s can probably not be achieved now by even the best-managed estates.

But these figures are computed from *Colombo* auction prices, and to that extent they should be treated with some caution. For the Colombo market is not competitive, and there is some slight evidence that the Colombo auctions were, and perhaps still are, manipulated as a means by which profits could be transferred out of Sri Lanka. It is not without interest that Colombo prices have fallen more than London prices—over a period during which wholesale United Kingdom prices increased by 9 percent. The significance of this divergent trend lies in the fact that a small group of interlocked British companies are involved at each stage of processing—from production to wholesale distribution. This does not prove that the foreign tea companies could, if they had wished, have increased the level of wages without increasing losses in Sri Lanka. But it suggests that unprofitability may be more an excuse than a reason.

But the foreign-owned companies produce only half of Sri Lanka's tea. To what extent Sri Lankan-owned estates made excessive profits—or any profits—through the 1960s is a more difficult question, not open to easy generalization. In 1969, nearly a quarter of estates replying to a questionnaire from the Estate Employers Federation claimed they were not covering direct costs. Some were and still are badly managed and starved of new investment. Many have been slow to replant with more productive (but less labour-intensive) hybrids, partly because of fears of land reform (since realized). Certainly, many Sri Lankan estate owners would have resisted attempt to raise wages, and it is probable that such attempts as were made led to falls in employment. The truth is that in the 1960s much of Sri Lanka's tea, especially low-grown, was going through a slow and painful metamorphosis, from high profitability to questionable viability. Under these circumstances, the break-up of estates and redeployment of land to food crops is the most satisfactory solution. But as it is being carried out in Sri Lanka, this is merely compounding the problems of the most vulnerable group of all—the non-citizen Tamils.

In Malaysia, both price and cost of rubber declined between 1955 and 1969. The fall in cost is explained by greatly increased yields, the conversion of low-productivity rubber land to oil palms, and the indexing of wages to the price of rubber, thus ensuring that labour costs fell as the price fell.* Profit margins were somewhat reduced from 1956 to 1966 and fell sharply from 1966 to 1968. Thereafter they recovered, pausing somewhat in 1971/72 but accelerating in 1973/74. Between 1964 and 1973, a random selection of four of the larger foreign-owned mixed plantation companies earned, after tax, a minimum of 32 percent on capital employed. It thus would be hard to sustain the argument that it was impossible to pay higher wages from 1956. The most immediate impact almost certainly would have been a fall in employment as managers tried to cut costs by raising labour productivity.

---

*This is the most direct link between the price of an internationally traded commodity and the level of living of labourers. Needless to say, there is no reason why domestic prices should fall when export prices fall. Although consumer prices in Malaysia were remarkably stable throughout the 1960s, this index link seriously reduced the real incomes of estate labourers. The link had the effect of transferring a major element of commercial risk from shareholders to labourers—a strange inversion of the classical account that can best be explained by differential bargaining power.

In general, then, the evidence is that, except perhaps on low-grown tea in Sri Lanka, it is false to argue that low profits produced low wages. But it is at least probable that higher wages would have reduced employment. Better wages for some would have produced the starkest poverty for others. Only in Malaysia, where urban (and perhaps rural) employment was growing rapidly, would the long-run benefits have been likely to exceed the costs. But even there the likely racial incidence of unemployment on the estates would have made redeployment long, slow, and painful. The social costs of estate capitalism are high indeed.

A final reason for the failure to enforce existing legislation is the close bond between the political oligarchs and the estate owners. In Negros, President Marcos himself owns at least one of the large sugar estates. In Sri Lanka, senior politicians of both parties—United National Party (UNP) and Sri Lanka Freedom Party (SLFP)—own substantial areas of tea, coconut, and rubber, as the recent registration of holdings in excess of 50 acres has amply demonstrated. In Malaysia, prominent Malays and Chinese have been co-opted onto boards of directors of estate companies, whose annual reports contain a coda of sycophancy for the existing leadership. Manipulation is mutual. The Malaysian government uses the estate companies as stalking horses for additional foreign investment. Their mutually good relations are a splendid advertisement for international financiers tired of sparring with less accommodating regimes.

Under these circumstances, no government had any incentive to pay the social costs of estate capitalism—or to persuade the capitalists to do so themselves. To risk personal and political humiliation for a distant group of aliens and migrants was, and remains, a wholly unacceptable proposition.

NOTES

1. C. Elliott (ed.), J. Bessell, R.A.J. Roberts, and N. Vanzetti, "Universities of Nottingham and Zambia Agricultural Labour Productivity Investigation (UNZALPI)," report to the Government of Zambia, mimeo., no. 3 (1971).

2. Cf. G. Cochrane, *Development Anthropology* (New York: Oxford University Press, 1971); Denis Goulet *The Cruel Choice: A New Concept in the Theory of Development* (New York: Atheneum, 1971), pp. 216-22, and sources there cited, particularly his own "Development for What?" in *Comparative Political Studies* 1, no. 2 (July 1968).

3. J.Y. Martin, "Sociologie de l'enseignement en Afrique noire," *Cahiers internationaux de sociologie,* 1972.

4. C. Crisostomo, W.H. Meyers, T. Paris, Bart Duff, and Randolph Barker, "The New Rice Technology and Labor Absorption in Philippine Agriculture," *Malayan Economic Review* 16, no. 2 (October 1971).

5. *Mid-Term Review of the Second Malaysia Plan 1971-75* (Kuala Lumpur: Government Press, 1973), p. 134.

6. "An Evaluation Research of the Philippine Rural Reconstruction Movement's Barrio Development Program in Laguna: Baseline Study" (a socio-economic and socio-psychological study of development in fifty barrios in the Province of Laguna), a report from the Asian Social Institute, mimeo. (Manila, January 1973).

7. *Population and Agricultural Change in Ceylon* (Colombo: Marga Institute, 1974).

8. H.N.C. Fonseka, "Problems of Agriculture in the Gal-Oya," *Modern Ceylon Studies* (Peradeniya) 2, no. 1 (January 1971): 70.

9. Richard T. Jackson, "Land Use and Social Stratification: Two Case Studies of Densely Populated Areas of Eastern Africa," mimeo., East African Universities Social Science Council, Eighth Annual Conference Proceedings, 1972.

10. R. Tindiduuza, *Essays on Land Fragmentation in Kigezi,* Occasional Paper no. 22 (Department of Geography, University of Makerere, 1972); E.R. Kagambirwe, *Some Causes and Consequences of Land Shortage in Kigezi,* Occasional Paper no. 23 (Department of Geography, University of Makerere, 1972), both quoted in Jackson, op. cit.; see Jackson, op. cit., and A.R. Kururagire, "Land Fragmentation at Rugarama, Kigezi," *Uganda Journal* 33, no. 1 (1969): 59-64.

11. S. Selvadurai and S. Jegatheesan, "An Economic Survey of Pineapple Small-holdings in Pontian, Johore" (Kuala Lumpur: Ministry of Agriculture and Co-operatives, August 1968).

12. See "Economic Survey of Fishing Communities of the East Coast of West Malaysia," mimeo. (Kuala Lumpur: Fisheries Division of the Ministry of Agriculture, July 1971).

13. Societe d'etude et de developpement economique et social, *Enquete sur le niveau de vie a Yaounde* (Paris, 1965); Institut national de statistique et d'etude economique and Office de recherche scientifique et technique outre-mer, *Le niveau de vie des populations de l'Adamaoua* (Paris, 1966); Societe d'etude et de developpement economique et social, *Le niveau de vie des populations de la zone cacaoyere du Cameroun* (Paris, 1966).

14. "UNZALPI," op. cit.

15. ILO, *Employment, Incomes and Equality: A Strategy for Increasing Productive Employment in Kenya,* report of an inter-agency team financed by the United Nations Development Programme and organized by the International Labour Organization (Geneva: ILO, 1972).

16. "UNZALPI," op. cit.

17. M.P. Cowen with Fred Murage, "Notes on Agricultural Wage Labour in a Kenya Location," in "Developmental Trends in Kenya," mimeo., proceedings of a seminar held at the Centre of African Studies, University of Edinburgh,

1972; W.J. Barber, *The Economy of British Central Africa* (London: Oxford University Press, 1961), pp. 77ff. But contrast: A. Mafeje and A.I. Richards, "The Commercial Farmer and his Labour Supply," in *Subsistence to Commercial Farming in Present-day Buganda: An Economic and Anthropological Survey*, eds. A.I. Richards, Ford Sturrock, and Jean Fortt (Cambridge: Cambridge University Press, 1974); basing their figures on Department of Labour returns, they suggest that unskilled agricultural labour rates doubled in Buganda in 1952-59. But the official figures are likely to be heavily influenced by public sector experience and are not a reliable guide to wages actually paid by peasant employers.

18. "The Patterns of Income and Expenditure of Coffee Growers in Buganda, 1962/63" (Statistics Division, Ministry of Planning and Economic Development, January 1967).

19. Cowen with Murage, op. cit. Cf. M.P. Cowen, "Concentration of Sales and Assets: Dairy Cattle and Tea in Magutu," Working Paper no. 146, mimeo. (University of Nairobi, Institute for Development Studies, 1974).

20. David Hougham, "Changing Patterns of Agriculture in South Kyagwe," mimeo. (Faculty of Agriculture, University of Makerere, 1966).

21. See B.E. Rourke, *Wages and Incomes of Agricultural Workers in Ghana*, Technical Publication Series no. 13 (Legon: Institute of Statistical, Social and Economic Research, University of Ghana, 1971); Polly Hill, *Migrant Cocoa Farmers of Southern Ghana* (Cambridge: Cambridge University Press, 1963).

22. Hill, op. cit., p. 188.

23. The proportions are from A.S. Appiah, "The Organization of Labour in the Production of Cocoa Beans: A Survey of Tepa District" (Department of Agriculture and Economics and Farm Management, University of Ghana, May 1970), and B.E. Rourke and A.S. Appiah, "The Organization of Labour for the Production of Cocoa Beans in Ghana," CMB *Newsletter* no. 44 (April 1970), both quoted in Rourke, *Wages and Incomes*, op. cit. Cf. N.O. Addo, *Social and Demographic Characteristics of the Cocoa Farming Population in Brong-Ahafo Region*, vol. 1 of *Migration and Economic Change in Ghana* (Legon: University of Ghana, 1971), pp. 5-8. Only 1 percent of 885 farmers were born outside Ghana. Granting of land to Voltaiques is more common in Ivory Coast.

24. Hill, op. cit., p. 188.

25. Rourke, *Wages and Incomes*, op. cit., p. 34.

26. Appiah, op. cit.

27. For instance, Polly Hill reported earnings of "over £30" (N₵60) in southern Ghana in 1960. See Polly Hill, "Social Factors in Cocoa Farming," in *Agriculture and Land Use in Ghana*, ed. Brian Wills (London/Accra: Oxford University Press for the Ghana Ministry of Food and Agriculture, 1962), p. 283.

28. N.O. Addo, "Some Employment and Labour Conditions on Ghana's Cocoa Farms," paper presented to the Cocoa Economics Research Conference,

April 1973; "Employment and Labour Supply on Ghana's Cocoa Farms in the pre- and post-Aliens Compliance Order Era," *Economic Bulletin of Ghana* (2nd series) 2, no. 4 (1972).

29. B.E. Rourke and S.K. Sakyi-Gyinae, "Agricultural and Urban Wage Rates in Ghana," *Economic Bulletin of Ghana* (2nd series) 2, no. 1 (1972).

30. B.E. Rourke and F.A. Obeng, "Seasonality in the Employment of Casual Agricultural Labour in Ghana," mimeo. (Department of Agricultural Economics and Farm Management, University of Ghana, Research Report no. 1, 1973).

31. Addo, "Employment . . . pre- and post-Aliens Compliance Order Era," op. cit.

32. Konrad Engleman, *Building Co-operative Movements in Developing Countries* (New York: Praeger Publishers, 1968), pp. 36ff. Cf. J.S. Owers, "The Impact of Land Reform on Egyptian Agriculture: 1952-1965," *International Economic Review* 11, no. 1 (spring 1971): 59.

33. A. Mohieldine, "Agricultural Investment and Employment in Egypt Since 1935," doctoral dissertation, University of London, 1966.

34. M. Abdel-Fadil, *Employment and Income Distribution in Egypt, 1952-70*, Discussion Paper (Norwich: University of East Anglia, 1974).

35. ILO, *Rural Employment Problems in the UAR* (Geneva: ILO, 1969), p. 69.

36. D. Mead, *Growth and Structural Change in the Egyptian Economy* (Homewood, Ill.: Irwin, 1967).

37. Bent Hansen, "Employment and Wages in Rural Egypt," *American Economic Review* 59, no. 3 (June 1969).

38. International Rice Research Institute (IRRI), *Annual Research Review: Agricultural Economics*, Los Banos, 1973.

39. R. Barker and V. Cordova, "The Impact of New Technology on Rice Production—A Study of Change in Three Philippine Municipalities from 1966 to 1969," International Congress of Orientalists, Canberra, January 1971; Aida Librero and Mahar Mangahas, *UNRISD Report on the Green Revolution in the Philippines*, part 2, as quoted in Ingrid Palmer, *The New Rice in Monsoon Asia*, part II (Geneva: UNRISD, 1974) and S. Selvadurai, "Padi Farming in W. Malaysia" (Kuala Lumpur: Ministry of Agriculture and Co-operatives, 1972).

40. IRRI, *Annual Report*, Los Banos, 1970.

41. R. Barker, *Labour Absorption in Philippine Agriculture* (Los Banos, IRRI, 1972).

42. J. Couston, *Introduction and Effects of HYV Rice in the Philippines* (Rome: FAO, 1970), p. 91. Cf. R.A. Guino and W.H. Meyers, *The Effect of the New Rice Technology on Farm Employment and Mechanization* (Los Banos: IRRI, 1971); they argue that even small tractors are not economic on holdings of less than four hectares.

43. Barker, *Labour Absorption*, op. cit.

44. Palmer, op. cit., p. 252.

45. Randolph Barker, William H. Meyers, Cristina M. Crisostomo, and Bart Duff, "Employment and Technological Change in Philippine Agriculture," *International Labour Review* 106, nos. 2-3 (August/September 1972).

46. Librero and Mangahas as quoted in Palmer, op. cit.

47. Keith Griffin, *The Green Revolution: An Economic Analysis* (Geneva: UNRISD, 1972), p. 68, quoting from an IRRI survey of 42 farms in Laguna between 1966 and 1969.

48. Asian Social Institute, "An Evaluation Research," op. cit.

49. U.N. Bhati, "Social and Economic Implications of Large Scale Introduction of HYVs—A Village Case Study in West Malaysia" (Penang, 1973), p. 103.

50. S. Selvadurai, "Padi Farming," op. cit.

51. Palmer, op. cit., p. 368.

52. Ungku Aziz, "Poverty and Rural Development in Malaysia," *Kijian Ekonomi Malaysia* 1, no. 1 (1964).

53. *Preliminary Report on the Socio-Economic Survey of Ceylon, 1969-70* (Colombo: Department of Census and Statistics, 1971).

54. See *Sri Lanka Labour Gazette* 24, no. 1 (January 1973).

55. ILO, *Matching Employment Opportunities and Expectations: A Programme of Action for Ceylon,* vol. 2: *Technical Papers* (Geneva: ILO, 1971), p. 51.

56. See Lucas Parsons, "There Is Blood in Your Sugar," *Ronin Magazine,* February 1974.

57. F. Lynch, S.J., "Beyond the Minimum Wage: Sugarlandia in the 1970s," *Philippine Sociological Review* 18, nos. 3-4 (1970).

58. See Shirle Gordon, "The Conditions of Our Plantation Workers: The Mothers and Fathers of the Children," *Intisari* 3, no. 4 (1970).

59. Lynch, op. cit.

60. P. Richards and E. Stoutjesdijk, *Agriculture in Ceylon Until 1975* (Paris: Development Centre of Organization for Economic Cooperation and Development, 1970), p. 67.

6

THE PRIVILEGED:
URBAN PROPERTY
OWNERS

In this and the next two chapters, we describe the establishment and growth of three groups of privileged urban dwellers. In this chapter, we shall concentrate on the property-owning elite with a rather limited objective in mind. As we emphasized in Chapter 1, we are not concerned in this volume with the classical Marxist analysis of the appropriation of the labour surplus. In this chapter, therefore, we do not ask the kind of questions that a classical Marxist would be interested in: For instance, how is the value added in production divided between the wage earner and the owner of the means of production? Our objective is necessarily more limited. It is to enquire how big the urban property-owning group is; whence it derives its income; how it relates to government both in terms of influencing government policy and in terms of benefitting directly or indirectly from changes in that policy. We shall relate this discussion to various processes of impoverishment in Chapters 12 and 13.

In the next chapter, we shall examine in more detail a privileged group that, at least in the early stages of industrialization, has more influence on the direction of government policy and, through its control of the administrative framework of the country, has its own corporate power. In Chapter 8 we shall look at a group that is not usually considered elite but certainly is privileged: those in full-time employment in larger establishments in the formal sector. The interest of this group is not that its members necessarily have great political *power* but that, being much more numerous than either the property-owning or bureaucratic elites, they have very considerable political and social *influence*. We shall not discuss in these three chapters a number of elites that might be thought relevant to our theme—the political elite, the military elite, or the intellectual elite. This is not to deny the importance of these groups within the general framework of differentiation and social stratification. But we would argue that they are less immediately relevant to the central thrust of our argument for they are not groups that inevitably impoverish others by their own enrichment.*

Before turning to a more specific examination of this group, three important general points must be made. First, we are concerned here with property owners who reside in the urban areas rather than with those whose income derives exclusively from urban assets. As we shall show, for example, in the Philippines and Ghana it is not unusual for even middle- or low-income urban residents to own rural assets. Indeed, there is evidence of a considerable flow of rents and cropshares from the rural areas to the urban areas. To this extent it is important to bear in mind that the arrangement of themes in the chapters of this book can give a misleading impression that the urban and rural sectors are independent.

Second, it is no less relevant to the next chapter than to this that many urban property owners do not derive their whole or even their main income from the earnings of their assets. A very typical reaction of the relatively well-paid bureaucratic elite is to invest savings either in rural assets, principally land, or in housing, urban land, or service industries such as taxis, bars, or hotels. Here again, then, the ordering of our exposition can give a false impression of separation and independence. Many, perhaps most, of the bureaucratic elite derive at least some income from property. Conversely, it is almost certainly true that the great majority of property-income receivers have other sources of income.

Third, it follows that the great bulk of the urban property-income receivers are not particularly wealthy. Even in the Philippines, where property incomes probably account for a greater proportion of total income than in any other country with which we are concerned, the median income of entrepreneurs and rentiers is not significantly different from the median income of wage and salary earners. It is thus false to imagine that all who receive "unearned" income are very wealthy. That their relationship with those from they derive that income—tenants, workers, or consumers—is qualitatively different from their own relationships to their own employers is not in doubt. The basic conflict

---

*It could be argued that, by insisting upon large military expenditures, the military elite impoverishes the country as a whole, but in the countries we are concerned with, that is a credible argument only in Amin's Uganda and perhaps the Philippines and post-insurrection Sri Lanka. As the effect is generalized, it is less analytically important than the issues with which we are mainly concerned.

between the enrichment of some and the impoverishment of others is fundamental to all those who receive this kind of income. As such we shall return to
them in Chapters 11, 12, and 13. But, as we shall emphasize again, it is principally when the holding of assets is highly concentrated in the hands of a small
minority that we would expect to see the development of defensive political
power. This is much less typically the case in Africa, even in relatively "laissez-
faire" economies, than in Asia.

THE URBAN PROPERTY-OWNING ELITE IN AFRICA

In all the African countries with which we are concerned, most rural land on
individual freehold and urban property, apart from housing, was held by Europeans or Levantines until independence. The only exception to this was the
rather limited number of successful export producers who had invested capital
in land or in urban assets such as housing, retailing, and a rather limited range
of activities in the informal sector. In quantitative terms, both the number of
such investors and the total value of assets they controlled were almost negligible.

This pattern of asset ownership presented to independent governments a major economic and political problem. For the initial development strategy in
every African country we have studied was to expand the urban sector through
import substitution and imported capital. The unacceptable implication was
that the potentially large profits to be gained from this strategy would accrue
exclusively to foreign capital owners, with the result that political independence
would be associated with increasing economic dependence.

The reaction to this dilemma naturally varied from country to country according to ideological perspectives, the self-interest of the political elite, and
the pressure that could be brought upon it by metropolitan and other foreign
agencies. At one extreme is Ivory Coast where, after a short-lived period of
nationalist rhetoric, the incorporation of a small number of leading political
figures within the structure of urban foreign-owned capitalism ensured that no
serious challenge to the interests of this group emerged. Wealthier salary earners
have invested in a rather limited range of urban assets—housing, commercial
property, and service industries. Neither in modern industry nor in importing
and exporting is there much evidence of Ivorien participation.

If the Ivorien response has been one of neglect, another more widely
adopted solution has been to make property ownership a more open access
cone for some Africans. Kenya is a good example of this process. Adjustments
were made to regulations on licensing of road transport vehicles, the issue of
import licences, and the structure of retail and wholesale trade, to give African

entrepreneurs either a total monopoly or at least significant protection from competition from aliens. This was supplemented by at least periodic bursts of easy credit from the nationalized Kenya Commercial Bank and (largely unsuccessful) attempts to train neophyte entrepreneurs in some of the more basic rudiments of commercial literacy.[1]

For a number of reasons, such an approach could not be strikingly successful in the short run and perhaps even in the long. First, despite attempts to limit it, entry into many of the fields reserved for Kenyan Africans was easy. This brought intense intra-group competition, a high rate of failure, and the erosion of monopolistic profits. Second, there was predictably an area of inter-group conflict between the local subsidiaries of foreign manufacturers and indigenous emergent merchant capitalists. In the issue of import licences, for example, manufacturers wanted to maintain a monopoly of the entire domestic market and therefore were much opposed to the continuation of imports. The (African) importers saw this as a threat, if not to their very existence, at least to some of their more profitable lines of business.

Third, and perhaps most fundamental, a relatively small "bourgeois" trader or merchant does not easily or naturally grow into a large-scale industrial capitalist. Easy analogies between the early industrial revolution in Britain and the emergence of indigenous manufacturing capitalism in East Africa are wholly misleading. By creating virtual trading monopolies and eliminating competition, the Kenyan government has been fairly successful in creating a small group of African traders and merchants; but there is no sign of a significant penetration of manufacturing industry by Kenyan citizens. True, a number of Kenyans are shareholders in local subsidiaries of foreign companies; but their number is very limited and the capital subscribed a tiny proportion of total foreign-owned assets. It may well be the case that, particularly among the Kikuyu, one of the major beneficiary groups of development in Kenya, investment of savings in land is socially and financially more attractive than investment in industry.* In this sense, the access cone does not lead very far.

Obote in Uganda and Kaunda in Zambia have shown themselves in different degrees to be aware of the inconsistencies implied in this attempt to Africanize property ownership. Further, they have seen very clearly the more fundamental contradiction between such attempts and a political commitment to any variant of socialism. Neither satisfactorily solved this problem. In Uganda, Obote

---

*When the sellers are expatriates, they are unlikely to be able to repatriate the total proceeds immediately. Some of those funds may be invested in foreign-owned industrial companies operating in Kenya, or in Kenyan government bonds. In this way, the financial flows may go into industry, but the racial pattern of the ownership of industrial assets does not change.

and the Uganda People's Congress warned that independence did not mean "that the well-to-do, the educated and the feudal lords must and should be allowed to keep what they have, and get more if they can, without let or hindrance." The "Move to the Left," outlined in the Common Man's Charter, was declared to be "anti-feudalism and anti-capitalism."[2] But Obote's flirtation with a socialist pattern of ownership was brought to a sudden halt by his overthrow.

Amin's hasty and brutal expulsion of the Asians received much more widespread grass-roots support than Obote's over-cerebral discourses on socialism. The effect seems to have been to concentrate the ownership of more profitable and less sophisticated ex-Asian assets in a rather limited number of hands, mostly those of Amin's military henchmen and/or fellow Muslims. The distribution of the smaller businesses has been more widespread, but it is clear that many of the new owners have found it difficult to make them profitable. The result has been a deterioration in the standard of service, gradual running down of assets or, in a rather limited number of cases, their acquisition by the small coterie of more successful Ugandan entrepreneurs who have been able to make their assets productive and profitable. For all the talk of "economic revolution," the effect of Amin's policies has almost certainly been to concentrate the holding of (fewer) productive assets, albeit in African hands.

In Zambia, the so-called Mulungushi and Matero Reforms in 1968 and 1969 attempted to do by less harsh means what Amin was later to do through the expulsion of Asians. They sought to break the monopoly power of the Europeans' middle-sized businesses, particularly in construction, transport, quarrying, distribution, and vehicle repair. The important difference is that, in Zambia, these businesses were taken over by the state and absorbed by the parastatal Industrial Development Corporation. Apart from shops, no businesses were transferred to individual ownership. But this does not mean that private entrepreneurs were excluded from the benefits of the reforms. Both government departments and the large copper companies were encouraged to make business available to small Zambian concerns, and the banks were obliged to lend to Zambian rather than European or foreign-owned businesses.

This encouragement of petty capitalism did not sit easily with Kaunda's nascent ideology of "humanism." But this should not be seen as an ideological compromise with capitalism, nor as a political compromise with the small group of Zambian businessmen who expected major pickings from an assault on the foreign domination of the economy. A more persuasive explanation is that it was a sensible recognition of the severe limitations on the ability of the state to absorb (and run properly) more than a very few of the larger firms. Thus on transport, the President had this to say:

The other two big road operators in the country are Smith and Youngson Ltd., and Central African Road Services Ltd. I am asking Central African Road Services Ltd. to offer the Government at least 51 per cent of their shares and I am asking Smith and Youngson Ltd. to do the same. It is my intention that when Government has taken over Central African Road Services Ltd., its activities will be confined entirely to passenger transport. In the past the Company has *failed to live up to the responsibility of its monopoly position to serve all sections of the community. By engaging in both passenger and freight transport it is running neither properly.* . . .

This is the way I want to rationalize the road transport system of the country. At the same time I want to see, as I said earlier, a great number of Zambian businessmen operating buses, taxis, lorries for distribution to the rural areas and so on. So from now on the transport pattern in the country will be three big State controlled organisations assisted by a large number of Zambian operators.[3] [Emphasis added.]

That a large monopoly was being replaced by a number of small monopolies is evidence perhaps of both a non-doctrinaire pragmatism and a failure to think through the likely long-term result.

For, as in Kenya, the major effect was to establish and protect a rather small group of petty capitalists, mostly in the service sectors and construction. At the lower end of this group, there is a high degree of competition, of enterprise mortality, and probably of low margins. At the upper end, the businesses are still dependent upon protection from competition from Asian- or European-managed operations by receipt of preferential access to credit and by discrimination in acquiring government or parastatal business. Despite these privileges, these businesses have not yet produced a significant group of wealthy, capital-owning Zambians who have effectively penetrated the processes of political and administrative decision making. This is emphatically not to argue that the small number of such Zambians have no influence in either of those arenas; but it is to suggest that they have less of both influence and power than the administrators of the parastatal organizations.

The policies in these three countries can be interpreted as con-mechs. They offered access to the ownership of sizeable business assets to a much wider group than could in fact achieve that ownership. A series of filters—"normal" banking practice of demanding collateral for loans, political influence, and experience in the relevant trade are three logically distinct categories—ensured that progress through the cone was highly selective; indeed, few were successful. But the access policies satisfied a real political demand and gave each government a greater legitimization with respect to its dealings with foreign interests entrenched in the economy. To most would-be entrepreneurs, the measures taken may not have been ideal—there was, for instance, much disaffection in Kenya over the issue of import licences and the selection of licencees—but at least they opened a way forward that had hitherto been effectively barred. In that attenuated sense, they commanded confidence from the proto-entrepreneurs, even though many of them have subsequently discovered from themselves the ferocity of inter-group competition at the "lower" end of the cone.

To the ruling groups, the benefits were substantial. There were first of all major political benefits, perhaps best exemplified by the euphoria the Mulungushi and Matero Reforms created (albeit rather briefly) for Kaunda and his philosophy of "humanism." In Uganda, the Common Man's Charter was Obote's desperate attempt to preserve a coalition of interest that would transcend tribal in-fighting and deny a large slice of ideological ground to his political critics, who were becoming increasingly critical, if in a very muffled way, of the regime's growing identification with property owners.

Second, the reforms in fact opened up a number of business opportunities that could be dispensed as political patronage or used directly for personal gain. This latter was not necessarily corrupt. Although there were examples of corruption at or near cabinet level in all three countries as politicians sought, sometimes with more naivete than malice, to exploit the opportunities presented to them, it is not a major part of our argument that these steps were taken in order that politicians and senior bureaucrats might benefit corruptly. But there can be little doubt that, in each country, the major beneficiaries of the easier access were those who already had considerable political and/or financial leverage. The rash of resignations from government posts, after the economic reforms in Zambia, was not accidental. The shuffling both of party hacks and of bright young bureaucrats into the parastatals in both Uganda and Zambia combined patronage with the opportunity for greater reward and the acquisition of relevant commercial experience.* In each capital, the boom in property values, fuelled by easier credit for a limited income group of nationals, brought major increases in both wealth and income to those who could take advantage of it.

In short, the creation of the bourgeoisie, with a light frosting of more substantial capitalists on top, is one of the classic examples of the con-mech. In all three countries it has been challenged—in very different modes. In no country has it been swept entirely away.†

---

*But see p. 169 below for the political leadership's later disillusionment with this group of beneficiaries.

†Indeed, it could be argued that Amin's "Economic War" was no more than this particular con-mech writ large by an illiterate hand.

The approach in these three countries lies in sharp contrast to that in Ghana under Nkrumah and in Tanzania. For there, the object of government policy has been to erect effective competition to national or non-national private capitalists by the creation of efficient publicly owned enterprises. Although Nkrumah's opposition to the development of a local capitalism was much less thoroughgoing in action, if not in rhetoric, than that of Nyerere,* in both countries the emphasis has been on capturing the maximum surplus for public distribution rather than in creating conditions under which the surplus can be appropriated by private individuals. (The generation of a surplus to capture is a necessary precondition that Nkrumah failed to achieve. On the only very questionable figures available, "income from property and enterprise" was negative in 1961 and 1962 and in 1965 was less than 12 percent of the value of all wages.[4])

We are not concerned here with an assessment of those policies or with the wide-ranging implications they have for efficient resource allocation. Our concern is rather to emphasize that in these countries the emergence and indeed survival of an indigenous group of capitalists has occurred despite official policy rather than because of it. In Ghana, the rapid political and economic mobilization of Ghanaian commercial, and to a much less extent industrial, capitalists after the resumption of civilian rule is eloquent testimony not only to their survival but to their entrenchment (and perhaps even their ability to profit from the inefficiencies of the state industries under Nkrumah).

In Tanzania, where the assault has been more consistent,† there is some evidence that the administrative influence of the tiny group of Tanzanian traders and merchants is not completely broken. For instance, the *Economic Survey 1971-72,* explaining low capacity utilization in manufacturing, criticized "an irrational import policy by which directly competing imports, usually low-priced, have pre-empted the market for such products as food, clothing, and light engineering goods."[5] This is good prima facie evidence of the ability of importing and distributing interests (dominated but not exclusively controlled by parastatals) to extort lucrative concessions.[6] But this should not be allowed seriously to qualify the fact that in Tanzania those deriving incomes from rents or profits are, in national accounting terms, wholly insignificant. According to the Household Budget Survey of 1972, only 5 percent of urban non-farm

---

*For example, Nkrumah pursued a "laissez-faire" policy towards the logging industry—a policy subsequently reversed by the military government, whose attempts to maximize local value added were maintained by the Busia government despite intense political pressure from the timber barons.

†Witness the prohibition of the ownership of second houses by politicians and public servants, a measure that Nkrumah was unable to implement.

households received rents, interest, and dividends. Twenty-five percent of the same group earned their living by trade, but as the average income of these traders was less than half the average level of wages and salaries, it is reasonable to assume that all but a tiny handful of these are very small-scale retailers or hawkers.

In Africa, then, the history of industrialization and urban development is still too short to have produced the kind of differentiation we shall find in Asia. But this should not be taken to mean that indigenous property owners are irrelevant. Small in number, modest in assets as they may be by comparison with the subsidiaries of multinational corporations, they have consistently shown their ability to extort from even the most ideologically unsympathetic government concessions, protection, and subsidies. But this has to be seen in the context of the post-independence emphasis on national participation: better a black capitalist than a white one. With the exception of Julius Nyerere, African leaders are only slowly feeling their way beyond that.

The vital question, and one that cannot yet be answered, is whether, when they are ready to act against the monopolies they have created, they will still have sufficient political elbow room to do so. The circumstances of Nkrumah's downfall and the support that the military quickly secured from Ghanaian urban capital owners are not promising omens.

THE URBAN PROPERTY-OWNING ELITE IN ASIA

In Asia, the process of the formation of an indigenous capital-owning group, or even class, is much further advanced. We have already seen how in Sri Lanka the Karavas emerged on the back of the coffee boom as the principal merchant capitalist group in Sri Lanka. Although the bulk of their interests remained in trade rather than manufacture, they nonetheless spearheaded what little industrial expansion took place in Sri Lanka in the 1950s. If the Karavas dominated both merchanting and industry largely because of their greater adaptation to British education and styles, the other major property-owning group in the urban areas, the Hindu Tamils, had neither of these advantages. While generalization on the scanty evidence is dangerous, it is almost certainly true that the Tamils are much more significant than the Karavas in small-scale industry and commerce. While few of them became very wealthy, they owned a large proportion of second-rate urban property and probably controlled the greatest *number* of urban businesses.

We do not have data by ethnic group or income class; indeed, data on property incomes are slight. According to the 1969-70 Socio-Economic Survey, 26 percent of urban incomes came from profits and less than 4 percent from rents. Half of these profits are earned in wholesale and retail trade, and only 11 percent in manufacturing. Nearly half accordingly accrue to "sales workers," less than 10 percent to administrative and managerial workers, and less than 5 percent to professional and technical workers. There is little evidence of a large group living entirely on profits and rents—i.e., having no stated occupation. Less than Rs4 million (3 percent of income accounted) goes to an "unspecified" category of income recipients, which presumably includes pure rentiers. Analysed by income group (throughout the island), barely a quarter of profits accrue to those above the threshold level at which income tax becomes payable. But it is the case that the richest 0.2 percent of households draw on average Rs500 per month from profits—or more than the total income of 85 percent of the population. Given that the figures are probably not very reliable in this respect (since profits may well be understated, especially by the richer groups), it would be foolish to draw bold conclusions. But the published data show little evidence of a large group of rich recipients of unearned income.

The political significance of the propertied groups can easily be overestimated. None are sufficiently large or sufficiently concentrated in their patterns of residence to be able to win a substantial number of constituencies on a basically ethnic appeal. Further, M. Singer has shown that the number of members of Parliament deriving the major part of their income from business was not large in the 1950s. Although it may well have increased in the 1960s, the bulk of these members have come from small-scale businesses rather than from the great trading houses. But it does not follow that these urban property owners had no influence; indeed, Singer suggests that some politicians, particularly lawyers, were directly financed by business interests.[7] It is clear that at least some present politicians, of both the United National Party and the Sri Lanka Freedom Party, are ready to represent the interests not only of Sri Lankan property owners but of local subsidiaries of multinational corporations.* It is not insignificant that Mrs. Bandaranaike, like her husband before her, has been able to make rather minor structural changes in the pattern of ownership of assets in the urban sector despite much socialist and, lately, Marxist rhetoric.

In Malaysia, the quantitative significance of urban property is much greater. Almost one half of total personal income is derived from the ownership of assets: "Inequality in the ownership of assets particularly in urban-based activities is far more pronounced than other forms of inequality."[8] Table 6.1 shows that the Chinese dominate the non-corporate industrial sector as well as the

---

*A good example of this was a debate in December 1973 on the plans to establish a national pharmaceutical company to distribute drugs and monitor prices. The vigour with which the plan was assailed is most convincingly explained by the direct representation of the interests involved.

TABLE 6.1

West Malaysia: Ownership of Assets in Modern Agriculture and Industry, 1970

| | Modern Agriculture (planted acreage)[a] | | | | Industry (fixed assets)[b] | | | |
| | Corporate Sector | | Non-Corporate Sector | | Corporate Sector | | Non-Corporate Sector | |
	Thousands of Acres	Percent	Thousands of Acres	Percent	$Million	Percent	$Million	Percent
Malaysians	515.0	29.2	697.6	94.1	559.7	42.8	167.2	97.6
Malays	(5.0)	(0.3)	(349.3)	(47.1)	(11.2)	(0.9)	(3.9)	(2.3)
Chinese	(457.0)	(25.9)	(243.3)	(32.8)	(342.3)	(26.2)	(158.0)	(92.2)
Indians	(4.9)	(0.3)	(74.8)	(10.1)	(1.5)	(0.1)	(3.9)	(2.3)
Others	(48.1)	(2.7)	(13.2)	(1.8)	(187.2)	(14.3)	(1.4)	(0.8)
Government[c]	—	—	(17.0)	(2.3)	(17.5)	(1.3)	—	—
Non-Malaysians	1,249.6	70.8	44.0	5.9	747.3	57.2	4.1	2.4
Total	1,764.6	100.0	741.6	100.0	1,307.0	100.0	171.3	100.0
Percent of total	70.4		29.6		87.4		12.6	

[a]Modern agriculture covers estate acreage under rubber, oil palm, coconut, and tea. FLDA is included in this category under the non-corporate sector. Ownership is in terms of total planted acreage.

[b]The industry sector covers manufacturing, construction, and mining. Ownership is in terms of fixed assets. Total excludes unallocatable assets amounting to $25.2 million.

[c]Government ownership of 17,000 acres in modern agriculture is included in the non-corporate sector; government ownership of $17.5 million of fixed assets in industry is included in the corporate sector.

Source: Mid-Term Review of the Second Malysia Plan 1971-1975 (Kuala Lumpur: Government Press, 1973), p. 12.

indigenously owned corporate sector. In terms of all indigenously owned industrial assets, the Chinese own nearly two thirds. If commercial assets were included, Chinese dominance would probably be further increased. Unfortunately,
we do not have the pattern of ownership of assets owned by size group, so we
do not know with any degree of certainty how far the assets of any one racial
group are concentrated. But a very rough guide to the concentration of total
wealth is furnished by returns for estate duty. In 1969 this showed that 14 percent of the estates declared for duty accounted for 50 percent of the net value.
If we include duty-exempt estates, the figure is even more striking: 6 percent of
wealth owners owned 40 percent of the net value of estates. Given the incentives of the very rich to avoid estate duty by prior disposal of their assets, it is
likely that this understates the true concentration. It is well within the bounds
of possibility that 5 percent of wealth owners own half the assets. (The Gini
coefficient was 0.58 for 1969; there is no evidence of significant changes in
concentration during 1964-69.)

We have here, then, a very unequal distribution of productive assets for all
racial groups. Since Chinese dominance of the urban sector is so marked, we
are probably safe in assuming that the concentration of assets of urban Chinese
is not much less than the national pattern. But the modalities by which that
concentration of wealth finds political expression are, given the nature of political power sharing in Malaysia, more subtle than in other countries. For example, a recent survey of larger businesses in Malaysia found that by comparison
with other businesses, Chinese-owned firms were less well-informed about government policy, less acquainted with politicians and civil servants (particularly
at the federal level), and less ready to use (or, perhaps, to admit to using) their
influence to affect government policy.[9] But the various Chinese associations,
and particularly the Chinese chambers of commerce, financed almost exclusively by wealthy Chinese businessmen, have continuously played a major part
in critical dialogue with government, largely, if obliquely, through the Malay-
Chinese Association; and it may well be that Frederick R. von Mehden's findings reflect preference to work through these formal and less formal associations rather than directly from a business base.

It would certainly be quite mistaken to interpret the Malaysian constitution
as the ossification of a division of spoils whereby Chinese are left in undisputed
control of the wealth of the country while Malays have the lion's share of direct
political power.[10] Indeed, it is not over-cynical to argue that the trauma of the
race riots in 1969 and the subsequent formulation of the New Economic Policy
(NEP), by which Malays are to be increasingly incorporated in the modern sector, was itself the result of the ability of the Chinese (and other non-Malay business interests) to convince the Malay political leaders of the wisdom of allowing
that division of spoils to remain unchallenged.

It is significant that the kernel of the NEP is not to redistribute assets in favour of Malays but to enable Malays to accumulate new assets. This is to be
achieved over time by discriminating in favour of Malays in, for instance, the
distribution of credit, commercial training, and government contracts. (Preferential treatment for Malays long predates the launching of the NEP. In transport licensing it has operated since 1960, but its effect on heavy haulage—as opposed to taxis—has been negligible, since Malays find it difficult to show that
they are adequately financed and, more particularly, that they have enough
business connections to ensure a proper volume of commissions.[11])

Whether preferential treatment will suffice to contain Malay aspirations or
to allay their resentment at Chinese domination of the economy is an open
question. What is likely to result is the creation of a rather small Malay bourgeoisie, dependent upon a pattern of discrimination for protection from Chinese competition. In other words, the distribution of assets owned by Malays is
likely to become more unequal as a result of the NEP, although the pattern of
inequality between races may be slowly modified.

Is the NEP a con-mech comparable to that we saw operating in Eastern Africa? That is a difficult question to answer, especially in the light of widespread
ignorance of the provisions of the NEP among Malays. It may well be that, as a
package of policies, it has not performed a confidence-winning, legitimacy-
bestowing function simply because it has not been adequately explained and
communicated as a coherent policy. The other difficulty is that it is hard to
argue that it has brought direct or indirect economic benefits to the ruling
groups of Malays. For the most part, they are already so well integrated into
the existing economic structure, both personally and corporately, that it would
be hard to sustain the argument that the economic benefits are significant to
them. The only major benefit is likely to be that of political patronage; of the
operation of that within the context of the NEP we have too little evidence to
reach even a tentative conclusion.

For the Philippines, we have rather fuller data on property incomes from the
Bureau of the Census and Statistics (BCS) in its Family Income and Expenditure Surveys of 1961, 1965, and 1971. By examining the sources and levels of
family income, we can see how large the urban property-owning elite is and
how it has changed in terms of size, structure, and income levels through the
1960s. Table 6.2 shows that in the urban areas the proportion of all urban families receiving entrepreneurial and rentier incomes has changed little—an increase of rather less than 2.5 percent between 1961 and 1971, vitually all of it
accounted for by an increase in those receiving entrepreneurial rather than
rentier income. But as we might expect, the great majority of these incomes
are low.

The entrepreneurial incomes, for instance, accrue to small traders and transport contractors, many of whom might reasonably be considered in the

TABLE 6.2

Philippines: Percentage of Urban Families with Income from Specified Sources, 1961, 1965, and 1971

	1961	1965	1971
Entrepreneurial incomes	31.7	32.7	34.0
from:			
Trading	(19.8)	(20.2)	(22.2)
Manufacturing	(8.6)	(9.4)	(9.4)
Transport	(3.3)	(3.1)	(2.4)
Rentier incomes	20.3	21.0	20.2
from:			
Crop-share	(11.1)	(7.8)	(5.8)
Rent	(7.2)	(8.1)	(8.5)
Interest and dividend	(2.0)	(5.1)	(5.9)
Total	52.0	53.7	54.2

Source: Family Income and Expenditures 1971, the BCS Survey of Households Bulletin (Manila: Bureau of the Census and Statistics, 1973).

informal sector. Although the median incomes of these entrepreneurs show quite vigorous rises through the 1960s, even in 1961 the median family income of all traders, for instance, was only P-3,100—not much above the median family income of P2,450 for the whole population. The median income of manufacturing entrepreneurs was even significantly *below* the median income for the whole population.

Perhaps surprisingly, the same is true of sharecrop landlords. The median income of this group was only P1,600—evidence that many of these landlords are, in fact, rather small landholders. The only certain exceptions to this pattern of modest unearned incomes are the "pure" rentiers, receiving rent for lands, commercial buildings, or residential properties. The haciendas of Negros, for example, would be included in this group. For them, the median income in 1971 was P6,200—a level of income enjoyed by only the top 15 percent of income recipients in the Philippines. (It is likely, but not certain, that the 2,000 families deriving most of their income from dividends would also have a high average income, but the numbers involved are so small that the BCS does not publish the distribution.)

But examination of median incomes is less revealing than an analysis of the high-income recipients of unearned incomes. If the data can be trusted—we have not been able to ascertain how far coverage and disclosure improved over the decade—most interesting is the fact that the number of families receiving both entrepreneurial and rentier incomes in excess of ₱10,000 a year more than tripled between 1965 and 1971. The number of these wealthy income receivers by source is given in Table 6.3. This shows that there was no major difference with respect to rentiers; the major increase is in the trading and manufacturing groups, where the later 1960s saw the emergence of a significant number of high-income receivers. This, together with the rather low median incomes in 1971, implies a very rapid and marked differentiation of these groups in the later 1960s, possibly associated with divestment by some major U.S. companies, fearful that their privileges would be curtailed in 1974, when the Laurel-Langley Agreement came to an end. The bulk of the entrepreneurial and rentier incomes were still received by middle- or low-income groups. But by the end of the decade there had emerged a group of between a third and a half of a million people in the urban areas receiving very high incomes from these sources.

How far these new wealthy entrepreneurs and rentiers reinforced the existing distribution of political power in the urban areas or in the country as a whole is difficult to say. Certainly there is no doubt that before martial law these interests were well entrenched in the legislature and hardly less so in the executive. Whether martial law itself has weakened that power, or indeed was ever intended to, is an open question. So far, the evidence on a wide range of issues from tax reform to wage legislation is that the President is reluctant to countenance the fundamental changes that are required to put substance into the rhetoric of the "New Society." Further, his tendency to pander to the Filipino commercial elite has shown itself no less under martial law than during the politically tense period of the Constitutional Convention. By a range of decisions, from repeated attempts to attract foreign (and particularly American) investment to a decree giving remarkable tax advantages to multinational

TABLE 6.3

**Philippines: Number of Families with Total Income Exceeding ₱10,000
a Year Deriving Income from Specified Sources, 1965 and 1971**

Source	1965	1971
Trade	12,046	37,240
Manufacture	1,728	13,930
Transport	1,711	6,889
Crop-share	3,502	6,206
Rent	1,768	1,717
Total	20,755	65,982

Source: Family Income and Expenditure 1971, the BCS Survey of Households Bulletin (Manila: Bureau of Census and Statistics, 1973).

corporations making Manila their headquarters, Marcos has shown both his dependence upon the U.S./Filipino business concerns and his eagerness to win from it both political and financial support.

The more interesting question is why Marcos had to resort to so unrefined a weapon as martial law, with all the risks attendant upon a military/police regime. To answer that question in full takes us beyond the scope of this book, but it is relevant to point out that the same kind of con-mech as we have already observed in Eastern Africa and Malaysia failed in the Philippines. Put shortly, there were throughout the 1960s a number of attempts to challenge the American domination of the urban economy. The Retail Trade Nationalization Act, originally passed in 1954 but due to take effect in 1964, was aimed primarily at the Chinese domination of trade, as was a similar law passed in 1960 with respect to rice trading and milling. Specifically anti-American legislation included measures by which certain sectors were either declared closed to foreign enterprises (e.g., financial services) or were closed for limited periods to allow national enterprises to become established (e.g., under the Investment Incentives Act of 1967).

Why did those measures not contain the forces of economic nationalism? There are many answers, at different levels of analysis. First, the conflict within the basic development strategy, adopted by the Macapagal administration and largely followed by Marcos, of attracting foreign (especially American) investment *and* encouraging Filipinization was too fundamental to allow an acceptable political compromise. For to achieve the former, the conditions of the latter, especially for the smaller companies, and incipient enterprises, were too rigorous. For example, a strict audit policy fell much harder on smaller local farms than on foreign farms. Tax treatment was much less severe for the latter than for the former. . The devaluation of the peso—in 1962, 1970, and 1972—allowed foreign firms to buy Filipino assets relatively cheaply, while making foreign inputs expensive for local firms.

Second, it is arguable that the Marcos regime was too dependent upon American financial and political support to refurbish the Filipinization programme in a way that might carry conviction.* With the slow-down of foreign investment in the later 1960s and the gathering pace of divestment by some of the most prestigious multinationals (including Exxon, Gulf Oil, and Chrysler), the whole strategy of economic growth was threatened—a threat made worse by the highest rate of inflation in Asia, widespread unrest and violence, and the

---

*There also was a legal problem in the "parity" clause of the Laurel-Langley Agreement. But the significance of this should not be exaggerated, given the fact that it had already been heavily qualified—and was due to end in 1974 anyway.

termination of the Laurel-Langley Agreement in 1974. Under these conditions, Marcos and his advisers may have felt that more emphasis on Filipinization could only make matters worse. It is significant that, since martial law, the word is hardly heard in official circles.

Third, the political force behind economic nationalism was too strong to be contained by the rather crude con-mech we have described elsewhere. Given real credibility by two major Supreme Court decisions in 1972—the Quasha and and Luzon Stevedoring cases*—and an effective organ of communication in the Constitutional Convention, the nationalists were able to discredit any confidence or legitimizing role the Filipinization measures may have had.

SUMMARY

We have tried to show that in both Africa and Asia much income from property accrues to middle- and lower-income groups. Both rural and urban assets are held by wage and lower salary earners who see the ownership of such assets as an attractive immediate investment, a possible alternative occupation, and perhaps increasingly as security in old age. But the fact that these assets are held by middle- and low-income groups does not imply that the users of those assets have or are able to mobilize reciprocal bargaining strength. We have already seen this with respect to landlord and tenant relationships in Asia and farmer/abusaman/labourer relationships in the cocoa belt in Ghana (see above, pp. 52-53, 65-69). In Chapter 11, we shall see the same phenomenon in relation to the informal sector in the towns. Indeed, it is arguable that the smaller capital owners—the owners of low-income houses, of small businesses, of small parcels of land—are more highly motivated and less inhibited to extort the maximum leverage from this basic non-reciprocity.

But the political and social influence of these petty capitalists is much less significant. In this respect, the Asian countries we have examined reveal to a much greater degree than the African the power and influence wielded by the urban owners of wealth. We shall return to a more detailed examination of the ways that influence and that power impoverish the poor in Chapters 10 to 13:

---

*By the former, the Court ruled that U.S. citizens and firms had no legal right to acquire land after Philippine independence in 1946 and that, when the Laurel-Langley Agreement ended in 1974, rights by which U.S. citizens had the same legal standing in the Philippines as Filipino citizens would be ended. By the second, the Court decided that firms operating in "closed" sectors could not have non-nationals as directors or management personnel.

for the moment, the important point to emphasize is that even in Sri Lanka two relatively radical governments have managed to make rather slight inroads on the accumulated wealth and power of this group despite a remarkably favourable conjunction of circumstances.* A ceiling on incomes, modest land reform, stricter control of consumer imports, very limited state intervention in manufacturing and commerce do not amount to the fundamental attack on one of the root causes of inequality and impoverishment in Sri Lanka. In Malaysia, a trauma similar to the insurrection in Sri Lanka has produced a very different reaction—a reaction that we have seen is common in some African countries. This involves the incorporation of some of the excluded into the property-owning privileged groups through a con-mech. We shall see in Chapter 11 that the most likely result of this policy is to distort income distribution further, increase the scope of non-reciprocal relationships, and reinforce the kinds of impoverishing pressure that we shall analyse particularly in Chapters 12 and 13.

But in both Africa and Asia (except perhaps in the Philippines) it is highly arguable that the property-owning elite is so small, inchoate, and dominated by foreign owners of domestic assets that its real significance is easily overstated. Of much greater significance in terms of their ability to affect government policy and urban styles of life are the bureaucratic elites. With the exception of the Philippines and possibly Malaysia, the civil service and the administrative and managerial groups in public and privately owned industry are not only much more numerous but also much more significant in determining political, economic, and social priorities. It is to this group, therefore, that we turn in the next chapter.

NOTES

1. For a detailed treatment of this, see Colin Leys, "The Limits of African Capitalism: Formation of the Monopolistic Petite Bourgeoisie in Kenya, " in "Developmental Trends in Kenya," mimeo., proceedings of a seminar held in the Centre of African Studies, University of Edinburgh, April 1972.

2. *The Common Man's Charter* (Entebbe: Government Printer, 1970), pp. 3-4.

---

*The 1971 insurrection, for instance, could have given Mrs. Bandaranaike carte blanche to institute far-reaching reforms. The only obvious fall-out has been the land reform measure of 1972 with, as we have already seen, rather generous ceilings.

3. K.D. Kaunda, "Zambia towards Economic Independence," in *After Mulungushi: The Economics of Zambian Humanism*, ed. B. de G. Fortman (Nairobi: East African Publishing House, 1969), p. 62.

4. T. Merritt Brown, "Macro-Economic Data on Ghana (Pt. II)," *Economic Bulletin of Ghana* (2nd Series) 2, no. 2 (1972).

5. *Economic Survey 1971-72* (Dar es Salaam: Government Printer), p. 94.

6. Cf. Leys, op. cit., p. 15.

7. M. Singer, *The Emerging Elite: A Study of Political Leadership in Ceylon* (Cambridge, Mass.: MIT Press, 1964), p. 88.

8. *Mid-Term Review of the Second Malaysia Plan 1971-75* (Kuala Lumpur: Government Press, 1973), p. 10.

9. Frederick R. von Mehden, "Public and Private Sector Relationships as Perceived by Companies and Associations in West Malaysia," mimeo. (Rice University Program for Development Studies, 1973).

10. See Gordon P. Means, *Malaysian Politics* (London: University of London Press, 1970), pp. 104-6; R.S. Milne, *Government and Politics in Malaysia* (Boston: Houghton Mifflin, 1967), pp. 87-113, and see particularly the influence of early Chinese business groups in ensuring the maintenance of the privileges of the old Straits Settlements.

11. See G. Naidu, "Rail and Road Transport in West Malaysia," B.Litt. thesis, Oxford University, 1972, pp. 53-64.

The growth of the bureaucracy in both the public and private sectors is one of the most widespread social changes that has accompanied the achievement of political independence and economic development. As structures of government and industry become increasingly complex, so the need for managers, administrators, and high-level technical personnel increases. But this is not a "neutral" change without fundamental repercussions on the processes of enrichment and impoverishment. We shall argue that its rapid growth and its ability to protect most of its inherited privileges gives the bureaucracy a central place in those processes. For it is at once the symbol and substance of privilege. But it is not the *only* such symbol: In the next chapter we shall examine white- and blue-collar workers in the formal sector to see how far those groups, sometimes called a "labour aristocracy," can be meaningfully said to be either symbolically or substantially implicated in the impoverishment of the poor.

Let is be said immediately that this threefold categorization of employees is crude and that a much finer distinction would be analytically desirable. The categories do, however, roughly correspond to consumption levels and even more roughly to education levels (at least after the worst manpower shortages are over; see below, pp. 177-79). Although the distinctions are neither watertight nor invariant, reward is clearly allied to function, in this hierarchical sense, and such a categorization therefore makes a useful frame in which to analyse the establishment, entrenchment, and protection of patterns of privilege.

What are those privileges? This can only be answered within a specified social context, for the perception of privilege is determined by a wide range of cultural, social, and economic variables. It therefore changes as one progresses along the socio-occupational spectrum. Basing our definitions of privilege on the revealed priorities of the young rural dwellers, we shall lay emphasis on three aspects.*

First, much recent empirical work has stressed the desire among low-income groups for income security.[1] A secure job in which the risks of sudden dismissal are minimized is a rational aspiration in a situation in which there can be no certainty that any new job can be found immediately, and in which the process of looking for a job is hard, slow, demeaning, and expensive. In Ghana, Tanzania, and Uganda, the almost total security of the teaching service makes it easily the most popular career choice among university students.[2]

If, by comparison with security, income level is a somewhat less urgent consideration, there are few workers indeed who do not seek to earn as high an income as lies within their reach and is compatible with security. It is not uncommon for young people to seek lower-paid, lower-risk jobs, usually in the public sector, precisely because constancy of income is more important to them than its level. But other factors associated with income are hardly less important, although seldom identified in questionnaires addressed to the unemployed. These include protection against rising prices, an incremental or age-related scale, the possibility of promotion, and fringe benefits. Ability to secure these is, by our definition, one of the marks of privilege since they critically affect a household's long-run consumption pattern.

Closely related to both security of employment and long-run real income is a third factor to which we shall give much prominence in the next two chapters: the ability to compete in a labour market that is in equilibrium or in chronic scarcity. For the man or woman who is able to sell skills in an undersupplied market is likely to have greater security, better prospects of promotion, and a more rapidly rising income than a worker who has to compete with others in a buyer's market. This is not to deny the many imperfections in the labour market, nor the protection that can be afforded an unskilled worker by a trade union or other organization. But the fact that such protection is necessary is itself an indication of the disadvantage of being obliged to compete in an over-supplied market.

---

*It may seem strange that we define the privileges of one group by the criteria of another group. But what is important from our standpoint is not what the rich regard as their own privileges but what the rest of the community covets and tries to secure.

THE COLONIAL HERITAGE

Necessarily, we begin with the closing years of the colonial period for, as we shall see in greater detail later, the patterns established by the colonial powers explain much of the form and consumption patterns of the present urban elite. Although there were great differences in style and long-term strategy between the colonial powers, three crucially important assumptions were held in common.

The first was the assumption that the colonizing power and its representatives in the colony were wholly different from the colonized people. They were different in culture. They were different in social mores. They were different in political structure. They were different in economic level. The colonizers not only differed from the colonized; they were superior to them. To protect their identity, they developed their own enclave society, even when (in India and Ceylon, for example) they were surrounded by a culturally rich and sophisticated civilization.

The second assumption of the colonizers was of a right to a standard of life not only higher than that of the colonized people—that followed inevitably from the assumption of superiority—but higher than they would normally expect to enjoy at home. This assumption may not have been unrealistic in the early colonial days when indisputably there were discomforts, dangers, and disruptions for the colonizers. Then high material rewards may have been necessary to attract an adequate flow of colonizers. The advent of air travel, the development of tropical medicine, the establishment of a critical mass of Europeans in each colonized country had by the end of World War II ensured that in most countries at most times the great majority of Europeans could look forward to a substantially higher standard of life than they could expect at home. This was still justified on the grounds of the need to attract European settlers and to compensate public and corporate servants for the disadvantages of living outside their country of origin.

The third assumption made by the colonial powers, and embodied by their representatives in the colonies, was that the European community, defined by the two previous assumptions as a social and economic elite, was also a political elite. While colonies varied in the extent to which power was gradually transferred from the metropolitan country, the essence of colonization was that the local colonists could dispose of the property and persons of the colonized peoples in a wholly non-reciprocal relationship. This could be illustrated in terms of land settlement in East Africa and the Philippines; in terms of the control of trade in West Africa; in terms of commercial policy in India; in terms of the control of natural resources in Malaysia. But the point needs no emphasis. Non-reciprocity of political relationship was the keystone of all colonial political architecture.

As independence became an increasingly real possibility, so these assumptions, never entirely static in conception, underwent more rapid metamorphosis. Naturally the evidence of this change varied from country to country, but nearly universal were increases in primary and secondary education of the indigenous population, increasing provision of technical training (or at least the removal of legislative constraints on such provision), and increasingly rapid promotion in the public service. By the time the colonial power had accepted independence as inevitable, this process of accelerated social mobility was proceeding at a rate related to the tardiness of its beginning. In Zambia, one of the least educationally prepared colonies in the modern history of empire, educational neglect combined with economic opportunity to trigger a frantic scramble for literate and trainable manpower from 1964 to 1968-69. By contrast, the African francophone countries and Ghana, Sri Lanka, and to a much less marked degree East Africa had, under colonial patronage, evolved a local variant of the lycee or the British public school—a highly selective process of cultural assimilation ideally suited to the preparation of a small elite-in-waiting.[3]

In Asia, the simple pattern of the replacement of a European elite by an indigenous elite is complicated by internal racial divisions. This is most clearly illustrated in Sri Lanka, where the Tamils, originally imported to work the plantations, remain a politically excluded and economically deprived minority. In Malaysia, the situation was more complex since the political, and to a lesser extent administrative, structure was bequeathed to a racial group that was economically dominated by the Chinese. In order to survive economically, the political masters of Malaysia were therefore obliged to find a modus vivendi with the conomic masters. The attendant fracturing of Malaysian society—e.g., by the granting of Malaysian citizenship to Chinese despite opposition from Malays—was thus already implied by the political settlement of independence.

As independence became more imminent, the European population was left in a somewhat anomalous position. Increasing deprived of real political power, the Europeans nonetheless controlled two essential elements of economic life: skills and real wealth. Finding themselves shorn of their other privileges, those in the European community increasingly sought to raise their incomes as compensation for the alleged political and social risks of living in an independent country. Rationalizing this by appeals to lack of job security in the face of rapid localization, Europeans exploited their monopoly position by demanding yet higher salaries and extensions of existing privileges in fringe benefits and social consumption.

Although in many countries the greatest porportion of the financial cost of this reaction was met by the metropolitan power in the form of technical assistance commitments or a short-run reduction of profits in the expatriate-owned private sector, the social cost to the newly independent country was a further increase in the consumption gap between the European elite and the

rest of the population. Within two years the wages and salaries of European
mine workers in Zambia increased by 41 percent. Although European government employees increased their salaries only half as fast in the same period,
that increase was nonetheless in marked contrast to the gentle rise in the pre-
independence period. In Tanzania, European salaries rose by over 20 percent
between 1962 and 1965, and in Ghana the government was persuaded to restore the value of real incomes of European civil servants to its 1951 level on the
the eve of independence and a year later greatly to increase overseas payments
to the same group.

The essential point of this reaction by those in the European elite is not that
it rapidly increased their level of overt consumption, for in many cases it did
not. Insecure and frightened, many highly paid Europeans greatly increased
their rate of saving. Much more important, these salary levels provided a target
for the new elite seeking to take over European jobs.

It is difficult to over-emphasize the historic importance of the assimilation
of a small number in the indigenous population into the ruling elite. With an
ideology that hardly transcended a narrow nationalism and in the majority of
cases paid only the most perfunctory lip service to principles of socialism (and
in some cases—Philippines, Malaysia, Ivory Coast—not even that), it was perhaps inevitable that the new leadership should be the object of a process of
economic osmosis by which the assumptions and patterns of the colonizers
were transferred virtually intact to the new masters. At that point the rhetoric
of development so liberally proclaimed by the new leadership contained within
itself the seed of its own destruction.

CO-OPTATION AND EXPANSION

In the private sector, the colonial heritage meant that the great majority of
the owners of the means of production, particularly industrial production, were
foreigners. But before independence the process of co-opting prominent local
figures into the capitalist sector had begun. This is especially true of metropolitan-owned companies, but much less true of companies owned by racial
minorities. Co-optation did not take place in Chinese-owned companies in
Malaysia or in Asian-owned companies in East Africa. In Uganda, for example,
in 1967 only 15 percent of senior executives in European-controlled firms were
Ugandan citizens. This contrasts with 65 percent in administration and executive posts throughout the economy. In larger Asian-controlled companies (the
largest group owned effectively by two families), employing altogether over
150 senior executives, only 10 were Ugandan citizens. In medium-sized firms
the proportion of Ugandans employed in senior executive positions in
European-controlled firms was 19 percent, but in Asian-controlled firms it fell
to 2 percent.[4]

Thus, it was thought desirable at the approach of independence, especially by the metropolitan-owned firms, to have a number of citizens either in senior executive positions or, better still, on the boards. They were placed there not only for window-dressing (although the importance of appearing to take nationalistic aspirations seriously was fully appreciated) but also because local directors were expected to bring local expertise—particularly knowledge of and friendship with important indigenous bureaucrats and politicians. At independence the need to co-opt local businessmen increased as the political demand for participation at every level of the country's economy mounted. Particularly in Eastern Africa, the acute shortage of qualified manpower meant that there was a very limited pool from which such local directors could be chosen. (And the manpower that was available was already highly selected socially, economically, and tribally; for a full discussion, see Chapter 12.) This meant that the same names appeared frequently, as a very small number of individuals established themselves as a dominant group. But their power in their companies tended to be more symbolic than real; their influence, particularly on matters relating to personnel, management, and relationships with government, was somewhat greater.

With the development of state-owned enterprises there came into being an important (to judge by the vehemence of the attacks upon them) new group of high-level employees, the parastatal managers. Drawing most of their personnel from the civil service, but much of their style from the private sector, the parastatals attracted mounting criticism in Ghana, Uganda, Zambia, and Tanzania, not only for their inefficiency but also for their alleged siphoning off of an investible surplus to build prestige offices, to pay high salaries, and to furnish their senior employees with a range of fringe benefits comparable to those provided by international corporations.[5] Although some of the heat of the criticism directed at them rose from the fear that they were becoming politically identified with the expatriate commercial community, the parastatal managers were perhaps those who benefitted most immediately from the scarcity of high-level local manpower.*

After the early years of co-optation, three factors combined to ensure that the bureaucratic elite grew rapidly: the need to replace Europeans (a need felt more keenly in anglophone than francophone Africa), the need to extend the

---

*The Caisse de Stabilisation in Ivory Coast has not, so far as we are aware, been attached by the government, but it is continuously criticised by opposition politicians and by more perceptive Europeans. It owns the largest and most flamboyant office block in Abidjan. For official complaints that parastatals were paying higher wages and salaries than both the public and private sectors in other countries, see below, p. 181.

range of government services (especially skill-intensive education), and the growth of industrial production. Table 7.1 shows the extreme dependence of francophone Africa on non-Africans in three high-level manpower categories, in stark contrast to Ghana. The rate of change of this dependence is also revealing. One would expect it to fall, as it has, for instance, at one level in Uganda. But it may be increasing in francophone Africa and at the professional level in Uganda.

The organic demand for high-level manpower hardly needs emphasis. It is a consistent refrain of early manpower reports, some of which show huge and lasting deficits in technical high-level skills. As predictions, and highly fallible predictions—an intensive study of Uganda's experience of manpower planning concluded that it was "futile"[6]—these are less interesting than data, even rough and scrappy data, on actual events. These are presented in Table 7.2. As the figures have been assembled from a variety of sources, they are not strictly comparable; for instance, the Zambian figures include a rather larger lower-level technical group than do the other figures. Further, the Zambian figures are less confined to those with post-secondary education since, in the early years immediately after independence, Africans with even some secondary education were extremely scarce.

Granted that these figures are no more than orders of magnitude rather than precise estimates, what conclusions emerge? The first and most obvious is that the size of the groups represented here is minuscule in comparison with the population as a whole. Even where rather wide definitions have been used in the enumerations, as in Ivory Coast, Ghana, and Zambia, the proportion of the adult population in these groups is less than 1 percent. The point needs no labouring: These elites are small.

But from our point of view the important fact is not that these groups are so small in relation to the rest of the population but that in most countries they have been growing fast—faster than total recorded employment. This is exactly what manpower planning theory would lead us to expect, for it has been almost universal experience that the rate of growth of demand for high-level manpower exceeds the rate of growth of GDP. As we show in Chapter 11, GDP growth rates have usually, but not universally, exceeded rates of employment growth as labour productivity rises. This implies a high degree of upward mobility for those able to exploit the opportunity presented by a greater proportionate increase in high-level employment.

Let us immediately recognize that the data base at this point is weak. The rate of growth of the elite can be exaggerated by changes in definition and by improvements in the coverage of manpower surveys and other sources of data from which Table 7.1 is constructed. Equally, there is no doubt that enumerations of employees, on which in general we rely for information about changes in total paid employment, usually underestimate the total level of employment

TABLE 7.1

African Dependence on Expatriate Skills
(percentages)

Country and Occupation	Year	Africans		Non-Africans
		Citizens	Non-Citizens	
Ivory Coast				
Professionals, Technicians, Man-	1963	18.4	3.2	78.4
agers	1970	17.6	3.7	78.7
Cameroon				
Professionals, Technicians	1972	18.5	8.4	73.1
Managers	1972	10.2	13.5	76.3
Upper Volta				
Professionals, Technicians,	1963	65.0	8.6	26.4
Managers	1965	67.1	4.0	28.9
Ghana				
Senior civil service	1968	94.7		5.3
Uganda				
Professionals	1959	33.7		66.3
	1967	26.0		74.0
Administrative and executive	1959	15.8		84.2
	1967	65.0		35.0
Zambia				
Professionals	1968	18.9		81.1
Administrative and executive	1968	71.3		28.7

Sources:

Ivory Coast	Ministere de l'enseignement technique et de la formation professionnelle et Ministere du plan, *Le secteur prive et para-public en Cote d'Ivoire, 1971,* part 2 (Abidjan).
Cameroon	Ministere du plan, *La main d'oeuvre salariee permanente en Republique du Cameroun, 1971* (Yaounde, 1971); Direction des Statistiques, *Enquete emploi 1972-73* (Yaounde, 1973, confidential in June 1973).
Upper Volta	Societe d'Etude pour le developpement economique et sociale, *Emploi et Formation en Haute-Volta* (Paris, 1970).
Ghana	Manpower Division of the Development Planning Secretariat, *High Level and Skilled Manpower Survey in Ghana, 1968* (Accra, 1971).
Uganda	Establishment lists as reproduced in *Annual Estimates of Recurrent Expenditure* (Entebbe).
Zambia	Development Division of the Office of the Vice-President, *Zambian Manpower* (Lusaka: Government Printer, 1969); *Report of the O'Riordan Salaries Commission* (1971).

TABLE 7.2

The Bureaucratic, Technical, and Professional Elite in Some African Countries

Country and Classification	Year	Number	Year	Number	Rate of Growth Per Annum (percent)
Uganda					
Professional	1959	1,660	1967	3,610	9.5
Administrative and executive	1959	622	1967	1,200	
Tanzania					
Professional and technical	1962	(8,679)	1967	11,912	(6.5)
Administrative and executive	1962	(3,204)	1967	7,824	(19.0)
Zambia					
Professional, administrative, managerial, and technical	1964	15,890	1970	25,000	7.5
Ghana					
Professional, technical, and related	1963	44,200	1969	58,400	3.6
Managerial	1963	10,700	1969	13,000	3.3
Ivory Coast					
Professional, technical, administrative, and managerial	1963	17,533	1970	26,918	6.3
Cameroon					
Professional, technical, administrative, and managerial (private sector only)	1965	1,886	1972	3,525	11.0
Upper Volta					
Professional, technical, administrative and managerial	1965	761	1969	1,152	11.0

Sources: As Table 7.1, plus population censuses and, in Ghana and Tanzania, annual labour enumerations.

in the formal sector. Furthermore, in many countries the coverage of these enumerations has improved. All this may be admitted, yet the differences in the rate of growth of the privileged groups featured in Table 7.1 and the rates of growth of formal total employment (which may understate the rate of growth of jobs for the non-privileged) are in many cases so large that even adjustments for the statistical oddities of the data do not seriously impugn the basic point.

For example, in Uganda recorded employment increased by somewhat less than 3.5 percent through the 1960s, and yet the categories of high-level manpower featured in Table 7.2 increased by nearly 10 percent a year between 1959 and 1967. In Zambia, the rate of growth of the professional, technical, administrative, and management groups seems to have been about 7.5 percent a year from 1964 to 1970, and yet recorded employment as a whole in that period increased by something less than 5.5 percent a year. In Ghana, where the relatively wide definition of this group would tend to understate the difference in rates of growth, the "professional, technical, and related workers" group grew at an average rate of 3.6 percent a year between 1963 and 1969 and the managerial group slightly more slowly. But recorded employment as a whole grew at a rate of less than 1 percent a year. The contrast in Cameroon and Upper Volta is even more striking. Here we seem to have evidence, then, controverted by no African country on which we have data, that the most privileged group of all employees has been growing faster than employment as a whole, i.e., that the highly privileged as a proportion of the enumerated work force has been increasing. The full ramification of that will become clear later.

But first we must ask whether this rapid growth of elite groups is not limited to Africa or to the early years after independence. For part of our explanation of such growth was the rapid extension of government services and localization—both phenomena that might be thought to be particularly associated with the immediate post-independence years. As a check, then, it is useful to look at four countries that have been independent much longer and in which these two particular factors may be presumed to be weaker.

We begin with Sri Lanka and the Philippines. Both have pressed ahead with educational expansion so that the manpower shortages so typical of Africa have been turned into manpower surpluses more characteristic of Asia and Latin America (see Table 7.3). The similarities are perhaps less striking than the differences between these two countries, but it is still fair to ask whether the elites seem to have been growing faster than total employment.

The evidence certainly is that the two elite groups—administrative, executive, and managerial on the one hand, and professional and technical on the other—have been growing somewhat faster in both Sri Lanka and the Philippines than have total employment or employment of unskilled labour. It is particularly surprising that this has been happening in Sri Lanka. Given the disappointing

TABLE 7.3

Sri Lanka (1963-69) and Philippines (1958-68):
Changes in the Occupational Structure
(percentages)

	Annual Rate of Growth	
Occupational Group	Sri Lanka	Philippines
Professional, technical, and allied workers	2.6	8.1
Administrative, executive, and managerial workers*	3.7	5.6
Clerical and allied workers	2.9	7.8
Sales workers	2.0	4.6
Workers in agriculture, forestry, hunting, and fishing	0.4	2.9
Miners, quarrymen, and related workers	21.4	3.4
Workers in transport and communication	4.3	6.0
Craftsmen, production process workers, and labourers not elsewhere classified	1.8	1.8
Service, sports, and recreation workers	-11.9	4.0

*In the Philippine classification, owner-operators of commercial and industrial concerns are included in this category.

Sources: Preliminary Report on the Socio-Economic Survey of Ceylon, 1969-70 (Colombo: Department of Census and Statistics, 1971); Melinda M. Bacol, "Inter-Generational Occupational Mobility in the Philippines," *Philippine Sociological Review* 19, nos. 3, 4 (1971): 192.

rate of economic growth and the very tight constraints on government finance, here if anywhere one would have expected to see the elite group growing slowly. Part of the explanation lies in the continued rapid expansion of education and therefore the employment of teachers, and part in the increasing technical sophistication of production techniques.

In the Philippines the explanation is less difficult, although the data in Table 7.3 must be treated with great care.* Relative capital intensity of much industry, particularly perhaps foreign-owned industry, the increasing sophistication of government, and the expansion of health and education services would all

---

*Not only are there the usual problems of under-enumeration but the classification of workers (and particularly the catch-all sub-category "related workers") may lead to an exaggeration of the size and growth of the two high-level manpower groups. However, the scale of the difference between the rate of growth of the professional group and all others, except the clerical group, suggests that the over-all trend is reliable.

lead one to expect a rapid rate of growth of the elite cadres by comparison
with lower-skill groups. It is no surprise to find, then, that the proportion of
the total population employed in these elite groups is higher in both Sri Lanka
and the Philippines than it is in any of the African countries. Although the difference is not so large as to make it worth straining the point (particularly in
view of the nature of the data), the relatively larger elite groups in the Asian
countries imply not only a greater concentration of income, a theme to which
we shall return, but also a proportionately greater degree of upward mobility.

Egypt is a third example of a country in which manpower is not a constraint
in the way that it is in sub-Saharan Africa. Although the data are seriously deficient, there can be little doubt that the same pattern has emerged there. Indeed,
one perceptive observer has written: "The increasing size and power of the
bureaucracy may be described as the most important institutional change to
have taken place in Egyptian society since 1952."[7] The 1950s saw a rapid expansion of the bureaucracy, but that was accelerated further as a result of the
nationalizations of 1961. During the first Five Year Plan, the cost of civil administration rose from 5 percent of GDP in 1959/60 to 10 percent of GDP in
1965/66. Table 7.4 shows that in the government service sector, the top bureaucracy not only grew faster than total employment but nearly three times
as fast as the more humble clerical group. Abdel Ghoneim has called these top
bureaucrats the "New Class."[8] Comprising active and retired military officers
and some well-connected senior civil servants, they not only have great power
and a well-articulated sense of their own identity and interest but also a very
much higher standard of living than the rest of the urban population—a theme to
to which we shall return.

Malaysia provides the one exception to the general pattern of a bureaucratic
elite growing faster than either formal employment in general or low-skill occupations in particular. The professional and technical groups grew during 1962-
68 at 2.5 percent per annum, but the managerial and administrative group actually contracted by 10 percent over the same period. By contrast, employment
of manufacturing manual workers (craftsmen, process workers, and labourers),
grew at over 3.5 percent per annum, but total non-agricultural employment at
only 1.7 percent.[9] The evidence, then, is slightly ambiguous. The rapid increase
in the number of production workers is explained by the growth of manufacturing output, which drew manpower from agriculture and from the "sales"
occupational group. But, simultaneously, the professional and technical groups,
rather a mixed bag in terms of qualifications and income levels, expanded,
partly to service the booming manufacturing sector and partly to man expanding government services. The decline of the managerial group is a mystery, just
possibly explained by concentration in the sales sector. (It is not likely to be
explained by changes in occupational classification, as the same directory was
used in 1962 and 1967/68.[10]) But it is clear that we cannot conclude that the

TABLE 7.4

Egypt: Structure of Employment in the Government
Service Sector, 1962/63-1971/72

Post	Number of Jobs			Average Annual Percentage Increase, 1962/72
	1962/63	1966/67	1971/72	
Top administrative	967	1,544	1,905	7.0
Highly specialized	71,661	103,589	137,814	6.7
Technical*	126,090	161,030	208,044	5.2
Organizational and administrative*	13,671	19,864	25,281	6.1
Clerical	63,451	76,011	85,928	3.1
All categories (including service workers)	707,312	1,035,747	1,290,538	6.0

*Middle grades.

Sources: Abdel Ghoneim, "On the Issue of the New Class in Egypt," Al-Tala'ia 4, no. 2 (1968): 88; and M.S. Al-Attriby, "Bureaucratic Inflation in the last Ten Years," Al-Tala'ia 8, no. 10 (1972): 74; both as quoted in M. Abdel-Fadil, Employment and Income Distribution in Egypt, 1952-1970, Discussion Paper (Norwich: University of East Anglia, 1974).

bureaucratic elites in Malaysia grew faster than other occupational groups in this period.

EDUCATION AND THE RECRUITMENT OF THE ELITE

How can the rapid rate of growth of these elites be reconciled with the extreme scarcity of educated manpower in the African countries we have mentioned? In conditions of extreme scarcity, educational requirements tend to be reduced or ignored. Provided the employer considers an applicant trainable, he will recruit him even if his formal qualifications are less than normally would be expected.[11] Thus, in the early years of accelerated differentiation we find very little correlation between educational level and occupation—as Table 7.5 illustrates.

Table 7.5 must be interpreted with some care as the occupational groups are broad. But the data show that, twelve years ago, over 60 percent of the "administrative and executive group" in Sri Lanka had no more than primary schooling. At the professional level, the contrast between Sri Lanka and the three African countries is, as one would expect, more marked. In Sri Lanka only 24 percent had not received secondary education; in Tanzania 62 percent. As the supply of educated manpower at the secondary level becomes more plentiful, so the educational requirements for given posts are increased. The premium upon education for those seeking selection or promotion thus increases. Education becomes a more important and more selective access cone.

There are signs that this is already happening. In Zambia, for example, the O'Riordan Commission specifically suggested that the government should *not* raise educational requirements for jobs in the civil service, much though that would be welcomed on efficiency grounds, because to do so would create

TABLE 7.5

**Tanzania, Ghana, Sri Lanka: Education and Occupation
of the Bureaucratic Elite
(percent)**

Occupation and Education	Tanzania (1967)	Ghana (1960)	Sri Lanka (1963)
Professional, technical, and related workers			
No schooling	5.7	8.0	2.1
Primary school*	56.5	43.9	21.5
Secondary school	24.6	19.9	65.5
Post-secondary	13.2	28.2	8.4
Unspecified			2.5
Total	100.0	100.0	100.0
Administrative, executive and managerial workers			
No schooling	13.1	5.0	1.6
Primary school*	52.0	35.6	63.5
Secondary school	26.9	38.1	24.7
Post-secondary	8.0	21.3	6.1
Unspecified			4.1
Total	100.0	100.0	100.0

*Includes Arabic and middle schools in Ghana.
Sources: Tanzania 1967 Population Census (economically active workers by occupation and education).
Ghana 1960 Census (selected occupations of employed persons aged 15 and over by type of school and sex and by the three cities: Sekondi-Takoradi M.C., Accra M.C., Kumasi M.C.).
Sri Lanka 1963 Population Census (educational profiles of occupational categories, 1963).

employment problems for less qualified secondary school graduates. It also
would threaten the less educated already recruited with retarded promotion.
There is no means of telling how far this consideration weighed with the official representatives of the junior civil servants who supported this recommendation. But it is very clear from an earlier investigation of the teaching service
that there was widespread disaffection among less educated teachers who saw
their promotion chances blocked by the rising standards of new entrants. This
was officially denied, but there is no reason to believe that the teachers' concern was misplaced.[12]

The wide range of educational attainment found in the elites, as illustrated
in Table 7.5, suggests that education has not been the only road into the elites
in the past. If there has been a fairly high degree of upward mobility not de-
determined by education, will there remain a chance for the bright but under-
educated man to work his way up? Although it is extremely hard to dogmatize
on this point, it does seem that, the greater the surplus of educated people, the
harder it is for the under-educated or under-qualified to win promotion on
merit and experience. An extreme example of this is Sri Lanka, where each
post in the civil service is graded by educational requirement and it is wholly
impossible for a man lacking the specified educational requirement to be promoted. A similar rigidity can be detected in India,[13] in the Philippines, and in
Egypt. Whether this comes about as a result of pressure from educated groups
wishing to maintain a monopoly of scarce jobs (as there is some evidence in Sri
Lanka), or as a result of governments wishing to minimize the frustration, and
therefore political inflammability, of educated manpower (as is the case in
Egypt), the result is the same. In either case, the possibility of upward mobility
is biased against the man who was excluded from educational opportunity in
his adolescence. This means that in the future, as the number of secondary
school leavers and then university graduates rises faster than jobs for them are
created, it is likely to become increasingly difficult for the less educated man to
work his way up into the bureaucratic elite. In other words, access to the elite
becomes more heavily dependent upon education, notwithstanding the survival
of other access cones.

For example, in countries where the army is in power, military connections
will no doubt continue to offer access as they have so conspicuously in Egypt.
But in countries with a surplus of educated manpower, social or occupational
promotion through the military becomes educationally selective. Contrast
Uganda, where the stock of educated manpower in or close to the army is
small, with Ghana or Egypt. Other forms of "indirect" recruitment through
brokers—e.g., tribal connections—also become biased in favour of the more
educated (see below, pp. 266-67). This is not to argue that, in conditions of
educational surplus, these routes of occupational promotion become closed or
inoperative, but rather that they no longer keep the bureaucratic elite as open
to the less educated as it was in the years of educational scarcity.

Educational scarcity and a tendency for the elite to grow faster than other socio-economic groups thus combine to create a doubly selective process. For those who are educated to a level that makes them competitive in the elite groups have a better chance of employment and a better chance of rapid promotion. Those who fail to acquire a competitive level of education, but nonetheless secure employment at the level of the bureaucratic elite, are likely to find increasing resistance to promotion within that elite. Those with neither the requisite educational attainment nor access to other routes of promotion are obliged to compete for a job in a labour market characterized by excess supply, slow growth, and increasing competition. It is this context that makes the selectivity of education so crucial (see below, pp. 244-57).

MONEY INCOMES OF ELITES

In terms of the basic analytical frame, we would expect to find that, given the political and administrative power and influence of this group, it has been able to increase, perhaps greatly increase, its share of total consumption in at least two senses. As the size of the group expands, we would expect the total consumption accruing to the group to expand nearly as fast (allowing for the fact fact that the age structure is likely to change in the years of rapid expansion). This implies a shift of consumption resources to this group as a whole. But, second, and more interesting, we would expect to find that in general the average per capita real incomes of this group have risen at least in line with the growth of national income, and perhaps even faster. For we would expect this elite to be adept at securing personal enrichment from the process of economic growth. Third, we might expect to find one or both of these patterns more marked in the "growth" group of countries than in the "equity" group.

We shall in fact find some evidence of the first pattern, very little of the second, and a rather confusing and inconsistent jumble in the third.

We have emphasized the impact on the process of elite formation of the change from extreme scarcity to over-supply of educated manpower. How far does this affect the level of living of these elites? This implies two questions: How far did elite salaries respond to the extreme scarcity of elite skills in the early post-independence period? And how far did the change in the market reduce salaries?

Here the evidence is nearly unequivocal. For despite the fact that such skills were in short supply and that the elite had control of the civil service, much of the legislature, and nearly all of the parastatal sector, the evidence strongly suggests that, in the public sector at least, colonial differentials have been gradually eroded.

In Africa, we have fairly satisfactory time series for the bureaucratic and technical elite for only three countries: Uganda, Zambia, and Ghana. All show a remarkably slow rate of growth of money income throughout the 1960s. The money income of an African graduate joining the senior civil service in Ghana, for instance, increased at less than 2 percent a year between 1953 and 1971. In Uganda, throughout the 1960s the top grade of the G.3 scale—the appropriate scale for higher executive officers—increased by less than one half of one percent per year. Even secondary school leavers, one of the groups in most critical shortage and a politically sensitive group, increased their money income by less than 2.5 percent a year from 1961 to 1967. Although there may have been some small acceleration thereafter, it lasted only until 1971. In Zambia, the data are less clear, but the effect of three commissions of enquiry into public service salaries since independence has been to increase top salaries by somewhat less than 5 percent a year, if one takes the whole period since independence, 1964 to 1973.

In Tanzania, it is government policy to peg senior salaries (and even, after the Arusha Declaration, to reduce them). Although, as we shall see, this policy has been difficult to enforce, money incomes in the public service are unlikely to have increased much. That is certainly the opinion of one of the government's senior economic advisers. Without specifying the data on which his conclusions were based, he wrote:

> In the public sector wage and salary group the maximum gross income differential for citizens is about 25:1 (Shs.60,000:2,400) in cash terms and perhaps 30:1 including fringe benefits. In post-tax private purchasing power the difference is of the order of 12.5:1 and 16:1. Using pre-Adu scales, direct substitution for expatriates by citizens on same terms and 1961 tax structure, the difference was, in 1960, about 70/80:1 cash a and 100:1 including fringes in post-tax purchasing power. This does *not* mean that there has been this great reduction because top posts were not citizen-held in 1960, *but* it does show how policies have both achieved an *actual* reduction and have altered the system to prevent the increases which would have resulted from unchanged wage, salary, fringe benefit and tax structures.[14]

Again we must ask whether this is a freak African occurrence related to the particular circumstances of Africa's colonial history, or whether this slow growth of money incomes among the elite is a more general phenomenon.

In Sri Lanka, where there has been a long tradition of trying to reduce some of the greater post-colonial differentials, the money income of professionals (class I, grade I) in the civil service has increased at less than 1.5 percent a year between 1948 and 1968. That of accountants and doctors has increased fractionally faster.

The only countries we have studied that seem at first sight to buck this trend are the Philippines and Egypt. In the Philippines, between 1954 and 1971 the professional groups actually suffered a fall in their money income but the managerial and administrative groups increased theirs by over 4 percent a year. The fall in the professional group in the Philippines is probably explained by the rather broad definition of the group, which includes technical and related workers. Over the last fifteen years, the structure of this group has changed with the adherence of a greater number of lower-paid workers. The effect of this has been to reduce the average income of the group. Whether or not this masks an increase in the money incomes of the high-level personnel in this group, we cannot say. We have seen evidence of entrepreneurial incomes rising rather rapidly in the 1960s, and this makes it at least probable that professionals who "service" enterprises—lawyers, accountants, brokers, consultants—will have benefitted thereby. In Egypt, the top bureaucratic elite in the public business sector follows the general pattern, with rather modest increases during 1962-67. But over the same period, the equivalent group in the government administration, jealous of its inferior position vis-a-vis the parastatals, rapidly increased its income, achieving an average annual rate of growth of nearly 11 percent. (There is an income ceiling in Egypt, but it is doubtful whether it applies to any public employees, as it is fixed at a level more than double the basic maximum salary, i.e., excluding allowances.)

With this exception, then, there is no evidence of these elite groups increasing their money incomes faster than average for the modern sector as a whole, despite their strong market position. Nor is there much evidence of a fall in *money* income after the market has become over-supplied, as in Ghana in the later 1960s; Egypt, Sri Lanka, and the Philippines somewhat earlier. Although this may have happened to a greater extent in the private secor, the very large proportion of workers employed by government in all these countries tends to ensure that private sector salaries do not move far from public sector salaries for any length of time. (The Mills-Odoi Commission in Ghana recognized that private and parastatal salaries were higher than public sector salaries, but refused to bid up the latter in the expectation that the former would decline at some point in the future.[15])

We seem, then, to have a remarkable constancy of money income, irrespective of market condition. In this case, the effect of the change from under-supply to over-supply is limited to that of raising educational qualifications for entrants. If demand for this level of labour is at all price-elastic (and it is hard to to see why it should be perfectly inelastic in either the public or private sectors in all but the shortest run), the less qualified would-be entrant is the unhappy victim of a double process of exclusion. He is excluded because he cannot compete under the raised qualifications. And he is excluded because the number of jobs available is not expanding as rapidly as it would if salaries fell in accordance with the new market condition. More significant from our point of view, structural adjustments that would be of immediate and direct benefit to the poor—most obviously an increase in the quantity of services and employment—are not made. We shall return to this point in more detail in Chapter 12.

REAL INCOMES OF ELITES

The near constancy of money salaries disguises substantial falls in real income. The average rate of increase of the cost of living of high-income groups is given in Table 7.6. Although there are severe problems about the price indexes in each of these countries, it seems reasonable to conclude that real incomes of most elite groups, for which we have adequate data on money incomes, fell over the post-independence period—with the possible exceptions of Egypt,* Sri Lanka (where the cost of living has risen slowly†), and the Philippines (where the incomes of the elites may have risen faster than 5.2 percent). In some cases, of which Ghana is clearly a leading example, that fall was prolonged and severe. Despite a strong market position in the early years after independence, then, there is no evidence in the public sector of market or political forces bestowing on these privileged groups rapid rises in income; nor is there evidence of a sharp break when the character of the market changed.

In other words, we seem to have an institutionalized salary level, initially inherited from colonial days, being gradually eroded. How can this be explained?

First and most important, the facts as we have presented them do not tell the whole story. For the relative constancy of money incomes is an illusion that can be supported only if one takes a given age or a given grade in a salary structure and observes it over a period. In fact, of course, a particular professional acquires seniority, and in nearly every case that we have examined seniority brings its own reward. In the public service in every country and in most private firms at this level of employment, an incremental scale is normal. These incremental scales can be long (and have in a number of cases been deliberately lengthened), progression up them is virtually automatic, and, unless

---

*The cost-of-living index is unsuitable as it is heavily weighted with subsidized or price-controlled essentials. Given the scarcity of luxury items and private urban housing or an appropriate quality, it would be very surprising if an urban high-income index did not show a higher rate of increase than top bureaucratic salaries.

†But the Colombo cost-of-living index is a particularly poor proxy for upper-income groups. Their cost of living has risen faster, and perhaps much faster, than the index suggests.

TABLE 7.6

Average Rates of Increase in Cost of Living

Country	Period	Percentage Increase Per Annum
Uganda	1961-71	4.3
Zambia	1960-73	4.8
Ghana	1957-69	6.2
Sri Lanka	1948-71	1.8
Philippines	1955-71	5.2

Note: High-income indexes have been used where available.

Sources:

Uganda   *Abstract of Statistics* (Entebbe: Government Printer).

Zambia   *Statistical Year Book* (Lusaka: Government Printer).

Ghana   *Statistical Year Book,* Quarterly Digest of Statistics (Accra: Central Bureau of Statistics).

Sri Lanka   *Central Bank of Ceylon Bulletin,* March 1973.

Philippines *Journal of Philippine Statistics* (Manila: Department of Commerce and Industry, Bureau of the Census and Statistics).

an officer commits some misdemeanour or lacks necessary qualifications, he is likely to be able to transfer from one grade to the next and thus achieve the benefit of a number of incremental scales over his working life.

The value of such increments obviously varies from country to country, but a value of between 3 percent and 6 percent seems to be average at this level. Thus a professional is assured of an increase in money income that for most countries most of the time has been enough to offset the rise of prices. Apart from periods of particularly sharp inflation, as for instance in Uganda in 1969 or Ghana after the devaluation of the cedi in 1967, those who have been able to progress up the incremental ladder will not have suffered a fall in their real income. In some countries, for example Zambia and, for the administrative group, the Philippines, real incomes will have increased, not dramatically but steadily. Only those who found themselves at the top of a scale or unable to progress up a further scale because they lacked the educational and professional qualifications were deprived of this source of increase.

In this connection, another consideration is relevant. In countries where high-level skills were in short supply, there is much evidence, usually in complaints by the representatives of governments to salaries commissions, of migration from the public sector to the private sector and even from ministry to ministry as the more mobile and ambitious officers used the market situation

to gain accelerated promotion. In the extreme cases of the East African countries immediately after independence, it was not unusual for a university graduate to progress from the entry grade of the civil service to a permanent secretary
or under-secretary in three or four years. This is only an extreme example of
what was for a time a common phenomenon.

The second qualification to the picture presented by the raw data is that the
value of some of the fringe benefits enjoyed by the elite groups increased markedly over the period. Again there are variations in fringe benefits from country
to country, but it is not unusual to find fringe benefits that include medical
insurance, pension rights, and, most important, housing.* Although we shall return to a more detailed consideration of public housing policies in Chapter 12,
it is worth emphasizing here that the distributional effect of the allocation of
houses to public servants tends to be highly regressive. The higher an officer's
status and income, the greater the likelihood that he will be allocated a government house. A relic of colonial days, the assumption that government is obliged to provide housing to its employees has been modified to a varying extent,
but nowhere has it been wholly abolished. In Zambia, for instance, at a time
when construction capacity was one of the most critical bottlenecks in the
whole development effort, and when, furthermore, government services were
near to breaking point as a result of the rapid expansion of the public service,
these two difficulties were compounded by the policy of providing houses to
nearly all monthly-paid government servants, and thus increasing their income
by an average of 15 percent.[16] When the government tried to end this practice
by passing all its stock of houses to a National Housing Corporation—which
would progressively introduce economic rents—the plan was first postponed
and then cancelled as a result of great pressure from civil servants. In Sri Lanka,
by contrast, some rationality has been introduced into the system of allocation
and, although there is no uniform pattern, there is at least some attempt to
ration government housing according to need. Thus, police and teachers in
remoter areas are housed, while senior government officers in Colombo are left
to find their own accommodations.

While most governments follow the colonial precedent of requiring officers
to pay either a notional rent or a proportion of salary, the subsidy element in
government housing usually is considerable. Even when tax is levied on the
notional benefit from the occupation of government housing, the real benefit
exceeds the taxed benefit.[17] Taken together, these fringe benefits amount to a
considerable value. In 1963, the Ugandan Treasury concluded that the value of

---

*Fringe benefits supplied to expatriates are usually more extensive and in-
clude, as well as those detailed above, free travel, home leave, subsidized education and free travel for children, and superior local services (particularly
education and health care).

fringe benefits in the public service rose from 35 percent of basic salary for those on salary levels of up to £266 a year to over 45 percent of basic salary for those with salaries exceeding £945 a year. Particularly in the case of metropolitan housing, it is likely that the value of these fringe benefits has increased.

Does the same conclusion apply to the private sector? On this we have very little direct data. Reports on parastatal organizations in Tanzania, Zambia, and Ghana have all made the point that fringe benefits in parastatals tend to exceed those in regular government employment precisely because the parastatals have to compete with the private sector. (R.H. Green stated that parastatal wage policy was to increase salaries but hold fringe benefits constant.) In 1970, non-agricultural public employees were nearly twice as likely to be given free housing in Tanzania as were those employed in the parastatals and private business.[18] But the private sector is not itself homogeneous. There is a great difference between the prestigious extravagance, the deliberate conspicuous consumption of the large multinationals, and the very much less extravagant policies of small and particularly locally-owned companies. Senior employees of the copper companies in Zambia, white and black, for instance, live in a style richly redolent of the colonial period. The same can be said of the larger number of international companies with manufacturing bases in Kuala Lumpur and Manila.

These two considerations taken together mean that data on money incomes must be carefully reinterpreted. Most elite groups benefit from incremental scales and a proportion, possibly higher in the public sector than in the private, from a panoply of fringe benefits. Thus, while it is true that the real income attached to a given post has declined over time, it is not in general true that the real income of any given individual has declined over time except during periods of unusually rapid inflation. These periods of inflation have in most cases been followed by increases in the basic scale, and therefore such falls in real income tend to be of limited duration.

We have here, then, the explanation of why the erosion of differentials, illustrated in Table 7.7, has been possible. A direct onslaught on the standard of living of the elite would have been politically impossible. Only in Tanzania was it partially successful. Even there, in 1968 ministers, regional and area commissioners "asked" for gratuities that would almost completely compensate them for the salary cuts they took after the Arusha Declaration. Further, widespread concern at the way the surpluses of the parastatals were dissipated by unauthorized payment of bonuses to employees of up to T.Shs.5,000 each resulted in the appointment in 1972 of a special commission of enquiry (of the party rather than the government) into this issue. But the overall pattern is clear enough. By ensuring that the real incomes of individuals were protected—and perhaps rose slowly—governments were able to ensure that differentials between posts were actually reduced.

TABLE 7.7

Ratios of National Elite Salaries to Minimum Wages

Country and Components	Dates		
Uganda	1961	1965	1971
Civil service grade 3/Kampala minimum wage	25.9	11.1	10.9
Zambia[a]		1965	1971
All African graduates/Lusaka minimum wage		9.3	10.7
Ghana	1953	1958	1968
Senior civil service—average salary of all			
graduates/urban minimum wage	14.5	11.1	10.2
Sri Lanka	1948		1967
Civil service class 1, grade 1/unskilled			
engineering workers (public sector)	20.8		11.3
Philippines[b]		1965	1971
Professional, technical/manual		3.0	2.2
Senior university professor/industrial			
minimum wage		7.4	
Egypt	1956		
Government administration: top			
grade/lowest grade[c]	24.1		
Ivory Coast			1971
Upper professionals/unskilled workers			
(private sector)			18.0
Ivorien upper professionals/unskilled workers			8.0
Cameroon			1972
Upper professionals/unskilled workers			
(public sector)			11.0
(private sector)			16.0
Upper Volta			1969
African upper professionals/unskilled workers			19.0

[a]The Zambian figures present a statistical difficulty: There is no figure for salaries of all African graduates in 1971. We estimated a figure on the known wage/salary awards in the public sector. This may overestimate the average earnings of all African graduates, given the rapid expansion of this group after 1969 and therefore the change in its structure following a reduction in the average of the group. But the source of error here is quite small and it does appear (as one would expect from other data) that the closing of the gap in Zambia

since independence certainly has been less vigorous compared with other countries.

[b] Although the change is in the right direction, these ratios are much lower than the other countries because the "professional and technical" group includes a large number of relatively low-paid workers.

[c] Excluding "representation allowances"; if these are included, the differential could rise to 40:1 (see A. Ghoneim, full source listing below, pp. 89-90).

Sources:

Uganda	Establishment lists as reproduced in *Annual Estimates of Recurrent Expenditure* (Entebbe).
Zambia	Development Division of the Office of the Vice-President, *Zambian Manpower* (Lusaka: Government Printer, 1969); *Report of the O'Riordan Salaries Commission* (1971).
Ghana	Data from Public Services Advisory Board.
Sri Lanka	ILO, *Matching Employment Opportunities and Expectations: A Programme of Action for Ceylon,* report of an inter-agency team organized by the International Labour Organization (Geneva: ILO, 1971).
Philippines	*Family Income and Expenditures,* 1965 and 1971, the BCS Survey of Households Bulletin (Manila: Bureau of the Census and Statistics).
Egypt	Abdel Ghoneim, "On the Issue of the New Class in Egypt," *Al-Tala'ia* 4, no. 2 (1968), as quoted in M. Abdel-Fadil, *Employment and Income Distribution in Egypt, 1952-1970,* Discussion Paper (Norwich: University of East Anglia, 1974).
Ivory Coast	Ministere de l'enseignement technique et de la formation professionnelle et Ministere du plan, *Le secteur prive et para-public en Cote d'Ivoire, 1971* (Abidjan, 1972).
Cameroon	Ministere du plan, *La main d'oeuvre salariee permanente en Republique du Cameroun, 1971* (Yaounde, 1971); Direction des Statistiques, *Enquete emploi 1972-73* (Yaounde, 1973, confidential in June 1973).
Upper Volta	Societe d'etude pour le developpement economique et social, *Emploi et formation en Haute-Volta* (Paris, 1970).

187

Although we lack earlier data against which to judge them, the figures for the francophone countries suggest that this generalization can be applied there with only the greatest caution. The continuing heavy dependence upon expatriates, the hangover of the effect of the colonial "code du travail" (tying public sector salaries to metropolitan rates), and the highly selective approach to localization all combine to ensure that crude differentials are high.

Tax policy could, in theory, have been used to close the gap even faster. In general, the effect of direct taxation has been small. There is also considerable variability between countries in the degree of progressiveness of taxation; in Egypt even after the "socialist reform" of the fiscal system in 1961, income taxes were less progressive than in either the United States or West Germany.[19] However, Table 7.8 suggests that the effect of direct taxation is certainly to reduce the differential with low-income earners, but by very little.* Again, this has to be seen in its political setting. Higher marginal rates for high-income groups would have been resisted—as they were in Zambia in 1968, Ghana in 1971, and Sri Lanka in 1972—and would perhaps have been self-defeating since they would have prompted demands for larger rises in money incomes. By allowing inflation to erode the real value of incomes and refusing to adjust tax schedules in line with inflation,† governments have avoided confrontation but have slowly begun to achieve the same purpose.

---

*The assumptions in the table are necessarily rather crude. They tend to overestimate the incidence of tax because they ignore all allowances that can be set against tax, except wife and children and earned income allowances. Additional allowances vary from country to country, but their effect is usually to subsidize the amassing of capital out of pre-tax income. Although the interest on the capital is taxable, often at higher rates than earned income, the net effect of these allowances is to reduce the tax burden by a greater proportion the higher the marginal rate of tax. The table also assumes that the high-income groups have no comparative advantage in evading taxation. Studies in rich and poor countries suggest that this is not the case: The higher the marginal rate of tax, the greater the incentive to evade.

†Tax rates have been amended, of course, but not at the same rate as inflation. The effective rate on real incomes has therefore risen. In some countries—Sri Lanka, the Philippines, Zambia, Tanzania—the effective rate on higher money incomes also has increased.

TABLE 7.8

Impact of Income Tax on Differentials

Country and Occupation	Year	Pre-Tax	Post-Tax Single	Post-Tax Married Plus Two Children
Uganda				
Civil service grade 3/minimum wages	1971	10.9	10.0	10.9
Ghana				
Senior civil service (average African salary)/urban minimum wage	1968	12.4	11.5	11.5
Zambia				
All African graduates/Lusaka minimum wage	1971	10.7	9.8	10.6
Sri Lanka				
Civil service class 1, grade 1/ public unskilled engineers	1967	11.3	9.9	10.3
Philippines				
Professional, technical/manual	1971	2.7	2.7	2.7
Senior university professor/ minimum wage	1965	7.4		6.3 (average)

Source: As Table 7.7, with relevant tax tables as supplied by ministries of finance or similar.

CONCLUSION

The evidence we have presented shows that, in nearly every country, the bureaucratic elite has grown fast, but that, contrary to what might be expected, it has in general not disproportionately increased its share of national consumption. It is true that differentials are still very high by the standards of industrialized countries (and even more so by those of Cuba and China) and that lower salaries would not produce shortages of this kind of manpower. In this sense, therefore, these groups are overpaid and consume more than would fall to them if differentials were effective in ensuring that no more sought employment at this level than could be employed there.

But such observations are not very helpful except in so far as they suggest that the corrections already under way have a great deal further to go. For, with some exceptions, notably Egypt and the Philippines (one "socialist," the other "capitalist"), governments have succeeded in slowly, very slowly, whittling away the consumption privileges of this group. But that does not mean that they have gone far, nor that the very large bias in the distribution of consumption, inherited from colonial times, has been much changed. It is not without significance that in Zambia from 1964 to 1967 imports of cheaper cotton textiles (ISIC 65241) increased by 42 percent while imports of household electrical equipment increased by 125 percent; nor that in Ivory Coast imports of refrigerating equipment more than doubled in 1966-70 while all textile imports grew only a third as fast. Perhaps an extreme example is Egypt. During the first Five Year Plan (1960/61-1964/65)—i.e., *after* the "radicalization"— consumption of washing machines increased 390 percent; of clothing, 26.7 percent. Sales of radios increased over sixfold; of footwear, only one tenth as much.[20]

How far is ideological position consistent with actual experience? Is it the case that the "growth" countries show both a higher rate of growth and a more general enrichment of the elite? The evidence is not sufficiently complete to allow dogmatism on the point, but there can be little doubt that in terms of size the differences that seem to emerge (see, for instance, Tables 7.2 and 7.3) are more explicable in terms of real growth and absolute level of GDP than in terms of ideological commitment. The two countries with particularly low rates of growth of GDP—Sri Lanka and Ghana—had little in common ideologically over the period, but both had low rates of growth of these elites. Cameroon and Upper Volta, with no very obvious ideological line, but certainly nearer Ivory Coast than Egypt or Tanzania, are fairly obvious cases of early post-independence correction of imbalances; the measurement of GDP in both is so unsatisfactory that it is unwise to try to relate the growth of the elite to that. Even if the 1962 figures for Tanzania are very badly underenumerated,* the rapid growth of these groups contrasts starkly with Ghana and Sri Lanka.

More interesting is the question of real incomes; for here, if anywhere, we would expect ideological patterns to be reflected. But again there seems to be no consistent pattern—in either absolute or relative terms. Two of the three countries in which we think elite real incomes may have increased belong to the "equity" group—Egypt and Sri Lanka. It is very possible, although we

---

*The 1962 figure is from the Employment and Earnings Survey; this tabulation was then discontinued. The 1967 figure is from the Population Census. There is no certainty that these two wholly separate enquiries used the same classifications.

cannot be sure, that to these should be added all the countries of francophone West Africa under study—all "growth"-oriented. In post-tax differential terms, we are at a disadvantage in not having fully comparable data for any of the "growth" countries. But the figures in Tables 7.7 and 7.8 do not suggest (except perhaps for Upper Volta) that differentials are significantly and consistently higher there. From very imperfect data from one region we would surmise that in Malaysia differentials between senior civil servants and unskilled workers in formal sector manufacturing employment are lower, rather than higher, than those in Table 7.7. Certainly there is not the contrast one might expect between Tanzania (as reported by Green) and the "middle ground," as represented by Uganda, Ghana, and Zambia. Indeed, if Green's figures are right, differentials in Tanzania are higher rather than lower.

The data, then, do not fit any easy pattern of political priorities. It does not seem to be the case that the more egalitarian-inclined governments have succeeded in reducing the consumption, in either absolute or relative terms, of this group any better than those whose priorities lie elsewhere. From this we would not wish to conclude that this group is universally well organized, politically conscious, and tireless in the defence of its own privilege.

Although no one can read the minutes of evidence of commissions of enquiry on the public service, or on parastatals, or on incomes policy in general without being impressed by the ability of this group to manipulate facts to fit its own special pleas, the fact remains that governments and their public and private advisers have consistently, if not dramatically, gnawed away at their privileges—or allowed time and inflation to do so. It is true that, when they have tried to go too fast, they have been rebuffed and have had to withdraw. For instance, the Zambian government eventually had to let drop one of the provisions of a 1964 agreement that would have resulted in net falls in the money income of citizen civil servants in senior posts.[21] The basic issue has been the gradual reform of a wholly inappropriate salary structure. In general, the need for that reform is granted; the elite does not expose itself by trying to defend the indefensible. But it does seek to ensure that the process of reform does not bring with it real and sustained losses of income. In that it has been remarkably successful.

It is therefore not a major point of our case that the bureaucratic elite is a greedy, self-serving monster, gobbling up scarce consumption resources and thereby impoverishing the rest of the community. The real significance of the bureaucratic elite in the process of impoverishment is more subtle. In later chapters, we shall show that, by using its power and influence, it distorts the allocation of resources and mis-specifies the nature of goods and services to be produced. It thereby impoverishes those who are excluded from that allocation.

To take one example from the rural sector, the elite impoverishes the less efficient farmers who are deprived of support services by the output-maximizing algorithm so wholeheartedly espoused by the bureaucracy, which judges itself by its ability to increase output (we shall examine other examples in Chapters 12 and 13). But it also impoverishes, in relative terms, those who legitimately aspire to join the elite and share its substantial privileges, but who find they are excluded by the processes of selection and exclusion we shall examine in more detail in Chapters 9 and 10. In both absolute and relative terms, then, this elite is one of the foremost of the poverty makers. In the next chapter, we see how far the same description can be applied to two other urban groups.

NOTES

1. Most recent sources for Africa are well summarized in J.M. Wober, *Aspirations: Africans' Ideas About Education and Work,* Occasional Paper no. 3 (Kampala: Makerere University, 1971). A useful source for Ivory Coast not mentioned by Wober is *Rapport de synthese sur les opinions et attitudes des paysans et ouvriers ivoiriens vis-a-vis du developpement* (Abidjan: Ministere du plan, Institut d:Ethnologie, Societe d'etudes techniques et financieres, 1972). For Asia, see Murad bin Mohd. Noor, *Lapuran: jawatankuasa di atas kajian pendapat mengenai pelajaran dan masyarakat (lapuran keciciran)* (Report on the "Study of opinion about education and society") (Kuala Lumpur: Ministry of Education, 1973); International Labour Organization, *Matching Employment Opportunities and Expectations: A Programme of Action for Ceylon,* report of an inter-agency team organized by the ILO and financed by the United Nations Development Programme (Geneva: ILO, 1971).

2. Jael D. Barkan, "African University Students and Social Change: An Analysis of Student Opinion in Ghana, Tanzania and Uganda," doctoral dissertation, University of California at Los Angeles, 1970.

3. M. Singer, *The Emerging Elite: A Study of Political Leadership in Ceylon* (Cambridge, Mass.: MIT Press, 1964); J.E. Goldthorpe, *An African Elite: Makerere College Students, 1922-60* (Nairobi: Oxford University Press for the East African Institute of Social Research, 1965).

4. *Report of the Committee on Africanisation of Commerce and Industry in Uganda* (Entebbe: Government Printer, 1968).

5. *Commissions of Enquiry into State Enterprises* (Accra, 1964, 1968, 1969); *The Common Man's Charter* (Entebbe: Government Printer, 1970); President Kaunda's attack on "the intelligentsia," reported by the *Times of Zambia,* December 1970; P.G. Packard, "Management and Control of Parastatal Organisations," in *Towards Socialist Planning,* Uchumi Editorial Board (Dar es Salaam: Tanzania Publishing House, 1972).

6. E.A. Ochieng, "High Level Manpower Planning in Uganda," master's thesis, Makerere University, 1973.

7. M. Abdel-Fadil, *Employment and Income Distribution in Egypt, 1952-1970*, Discussion Paper (Norwich: University of East Englia, 1974).

8. A. Ghoneim, "On the Issue of the New Class in Egypt," *Al-Tala'ia* 4, no. 2 (February 1968).

9. *Socio-Economic Sample Survey of Households: Malaysia, 1967-68* (Kuala Lumpur: Department of Statistics, 1970).

10. Ibid., p. 13.

11. The best empirical investigation of this is *Zambian Manpower* (Lusaka: Government Printer, 1967).

12. *Report of the Commission Appointed to Review the Grading Structure of the Civil Service, Under the Chairmanship of Mr. Justice Whelan* (Lusaka: Government Printer, 1966), p. 16.

13. Marc Blaug, R. Layard, and M. Woodhall, *The Causes of Graduate Unemployment in India* (London: Allen Lane, 1969).

14. R.H. Green, "Income Distribution Policy," paper for Mid-Plan Review: Working Party I and IV, mimeo. (Dar es Salaam, 1971), p. 3.

15. *Report of the Commission on the Structure and Remuneration of the Public Services in Ghana* (Accra: Government Printer, 1967), pp. 27-28.

16. *Report of Enquiry into the Mining Industry, 1966* (The Brown Report) (Lusaka: Government Printer, 1966).

17. J.B. Knight, "The Determinants of Wages and Salaries in Uganda," *Bulletin of the Oxford University Institute of Economics and Statistics,* August 1967, p. 257.

18. *Survey of Employment and Earnings, 1970* (Dar es Salaam: Bureau of Statistics, Ministry of Economic Affairs and Development Planning, 1972), p. 21.

19. See Patrick O'Brien, *The Revolution in Egypt's Economic System: From Private Enterprise to Socialism, 1952-1965* (London: Oxford University Press for Royal Institute for International Affairs, 1966), p. 205.

20. *Follow-up Report of the First Five Year Plan* (Cairo: Ministry of Planning, 1966), quoted in Abdel-Fadil, op. cit.

21. *Establishment Circular B. 275,* June 26, 1966, quoted in Whelan Report, op. cit., p. 10.

The top bureaucratic elite is tiny in Africa and small in Asia. In numerical terms, the addition of the more substantial local entrepreneurs makes a perceptible, rather than dramatic, difference. The significance of these two groups derives less from their numbers than from their power and influence—in economic, political, and social terms. They are the establishment whose non-resistance, if not co-operation, is a necessary condition of change in, or even survival of, the basic institutions and relationships of the modern urban economy.

In this chapter, we examine three quite separate occupational groups: middle- and lower-level white-collar workers (clerical and sales); skilled blue-collar workers; and finally, much more shortly, unskilled workers employed in the formal sector. Analytically, we must do two operations at once. First, we must ask how far these groups are themselves involved in the processes by which the poor are impoverished. Second, we must ask how they are manipulated and controlled by the ruling groups, of which the larger property owners (domestic and foreign) and the bureaucratic elite are the two most significant. For in terms of our frame, the groups with which we are concerned here is, as it were, in the middle of the system. They aspire upwards and may feel that they are powerless vis-a-vis the topmost elites. But simultaneously, so we shall argue, they are themselves compromised in a set of relationships that have the effect of reinforcing the poverty of the poor.

It is clear that these groups are cardinal in the process of economic development as conceived (usually implicitly) in national development plans. Without them, industrialization and the modernization of institutions is impossible, even if a high level of dependence on non-nationals is acceptable. Accordingly, the manipulation of access cones in such a way as will meet the projected demand (net of foreigners) becomes enshrined as an important part of policy. Manpower surveys are made, manpower projections are prepared (usually by Western experts of varying degrees of competence), education and training plans are in theory made mutually consistent. These normally (in our experience universally) ignore non-formal, non-Western institutions and traditional training environments, and concentrate large quantities of resources on replicating the more prestigious Western-style institutions: e.g., universities rather than technical colleges; agricultural colleges rather than model farms at the appropriate technical level and scale; teaching hospitals rather than rural health clinics with minimal teaching provision. More particularly, since they provide the basic feedstock for these tertiary institutions, secondary and primary schools are expanded to a point at which they may be absorbing 5 percent or more of GDP.

After a period, usually rather short, of intense scarcity of this level of manpower in quantitative terms and another period, usually rather longer, of some qualitative shortcoming, adequate supplies of manpower become available. It is at this point that the ruling elites in general, and the politicians in particular, are faced with a seemingly insurmountable problem. Having widened the access cone (or having provided quite new ones) to promote "development," they find that these access cones cannot be reduced at an acceptable political cost. Although clearly an immediate waste of economic resources and potentially a social and political threat of the greatest magnitude, the production of a surplus of those with qualifications at this level simply cannot be corrected.

Various devices are then employed to meet the situation—from guaranteed employment of university graduates in Egypt to attempts to reimpose control on access, as in Tanzania. These are not successful, partially because they are internally inconsistent and partially because they conflict with the structure (and sometimes changes in the structure) of rewards. To put it at its simplest, it is politically difficult to close access cones when the differentials between "bowls" are high; it is even more difficult when such differentials are rising. The political problem is then to secure confidence in a system in permanent and deepening imbalance. We shall argue that this is a problem that has not been solved in any of the countries we have examined; in some it is a problem that is now becoming uncontainable.

With this basic frame in mind, let us now review the data. We deal first with the structure and incomes of sales and clerical workers—middle- and lower-level white-collar employees. We then turn to blue-collar workers, dealing first with the skilled and semi-skilled and concluding with a short consideration of the unskilled.

CLERICAL AND SALES WORKERS

Usually lacking university training or higher professional qualifications, middle-level white-collar workers are the products of secondary education (when the labour market is in equilibrium) who comprise at the most junior level clerks and stenographers, and, at the more senior level, the middle echelons of management. Usually urban in residence (and almost invariably urban in consumption patterns), this group no less than the top elite results from the processes of industrialization and modernization. Mobile within their categories, the limits of mobility are nonetheless well defined for those in this group. If they lack appropriate educational qualifications, they may be unable to to aspire to the heights of the administrative or technical pyramid, especially after the period of educational scarcity has passed. They can then readily find themselves, even early in their lives, at a dead end.

At the lower end of the scale they may be economically little differentiated from skilled manual workers. This often has the result of making the junior white-collar worker more conscious of his supposedly superior status, more determined to emphasize that status by his consumption pattern, his choice of friends, his place of residence, and his aspirations for his children. At least some of these drives make him espouse, almost aggressively, Western styles of consumption and behaviour. He is the target of the bulk of consumer advertising. He is more likely than the manual worker to cut himself off from his village roots and seek security in his urban environment, and particularly in his employment, rather than in kin groups based in the village.

It is this security of employment, and therefore of consumption and status, that makes the middle-level white-collar worker the cynosure of secondary school leavers. For as we emphasized in the last chapter, study after study of the expectations and aspirations of secondary school leavers has shown that they aspire (but do not necessarily expect to reach) to the ranks of middle-level white-collar workers. And the principal attraction is less the level of salary than its security. In this respect, the civil or teaching services are preferred to the private sector. It is not often that a civil servant or teacher is dismissed. Even if, job for job, the level of salaries is lower, the moral certainty of continued employment, at a salary that (at least in money terms) is likely to rise gently, with the added attraction of a pension at the end of one's career, makes the civil service a natural choice for secondary school leavers, who want, perhaps above anything else, to leave forever peasant agriculture and the village environment.

In this group we shall also include primary school teachers. It is still relatively rare for primary school teachers to have completed the full cycle of secondary education, and have received a two-year teacher training course. Nonetheless, they fit better into this group than into the two remaining groups we shall be considering. They enjoy greater security of employment. They have been able, in most countries, to greatly improve their terms and conditions of service. They tend to identify much more readily with the lower end of middle-level white-collar workers than with manual workers. One great difference is that primary school teachers are not as urban-centered as are middle-level white-collar workers. Since independence, all the countries under study have greatly increased the number of rural primary schools. While it often remains true, as we shall see in a later chapter, that metropolitan and urban areas are better served proportionately, the great majority of primary school teachers now live and work in rural rather than urban areas. Sociologically and to some extent economically, this separates them from middle-level white-collar workers, but they remain much closer to that group than to the farmers and peasants in the rural areas.

The figures in Table 8.1 can again only be taken as orders of magnitude. They are liable in general to be underestimates as a result of the inadequate coverage of labour enumerations. The figures for sales workers in Ghana give an exceptional but salutary reminder of how inadequate that coverage can be. It is, however, clear at a glance that this group is very much bigger than the elite groups and that, apart from primary teachers, it is growing at rates varying between 2.5 and 6.5 percent a year. The rapid expansion of education in the post-independence period is reflected in much higher rates of growth of the numbers of primary teachers.

How far are expatriates included in the groups enumerated in the Tables 8.1 and 8.2? This is an important question if we are correct in believing that the presence of expatriates tends to reinforce the processes by which privileges are protected. The number of African non-nationals in these groups in African countries is surprisingly high, but that of Europeans moderate except for countries of particular educational deprivation or those that have given a low priority to localization.. The case of Ivory Coast, with its net increase in the number of expatriates employed in the middle-level white-collar group, is extreme. This example of increased dependence as a result of both high rates of economic growth and a prolonged insistence on the maintenance of perhaps inappropriately high standard is in obvious contrast to Tanzania and, in some ways a less auspicious example, Uganda.

If we ask for the origin of this group in educational terms, Table 8.2 shows a fairly broad spectrum within any particular country. At the clerical level, an educational surplus country such as Sri Lanka has a much higher level than, say, Ghana. This contrast is less marked at the sales level, partly because this includes low-level skills in the informal sector and partly because by its nature the educational requirements of this group are lower.

In what sense is this a privileged group? If we take the major privileges to be above-average income insulated from inflation, an incremental scale, obligatory

TABLE 8.1

Number and Growth of White-Collar Workers

Country	Occupation	Period	Number in Last Ob- served Year	Average Annual Rate of Growth (percent)
Uganda	Primary teachers	1959-71	22,558	6.2
	"second level"	1963-67	8,600	4.2
Zambia	Primary teachers	1964-70	12,200	8.7
	Clerical, sales, and technical workers	1964-70	43,000	6.4
Ghana	Clerical workers	1960-69	54,341	2.6
	Sales workers	1964-69	5,613	5.1
	Primary and middle school teachers	1963-69	47,877	7.0
Ivory Coast	Lower-grade white- collar workers	1963-70	15,216	4.3
Sri Lanka	Clerical and allied workers	1963-69	139,650	2.8
	Sales workers	1963-69	238,640	1.9
Philippines	Clerical, office, and related workers	1958-68	412,200	7.8
	Salesmen and related	1958-68	937,400	4.7

Sources:

Uganda   E.O. Ochieng, "High Level Manpower Planning in Uganda," master's thesis, University of Makerere, 1973.

Zambia   *Manpower Report* (Lusaka: Government Printer, 1966); *Zambian Manpower* (Lusaka: Government Printer, 1969); Second National Development Plan (Lusaka: Government Printer, 1970).

Ghana   *Labour Statistics* (Accra: Central Bureau of Statistics, annual); 1960 Population Census (Accra: Central Bureau of Statistics, 1963).

Ivory Coast   *Statistiques Repartition de la main d'oeuvre au Cote d'Ivoire* (Abidjan: Office de la main d'oeuvre, 1963-70).

Sri Lanka   *Preliminary Report on the Socio-economic Survey of Ceylon, 1969-70* (Colombo: Department of Census and Statistics, October 1971).

Philippines   Melinda M. Bacol, "Inter-Generational Occupational Mobility in the Philippines," *Philippine Sociological Review* 19, nos. 3, 4 (1971): 192.

TABLE 8.2

Tanzania, Ghana, Sri Lanka: Education of Clerical and Sales Workers
(percentages)

Occupation and Education	Tanzania (1967)	Ghana (1960)	Sri Lanka (1963)
Clerical workers			
No schooling	3.3	0.9	0.4
Primary school*	57.4	69.5	49.4
Secondary school	36.5	21.0	47.3
Post-secondary	2.8	8.6	0.7
Unspecified	—	—	2.2
Total	100.0	100.0	100.0
Sales workers			
No schooling	34.8	79.9	6.0
Primary school*	57.4	18.5	82.6
Secondary school	7.4	1.3	5.9
Post-secondary	0.4	0.3	0.1
Unspecified	—	—	5.4
Total	100.0	100.0	100.0

*Includes Arabic and middle schools in Ghana.

Sources:

Tanzania   1967 Population Census (economically active workers by occupa-
            tion and education).

Ghana   1960 Census (selected occupations of employed persons aged 15
            and over by type of school and sex and by the three cities: Sekondi-
            Takoradi M.C., Accra M.C., Kumasi M.C.).

Sri Lanka   1963 Population Census (educational profiles of occupational cate-
            gories, 1963).

membership in a social security system, some kind of organization for the protection of workers' interests, and, perhaps most important of all, ability to
compete in a non-saturated labour market, then we must distinguish sharply
between clerical workers and sales workers.

In the sales sector, the situation varies greatly. This is partly because a much
higher proportion of the sales sector is privately owned; partly because unionization is less far advanced; partly because the level of skill involved is usually
lower; and partly because the definition of the sales sector is somewhat vague
anyway, spanning sales staff of state importing agencies to family assistants on
a market stall. In Sri Lanka, for example, the shop workers and storekeepers of
Colombo are well organized and have achieved considerable advances of income

and benefits, including the coveted "thirteenth month." But the union does not cover all shop workers in Columbo, much less in the rest of the island. Family assistants and hired labour in small establishments may thus have neither the security nor the income enjoyed by their fellow workers in larger, urban establishments.

Such a range of economic and social status is not, of course, confined to Sri Lanka. Such countries as Ghana and Cameroon, with a long tradition of traders or "mammies," introduce a further complication. For some of these traders, lacking even modest educational qualifications, are able to earn incomes and build up a capital stock that, in those terms—but in virtually no others—puts them on a par with the bureaucratic elite.[1] Others, of course, earn very little and regard trading as a stop-gap to eke out a living between jobs.

Within this group, then, we begin to encounter the first elements of those who have none of the privileges we have identified. How far this "submerged" group is picked up in the data of Table 8.1 is far from clear. The large discrepancy in the figures for Ghana—with the census revealing all sales workers and the labour enumerations tracing only those in registered establishments—gives an idea of the order of magnitude of this group. To them we shall return.

For the moment, our purpose is to emphasize the distinction between those employed in larger establishments, who generally have conditions of employment that compare with the lower end of the spectrum of clerical workers, and those who, servicing the "informal" retail and wholesale trade, have few privileges indeed. They are the vanguard of the poor. But their very presence constitutes a threat to the "established" sales workers. There is here an element of intra-group competition for employment in the formal sector. We know very little about upward mobility within the sales sector, but the wide range (and rather low median) of education revealed in Table 8.2 suggests that lack of formal education is less a barrier to entry here than in the clerical grades. Other barriers doubtless exist—notably tribal and kin connections in West Africa (perhaps in Cameroon even more than in Ghana) and racial origin in Malaysia and, to a lesser extent, Sri Lanka.

But within a given ethnic, tribal, or kin group, mobility seems to be freer. This suggests that the sales workers certainly do not enjoy the great benefit of the elites in competing in a market where the demand for employees outstrips the supply. To that extent, such security as they do have is much tempered, unless their tenure is protected by law—as in Egypt, Sri Lanka, and (intermittently in the last decade) Ghana, Uganda, and Zambia. The fact that they can gain such legal protection does itself constitute a major advantage.

But this raises a dilemma that will recur as we discuss other groups. If the employed sales workers are protected either by the law or by tight and effective uniozation, what effect does that have on those who might compete for their jobs? If the "established" sector is somewhat insulated from the market, does the "informal" sector pay the price? A good example of such a process would be the "established" sales sector, securing rapid rises in income—and thereby constricting the growth of employment in the sector. We shall show that, in general, this does not seem to have happened except in the one case where legal protection and vigorous unionization have given the "established" sector a most unusual degree of monopoly power. In all other cases, on the slender and ambiguous evidence available, it seems that the "openness" of the employment in the established sector has been maintained—with predicatably unwelcome results for employees.

As far as clerical workers are concerned, in nearly all the countries in Table 8.1 the market situation has changed from one of relative scarcity to one of chronic surplus. As we suggested in the first paragraphs of this chapter, this poses a major problem for governments. Some countries have tried to respond to this situation by reducing or even reversing the rate of expansion. For instance, in Uganda, John Smythe has shown that in every postwar education development plan there has been overfulfillment of secondary education targets. In his view, both colonial and independent governments have needed "to establish visible evidence of . . . ultimate worth to the populace." Given widespread popular demand for education, particularly secondary education, targets have had to be consistently ignored.[2] This continues.* The Third Development Plan reduced the planned rate of increase of secondary school enrolments in 1971—but, revealingly, failed to reduce the actual rate.

Tanzania, not represented in the table because the data are inadequate, faced an emergent school leaver employment problem and proclaimed the policy of expanding enrolments in line only with the demand for educated manpower. But again the poltics of expansion have ensured that in fact enrolments have risen ahead of manpower demand.[3] In Ghana, the popular political demand for education was overpowering; any suggestion that enrolments should be reduced was greeted with hostility by the teaching profession and politically conscious public alike.[4] The result is well known. Particularly after the post-Nkrumah retrenchment, the employment possibilities for middle school leavers and secondary school drop-outs have become severely restricted, and there is some evidence that, in the north at least, parents are no longer so willing to make what now appears to be a high-risk investment in educating their sons.

But perhaps the best example of this particular problem is Sri Lanka. We shall return to a more detailed consideration in Chapters 10 and 11, but for the moment we can observe that very low rates of growth of employment creation in these categories in Sri Lanka have gone along with the rapid expansion of

---

*Or did until the Amin coup; no reliable education data are now available. Temporary shortages of teachers are said to be imposing a real constraint.

education. For many years now, the fundamental disequilibrium has been apparent.[5] But neither major party has been able to suggest that expansion, even at the university level, should cease. Indeed, as we shall see later, the irony of the situation is that government's desire to reduce inequalities in access to and performance in education—a desire seemingly shared by much of the electorate—makes expansion the more unstoppable.

The failure of governments to control access has two effects. First, it ensures the continuation of a surplus supply of persons educated at these levels and looking for this type of job. It thus increases the relative privilege of those who can secure employment at these levels. More fundamental, and perhaps in the long run more damaging, this relative privilege, precisely because it is so vulnerable, has the effect of building into the system political resistance to changes in education, in terms of both quality and quantity, and changes in the structure of effort and reward.* From the structured inequities that result comes the beginning of the identification of group interest and *perhaps* ultimately of class interest. The re-direction of resources to the poor or the rapid and radical dismantling of differentials can then only be achieved with the greatest difficulty.

The very scrappy evidence certainly suggests that clerical grades (on which we have better data) have protected their real incomes, partly by greater success than the bureaucratic elite in forcing up rates, and partly by devices similar to those the elites have used, such as seniority scales, promotions, and fringe benefits. Only in the Philippines, as we shall see, is there any persuasive evidence that real incomes fell significantly.

Let us illustrate these points. In Uganda, it was clear by the late 1960s that the supply of young people able to meet the educational requirements of this group was growing faster than job opportunity. And yet, between 1965 and 1970 the money income of senior clerical officers increased by 3.7 percent a year and of pool stenographers by 4.2 percent a year. In Zambia, over a slightly later period but again then the extreme educational bottlenecks had begun to break, the money incomes of clerical officers in the civil service (requiring a modest performance at "O" level) increased by 3.3 percent a year. In Kenya, the same general pattern emerges, and only in Tanzania is there some (inconclusive) evidence that the increases in the money income in the public sector of

---

*The classic example of such resistances is Sri Lanka, where the ILO mission's recommendations on educational reform were opposed less by the educational planners than by local politicians, who saw in them a threat to existing employees and to the privileges that new recruits would prospectively enjoy; see below, p. 239. On the "stickiness" of wages in over-supplied labour markets, see below, p. 239.

this group have been less than 2 percent a year. In Ghana, the money incomes of this skill group in the public sector seem to have increased at the same rate as salaries of the high-level skilled. Despite occasional exceptions, such as primary school teachers in Zambia (who increased their money income through the 1960s by nearly 9 percent a year), the general pattern that emerges is that the money incomes of this group rose slightly faster than those of the high-level elite in the public sector.

The mechanisms at work in the public sector are very similar to those we saw in the last chapter; indeed, in most countries the clerical and bureaucratic elites have the same negotiating and/or arbitration machinery in the shape of independent or semi-independent enquiries into the pay and conditions of all monthly-paid employees. That largely accounts for the familiar pattern, but it is worth emphasizing that in most African countries the structure of awards in the public sector usually was designed to raise the lower wages and salaries more than the higher ones. This same pattern can be detected in Ghana, Zambia, Uganda, Tanzania, and Ivory Coast.

But this desire, motivated at least in part by a realization of the actual or possible political strength of this group, was moderated by a realization of the financial cost of generous wage settlements to groups growing very rapidly in volume. More particularly, many governments pointed out, either in evidence to commissions or subsequent white papers, that higher current expenditures jeopardized the level of capital expenditures, both because they absorbed present resources and because they raised the implied future commitment of current expenditures, associated with any capital project. In Cameroon, Tanzania, and Ghana from 1966, the extreme scarcity of public resources has been the major official justification for low awards that may have strained confidence to the limit among many junior civil servants.

In Sri Lanka, the rate of growth of money income of this group has been extremely slow in the public sector and somewhat less slow in the private sector. A significant proportion of the labour force in these skill groups in Sri Lanka is covered by two unions well known for the political orientation. Their effectiveness is demonstrated by their ability to withstand market pressures and to increase the money and real income of this group at a time of a gross over-supply of young persons with secondary education.

In the private sector, the data are inferior in quantity and quality but, except perhaps for the immediate post-independence period in those eastern African countries marked by both educational unreadiness and the post-independence boom, the rate of growth of private sector salaries was probably only slightly higher than that of the public sector. There is little evidence here, then, of a major shift of resources from other sections of the community to this particular group, except in so far as the size of the group was growing.

Given the rather modest increases in money incomes and the price changes shown in Table 7.6 in the previous chapter, what is the likely pattern of real incomes? The real incomes of individuals in this group are unlikely to have declined. As a result of incremental scales and fringe benefits and, perhaps most important in Africa until the end of the 1960s, as a result of opportunities for accelerated promotion (at least for those prepared to move from one job to another), most persons within these groups are likely to have at least maintained their real income levels.

The one country where this seems to be less true is the Philippines. According to the BCS data, the average money incomes of clerical, office, and related workers increased by about 3.5 percent a year over the same period. This increase may, however, be something of an illusion, for inspection of the data suggests that the bulk of the increase has accrued to a rather limited group in the financial sector, most of whom are university graduates. If we take out this group and concentrate on retail sales workers, for instance, the increase disappears almost entirely. Real incomes are therefore likely to have fallen quite sharply.

The fact that there is no evidence in the data for a major redistribution of purchasing power to this group would suggest that, like the elites we described in the previous chapter, this group has seen differentials with the low-paid fall over time. Table 8.3 shows this to have been happening in those countries for which we have adequate time series. On the one hand, the differentials with the elite groups contracted; on the other, the differentials with the low-paid have been reduced, although, as one would expect, not quite so quickly.

It is dangerous to compare the differentials between countries because the precise level at which the ratios are calculated varies according to what reliable data are available. Perhaps oddly, it does not seem that the differentials in francophone Africa are very much higher than anywhere else. This seems to be the result of two factors. The first is the high level of expatriate salaries in francophone Africa and the effect that these and the "code du travail" have had on local salary scales at this level. Although too much should not be made of such comparison, it is not without interest that a secondary school teacher in Ivory Coast is paid two and a half times as much as a judge in Ghana. Second, as we shall see later, minimum wages in Ivory Coast, and to a lesser extent in Cameroon, increased rapidly in the 1950s, decelerated in the early 1960s, but rose rapidly to 1973. This pressure on the differential from the bottom has been enough to maintain seemingly average differentials.

To summarize the argument on these two groups, then, it is that a rising supply of adequately qualified manpower has sharpened intra-group competition. This is a point to which we shall return in Chapter 10, but for the moment we emphasize that, with the exception of the Philippines, this competition does not seem to have reduced real incomes. Differentials between

TABLE 8.3

Differentials—Ratios of Salaries of the Bureaucratic Elite, Middle-Level White-Collar, and Low-Income Groups

Country and Occupation	Dates	
Uganda	1961	1971
Civil service grade 3/pool stenographer	3.7	2.6
Pool stenographer/minimum wage	5.6	5.0
Tanzania		1971
Managerial and administrative/clerical		3.7
Clerical/Dar es Salaam minimum wage		2.7
Zambia	1961	1971
Clerical officer/minimum wage	4.5	3.9
Ghana	1961	1970
Senior civil service grades/middle school teachers	3.6	4.0
Middle school teachers/minimum wage	3.3	3.3
Ivory Coast		1971
Managers/secretaries, nurses (public sector)		3.6
Secretaries, nurses/minimum wage		3.2
Cameroon		1972
Upper professionals/qualified manpower		5-7.5
Qualified/unskilled		3.0
Sri Lanka	1948	1967
Civil service class 1, grade 1/primary teachers	6.7	4.9
Primary teachers/unskilled general workers	3.1	2.3
Philippines	1965	1971
Professional, technical/clerical	1.8	1.1
Clerical/manual labourers	2.3	2.4

Sources:

Uganda   Establishment lists as reproduced in *Annual Estimates of Recurrent Expenditure* (Entebbe).

Tanzania   M.A. Bienefeld and R.H. Sabot, *The National Urban Mobility Employment and Income Survey of Tanzania* (Dar es Salaam: Economic Research Bureau, University of Dar es Salaam, September 1972).

Zambia   Development Division of the Office of the Vice-President, *Zambian Manpower* (Lusaka: Government Printer, 1969); *Report of the O'Riordan Salaries Commission* (1971).

Ghana   Data from Public Services Advisory Board.

Sri Lanka   ILO, *Matching Employment Opportunities and Expectations: A Programme of Action for Ceylon,* report of an inter-agency team organized by the International Labour Organization (Geneva: ILO, 1971).

Philippines   *Family Income and Expenditures,* 1965 and 1971, the BCS Survey of Households Bulletin (Manila: Bureau of the Census and Statistics).

Ivory Coast   Ministere de l'enseignement technique et de la formation professionnelle et Ministere du plan, *Le secteur prive et para-public en Cote d'Ivoire, 1971* (Abidjan, 1972).

Cameroon   Ministere du plan, *La main d'oeuvre salariee permanente en Republique du Cameroun, 1971* (Yaounde, 1971); Direction des Statistiques, *Enquete emploi 1972-73* (Yaounde, 1973, confidential in June 1973).

rates, but not necessarily between individual incomes, have been reduced for both the elite and the unskilled. They are, however, still large—at a time when supply already exceeds demand at this level in nearly all countries. The neo-classical economist may say that the market is responding to a basic imbalance. The structuralist will say-that it is doing so only very slowly and that there are already well-entrenched interests to ensure that it does not adjust rapidly.

We shall see these themes better illustrated in the next section.

SKILLED AND SEMI-SKILLED BLUE-COLLAR WORKERS

If the group of sales workers includes the tip of the pyramid of non-privileged groups, it does not follow that skilled blue-collar workers, usually ranked below clerical and sales workers in occupational tables, should also be included among the non-privileged. Quite the contrary. Despite lack of secondary education (see Table 8.4), the *skilled* blue-collar workers include some highly privileged groups in terms of job security, skill scarcity, rate of increase of wages, access to social consumption, and urban residence. These are workers who have undergone some formal training, had long experience in highly technical jobs, and whose accumulation of skill is literally indispensable to the smooth functioning of industrial plants. At the other extreme are young men with no formal training. These have picked up the initial elements of skill or craft on the job, largely by a process of observation and emulation. They are differentiated from the unskilled only by their ability to handle a small part of a production or engineering process. It is this heterogeneity that makes this group difficult to analyse.

The crucial distinction within the group is between skills that take a moderately high level of formal education, some formal training, and particularly a substantial length of time on the job to perfect the necessary practical abilities, on the one hand, and on the other, those that can be achieved quite quickly. (But not all skilled workers necessarily have a high level of formal education; Margaret Peil's Ghanaian sample of factory workers suggests the reverse.[6]) Concretely, this skill distinction is the distinction between the leading electrical maintence engineer on the production line or in a mine, on the one hand, and the technical illiterate with grease on his hand on the other. By definition, the supply of the former cannot be increased quickly; the supply of the latter is high elastic.

As we shall see, the markets are not, in fact, as mutually independent as this suggests, but this distinction is crucial from the perspective of differentiation.

TABLE 8.4

Tanzania, Ghana, Sri Lanka: Education of Skilled
Blue-Collar Workers
(percentages)

Education	Tanzania[a] (1967)	Ghana[b] (1960)	Sri Lanka[c] (1963)
No Schooling	27.4	48.5	12.3
Primary[d]	68.8	48.5	77.3
Secondary	3.3	2.2	5.3
Post-secondary	0.5	0.8	0.1
Unspecified			5.4
Total	100.0	100.0	100.4

[a]Process workers include those working in textile, textile processing, leather, metal, electrical, woodwork, construction, printing, food, beverages, chemical industries.

[b]Includes workers in transport and communications, craftsmen, service, sport, and recreation workers.

[c]Includes workers in transport and communications; craftsmen; production process workers and labourers; service, sport, and recreation workers.

[d]Includes Arabic and middle schools in Ghana.

Sources:

Tanzania	1967 Population Census (economically active workers by occupation and education.
Ghana	1960 Census (selected occupations of employed persons aged 15 and over by type of school and sex and by the three cities: Sekondi-Takoradi M.C., Accra M.C., Kumasi M.C.).
Sri Lanka	1963 Population Census (educational profiles of occupational categories, 1963).

For it implies two things. First, the highly skilled group is still small in all the countries we have studied. Precise figures are extremely difficult to pin down, because of differences in definition and problems of enumeration. But the man-power survey of 1966 found only 6,600 in Uganda, and a more limited one in Ghana of 1963 found only 4,700 in the three major sectors of mining, manu-facturing, and construction. In Ivory Coast, the 1963 survey found only 3,000 foremen and nearly 9,000 skilled men, and in Tanzania an incomplete survey found only 3,500 highly skilled manual workers in 1963. In Zambia, the group was, of course, bigger, and a more comprehensive survey (and a less restrictive definition) counted 31,000 skilled *and semi-skilled* artisans in 1964.

Small though this group of highly skilled manual workers in Africa was at independence, it included a significant proportion of non-citizens. An extreme example is again Ivory Coast, with fewer than 25 percent of foremen being Ivory Coast citizens in 1963. Only slightly more than three quarters of all skilled blue-collar workers were citizens in the same year. Ten years later, the picture was confused. In general, low-skill jobs at this level had been almost universally Africanized, but supervisory and high-skill jobs were to varying degrees still per-formed by Europeans—in Ivory Coast, 55 percent of foremen were Europeans in 1970. In Cameroon, 30 percent of foremen were Europeans in 1972. In Zambia, there were—in absolute terms—more Europeans employed in the construction industry than there had been in 1967. Even in mining, the pro-portion of Europeans to Africans had declined little. There is little evidence, then, of excess supply at this level.

But attempts to increase supply and change the structure of demand were well under way. Political pressure in all East African countries had found more efficient expression in the control of work permits and the functioning of joint government-private sector working parties. Employers had begun to seek more actively to redesign job specifications to ensure that Africans were promoted as rapidly as their skills allowed and that Europeans were employed only out of genuine necessity. Thus by 1971 Africanization was complete in Tanzania in such jobs as painting and plastering, but had hardly begun in radio repair and precision instrument maintenance.

There can be little doubt that governments played a significant and perhaps even major role in thus trying to widen access cones. In this they were respond-ing to urban grass-roots pressures. For those citizens with the beginnings of a skill were increasingly impatient, both of demanding European supervisors and of promotion chances blocked by colonial left-overs. Party conferences, com-missions of enquiry, and the correspondence columns of newspapers are replete with articulate and even aggressive protests, not only against racial income dif-ferentials but also at the survival, ten or fifteen years after independence, of pre-independence relationships at work. Under this kind of pressure, anglophone governments were in general ready to sacrifice efficiency, especially in the public and parastatal sectors. Where the political threat was real, immediate, and vocal, the efficiency algorithm was jettisoned. In Ivory Coast and Cameroon, by contrast, the political threat was much less real, not because racial domination was less resented but rather because the political structures were less open to hear such resentment expressed and less responsive to such as was expressed.

The effect has been to greatly increase employment of nationals in skilled jobs and, to a lesser extent, by job fragmentation to raise the demand for semi-skills rather than skills. But in Africa, although not in Asia, it is at the semi-skilled rather than the skilled level that we again encounter surplus labour. The problem here does not arise from the fact that governments have consciously increased access, except in to far as they have expanded education. Indeed, we shall see later that formal training institutions at this level (as opposed to the highly skilled and elite) usually have been meagre in quantity and quality. Much of the semi-skilled labour force is self-taught, often in the informal sector. Because competition for employment is less severe with some skill rather than with none (and less severe still if, as is not unusual, the worker has a number of semi-skills), there is every incentive to acquire at least the rudiments of a trade. The expansion of semi-skills has thus largely been an autogenerative process, more vigorous in some countries than in others.

As such, it has brought political problems with it. In 1963 in Ivory Coast, over half of the semi-skilled jobs were taken by non-Ivorien Africans. This represented a continuation of the tradition of the importation of manual workers from the north. Originally regarded as a source of agricultural labour, as industrialization proceeded many of these Voltaiques and Malis had come to occupy semi-skilled jobs. This has shown little sign of changing despite earlier riots against Dahomeyans and Togos. Between 1963 and 1970, the proportion of semi-skilled jobs held by non-Ivorien Africans remained virtually unchanged. In Upper Volta, the proportion of semi-skilled, skilled, and foremen's jobs held by African non-citizens doubled between 1963 and 1965.

In Ghana, by contrast, semi-skilled employment was dominated by the (citizen) Ewe, but significant numbers of skilled and semi-skilled jobs were held by (non-citizen) Voltaiques, Malis, and Togos. With the sharp contraction in employment in the mid-1960s, rapidly falling real incomes even for those in full-time employment, and an ever larger volume of middle and secondary school leavers entering the job market, the government badly needed to show that it had policies that would meet the situation. In May 1968, non-citizen Africans were required to have work permits and severely to limit their participation in the informal sector. Eighteen months later, all those without work permits were given two weeks to leave the country. Probably a quarter of a million had gone by the end of 1969, often the objects of brutal popular harassment.

But Africanization, localization, or nationalization of employment is a very limited strategy. Once aliens have been expelled and replaced by citizens, the fundamental disequilibriums begin to reappear and creep up the skill ladder as formal and informal training takes place. In bureaucratic and clerical occupations, educational levels can be raised and access cones thus reduced—although this is merely likely to transfer demand back to the educational system. In the blue-collar occupations, some limited educational selectivity may perform the same function, particularly in training institutions, but the same basic problem remains. We thus have two sets of forces. The first is intra-group competition for the education and jobs that are available; the second is the conflict between the ability of the formal sector to create jobs (essentially an economic problem) and the popular demand that education and training (with more emphasis on the former) be widely available. We shall return to the intra-group competition in Chapters 9 and 10. Before we analyse the second conflict, we must briefly review the experience of our Asian countries and changes in the income levels of these groups.

The scarcity of blue-collar skills that is still a feature of most African economies is considerably less present in the three Asian countries we have examined. Although in each country there are certain categories of workers in short supply, a longer history of industrialization, a higher level of education, and perhaps (although data on this are far from conclusive) a greater training capability have together ensured not only that this group is proportionately bigger than in the African countries but also that it can be increased more quickly. Indeed, from the fact that as many as one in three skilled workers are self-employed it follows that there is a major over-supply of this group. Data for Sri Lanka and Malaysia are less specific but the same pattern persists, namely, that a significant proportion of blue-collar skilled workers establish their own workshops or small enterprises. At the worst, these form a reserve army of the under-employed ready to go back into formal employment as employees if the chances of finding employment and the level of wages and security are substantially better than what they can achieve on their own.

The existence of this large group of self-employed is not inconsistent either with shortages of specific skills (particularly those in which training facilities have lagged behind demand) or with rising wages for skilled blue-collar workers in general.* In Sri Lanka, for instance, certain groups of skilled workers are highly unionized and have, as we shall see, achieved remarkable increases in real income. But the same workers, e.g., heavy transport drivers, are to be found in the informal sector and are, in market terms, in excess supply.

This therefore suggests that in these countries the possession of blue-collar

---

*It goes some way towards explaining somewhat *lower* rates of absolute unemployment among primary school leavers in Sri Lanka and Malaysia; see below, Chapter 11; p. 300.

skills is not by itself a guarantee of the privileges we mentioned with respect to Africa. We must make two sets of distinctions. First, we must distinguish between those who possess skills that are in general short supply and who therefore command a scarcity rent, and those who possess more generalized skills with no such scarcity. Second, we must distinguish between those who practice those skills in formal employment, particularly if they are protected by some kind of union or statutory provisions, and those who practice their skills either as self-employed or as the employees of very small family businesses that are able to ignore many of the legislative and organizational defences of the workers. The importance of these distinctions will soon become apparent.

Is the difference in structure reflected in differences in the behaviour of wages of these groups? The greater elasticity of supply would suggest that wages of semi-skilled groups would increase less rapidly than those of skilled workers. Certainly, this difference is reflected in conditions of employment. To take an extreme example from Uganda, there one favoured group of senior skilled blue-collar workers has a ten-point incremental scale and other conditions of service almost identical with those of senior white-collar workers. By contrast, semi-skilled employees were until 1970 on a daily-paid basis and as such could be fired without notice.

But has this distinction in market characteristics been reflected in the level and rate of growth of wages? For no country where we have adequate time series data is this the case. In every case that we have examined, the rate of growth of *rates* has been higher for the semi-skilled than for the highly skilled. To take two examples from East Africa: In Uganda, the annual rate of growth of the wage rates for the most senior skilled group of the public sector was 2 percent per year from 1963 to 1973; that compared with an average rate of 2.4 percent a year for a large and (so far as we can tell) representative group of semi-skilled workers. In Zambia, the average rate of growth of wages of surface artisan foremen in the copper mines from 1964 to 1972 was 6.1 percent; the very much less qualified and less highly paid group, handymen grade 1, enjoyed an average rate of increase of over 12 percent a year in the same period. Although regradings make similar comparisons difficult in the public sector in Zambia, the same broad conclusion seems secure, namely, that the more lowly paid semi-skilled workers enjoyed more rapid rates of growth in money incomes than the more skilled workers.

In Ghana, the time series are much less satisfactory, but the structure of the Mills-Odoi awards in 1967 makes it clear that the intention was precisely to give both a higher immediate award and the prospect of a higher utlimate award to the lower-paid semi-skilled workers than to the skilled.[7]

This pattern is consistent with the trend that we examined in the earlier chapter. Aware of their power as large employers, and perhaps aware of their position as wage leaders, governments were able to hold rates for skilled workers, if not constant, at least to a lower rate of growth than for semi- and unskilled workers. These represented both a direct political threat to government—as in Ghana in 1960 and 1971-72, and Zambia in 1966 and 1969—and a challenge to the government's own proclaimed desire to erode the differentials between the high-paid and the low-paid. In all the major commissions of enquiry into wages in the countries under examination, one of the major complaints of the labour force has been rising prices. In general, governments have been sympathetic to the argument, but have heavily qualified their sympathy with the observation that rising prices, particularly food prices, hit the lowest-paid hardest. Thus the Ani Salaries Commission Report of 1963 defined Uganda government policy, reaffairmed by the Mayanja Report three years later in these words:

> As existing incomes at the higher level not only afford wide scope for adjustments to meet changing circumstances, but also amply accommodate different standards of living compatible with the social standing and other commitments of the class which earns them, it will be a wise policy, consistent with the principle of narrowing the gap in the salary structure to more realistic proportions, that unless new circumstances arise of a kind which overwhelmingly compel a   review, salaries at those levels should be fixed or "pegged" over a considerable period of time; that in future additions made to incomes at the lower levels for whatever reasons, should be tapered off to nil at the highest point immediately below the line at which the top incomes are "pegged."[8]

The desire to reduce differentials and protect the living standards of the most vulnerable groups have conspired to raise the money rates (but not necessarily real incomes) of the lower-skill groups faster than the high-skill groups.

In view of the market situation, this may seem paradoxical. One would expect it to lead to a continuous drain of skilled blue-collar workers (and middle-level white-collar workers) from the public sector to the private sector. To some extent, this has indeed happened. In Ghana, in 1967 the Mills-Odoi Commission thought that the private sector was paying about 20 percent more than the public sector, and that the parastatals were paying even more than the private sector. Certainly for some specialist skills this had led to a shortage in government service, but the Commission thought it undesirable, and in the long run self-defeating, for government to enter an auction with the private sector. This indeed seems to have been a common theme. Merely increasing wages for the higher-skill groups does not increase the supply (except in the very long run), and therefore most governments have refused to be lured into a bid and counterbid situation with the private sector. Rather, they are prepared to delay localization and put up with expatriates and/or unfilled vacancies—albeit at the cost of reduced efficiency.

The stickiness of skilled workers' rates is the more surprising in view of the remaining high racial differentials at this skill level, illustrated in Table 8.5. Although governments and employers took steps to disguise these differentials by such devices as negotiating a common basic scale and paying an overseas supplement to expatriates or giving a compound bonus at the end of the contract period, the more sophisticated workers, union leaders, and (opposition) politicians could not be taken in so easily. But in francophone Africa the unions were, by the mid-1960s, of little account; the political opposition was muzzled and the workers themselves had few effective channels of protest. In Zambia, the picture was slightly less bleak and skilled workers did achieve high rates of growth of real and money income in 1965-70.

TABLE 8.5

Racial Differentials Among Skilled Workers in Africa

Country	Grade	Year	Europeans/ African Non- Citizens	Europeans/ African Citizens
Upper Volta	Qualified employees (white-collar)	1969	2.2	2.7
Cameroon	Foremen	1972	2.4*	3.9
Ivory Coast	Qualified workers (blue-collar)	1971	2.7	2.8
Zambia	Skilled workers	1965		2.2
	Supervisory skilled workers	1965		2.7
	Skilled workers	1967		1.8
	Supervisory skilled workers	1967		2.2

*This ratio is unrealistically low as non-French Europeans are included in the denominator.

Sources:

Upper Volta	Societe d'etude et de developpement economique et social, *Emploi et Formation en Haute-Volta* (Paris, 1970).
Cameroon	Direction des Statistiques, *Enquete emploi 1972-73* (Yaounde, 1973).
Ivory Coast	Ministere de l'enseignement technique et de la formation professionnelle et Ministere du Plan, *Le secteur prive et para-public en Cote d'Ivoire,* part 2 (Abidjan, 1972).
Zambia	*Report of the Commission of Inquiry into the Mining Industry, 1966* (Lusaka: Government Printer, 1966), and subsequent years of *Annual Report of the Ministry of Labour and Social Welfare* (Lusaka).

The acquiescence of the high-skill groups in the erosion of skill differentials and the consequent constancy of or even fall in their real incomes can probably be explained in the same way as that of the bureaucratic elite. For such a fall is more apparent than real, for the reasons we sketched at some length in the last chapter. Because these high-skill grades tend to be career grades, they frequently have an incremental scale (or, in francophone countries, a 1 percent per annum "prime d'anciennete"). These scales are vigorously defended by those who benefit from them, and indeed are lengthened. On the grounds that "a long scale means an adequate [sic] career for an officer," the Whelan Commission in Zambia yielded to pressure from junior civil servants to lengthen the incremental scale.[9] The same argument was used with equal effectiveness two years later before the Rogers Working Party.[10] Further, because skills are cumulative, it is often possible for all except the most senior to be re-graded within a particular occupation. Two careful studies of the relationship between length of employment and income in Ghana and Tanzania have both shown that, for men at least, seniority is rewarded. As one concluded: "The picture which emerges from this survey is of a labour force which is stable and in which experience is valued and remunerated accordingly, though . . . in the *occupational* hierarchy there are still relatively rigid education-related barriers to mobility based on experience."[11] Furthermore, because the market for skilled manpower has been in chronic shortage, the individual can protect his real income by moving from one employer to another. Even within government there is evidence of much inter-ministry mobility, often achieved with the connivance of the official regulatory body.

Can the same pattern be observed in the Asian countries we have examined? If so, how has this affected differentials with other groups? In Sri Lanka, the pattern is confused and, given the wide variance in wage rates between sector and between employer and the extremely complex system of fringe benefits and bonuses, the data must be treated with unusual caution. In Table 8.6 we present data on earnings of skilled and semi-skilled engineers between 1963 and 1969. These suggest that earnings of skilled engineers were rising somewhat faster than those of semi-skilled engineers, and that both groups were increasing their earnings faster than either the bureaucratic elite or the white-collar workers.

If we look at data over a longer period, according to public and private sector, we must be content with the distinction between skilled and unskilled. On this basis, it looks as though unskilled workers were increasing their wages faster in the public sector than skilled workers, but among larger employers, skilled workers were increasing their wages faster than unskilled workers. In either case, wages were rising faster in the private sector than in the public sector. In the case of skilled workers, this difference seems to have been a multiple of nearly two. Although there are problems of making the two series wholly

TABLE 8.6

Sri Lanka and Philippines: Blue-Collar Workers' Wages

Country and Grade	Period	Rate of Wages	Wages During Final Observed Year	Rate of Annual Growth (percent)
Sri Lanka				
Skilled engineers	1963-69	Rs/month	262	6.0
Semi-skilled engineers	1963-69	Rs/month	197	4.0
General skilled workers				
(public sector)	1953-69	Rs/month	220	3.0
General skilled workers (CMU)*	1953-69	Rs/month	261	5.7
General unskilled workers				
(public sector)	1953-69	Rs/month	175	4.5
General unskilled workers				
(CMU)*	1953-69	Rs/month	171	5.3
Philippines				
Craftsmen, production process,				
and related workers	1965-71	P/week	2,530	1.9

*CMU is the Ceylon Mercantile Union, whose rates were taken (after ILO Report Technical Paper 6) as representative of wages paid by "better employers" in the private sector.

Sources:

Sri Lanka   International Labour Organization, *Matching Employment Opportunities and Expectations: A Programme of Action for Ceylon,* report of an inter-agency team organized by the ILO (Geneva: ILO, 1971).

Philippines *Family Income and Expenditures,* 1965 and 1971, BCS Survey of Households Bulletin (Manila: Bureau of the Census and Statistics).

consistent, the general pattern of unskilled wages rising somewhat faster in the public sector but wages of skilled workers rising faster in the private sector is consistent with what we know of Sri Lankan wages policy. But the main point for the purposes of this chapter is to note that all manual workers have gained higher rises than the middle-level white-collar workers and the top elite.

In the Philippines, such fine distinctions are impossible. Data from the Bureau of Census and Statistics sample survey suggest that the money earnings of a rather wide group of craftsmen, production process workers, and a catch-all category of related workers increased by 1.9 percent a year between 1965 and

TABLE 8.7

Differentials—Ratios of Salaries of Elites, Blue-Collar Workers, and Unskilled

Country and Occupation	Dates	
Uganda	1961	1971
Civil service grade 3, local/"G" group semi-skilled	5.9	4.7
"G" group semi-skilled/Kampala minimum wage	4.4	2.3
Tanzania		1970
African managerial, administration/craftsman		4.7
Craftsman/Dar es Salaam minimum wage		1.6
Zambia	1964	1971
European rock breaker/surface foreman (copper)	10.6	6.4
Surface foreman (copper)/Lusaka minimum wage	1.2	1.6
Ghana	1958	1969
Civil service graduate/senior electrical maintenance worker	2.0	2.0
Senior electrical maintenance worker/Accra minimum wage	6.5	6.7
Ivory Coast (only Ivory Coast citizens)		1971
Upper-class professional/qualified worker		3.9
Qualified worker/unskilled labourer		2.1
Cameroon		1971
Upper-class professional/foreman, technician		3.1
Foreman, technician/unskilled labourer		1.7
Upper Volta		1969
Voltaique upper-class professional/qualified worker		7.3
Qualified worker/unskilled labourer		2.7
Philippines	1965	1971
Professional, technician/craftsman, production worker	3.4	2.2
Craftsman, production worker/manual labourer	1.3	1.2
Sri Lanka	1948	1969
Civil service class 1, grade 1/general skilled engineering worker	15.1	6.5
General skilled engineering worker/ general unskilled engineering worker	1.4	1.5

Sources:

Uganda   Establishment lists as reproduced in *Annual Estimates of Recurrent Expenditure* (Entebbe).

Tanzania   M.A. Bienefeld and R.H. Sabot, *The National Urban Mobility Employment and Income Survey of Tanzania* (Dar es Salaam: Economic Research Bureau, University of Dar es Salaam, September 1972).

Zambia   Development Division of the Office of the Vice-President, *Zambian Manpower* (Lusaka: Government Printer, 1969); *Report of the O'Riordan Salaries Commission* (1971).

1971. In fact, this is likely to underestimate the increase in the money earnings of the skilled and semi-skilled group, but not by enough to compensate for the rise in the cost of living. In absolute terms, the real incomes of both these groups seem likely to have fallen.

Data on differentials are presented in Table 8.7, but unfortunately we have no adequate time series for any of the francophone countries. Although the category "qualified workers" is wide, it is roughly equivalent to those who have passed a trade test. The relatively low differential between this group and the upper-class professionals in Ivory Coast is somewhat surprising; the much higher differential in Upper Volta would be more in accordance with what we have found hitherto. A possible explanation is that Ivorien upper-class professionals are still young and at the low end of their scales. Despite this oddity, a reasonably consistent general pattern of differentials seems to emerge from the diverse experience of all these countries. It is, as one would expect, that the differential between the elite and the skilled manual workers has fallen, although naturally at very varying rates—very slowly in Ghana, perhaps more rapidly in the Philippines. On the other hand, differentials between skilled manual workers and minimum wage earners have changed much less. The only exception seems to be Uganda, where a rather rapidly rising minimum wage has nearly halved the differential in eleven years.

Taking these two groups—middle-level white-collar workers and skilled and semi-skilled blue-collar workers—together, then, the basic pattern that seems to emerge, qualified perhaps only by the Philippines, is that money rates have risen

---

Ghana   Data from Public Services Advisory Board.

Sri Lanka   ILO, *Matching Employment Opportunities and Expectations: A Programme of Action for Ceylon,* report of an inter-agency team organized by the International Labour Organization (Geneva: ILO, 1971).

Philippines *Family Income and Expenditures,* 1965 and 1971, the BCS Survey of Households Bulletin (Manila: Bureau of the Census and Statistics).

Ivory Coast Ministere de l'enseignement technique et de la formation professionnelle et Ministere du plan, *Le secteur prive et para-public en Cote d'Ivoire, 1971* (Abidjan, 1972).

Cameroon Ministere du plan, *La main d'oeuvre salariee permenente in Republique du Cameroun, 1971* (Yaounde, 1971); Direction des Statistiques, *Enquete emploi 1972-73* (Yaounde, 1973, confidential in June 1973).

Upper Volta Societe d'etude et de developpement economique et social, *Emploi et formation en Haute-Volta* (Paris, 1970).

faster among the semi-skilled (and, as we shall presently see, the unskilled), but individual money incomes of the higher groups have in general been kept rising slowly. Trends in real terms are difficult to determine because of the inadequacies of price indexes and a higher proportion of subsistence income among some lower-income urban groups. But the better organized, more articulate, lower-income skill groups—primary school teachers, junior civil servants, at least some semi-skilled groups—have almost certainly secured significant increases in real terms of both rates and individual incomes. The major losers seem to have been:

1. Those whose seniority was not rewarded.

2. Those whose money incomes were not considered so low as to be obvious "hardship" cases.

3. Those who presented no political threat.

4. Those who could not make proper representations to the existing wage-fixing machinery.

5. Those who were reluctant to change jobs to increase their incomes.

6. Those whose skills or semi-skills became increasingly widely available, but who fulfilled conditions 2, 3, and 4.

There is no simple one-to-one relationship between these conditions and occupational groups, but in very broad terms we have argued that differentials have fallen slowly, less because money or real incomes of the privileged have fallen, but because the money incomes of the lowest-paid have risen fairly fast.

It is to a further consideration of that point that we now turn, before trying to explain the over-all picture in terms of our frame.

UNSKILLED WORKERS

In what sense is it meaningful to include unskilled workers in this consideration of privileged groups? At first sight, it would seem absurd to regard the unskilled worker as having any privileges. Particularly in developing countries, for instance, it could be argued that the unskilled worker, necessarily selling his labour in a market in chronic over-supply, is the least privileged of all urban groups. With little security of tenure, low wages, long hours, and poor working conditions, he is the paradigm case of the non-privileged. Such generalities, however, do not stand up to empirical investigation.

Table 8.8 presents rates of growth of minimum wages in money and real terms in all the countries for which we have adequate data. Although the table begs the question of what precisely is the significance of the minimum wage, in particular in countries where enforcement mechanisms are weak outside the

TABLE 8.8

Average Annual Rates of Growth of Minimum Wages

Country and Period		Average Annual Rate of Growth	
		Money Terms	Real Terms
Uganda	1949-59	8.4	
	1959-71	7.7	2.5
	1949-71	8.1	
Tanzania	1962-70	6.5	4.7
Zambia	1961-71	4.7	0.2
Ghana	1949-59	7.4	3.3
	1959-69	3.1	-4.4
	1949-69	5.1	-1.1
Sri Lanka	1952-62	2.6	
	1962-72	3.5	
	1952-72	3.1	2.5
Philippines	1951-64	2.4	1.7
	1964-73	4.3	-1.0
	1951-73	3.4	0.4
Ivory Coast	1954-60	9.7	
	1961-68	2.3	-1.4
	1968-73	9.4	6.7
Upper Volta	1954-60	15.6	
	1960-70	0.6	-3.5

Sources: Annual reports of Ministry of Labour or other body responsible for legislation.

public sector,* its interest lies in the fact that in all countries except for the Philippines the rate of growth of minimum wages in money terms has been higher, and in one or two cases much higher, than that of the other groups that we have looked at so far. This increase in money wages, often inadequate as it has been in the face of inflation, makes even unskilled labourers who are

---

*It is difficult to check how far minimum wages are in fact paid in the private sector. Labour enumerations (e.g., in Ghana, Tanzania, and Uganda) suggest that compliance is general but not universal, with lags whenever the rate is changed. But this is not very helpful as returns are made by employers who are unlikely to admit to an official body that they are breaking the law.

covered my minimum wage legislation a relatively privileged group vis-a-vis those who are not.

The argument is not that unskilled labourers on minimum wages are well off or adequately paid or able to enjoy a fully human existence; much less that real incomes have risen in every case. Sharp falls in real income of minimum wage earners are not uncommon, and in Ghana minimum wage earners were 40 percent worse off in 1969 than they had been in 1949. (On one reckoning, real wages had not increased between 1939 and 1970. But such a statement is highly misleading since it assumes consumption patterns remained unchanged.[12]) Still, they were, in common with all minimum wage earners, better off than those who did not have any legislative floor to their standard of living and who were therefore obliged to compete in an over-supplied market with no protection at all from the pressure of employers to fix a rate no higher than that required to fill the post. The gradual extension of the number of trades and sizes of establishment covered by minimum wage legislation has had the effect of increasing the number thus protected more rapidly than the rate of growth of employment alone. But even in countries where this process has gone relatively far, as in Sri Lanka, difficulties of enforcement, particularly outside the capital city, mean that a large number, and in some countries at least a majority, of unskilled employees in the formal sector are without such protection.

Of particular interest is the mix of countries in which minimum wages seem to have risen rapidly and consistently. Predictably, the Philippines, Ghana, and (since 1960) Upper Volta are not among them. Much less predictably, nor is Zambia. By contrast, Ivory Coast, Uganda, Tanzania, and Sri Lanka, all countries where minimum wages have risen fairly consistently, represent no obvious political grouping. In Ivory Coast, unions are of negligible significance and urban workers (apart, possibly, from 1958) have not posed much of a threat to the regime. At the other end of the spectrum is Sri Lanka, where unions are powerful but economic growth has been slow. It is simply not consistent with the facts to suppose that minimum wage earners achieve rising living standards only from exercise of naked power.

But it is also not consistent with the facts to suppose that economic growth alone will automatically deliver real wage rises to the unskilled. A recent survey in Malaysia, a country where unions are weak and politically divided and/or uncommitted, and where there is no minimum wage legislation, enables us to see what proportion of the relevant occupational groups are among the poorest urban dwellers. The data must be treated cautiously because they do not distinguish between the formal and informal sectors in the occupational analysis, and it is highly probable that many of the poorest service workers are self-employed in the informal sector. But, most revealing, the great bulk of the urban poverty problem in Malaysia (defined as those receiving less than SM25 per month, comprising 15.8 percent of all urban households and thus hardly an over-generous estimate) is not the self-employed, but employees. The self-employed account for less than one third of the urban poor; employees for more than one half (32.7 percent and 52.9 percent respectively).

If we may assume that the incidence of self- or "informal" employment is low among production workers, we begin to glimpse something of the cumulative effect of Malaysian labour legislation in the fact that, of those who are poor on this definition, more than one in three is a production worker. Indeed, more than one production worker in seven is poor on this definition. Many of these are in the manufacturing sector (which accounts for 15 percent of the sectoral distribution of the urban poor), but in relative terms the public utilities sector is a more obvious concentration of urban poverty (with 3.1 percent of the enumerated population but 4.4 percent of the poor). This strongly suggests that to explain the poverty of employees mainly by the activities of multinational corporations exploiting cheap labour or of unscrupulous Chinese sweat-shops is wide of the mark. For public-owned concerns are proportionately the lowest payers. And this almost certainly cannot be explained by differential skill patterns, for international comparisons suggest that public utilities are more skill-intensive than construction or the assembly-type of manufacturing that is so common in Malaysia.[13]

CONCLUSION

What conclusions, then, emerge from these two chapters on urban differentiation? Most striking is the fact that the wholly inappropriate wage and salary structure inherited from the colonial period has been modified in the post-independence period. The extent and speed of this modification naturally varies considerably from country to country. Nowhere has it been fast. It has been less rapid in francophone Africa than in anglophone Africa. It has gone further in Sri Lanka and the Philippines than in most African countries. But in no country is there evidence of differentials increasing within the formal urban sector and among those effectively covered by minimum wage legislation.

If we ask why ruling groups have been so anxious to reduce differentials by raising the income of those whose skills are already over-supplied—and thereby incidentally almost certainly adding to rural-urban migration—we have suggested that an answer based purely on the distribution of political power hardly fits the facts; the ability of interest groups to use wage-fixing machinery is at least as important. This is a form of social skill or influence that seems effective irrespective of the ideology of government or the naked actual institutional power of unions or other groups. Although any individual may feel quite powerless vis-a-vis government and its administrative machinery, this kind of social influence, often using ideological categories that no government wishes to deny, can be very effective. But it is an influence that the poorest, even in the urban areas, are unlikely to use. Although more open in fact that one might expect, these structures demand a level of social skills and articulation that most of the poor do not have. Inevitably, their case, often much stronger than those presented, goes by default. And even where it is represented by proxy, governments can ignore it purely because it is a pseudo-representation: A good example is the neglect of a suggestion in the Brown Report in Zambia that a rural development fund be financed out of the copper companies' "surplus" from using local rather than expatriate labour.[14]

The groups among which this contraction of differentials has taken place are typically less than 20 percent of the active labour force in Africa, and less than 35 percent in Asia. It is quite false, then, to deduce from these last two chapters that income has become less concentrated in the population as a whole. Furthermore, the reduction in differentials is not inconsistent with an increasing concentration of income, if the higher-income groups are growing rapidly, the original skew is marked, and the differentials are moderating slowly. Indeed, in Ghana, Malaysia, and the Philippines, these conditions have been fulfilled and there is (highly imperfect) evidence that the distribution of urban, formal sector, income has become more concentrated.[15]

But there are contrary examples, where the original elite was small, where it has not grown very rapidly, and where rates of growth of income among blue-collar workers (particularly the unskilled) have been high. In those cases, we would expect the concentration of "formal" urban income to fall. This is well attested in Sri Lanka,[16] and may have occurred in the Ivory Coast (except, perhaps, during the cocoa crisis of the mid-1960s).

Still, in all countries the reduction in differentials, achieved by the rising incomes of limited categories of manual workers, has almost certainly increased differentials both within the total (i.e., formal and informal) urban labour force and between the privileged urban groups and rural labourers and technically conservative small farmers. (The only cases where they may not be true is where real wages of even the privileged groups fell rapidly during periods of rapid inflation. Small farmers and those labourers either provided with, or able to grow, their own subsistence may during these periods have enjoyed a relative advantage, particularly if their consumption of modern sector goods was relatively limited.)

If, in general, unskilled workers have been relatively successful in inter-group competition for increased consumption resources, at whose cost has this been achieved? In the light of this chapter and the last, it is difficult to sustain the argument that it has been at the cost of more highly skilled or educated groups. There is no evidence to suggest that salaries would have risen faster if wages had risen more slowly.

More difficult is the question of profit receivers. Reliable quantitative evidence is practically non-existent, but we do not believe that wage rises in money terms have reduced profits. Indeed, the argument that they have played a part in raising productivity, especially in Africa, is persuasive, although attempts to measure this effect are not convincing. Domestic product markets in the formal sector are so imperfect that entrepreneurs have little difficulty in passing on costs, even under conditions of price control. Only where demand is highly price-elastic are total profits likely to fall. Given the modest rises in money wages we have seen and the usually small component of total costs represented by wages, increases in wage cost are unlikely much to reduce demand. Where products are sold on international markets, management is usually sufficiently sophisticated to adapt production techniques to new cost conditions and thus preserve profit margins. While we would not pretend that the empirical evidence exists for a final judgment, then, it is surely far-fetched to argue that profit receivers have paid for the rising consumption (where it has occurred) of the lower-skill groups..

We find more compelling the view that it is the excluded who have paid these costs. There are two separate arguments: One centres on employment; the other on capital expenditures.

Has the attempt by governments to increase the money incomes of the semi-skilled had an adverse effect on the creation of employment? This is a question that ought to be open to statistical analysis, but such analysis depends upon all other things remaining equal—a condition that is never fulfilled. Further, official statistics do not usually distinguish between skilled, semi-skilled, and un-skilled workers, and thus make impossible a detailed investigation of the effects of any given wage awares. However, it is clear that in Ghana, Uganda, Tanzania, and Zambia, large pay awards for the more lowly paid (usually including un-skilled workers) have been followed by either net falls in employment or marked decelerations of the rate of growth of employment. In Uganda, there is good evidence that the introduction of minimum wage legislation reduced employment of lower-income groups, especially the urban unskilled and employees of local government.[17] In Ghana in 1960 and in Zambia in 1966, large wage awards were followed by rapidly falling prices for major export crops. In the ensuing retrenchment, the higher level of wages in the public sector acted as a constraint both on employment and on capital expenditure. In Uganda, the Mayanja Board of Enquiry in 1966 drew attention to the fact that group employees (covering all manual grades) could not expect employment to rise if wages were continuously bid upwards:

The figure of 20,317 employed at the end of 1965 shows a reduction of some 5,500 on the previous year—a response presumably to the need for economy in the face of increased levels of pay and a tight

financial situation. The government's financial position has also necessitated during the last year an embargo on the filling of vacant posts.
It is highly likely, therefore, that further increases in wage levels will
have a negative effect on the numbers employed, a fact which the
public employees' union should keep firmly in mind.[18]

In the private sector, the classic defence against rising wages is substitution
of capital for labour, and an increase in the productivity of labour. Only if output rises enough to offset this increase in productivity is there likely to be an
increase in employment. Again the evidence is difficult to handle. In Uganda in
the earlier 1960s, and in the Zambian copper mines and construction industry,
such substitution and an associated deceleration of employment creation can
be seen.

It is usually the unskilled who bear the brunt of this substitution. As production becomes more capital-intensive, so it becomes more skill-intensive. It
is, therefore, highly possible that a wage award that covers the unskilled and
the semi-skilled will increase the demand for semi-skilled employees and decrease the demand for unskilled employees. In this case, the effect of attempting to erode differentials between skilled and unskilled workers is to change the
nature of the differential. The income differential may be reduced, but the
probability-of-employment differential may be increased. Although hard evidence on this is scarce, the 13 percent decline in the ratio of unskilled to
skilled production workers in Ghana between 1965 and 1969 is evidence that
points in this direction. The 1966 manpower projections for Zambia are perhaps an even more striking example.

As Table 8.9 shows, the past and projected rate of growth of demand for
"all other manual workers" (i.e., semi- and unskilled) is much below that of
skilled workers. It would be incorrect to conclude that this is directly and
uniquely the result of the movement of wages in Zambia since 1964, but it is
significant that the projections, which turned out to be over-optimistic, were
based on the assumption of constant real wage rates. (It is also true that the
projections were based on a much higher rate of growth of output than was
achieved after 1968.) In an economy where employment in mining and construction—both industries in which capital substitution is technically easy—
accounts for a large proportion of jobs, there is a strong probability that wage
increases have been achieved at the cost of employment opportunities for
semi- and unskilled workers.

The second argument in favour of the view that increases in the income of
any public employee impoverishes the poor is simply an accounting matter. If
revenues are more or less fixed, the greater the proportion of those revenues
that is spent on wages and salaries of public employees, the less that can be

TABLE 8.9

Zambia: Estimated Distribution of Industrial Employment
by Occupational Group

		1970		1980	
	1964		Rate of Growth		Rate of Growth
Occupational Group	Number	Number	(Percent)	Number	(Percent)
Manual workers	165,300	253,000	7.4	342,000	3.1
Skilled	31,200	64,000	12.7	116,000	6.1
All other	134,100	189,000	5.9	226,000	1.8
Service workers	52,000	70,000	5.1	94,000	3.0
Other than domestics	16,600	32,000	11.6	62,000	6.8
Domestics	35,400	38,000	1.2	32,000	-1.7

Source: Development Division of the Office of the Vice-President, *Zambian Manpower* (Lusaka: Government Printer, 1969).

spent on capital development.* This argument assumes that it is the poor, either in the urban or rural areas, who will benefit from such capital development. We shall argue in Chapters 9 and 12 that that is an assumption that needs much more critical examination; indeed, we have already seen evidence that rural development expenditures tend not to reach the poorest. To this extent, the argument must be recast.

If public sector salaries rise, either employment falls in order to protect capital expenditures (the earlier point), or capital expenditures fall (or are "rephased"). Unless there is strong political and administrative pressure to ensure that programmes and projects that do in fact (and not only in theory) reach the poor are maintained, the likelihood is that economies will be made here rather than on programmes that, while theoretically servicing at least some of the poor, actually benefit one or more of the elite groups. There are allegedly sound, efficiency-type economic and administrative arguments for giving these projects a lower priority; if they are in the plan at all, they are more vulnerable during a budgetary squeeze unless there is strong political pressure to maintain them. We shall see in Chapter 12 that sometimes even that pressure cannot withstand structural and administrative forces. This suggests that we can

---

*A slight variant of this argument, presented in Chapter 12, is that rising costs make the expansion of a given service more difficult. As the poor are at the margin of the service, it is they who are thus deprived; see below, pp. 333-35.

conclude no more than that higher wage and salary costs are likely to be paid, in the form of consumption forgone, by actual or potential consumers. To identify them with the poor is not justified, even in countries where there is much rhetoric of social redistribution.

NOTES

1. P. Garlick, *African Traders and Economic Development in Ghana* (London: Oxford University Press, 1971); A. Nypan, *A Sample Study of Market Traders in Accra* (Accra: Economic Research Division, University College of Ghana, 1960), p. 37, where she makes the point that Ghanaian market traders regard education as a "business expense" in marked contrast to other types of consumption.

2. John Smythe, "Educational Planning in Uganda," *Comparative Education Review*, October 1970, pp. 360 ff. See also Bowman's comments thereon, pp. 365 ff.

3. R.H. Sabot, "Education, Income Distribution and Rates of Urban Migration in Tanzania," mimeo. (Economic Research Bureau, University of Dar es Salaam, and Institute of Economics and Statistics, Oxford University, March 1972).

4. See, for instance, the contrast between the *First Annual Report of the Ghana Manpower Board* (Accra, 1968) and *One Year Development Plan, 1970-1* (Accra, 1970), p. 166.

5. See E.L. Wijemanne and M.E. Sinclair, "General Education: Some Developments in the Sixties and Prospects for the Seventies," *Marga* 1, no. 4 (1972): 1-3.

6. Margaret Peil, *The Ghanaian Factory Worker* (Cambridge: Cambridge University Press, 1972).

7. *Report of the Commission on the Structure and Remuneration of the Public Services in Ghana* (The Mills-Odoi Report) (Accra: Ministry of Information, 1967).

8. *Report of the Board of Inquiry into a Claim for a Rise in Salaries of "E" Scale Public Officers* (Entebbe: Government Printer, 1966), p. 11.

9. *Report of the Commission Appointed to Review the Grading Structure of the Civil Service* (Lusaka: Government Printer, 1966), p. 11.

10. *Education in Transition: Report of the Administrative Working Party Appointed to Examine Certain Aspects of the Teaching Service* (Lusaka: Ministry of Education, 1968), p. 19.

11. M.A. Bienefeld, *The Wage Employed*, vol. III of *The National Urban Mobility, Employment and Income Survey of Tanzania* (Dar es Salaam: Ministry of Economic Affairs and Development Planning, 1972), p. 92. Cf.

C.A. Greenhalgh, "Income Differentials in the Eastern Region of Ghana," to be published in the *Economic Bulletin of Ghana*, kindly made available before publication by the author. The Ghana data are more skill-specific than the Tanzanian. Margaret Peil's data suggest less occupational rigidity and a lower *general* level of differentials, but she has detailed data for only one period and her excellent survey covered only factory workers. But they certainly suggest that the differentials in Table 8.7 may be on the high side, most probably because the representative blue-collar skilled worker is unusually well paid. See Peil, op. cit., p. 78.

12. See Tony Killick, "Labour: A General Study," in *The Economy of Ghana*, vol. I of *A Study of Contemporary Ghana*, eds. Walter Birmingham, I. Neustadt, and E.N. Omaboe (London: Allen and Unwin, 1966).

13. Sudhir Anand, "The Size Distribution of Income in Malaysia," draft report to International Bank for Reconstruction and Development, 1974. We are grateful to the author for allowing us to sees this work in draft.

14. *Report of the Commission of Enquiry into the Mining Industry, 1966* (The Brown Report) (Lusaka: Government Printer, 1966), p. 51

15. Kodwo Ewusi, *The Distribution of Monetary Incomes in Ghana*, Technical Publication no. 14 (Legon: Institute of Statistical, Social and Economic Research, 1971); C.B. Edwards, "Protection, Profits and Policy: An Analysis of Industrialisation in Malaysia," dissertation submitted for Ph.D., University of East Anglia, 1974.

16. Warnasena Rasaputram, "Changes in the Pattern of Income Inequality in Ceylon," *Marga* 1, no. 4 (1972).

17. Azarias Baryaruha, *Factors Affecting Industrial Employment: A Study of Ugandan Experience, 1954-1965*, Occasional Paper (Makerere: East African Institute of Social Research, University of Makerere, 1965).

18. *Report of the Board of Inquiry into a Wages Increase Claim in Respect of Group Employees in the Uganda Public Service* (Entebbe: Government Printer, 1966), pp. 6-7.

Formal education is a classical example of the con-mech. It is a competitive access cone, open enough to maintain confidence but actually highly selective. It imparts legitimacy, as well as some material rewards, to those who benefit from it. But it also imparts major benefits to those who control it. These benefits are political: a new school, even a new classroom, is an important piece of political patronage. They are also economic. Not only does the kind of economic growth on which the elites depend require an educational system to deliver the manpower we were considering in the last chapter but, as we shall show, the educational system itself becomes one of the principal means by which the privileges of the elite are continuously reinforced.

The object of this chapter is to examine the causes and nature of the biases in the formal education system. The basic argument is that the urban and particularly rural poor are excluded from access to education; that even where they have physical access, they are less likely to make use of it; that they are more likely drop out; that they are less likely to perform well; and that they are therefore much less likely to be found in the upper reaches of secondary schools or universities. Education thus acts both as a reinforcing mechanism for those already privileged and as a highly biased access cone for the excluded.

But since the poor do not fully appreciate these biases and regard the system as basically fair because competitive, they tend to greatly overestimate the likely benefits of schooling. The argument of this chapter is not that the poor overestimate the chance of getting a job once education is terminated; that is a quite separate issue to which we turn in the next chapter. Here we are concerned only with analysing the sources and scale of the biases that exist within the educational system. We do so under six headings: geographical distribution of schools; financial constraints on take-up; biases arising from mis-specification of education; the effect of social status on performance and drop-out; the biases in the selection process; and, finally, the social composition of secondary school and university populations.

SPATIAL DISTORTION

The present spatial distribution of educational facilities is the result of a number of forces that have sometimes acted together and sometimes in opposition to one another. First, the colonial period saw the establishment of mission schools and later of independent schools founded, or substantially aided, by the colonial authorities. To some extent the latter were designed to fill some of the more glaring gaps left by the former, gaps that were of particular political or commercial interest to the colonial powers. For the distribution of mission schools was determined to a very large extent by the eagerness with which the population responded to the overtures of the missionaries. (It also was influenced by the climate of the region. The degree of missionary activity in Tanzania, for example, is highly, but not perfectly, related to altitude above sea level.)

In areas in which the early Church took hold quickly and easily, missionaries spread a network of catechetical classes and primary schools. In areas that were more resistant to Christianity, the provision of schools was much delayed.

The result was that at independence in most countries the spatial coverage of the population with primary schools, and much more with secondary schools, was extremely spotty. In West Africa, the adequacy of educational provision was directly related to the proximity of the coast. The further north one went, the fewer schools one found. In East Africa, some favoured tribes— the Buganda in Uganda, the Chewa in Zambia, the Kikuyu in Kenya—were well educated by comparison with other tribal groups.

If in the non-Christian countries of Asia the impact of the missions was somewhat less marked (but no less in the Philippines, for example), it is still true that the effect of the colonial period taken as a whole was to bestow an education upon those groups that were particularly responsive or particularly useful and/or important to the colonial administrators. In Malaysia, this discrimination took a racial form with the result that the Chinese, and particularly the urban Chinese, were given much greater opportunity than all Malays, and particularly rural Malays. In Sri Lanka, we have already seen how at the secondary level the colonial regime and the missionaries combined to produce an educational structure not dissimilar to that of contemporary Britain. At the apex stood a small

number of highly selective fee-paying public schools, attendance at which was
at once the mark and the guarantee of privilege.

Upon independence, one of the major tasks facing all governments was a
rapid expansion of primary and secondary education and, to a greater or lesser
extent, the removal of the worst of the distributional biases inherited from the
colonial regime. The means by which this was undertaken varied a good deal,
from complete centralization of educational administration in Uganda to the
encouragement of local initiative in Kenya and Ivory Coast. But either approach
brought with it its own demonstration of the conflict between the need to expand education rapidly at the national level (and therefore to keep unit costs
low) and the need, pressed with very different degrees of political vigour, to
remove inequalities of access. A highly centralized approach heightened the
classical conflict between equity and efficiency. Even at primary school level,
considerable cost savings could be achieved by building larger and fewer
schools or amalgamating existing schools where denominational rivalries had
duplicated facilities in the same locality. But such a strategy conflicted directly
with the demands of equity, for distance from school is one of the strongest
determinants of enrolment and drop-out. For example, a study of primary
schools in Tanzania showed that attendance at school declined very markedly
for children more than a mile from school and that absenteeism was much
better explained by distance than by socio-economic characteristics of the
home; absenteeism was positively related to socio-economic status as demonstrated by ownership of modern household goods and to an instrumental view
of education.[1]

The trade-off between equity and efficiency has been solved in a variety of
ways, but in every country a critical variable is population density. For as density declines, the possibility of siting primary schools in such a way that all
children in the region are less than two miles from school disappears. Even if
remote, thinly populated areas receive a proportionate share of educational
resources, it follows that education will be distributed less equitably in those
areas than in the more densely populated areas. (And as building costs and costs
of supplies are higher in the remote areas—sometimes more than double—a proportionate distribution of the education budget will anyway mean that those
areas have fewer real resources per head than areas where costs are lower.)

A decentralized approach relying heavily upon local initiative is clearly no
solution to this conflict. For such initiative will come most readily from areas
in which there is a combination of an active desire for improvement in educational facilities and sufficient resources to secure that improvement. In Ivory
Coast, for example, it is clear that higher enrolment ratios in primary schools in
the cocoa-growing area are explicable primarily by the fact that cocoa farmers
have long been better educated and have high enough incomes to build and
maintain self-help schools. Much the same can be said of Harambee secondary

TABLE 9.1

**Primary Education Enrolment Ratios in Rural Areas as
Percentages of Enrolment Ratios in the Capital**

Country	Year	Top Rural			Bottom Rural		
		Male	Both Sexes	Female	Male	Both Sexes	Female
Kenya	1970		162.7			13.6	
Tanzania	1969	159.5	161.0	162.9	41.9	40.8	20.7
Uganda	1968		89.1			22.0	
Zambia	1969		106.3			68.8	
Ghana	1970		98.1			23.7	
Cameroon	1971-72[a]					24.5	12.3
Ivory Coast	1969		116.7	77.8		27.8	13.4
Upper Volta	1971	51.0	41.6	37.7	5.7	3.7	2.8
Tunisia	1969-70	208.0		104.4	80.0		13.8
Sri Lanka[b]	1972		104.1			50.5	

[a]Using Centre-South with Yaounde as reference.

[b]All grades of education.

Sources: Annual reports of ministries of education.

schools in Kenya. In this respect, there is a close analogy between private education and variants of self-help: Access to both depends upon parental initiative and resources and, as such, is more likely to increase inequities than to reduce them.* The fact that the quality of such education is often low may to some extent reduce the effect of such inequities, but it does not itself reduce the distortions in access to education.

Table 9.1 must be interpreted in the light of these remarks. Predictably, spatial inequalities are marked. But, since the unit of analysis is large, their full extent is not revealed. Most obviously, the rural area with the lowest enrolment ratio usually includes at least one sizeable town in which enrolment ratios are much higher than in the surrounding rural areas. Equally, the metropolitan area may contain within it peri-urban villages that are hardly better served than the worst of the rural areas.

This raises a further point: the relationship between the metropolitan areas and the squatments. We shall emphasize in Chapter 12 the ambivalence of the

---

*But self-help schools may improve *intra*-regional equity, at the same time as it increases *inter*-regional disparity. Further, the effect is heightened by the ability of self-help areas to pre-empt recurrent expenditures.

relevant authorities to these squatments; here we illustrate that ambivalence with respect to one revealing case study against which the figures for the metropolitan area in Table 9.1 must be interpreted. The study relates to two neighbouring suburbs of Lusaka in Zambia.[2]

One of these, Matero, is a well-established suburb, highly organized, integrated into the municipality, and inhabited by clerical, skilled, and some unskilled, labour commuting daily to Lusaka. Although on our last visit we were surprised to see a large white Rolls Royce being driven from a home in Matero, it is a district that neither attracts the very wealthy nor tolerates the wholly indigent. In so far as the term has any meaning at all, it is an African middle-class suburb. Hard up against it is Kapwepwe. Until 1970, this was an illegal settlement outside the city boundary. It has seen phenomenal growth in the last five years and is typical of many shantytowns or bidonvilles on the edge of large African cities—untouched by officialdom, with low-quality houses, virtually no services, a high rate of turnover, and a generally lower economic level than established suburbs such as Matero.

Perhaps unsurprisingly, the primary education survey points to a much greater access to and take-up of primary education in Matero than Kapwepwe. Although the survey itself is not without its methodological difficulties, it is surely significant that in Matero only one child out of 385 covered in the survey had been unsuccessful in finding a primary school place at the first attempt. By contrast, in Kapwepwe 43 children out of the much lower sample population of 237 (18 percent) had had that experience. This finding must be set against the extraordinarily dense pattern of settlement in these suburbs. It is certainly not explicable in terms of geographical accessibility since the distance from the centre of Kapwepwe to the nearest school in Matero is only 700 yards, and the furthest school from the centre of Kapwepwe is barely a mile away. While it may be true that primary schools recruit children on the basis of geographical proximity, the evidence suggests that the criterion is less that of proximity than that of residence in Matero. Thus, at the margin a child who lives further away but in Matero will be preferred over one who lives more close at hand but outside the suburb boundary.

There is little reason to believe that this contrast between Kapwepwe and Matero is unusual. But the difference is not purely one between supply of educational facilities. Since the families' economy in Kapwepwe, as in almost any squatment,* tends to be precarious, there is a much greater tendency to seek

---

*This is not universally true. Some squatments contain a significant proportion of persons with full-time employment in the formal sector. But the new squatments, often inhabited very largely by migrants, tend to have a higher proportion of persons who have not yet found jobs in the formal sector and who are therefore dependent upon less regular earnings.

employment for children or employ them directly on domestic production of handicrafts. In Mary Hollnsteiner's survey of Tondo in Manila, it is significant that, although the average age of families in the squatter area of Tondo is much lower than in the other areas, over a third of the surveyed families had children in employment.[3] Particularly in the new squatments, then, the effect of demand for education is likely to be lower and the incentive to voluntary organizations to establish alternative schools thus much reduced.*

Table 9.1 highlights the relative deprivation of the worst of the rural areas in relation to the metropolitan area and the best-provided rural area. Although the data are not wholly comparable, a number of conclusions emerge. The first is that in almost all cases the most deprived rural area has an enrolment ratio less than half that of the metropolitan area. But there are some significant exceptions. These include Tunisia, Zambia, and Tanzania in Africa and Sri Lanka in Asia. If comparable data were available for Malaysia, that would be included, too.† It is also possible that at the primary level the Philippines would be an exception to this generalization.

We thus seem to have two quite different groups of countries in which spatial deprivation is less severe. First, there are countries, in this case the predominantly Asian ones, in which there has been a long history of primary education with the result that over time the grossest spatial distortions have been removed. The second group is in some ways more interesting. These are all African countries that have given a particularly high political priority to removing spatial distortion inherited from colonial times. These contrast with others, such as Ghana and Kenya, where there has been some rhetoric of equality—more in the former, particularly under Nkrumah, than in the latter—but in which the figures suggest action has lagged far behind words. In Ghana, the distribution of education is still highly correlated with the distribution of non-agricultural jobs.

---

*It is, of course, very possible that there is a dialectic interaction here: Children are employed because there are no schools and there are no schools because children are employed. But even if there were schools, some of the poorest families would be less likely to use them, not only because of the loss of children's earnings but also because the poorest tend to be the most mobile and therefore have less opportunity and less incentive to enrol their children in school.

†The only relevant data to which we had access were enrolment ratios by zones. These are very large units, usually including two states. But the two poorest states, Kelantan and Treqganu, had average enrolment ratios only slightly less than those of the richer states.

For every 5 percent of the population thus employed, the proportion of children at school rises by over 10 percent.*

The feature that is perhaps surprising is the number of countries in which the enrolment ratios in the best endowed rural areas exceed those in the metropolitan areas. There are two explanations for this. The first is that, in such countries as Ivory Coast, Kenya, and Tunisia very high rates of urban migration have meant that primary provision in the urban areas has not been able to keep pace. This is a statistical reflection of the bias against the squatments and the peri-urban villages that we have examined in the Kapwepwe case study. The other part of the explanation, of which Tanzania is a particularly good example, is that some rural areas have had a long history of educational provision, partly because they were intensively covered by missions—as the Pare district—and partly because they were densely settled and therefore a higher proportion of the population lives within walking distance of a primary school.

The data on secondary education are less satisfactory.† But, as we would expect, Table 9.2 does suggest that regional inequalities are much greater in secondary education than in primary. This is partly because secondary education is less well developed, with the result that most secondary schools are in urban areas and in the more highly developed rural areas, and partly because in many countries all secondary schools are boarding schools. For them, situation is not a good guide to geographical distribution of students.

A final feature of the tables is the predictable difference between enrolment ratios for boys and girls. In every case, this is more marked in the deprived rural areas than in either the metropolitan areas or the best endowed rural areas. In nearly every case, the enrolment rate for boys is more than double that of girls. Gender is almost as much a bar to education as location.

What the tables do not adequately bring out is the effect of distance on quality of schools. Although this relationship may not be as simple or as strong as one might imagine,[4] there can be little doubt that, at both primary and secondary levels, quality is heavily influenced, if not actually determined, by distance from the metropolis and/or the regional capital. The level of supervision, the supply of equipment, the ease with which first-rate teachers can be recruited and retained—all these tend to ensure that the schools in the more developed areas are qualitatively superior to the "bush" or "jungle" schools. This means

---

*Data from the 1970 census, with Greater Accra excluded. The regression equation was $y = 2.45x - 9.16$, when y is percentage attendance at school and x is non-agricultural employment. Coefficient of determination: 0.74.

†In the case of Zambia, for example, we have data only on age groups. But in the worst rural areas, many children in the secondary age group are in fact enrolled in primary schools. This means that the secondary enrolment ratios in deprived rural areas are almost certainly overstated.

TABLE 9.2

Secondary Education Enrolment Ratios in Rural Areas as Percentages of Enrolment Ratios in the Capital

Country	Year	Top Rural			Bottom Rural		
		Male	Both Sexes	Female	Male	Both Sexes	Female
Kenya	1970		35.2			21.4	
Tanzania	1969	92.9	64.8	28.7	0.0	0.0	0.0
Uganda	1968		43.0			2.6	
Zambia	1969		82.4			41.2	
Cameroon[a]	1965		128.0			7.0	
Ivory Coast[b]	1968		—			17.3	

[a]Using Centre-South with Yaounde as reference.

[b]Comparing the Northern Region with the whole of the Southern Region, including Abidjan.

Sources: Annual reports of ministries of education.

that children in the poorest rural areas not only have less chance of going to school; they have much less chance of going to a good school.

FINANCIAL CONSTRAINTS ON TAKE-UP

There are three important types of financial constraint—overt private cost (fees), covert private costs (books, uniform, transport), and earnings forgone. Of the last we shall have little to say here, principally because we have found no hard evidence that earnings forgone, although they may be highly valued, are commonly valued more highly than education. We have already seen that there are examples of a high rate of employment of children by low-income families (and even of older children by middle-income families), but that cannot be taken as evidence that families refuse to send their children to school *because* of the earnings that would thereby be lost. All that can fairly be said is that, for low-income families, the loss of children's earnings is a greater proportionate cost than for middle-income families and may contribute powerfully to the premature withdrawal of some children who are needed to earn money to pay for the primary education of siblings. But in general, all the evidence suggests that even low-income families are very well aware of the financial advantages of education and are ready to forgo any contribution to family income from children in the hopes that they will realise those advantages.

Before we turn to private costs, it is relevant to put educational finance in a wider setting. The precise system of educational finance naturally varies from country to country. In most, there is a commitment to free primary education but charges are more common at secondary and tertiary levels.* In the same way, the division of financial responsibility between central government and local government varies. In general, the greater the political determination to reduce regional disparities, the greater the degree of centralization.

This is significant, for dependence upon local finance tends to perpetuate regional variations in both quantity and quality of services. In the Philippines, for example, central government accepts responsibility under the constitution for primary education but secondary education is financed by local authorities. Furthermore, local authorities tend to raise finance for secondary education through a land tax or other forms of property taxation. Since local government tends to be controlled by those on whom such taxation would fall most heavily, it is no surprise to find that secondary schooling in the Philippines has been consistently starved of funds and has had to rely to an increasing extent on tuition fees at this level. The Presidential Commission of Enquiry was under no illusions about the results: "Support for public secondary education . . . has never been adequate. Thus public secondary institutions are dependent on tuition fees. Most are poorly housed and equipped with no provision for library facilities."[5]

The perpetuation, and indeed aggravation, of regional variations in quality is only one result of charging fees. The more immediate one, and from our point of view the more relevant one, is the inevitable pressure of fees on the poor. Secondary education in Uganda, for instance, can cost as much as 40 percent of the minimum wage in Kampala for overt costs alone—a level of income that greatly exceeds the cash earning of the great majority of rural people and nearly all those employed in the informal sector. It is true that Uganda may be an extreme case; equivalent figures for Cameroon (where 65 percent of secondary pupils are at private, fee-paying schools) are about 22 percent, and for the Philippines about 12 percent. It is also true that financing education is an obligation on the whole kin group and not purely on the nuclear family. It is no less true, however, that most families have more than one child and that, as we

---

*Uganda is a bizarre inversion of this pattern. There the proportion of costs borne by the state increases as one progresses up the system. The present government is committed to changing this system.

have already seen, food alone can take over 60 percent of income. Under these conditions, it is no surprise that parents and pupils give as one of the major reasons for dropping out of school inability of the family to meet the fees. (It is also true that the same reason is given even when no fees are charged—evidence that the hidden costs for books, transport, and food can be considerable; see below, p. 238.)

It is extremely difficult to quantify the extent to which the charging of fees acts as a further process of exclusion of the poor. If we assume that family size is similar (except for the lowest income group, which comprises single-member families) then equality of take-up of education would produce roughly similar absolute expenditures on education. But, of course, what we find is exactly the reverse. In the Philippines, for instance, the poorest families (those with incomes of under ₱1,500, comprising 45 percent of the population in 1965) spent less than ₱15 per child on education, while the richer groups (those with incomes of over ₱4,000, comprising less than 14 percent of the population) spent more than ₱75 per child. We have very interesting corroborative evidence from a very different setting, namely, the Mwanza and West Lake areas of Tanzania. This is a relatively rich area in which there is less tendency to remit fees for poorer children.[6] According to the Household Budget Survey, the richer inhabitants of this region (those receiving between Shs.10,000 and Shs.25,000 a year) spent over a hundred times as much on education as the poorest groups. Even allowing for differences in family size and structure, and for the fact that some poor children are paid for by richer kinsmen, the big discrepancy in the payment of fees is evidence, although not proof, of poorer children being excluded from education.*

The best direct evidence we have comes from rather old data from Sri Lanka. There a large survey of children not attending school revealed a very close relationship between attendance and the income of the household head. For every Rs.20 increase in his weekly wage, the chances of a child attending school increased by 1 percent for the youngest to 3 percent for the 12-14 age group.†

---

*It is not, however, evidence of poor children being excluded by poverty alone. It could be objected that the poorest income group is of primarily single-person households with a small number of children and therefore a low average expenditure on fees. But it is interesting that those in the expenditure bracket Shs. 2,000-4,000 (not among the very poor) spent less than one twentieth of those in the higher expenditure bracket. An analysis of household size by expenditure group is not available.

†Coefficients of determination were: 7- 9 years 0.76
                                   10-11 years 0.85
                                   12-14 years 0.96

To some extent, it is true, this association reflects the influence on attendance of area of residence, race, and education of parents—and not poverty alone. As we have no means of separating these influences out—and even if we had the data, their mutual interaction would make interpretation hazardous—it is worth quoting the comments of the official report. If the language is quaint, there is no reason to assume that the analysis is incorrect. It gave poverty as the major reason for non-attendance in these words:

> It is well known that attendance in recent months has increased since the introduction of the mid-day meal. If poverty means only hunger, why has the increase not been as well marked as it should have been? Surely a fair meal a day should have been a sufficient attraction for those who live below subsistence level. The question had been put to a large number of parents by our enumerators and their replies have almost invariably been the same. How could they send their children to school in the rags they wear and expect them to sit with those who are comparatively better off? We are informed that some have never known a change of clothes for years on end. We are, therefore, convinced that it is not indifference on the part of most parents that their children do not attend school. Despite poverty so abject as would smother every decent human emotion, they are yet not entirely devoid of some vague notions of self-respect. They would not wish their children to be the subject of scornful comment of other children or of teachers. A good number of parents have expressly admitted that this was the real cause of their inability to send their children to school. The reticence of many others can only be interpreted in similar terms.[7]

This is one graphic example of the influence of covert charges—in this case, the need to clothe children up to a certain standard and to ensure that they are adequately equipped in other respects. This suggests that absolute poverty is not the only bias; relative poverty may be at least as important.

MIS-SPECIFICATION OF FORMAL EDUCATION

The problem of the type of education—academic, vocational, informal, community-based—that would best suit the conditions of poor countries has received much comment, and it is no point of our purpose to become involved in that debate. But we do have to ask whether there is evidence that the type of education currently offered acts as a greater deterrent to the poor than to the rich. If vocational schools were more common, or if curriculums were more "relevant," would poor parents keep their children in school longer?

We have seen no conclusive evidence that this is so. Indeed, there is some evidence that, at least in the short run, all parents regard such innovations with great suspicion. Even attempts to adapt the curriculum to local conditions may be resisted. Believing that foreign is best, parents are highly dubious of attempts to indigenize either the syllabus or the form of education. This is not an irrational reaction. On the contrary, it follows directly from the observed relationship between possession of an internationally recognized education qualification and employment and promotion. With the abolition of that qualification, parents assume (perhaps not wholly incorrectly) that the employment prospects of their children are jeopardized.

Assuming that their children will be successful in school (since, if they did not assume this, they would presumably be reluctant to allow them to continue), parents resist even more fiercely than teachers moves that they see as directly threatening the future security of their children. There is evidence of this from Kenya, from Uganda, from Zambia, from Ghana, and from Sri Lanka. To quote one example from Sri Lanka: When the Committee to Enquire into and Report on Public Examinations at Secondary School Level issued its interim report in August 1972 (in which it suggested the decentralization of secondary examinations in Sri Lanka),[8] it was greeted by intense political opposition. This came particularly from the more depressed parts of the island, because it was assumed that decentralization would be attended by local variations in standards and objectivity, with easily foreseeable implications for finding clerical employment. Yet the whole objective of decentralization was to make possible a more flexible examination system with greater stress on pre-occupational studies related to the local environment. Thus a highly progressive and desirable (if hardly revolutionary) educational reform was threatened by those who thought they stood to gain from the existing patterns of privilege.*

The problems of an over-academic secondary education dominated by an examination system are not unknown in rich countries. One approach to a solution that has been followed in the rich countries has been a two-stream system in secondary education: an academic stream and a vocational stream. The justification for this is that the brighter child is able to continue with an academic education, perhaps leading on to tertiary education, while the less bright child is not squeezed out of the educational system by the content of the syllabus,

---

*How far lower-income groups were involved in this protest is extremely difficult to say. Certainly it seems to be the case that in many African countries the protest against reform has come from grass roots in rural areas. But given a small proportion of children from very poor homes who go to secondary schools, it is unlikely the protests had major backing from the urban and rural poor.

but rather is given the opportunity to develop other talents in the context of vocational training. Thus, he is enabled to acquire skills that allow him to compete more favourably for employment when he leaves school.

There are, of course, profound ideological objections to this system in the rich countries. They need not detain us here. What is significant from our point of view is that this approach has been adopted by a number of poor countries—ins our sample, most notably by Egypt and Tunisia. How far is it the case that this system reduces the bias against the children of poor families in secondary education? That is a question that we cannot answer. But there are at least three reasons for believing that such a system reinforces biases rather than removing them.

First, we shall see that the Tunisian data suggest that children of manual workers (particularly boys) tend to opt for vocational schools rather than academic schools, either as a result of parental pressure or because they can see their future in terms of their parents' occupation. Second, the vocational schools tend to be biased towards the urban areas, both in terms of recruitment and in terms of skills taught. Third, the manpower requirements of vocational schools seriously constrain their rate of expansion and/or the quality of education offered. If they are expanded as rapidly as they were in Egypt in the early 1960s, they become little more than inferior industrial training departments. If they are not expanded sufficiently rapidly, the urban bias, already strongly marked, tends to be reinforced.

Above all, the whole streaming system, particularly when the vocational schools are more vocational than school, is open in the poor countries to the same objection to which it is subjected in the rich countries—namely, that it is a training for subservience. The streaming system reinforces the cleavage between the privileged child who is receiving an academic education and seeking white-collar employment and the non-privileged child whose education does not fit him for more than manual or supervisory employment. It is not insignificant that the independent Zambian government closed all vocational schools within a year of independence. However desirable they may be from the perspective of the manpower planner, to the politician and parent they embody a principle of differentiation that only those who benefit by it are likely to find appealing.

SOCIAL ORIGINS, PERFORMANCE, AND DROP-OUT

Before we come to see the cumulative effect on school populations of differential take-up and differential access, we must see what evidence there is for believing that performance in school is influenced by the social origins of the students. Is the bright student from a poor home likely to do less well than the bright (or mediocre) student from a "good" home? It would be absurd to try to draw major conclusions from the scrappy data at our disposal. Although many studies in rich countries have been fairly consistent in suggesting that the home is a far more important factor than the quality of the school (a notoriously difficult variable to quantify), the data from our countries are not unambiguous.

For instance, in Tunisia (a particularly interesting country in this respect with, as we shall see, one of the least inequitable educational systems), A. Bsais and C. Morrisson found no straightforward correlation between performance in examinations (at the end of the third year for those in shorter and technical training and at the end of the sixth year for academic teaching) with social origins as defined by income group.[9] Girls in technical schools and boys in academic schools seemed to follow the "normal" hypothesis: the higher the social origin, the better the scholastic performance. But for boys in technical training and girls in academic teaching, the reverse was the case—those from poorer families perform better than those from richer families (but the sample of girls was very small, only 38). Bsais and Morrisson explain this by the fact that in technical schools, poor boys are more highly selected than rich boys, especially by the need to compete for scholarships.

This may be part of the reason, but it does not furnish a complete explanation. For if competition for scholarships raises the average intelligence of poor boys (by eliminating the less intelligent), this merely means that poor boys who are not bright enough to win scholarships do not go to secondary school—but rich boys of similar intelligence do. In other words, we have here an economic filter rather than evidence that performance is not affected by status.

But there is independent evidence that the level of education of parents has little impact on performance at secondary school—as measured by the ability of children to remain at school or in full-time education.[10] In other words, low parental education (which we may take to be closely related to parental income and occupation) does not seem to lead to a differential rate of drop-out or terminal failure. If children (or at least boys) from such families are already highly selected by the need to compete for scholarships, this is hardly surprising. But from this it does not follow that there is no bias in the system against such children. This is demonstrated by the distribution of students in secondary schools of different types. There is a much higher proportion of students from low-income families in courses that give a diploma *without access to university.* Further, as we have already mentioned, within technical training, low-income students are more likely to be found in the relatively low-skill (and low potential income) courses rather than in the high-skill courses that will give access to high-income jobs.

The Tunisian evidence, then, is that social origins do not seem important in excluding low-income children from school, but the evidence is ambiguous. What does seem fairly well established is that there are economic pressures that exclude less bright children from secondary school and less wealthy children from more potentially profitable training. That these pressures are better contained in Tunisia than in any other country we have examined is an important consideration to which we shall return.

Before doing so, we must review more evidence of the effect of social status on performance. A recent study of education in Uganda suggests that these factors have only a slight effect; economic pressures, on the other hand, make themselves felt both more strongly and more directly.[11] Parental education, father's occupation, and the "economic modernity" of the family (as indicated by the possession of modern consumer durables) are all uncorrelated to performance in the primary leaving examination—except the performance in the English language tests. S. Heyneman explains this by the differing skills required for this part of the examination. Unlike maths and the general paper, which require ability to apply fairly standard problem-solving techniques memorized from approved texts, the English exam requires "a high degree of inference and logical reasoning," which cannot be learned by rote.

If this is the right explanation, it is surprising that there is no correlation between a child's performance in English and parental capability in English, or the frequency of English usage in the home. The most we can say, then, is that there is again some meagre, rather unsatisfactory evidence that the privileged environment bestowed by elevated socio-economic status is one factor, but one factor among many, that enables children to develop powers of intellectual creativity and adaptability. If this is correct, we would expect this advantage to be greater as a child progresses up the educational ladder. Unless university education is of exceedingly low quality, the relative importance of those intellectual gifts over the ability to memorize should increase—thus bestowing greater benefit on children from elite groups. Whether this in fact is the case in Uganda we have no means of establishing, but, as we shall see, the elite is already heavily overrepresented at the university level.

In Ghana, we have evidence of a rather different character that encourages us to come to a less cautious conclusion. It takes further the distinction between different qualities of school at the secondary level and asks whether there are systemic biases that ensure that children from more elite backgrounds gain admission to the higher-quality schools while those from lower socio-economic origins are disproportionately likely to be found in the low-quality schools. This implies looking at the relationship between socio-economic status and factors that are likely to ensure that a child does sufficiently well in the qualifying examination to pass into one of the better schools. We find that higher-status groups* are more likely to send their children to nursery school;

---

*Status groups were defined only in terms of occupation. "Upper professionals" include doctors, lawyers, teachers, clergy, higher civil servants,

exclusively send their children to private, high-quality primary schools; are more likely to send them to an urban and better middle school; are more likely to use English in the home; and are less likely to disrupt their children's home life by sending them to live with relatives.[12] Now we do not know with certainty how far these features, either individually or in the aggregate, improve the chances of a child from a high-status home, because we do not know the distribution of innate ability. But it would be surprising, to say the least, if these advantages made no significant difference.

Certainly we find not only that high-status families are over-represented in secondary schools taken as a whole but, more interesting, that they are over-represented in the "top-quality" secondary schools. Thus, 34 percent of enrolled children from upper professional groups are in these schools; only 20 percent of farmers' children and 19 percent of blue-collar workers' children are successful in winning a place—and thereby a higher probability of a university education.* The inverse is true: The blue-collar workers have nearly half of their children in low-quality schools; upper professionals only a quarter. Since the top schools achieve results more than twice as good as the bottom schools in the terminal exams, it is hard to avoid the conclusion that there are indeed systemic biases against children from humbler homes.

From the three Asian countries we have studied, only Malaysia has adequate detailed data to allow us to investigate the effect of social status on a child's ability to stay in school. An intensive study of nearly 10,500 youths (made up of 4,500 youths at the age of 15+ and 6,000 at 11+ in 1972) showed that "parental advantage" was the most powerful factor in explaining why some children had dropped out of school while others had not.† It was more powerful than medium of instruction, socio-economic status, distance, urban residence, sex, or ethnic group. It alone explained 23 percent of the variation in drop-out, while that of socio-economic status explained only 10 percent (both statistically significant at the 0.001 level). In other words, the data are certainly consistent with the view that poverty alone explains—much more than status,

---

politicians, administrators, and managers. "Low-status groups" include blue-collar workers traders, farmers, and fishermen.

*For the whole sampled population, 22 percent were in "top" schools, 35 percent in "bottom" schools.

†But the index used to measure "parental advantage" is based on the youths' answers to questions that are not wholly independent of each other and depend upon a rather arbitrary scoring and weighting system. Although quite sophisticated statistical analysis revealed a significant difference between this index and socio-economic status, it is dangerous to draw major conclusions from so crude an index.

culture, or ethnic origin—why children drop out of school. But the data should not be taken to prove this point.

Taking these very different countries together, then, the evidence seems to suggest that, once a child is in school, performance will be affected relatively little by social background. It does not seem to be the case that elite children perform better than non-elite children because of their social origins. Rather, in so far as they perform better at all, they do so because elite status brings with it greater wealth. And this is what enables children to stay longer, attend better schools more regularly, equip themselves better, and choose more advantageous courses. If this is correct—and it is important to re-emphasize the weakness of the evidence—then the pressures upon a child once in school are similar in origin and direction to those in access and take-up.

BIASES IN THE SELECTION PROCESS

But is exclusion a wholly determined process? Or is it, rather, at least in part a random process in which intelligence, status, and origin are irrelevant? As Table 9.3 shows, competition for promotion from one level to another is intense. One (but only one) factor that determines success or failure in that competition is the examination system. For, in an effort to ensure equality of opportunity, every country "rations" post-primary education by a test of ability to profit from it.

This presupposes that the examination system is an effective method of ranking children according to their ability to benefit from a higher level of education. But is it? If it is not, and the process of selection and exclusion is little more than a lottery, then the randomness is a source of both inefficiency and injustice.

There has been very little scientific study of examinations in developing countries, but from both Uganda and Kenya we have some evidence that the system is both inefficient and unjust. In Kenya, Tony Somerset has shown that pupils in high-cost primary schools perform much better in the exam at the end of primary school than do pupils in low-cost schools. This is partly because the high-cost schools provide a higher quality of education. But is is also because they are particularly adept at preparing students for the exam. In other respects, the exam is revealed as a very inefficient selector for, although it chooses good students from good schools, it complements them by an entirely random selection of students from the rest of the school population. So a good student from a bad school has the same chance of being selected as a bad student from a good school—or as a bad student from a bad school. Thus, an intelligent pupil from a low-cost school is doubly unfortunate. He suffers from poorer teaching and less encouraging learning conditions; and his chances of being identified as a pupil

TABLE 9.3

Crude Enrolment at Indicated Level as Percentage of Enrolment at Immediately Lower Level, 1970 or Nearest Available Date

Country	Secondary	Higher Vocational/Academic
Tanzania	n.a.	0.5
Uganda	5.6	1.3
Zambia	9.0	0.7
Ghana	4.6	3.3
Cameroon	10.5	0.3
Ivory Coast	8.0	0.3
Upper Volta	8.1	n.a.
Tunisia	19.6	0.8
Malaysia	35.6	1.2
Philippines	29.5	10.8
Sri Lanka	13.8	n.a.

Note: Figures are "crude" because no adjustment is made for size of age cohorts.

Sources: Annual reports of ministries of education.

of high ability are much reduced because of the lower efficiency of the examination.[13]

In Uganda, both J. Silvey and S. Heyneman have shown that the primary leaving exam is dependent less upon intellectual ability than upon a capacity for regurgitating the contents of a standard text: "Cramming, rote learning, and memorizing are encouraged . . . while the ability to think logically, to distinguish the relevant from the irrelevant detail in problem-solving or to observe critically tend to be neglected."[14] The exam "demands factual knowledge and problem-solving techniques which have been routinized to the point of an automatic reaction. Answers . . . are elicited from countless hours of memory drill."[15] Such an exam is unlikely to achieve the objective of selecting those who will benefit most from post-primary education.

There is no reason to assume that Uganda and Kenya are unusual in this respect. There is less detailed evidence to the same effect from Sri Lanka, Malaysia, and Ghana.[16] Indeed, the design of efficient and equitable exams is a major educational problem in many countries.[17] The present regime of inefficient and inequitable exams randomizes the process of exclusion, except for the very best students. This implies that, in all countries, but particularly those with a much underdeveloped secondary level of education, the excluded include a disproportionate number of highly intelligent and able children. Ejected from school, they are left to compete for employment.

The second obvious discontinuity in Table 9.3 is from secondary to higher education. Of the efficiency of selection at this level we have no indication; indeed, the different structure of selection makes analysis unusually difficult.* But the very intensity of competition suggests that in every country, except perhaps the Philippines, those who are excluded from higher education include young men and women of very considerable creativity and intellectual capacity.

This is significant for two reasons. First, it means that the excluded at every level contain a wide range of ability, both actual and potential. The myth that "cream rises to the top" is even less true in these countries than it is in industrial countries. Second, in so far as the selection/exclusion process is seen to be random, or biased against particular groups, it is likely to cause resentment and frustration. That alone can threaten the survival of the con-mech.

SELECTIVITY: THE EVIDENCE

Despite the randomness introduced by inefficient exams, it comes as no surprise to find that, when we compare the socio-economic composition of the school population with that of the population as a whole, we find occupations associated with low incomes consistently under-represented. We shall present data that illustrate this from a number of countries, and then conclude this section with a consideration of what this implies for the processes of selection, mobility, and exclusion.

It is important, first, to make a preliminary methodological point in qualification of much of the evidence we shall examine in the rest of this chapter. The main tool we shall use is the social selectivity ratio, which expresses the proportion of a school population in a given social group as a ratio of that social group as a proportion of the population as a whole. Since we shall want to see how far social groups are under- or over-represented in the school population, we shall have to use the father's socio-economic characteristics (education, occupation, income group) as a proxy for that of the child.

---

*For example, universities may set academic entry qualifications so high as to make it appear that all who are "qualified" are awarded a place. From this it does not follow that the "unqualified" would not have benefitted from a university education. Further, in some countries, notably Ghana, a surprisingly high proportion of university entrants do not come through the "regular" academic channels.

In Western culture this is an acceptable technique, for the importance of the nuclear family and the rather slower processes of mobility tend to ensure that parental characteristics are a fair indication of a child's origins and domestic environment. But in developing countries, neither of these conditions is fulfilled. "Faute de mieux," we are obliged to use a technique that has proved helpful in Western countries and apply it to poor countries, where it is certainly less appropriate. For example, the survival of the extended family is nowhere better seen than in the financial and social arrangements surrounding education. Very rapid inter-generational mobility can produce a child with an elder brother who is a senior civil servant and a father who is a peasant farmer. To classify that child by his father's occupation may be analytically convenient, but it is not unambiguous. This is the more obvious with respect to income levels. A father's income may be literally irrelevant in a situation where education costs are seen and accepted as a legitimate claim on the whole kin group.

In a field that is much under-researched, we are obliged to use what material is available; these remarks should make us even more tentative in the conclusions we draw. The saving grace is that they tend to understate the phenomenon we are looking for. We expect to find small farmers and manual workers under-represented. If the effect is to put students into, for example, the peasant group who "belong" to an elite group, the under-representation of the sons of peasants is thereby under-recorded. Intra-kin group financial transfers operate in the same way. To this extent, the methodology is biased against our argument and can therefore be accepted.

But first we have to ask whether the situation we have described—three processes acting in concert to exclude the poor from education—is a static, constant fact of life, or whether it changes over time. To take the simplest case, one might argue that in the colonial period, when secondary education was extremely limited and functionally directed (i.e., intended to produce middle and lower white-collar workers who would be of use to the colonial regime), the system would be highly selective, since only those who sought the functions allowed them by the colonial regime would wish to secure secondary schooling. This would be much reinforced if the secondary schools, whether private or public, were deliberately elitist as St. Andrews in Sri Lanka or Achimota in Ghana. As the system expanded after independence, however, we would expect the degree of selectivity to be slowly moderated—slowly because, as we saw in Chapter 3, one of the effects of independence and associated economic and social development is to increase the size of the elite groups that are likely to be able to commandeer a disproportionate amount and a disproportionate quality of secondary education. In this case, the rate at which the biases against the poor were removed would depend, in the absence of countervailing political initiatives, on the size and rate of growth of the elites and the speed with which total enrolments were increased. Now in countries where secondary education has not grown very fast (perhaps

because priority has been given to primary education), and where the elites have developed rapidly (a situation rendered the more probable if we include in the elites, for this purpose, the richer farmers), it is not inconceivable that an expansion of the secondary system may be accompanied by *increasing* selectivity.*
Thus Philip Foster has argued,[18] from a rather shaky empirical base to which we shall return, that so far from there being a general, if rather slow, trend towards democratization of the secondary schooling, the schools become more, not less, socially selective, with very serious repercussions on mobility and exclusion.

An extreme illustration of the basic point is Upper Volta, where the continuing paucity of educational resources of all kinds, their concentration in the towns, and, in relation to the growth of formal employment as a whole, the rapid development of a bureaucratic elite have ensured the persistence of extreme selectivity—and therefore, we may presume, very limited upward mobility. As can be seen from Table 9.4, the son of an official in the public administration is 60 times more likely to go to secondary school than the son of a farmer. In Niger, another country with a tiny educational system and a large elite in relation to the resources available, the inequalities may be even more marked.[19]

But the more difficult question is whether, in less extreme cases, selectivity and inequality actually increase over time. This is such an important issue that one would naturally want to test it against high-quality data over a long period from a number of countries. Inevitably, such rigour is impossible. We have perfect data for no country, and passable data for only two that allow us to get any feel for what has been going on over time.

The first of those countries is Ghana. As is evident from Table 9.5, we have data over time for only a rather coarse classification of occupational groups. Further, we have had to use census data for 1950 and 1960 at a time when the occupational structure of the country was changing very rapidly. This is likely to lead to some overstating of the values in the third (elite) row, and perhaps to a rather lesser extent in the second (manual workers) row. To this extent, the table may overstate the differences between groups at any one time but understate differences over time.

Nonetheless, the change recorded in the table is substantial. (It is supported by D.A. Shiman's finding that the over-representation of high-income/status families declined by about 7 percent, and the under-representation of farmers

---

*To some extent, the rapid social change at independence may produce a misleading statistical appearance of increasing selectivity. Indeed, if in the colonial period sons of tribal dignitaries, occupationally classifiable as farmers, formed a major cohort in the secondary schools, their co-optation into the post-colonial system will appear in the statistics as an increase in the selectivity of secondary education.

TABLE 9.4

Upper Volta: Secondary Education Selectivity Ratios, 1970

Sector or Socio-Professional Group	Whole Country	Occupation	Ougadougou (1 college)
Primary sector	0.6	Farmers	0.7
Traditional secondary and tertiary sector	4.0[a]	Handworkers, employees, traders	7.0[b]
Modern secondary and tertiary sector	8.0[a]		
Public administration	36	Public officials	30

[a]All traders are included in the traditional sector, so in reality the first ratio is above 4 and the second one below 8.

[b]Included employees of the modern private sector.

Note: Active population figures are 1969 data from Societe d'etude et de developpement economique et social (SEDES):

Population in:	Percent
primary sector	97.6
traditional sector (secondary and tertiary)	1.2
modern (secondary and tertiary)	0.4
public administration	0.7

Sources: Ministere de l'Education Nationale, *Statistiques scolaires* (Ougadougou, 1966/67-1969/70); SEDES, *Emploi et Formation en Haute-Volta: Analyse et perspectives* (1970).

TABLE 9.5

Ghana: Selectivity Ratios of Sample Secondary School Population

Father's Occupational Group	1953	1963	1964	1966
Agriculture, fishing	0.37	0.61	0.60	0.66
Manual crafts, skilled and semi-skilled	0.32	0.44	0.48	0.66
All others including civil servants, teachers, professionals, and businessmen	9.54	3.94	3.93	3.28

Source: R.E. Koplin, "Education and National Integration in Ghana and and Kenya," doctoral dissertation, University of Oregon, 1968.

and fishermen improved by about 8 percent, both as proportions enrolled, during the period 1960-69.[20]) The biases against children of farmers, fishermen, and manual workers as measured by the selectivity indexes in Table 9.5 roughly halved between 1953 and 1966, while the privileges of the children of the elite, so very marked in 1953, were on this measure reduced by a factor of three over the same period. If we regard the ratio of the selectivity indexes as a measure of inequality, then it is true that this had declined from roughly 30 in 1953 to 5 in 1966—a rather considerable achievement given the very much greater absolute rise of the non-elite groups than of the elite groups even in Ghana.

We seem to have evidence here, then, of quite rapid erosion of the privileges of the elite in terms of access to secondary education with no evidence of the reverse procedure as suggested by P. Foster. But before we can reject Foster's hypothesis, we would need to know very much more about the composition of the "agriculture" group. As we emphasized in Chapter 3, differentiation has gone far in Ghanaian farming and it would be quite wrong to conclude that an increase in the selectivity indexes for farmers is the same as an increase in the provision of education for *poor* farmers. But, given the rather small number of very rich cocoa farmers and the fact that absentee landlords would not necessarily be classified in the census as farmers at all, it would be surprising if all the improvement in this group had been annexed by rich farmers. There is rather less ambiguity about the manual workers. So, with as little dogmatism as benefits a complex subject illuminated by inadequate data, we have to conclude that the evidence does not support Foster. But it does not finally refute him, either.

The only other country for which we have comparable data is Ivory Coast. This is fortuitous since it was comparing the experience of Ghana and Ivory Coast that originally led Foster to his hypothesis. But his hypothesis was based on the methodologically suspect assumption that comparing two countries at different levels of their educational development is a good proxy for comparing one country over time. Having found that Ghana was more advanced in its educational development than Ivory Coast but that the Ivory Coast system was more democratic than the Ghanaian, Foster put forward the hypothesis that inequalities increased. But when we look at these two countries over time, we find a very different picture. As we have already stressed, there is little evidence for the Foster hypothesis from Ghana. In Table 9.6, there is some evidence of increasing inequality in Ivory Coast. Despite some methodological difficulties in the table (which in fact tend to bias the figures against our argument and are therefore "safe"), there is evidence that the secondary system in Ivory Coast has indeed become less open to the rural population and more favourable to the urban population. If we assume that we can equate the modern sector with the urban sector, and the traditional sector with the rural sector, then the percentage of pupils from the urban areas has jumped from 27.5 percent to 37 percent in seven years. In this urban group, children from elite families have increased

TABLE 9.6

Ivory Coast: Selectivity Ratios of Sample Secondary School Population

Group or Sector	1963[a]			1969-70[b]
	Both Sexes	Male	Female	
Whole of primary sector	0.80	0.85	0.35	<0.67[c]
Whole of traditional sector (farmers, traders, handworkers)	<0.81[d]	0.85	0.45	0.72
Modern sector	>2.65	2.25	5.85	3.00
Private and professional services and public administration	8.30	6.70	20.45	9.10

[a]Sample of secondary school students from the second cycle (second, first, and terminal).

[b]Distribution of student population among the different socio-economic groups after figures for the entire 1969-70 student population.

[c]Less than 0.67 because 0.67 also includes traders of the traditional sector with the commercial farmers, and the ratio for traditional traders alone is likely to be above 0.67. The ratio for subsistence farmers is 0.20.

[d]Less than 0.81 and greater than 2.65 because all manual workers accounted for are included in the modern sector in the working out of ratios.

Sources: R. Clignet and P. Foster, *The Fortunate Few—A Study of Secondary Schools and Students in the Ivory Coast* (Evanston, Ill.: Northwestern University Press, 1966); also, unpublished data from Institut de recherche pedagogique, Abidjan, 1973).

from 21 percent to 28 percent, and children of urban manual workers from 7 percent to 9 percent. By contrast, in the rural areas, farmers' sons decreased from 67 percent to 56 percent.

This suggests that the main beneficiaries of the system have been in the urban population, particularly the elite groups.

Is it the case that this bias is associated with tribal discrimination, in Ivory Coast and elsewhere? If so, we might expect at leasts that aspect of bias to be more quickly perceived than socio-economic biases we have already discovered. We would expect that tribal groups that integrated most rapidly into the colonial system were those that ultimately took power, as politicians and administrators, at independence. Having perceived at first hand the benefits of education, they not only would want their children to go to school but would have the politico-administrative leverage to see that they were given the opportunity.

Table 9.7 bears out that expectation fairly clearly. In Ivory Coast, the Akan groups (Agni and Baoule) are over-represented, but not as much as the Lagoon

TABLE 9.7

Ivory Coast, Ghana, Tanzania, Uganda: Ethnic Selectivity
of University Students

Country and Tribe		Selectivity Index
Ivory Coast[a]	Agni	1.3
	Baoule	
	Lagoon cluster	2.0
	Kru	1.2
	Mandefou	0.6
	Senefou-Boli-Haipus	0.3
Ghana[b]	Asante	1.2
	Brong	0.5
	Ewe	1.1
	Fante	1.1
	Ga-Adangbe	2.0
Tanzania[b]	Asians	20.6
	Chagga	4.3
	Haya	1.8
	Nyakusa	1.7
	Nyamwezi	0.7
	Lukuma	0.4
Uganda[b]	Acholi	1.3
	Asians	4.6
	Ganda	1.7
	Kiga	1.3
	Lango	0.5
	Nkole	0.9
	Nyoro	1.4
	Teso	0.7
	Toro	0.6

[a]1969-70 data.

[b]1966 data.

Sources: Ivory Coast—unpublished data from Institute de recherche peda-gogique, Abidjan, 1973. Other countries—J.D. Barkan, "African University Students and Social Change: An Analysis of Student Opinion," doctoral dissertation, University of California at Los Angeles, 1970.

cluster, suggesting perhaps that geographical considerations are more important than political. In Ghana, the Ga and Asantes reveal the same pattern. In Tanzania, the Chagga have had long experience of education and were one of the first tribes to be widely educated by missionaries. Rather different, the Ganda not only were much more eager for education than other tribes in Uganda but also were quickly employed by the colonial regime as the local agents of administration. Although they have never had total control of national politics since independence, they have always (except perhaps in 1965-67 and 1972-73) been so politically influential that their interests have been well served. It seems clear, then, that ethnic inequalities persist. In all three countries, the tribes overrepresented are those that historically have had the greatest access to Western education. Conversely, those that are under-represented have not had as many schools in their respective localities.

It is much more difficult to be dogmatic about how those inequalities have changed over time. J.E. Goldthorpe has shown both that Ganda domination was much reduced (from 78 percent to 50 percent of Ugandan entries to Makerere) between 1922 and 1953 and that Kikuyu domination increased (from 32.5 percent to 44.5 percent of Kenyan entries) between 1930 and 1953.[21] This should at least put us on our guard against assuming too readily that growth in enrolments will eventually remove such disparities. At secondary school level, for instance, despite a decade of rapid growth in Ivory Coast, the pattern of tribal recruitment changed hardly at all. This suggests, and Malaysian evidence tends to confirm, the need for prolonged and determined political intervention before these inequalities are reduced. In Malaysia, for instance, the urban, English-medium nature of secondary school teaching has meant serious under-representation of Malays at the university level. In 1961, only 21 percent of university students were Malays. Partly as a result of the foundation of a new university with Malay-medium teaching and partly as a result of consistently improving Malay education at the secondary level, nearly half the student population was Malay in 1974. (Malays are 51 percent of the population; the shift from 1961 to 1965 occurred at the expense of Indians rather than Chinese.)[22]

It seems, then, that we should be reluctant to accept any general law about growing or diminishing inequalities in education over time. If high priority is given to industrialization, urbanization, and modernization, with all that they imply in terms of the distribution of political power between social groups, it is quite conceivable that inequalities will increase. If, on the contrary, high priority is demanded by the rural population, they may be much attenuated very quickly. It would be very surprising, for instance, if Tanzania, Zambia, and Sri Lanka demonstrated this increasing inequality, while it would be much less surprising if Malaysia and the Philippines did. Indeed, as we have already seen in Malaysia, poverty, socio-economic status, and urban residence together explain nearly 45 percent of differences in drop-out from schools. If it is the low-status rural poor who are dropping out of the Malaysian schools, it follows that they are likely to be seriously under-represented in the higher strata of the educational systems. This is illustrated in Table 9.8, which shows quite clearly that socio-economic status is directly related to enrolment for each of the three ethnic communities in both urban and rural areas.

In the Philippines, we have very little information on the way social selection operates in the schools. We have seen that the paucity of scholarships implies serious financial constraints for low-income families. Additionally, the very weak educational planning mechanism in the Philippines has introduced serious regional disparities.

Given the high correlation between regional origin, occupation, and income in the Philippines, it follows that access as well as take-up for low-income families is poor. We have no data on the determinants of performance in school, but we can examine the combined effects of the three types of bias—access, take-up, and social status—against low-income families at the university level.

As one would expect, Table 9.9 shows a heavy bias against the rural poor. Despite a long history of educational expansion and a rate of enrolment in

TABLE 9.8

Malaysia: Enrolment Percentages by Social Characteristics, 1972

Socio-Economic Status (combined scales*)	Urban				Rural			
	Malay	Chinese	Indian	Total	Malay	Chinese	Indian	Total
High	88	59	77	67	67	53	54	63
Medium	54	39	47	43	28	30	28	28
Low	27	22	21	22	14	18	16	15
Total	63	42	42	47	28	31	22	28
(absolute)	(503)	(1,294)	(140)	(1,937)	(1,776)	(544)	(235)	(2,555)

*Combined from socio-economic and "parental advantage" scales; weighting unspecified.

Note: Figures show percentages of youths (age 15+) still in form III or below, currently (1972) enrolled, by urbanization, socio-economic status, and community.

Source: Murad bin Mohd. Noor, Lapuran: jawatankuasa di atas kajian pendapat mengenai pelajaran dan masyarakat (lapuran keciciran) (Report on the "Study of opinion about education and society") (Kuala Lumpur: Ministry of Education, 1973).

TABLE 9.9

Philippines: Selectivity Ratios of University Students, 1969

Father's Occupation	State Colleges	Religious Colleges	Proprietary Colleges*
Professional, technical, managerial	5.2	5.3	3.2
Clerical, sales, service	4.1	4.2	4.3
Agriculture and related	0.19	0.16	0.31
Skilled and other	0.35	0.35	0.77

*Private non-religious colleges.

Note: The university structure is similar to that in the United States. Active population figures are the official 1968 Philippine labour force figures.

Source: Computed from data from Evelyn Miao, "The Structure and Performance of the Proprietary Institutions of Higher Education in the Philippines," doctoral dissertation, University of Wisconsin, 1971.

higher education that compares favourably with developed countries,* the sons of farmers and farm workers have in relative terms one twentieth the chance of reaching a state college that the sons of professional and technical groups have.[23] This pattern is less marked in proprietary colleges, partly because they are academically easier to enter and partly because they offer greater facilities for a limited range of non-technical vocational subjects, such as commerce and law. The exclusion of the poor is most marked in the religious colleges. In Ateneo de Manila (admittedly one of the most prestigious Church-related colleges), 82 percent of students come from families with yearly incomes exceeding ₱10,000. In 1971, only 6.1 percent of families were in this income category.[24]

It is extremely dangerous to compare selectivity ratios between countries because of the difficulties of defining social groups sufficiently rigorously. Interpretation of Table 9.10 must therefore be cautious—only groups I and V are reasonably homogeneous and comparable, although even here the wider definition of group I in Ghana and the very narrow definition in Kenya makes strict comparison ill advised. It is also relevant to re-emphasize the diversity to be found within the farmers' group in any one country, and much more between

---

*For instance, in 1965/66 the only country with a greater rate of enrolment in higher education was the United States, while enrolments in Sweden and Germany were roughly half and one third, respectively, that of the Philippines. At lower levels of education the developed countries had a slightly higher rate of enrolment, but the Philippines is not much lower.

TABLE 9.10

Summary: Selectivity Ratios of University Students

		Social Group				
Country	Year	I	II	III	IV	V
Ivory Coast	1974	14.4[a]	0.4			0.6[b]
Ghana[c]	1964	6.6	0.9	0.5	0.5	0.6
Kenya[c]	1966	227	74		0.59	0.3
Egypt	1968					
Cairo Univ.		8.97	3.62		6.05	0.2
Azhar Univ		4.84	2.42		0.47	0.25
Tunisia	1963/64	>2.8	2.1		1.1	<0.8
Philippines	1965	3.2	4.3		0.77	0.31

	Coverage of Social Groups				
	I	II	III	IV	V
Ivory Coast	Modern sector, public and private	Traders and craftsmen, mostly traditional			Farmers, fishermen
Ghana	Professional, administration, higher technical clerical	Traders	Skilled	Semi-skilled, Unskilled	Farmers, fishermen
Kenya	Professional, civil service, teaching	Business technical, semi-skilled		Unskilled agricultural	Farmers,, farm labourers
Egypt	Professional	Landowners, business		Labourers	Fellahs
Tunisia	Professional	White-collar workers		Hand-workers, traders, blue-collar workers	Farmers, farm labourers
Philippines	Professional, technical, managerial	Clerical, sales, service		Skilled, other	Agricultural and related

[a]Private 13.8; public 15.6.
[b]Smallholdings 0.6; estates 0.7.

countries. The table shows, at this level of generality, no more than that structural biases against the unskilled and the rural dwellers are strong, hierarchically ordered, and common to all six countries for which we have reasonable data.

This suggests that we should not assume that, as university education expands, it will become more democratic. It will only become more democratic if there is strong political determination to make it so.

CONCLUSION

With what conclusion, then, are we left? It is surely this: The three processes by which the poor are excluded from education—access, take-up, and differential performance—are strong and enduring. They are not overcome by the natural force of expansion. Indeed, expansion alone is consistent with increasing inequality. The removal of inequalities may be made easier in an expanding system, but growth alone does not produce equality; it must be accompanied by legal and administrative action that will ensure radical redistribution of educational opportunity to the poor. This action must be taken at many levels—at the level of

---

[c]Selectivity ratios at university level are lower than at secondary school level because in both countries access to university may be by parallel, non-secondary school, channels.

Sources:

Ivory Coast	Robert B. Charlick, "The Socio-Economic and Regional Origins of Ivorien Students at the University of Abidjan," mimeo. (Abidjan: Centre Ivorien de recherches economiques et sociales, March 1974).
Ghana and Kenya	R.E. Koplin, "Education and National Integration in Ghana and Kenya," doctoral dissertation, University of Oregon, 1968..
Egypt	Quoted by M. Abdel-Fadil, *Employment and Income Distribution in Egypt, 1952-70,* discussion paper (Norwich: University of East Anglia, 1974), from sample study by the National Centre of Social and Criminal Research, Cairo, 1968.
Tunisia	L. Ben Salem. *Democratisation de l'enseignement en Tunisie: Essai d'analyse du milieu d'origine des etudiants tunisiens, Revue tunisienne des sciences sociales* no. 16 (Tunis: Centre d'etudes et de recherches economiques et sociales, 1969).
Philippines	Evelyn Miao, "The Structure and Performance of the Proprietary Institutions of Higher Education in the Philippines," doctoral dissertation, University of Wisconsin, 1971.

TABLE 9.11

Tunisia: Selectivity Ratios of School and University Populations

| Socio-Professional Group of Fathers of School Children | 1969/70: Pupils of Sixth Form at End of: | | 1967/68: All Last-Year Students (Sixth and Third Year) | | | | | | 1963/64: Sample of University Students | | |
| | Primary | Secondary | Secondary Technical | Secondary | | | Sixth Technical Third | | Average | Male | Female |
	(1)	(2)	(3)	Average (4)	Male (5)	Female (6)	Male (7)	Female (8)	(9)	(10)	(11)
Upper-class professionals	≥1	2	>1.05	1.95	1.4	4.15	0.55	1.1	>2.8	2.1	6.8
White-collar workers, workers in services	1	2	<1.3	1.4	1.05	2.9	0.90	2.25	2.1	1.9	2.9
Handworkers, traders, blue-collar workers	1.5	1	<1.65	1.5	1.6	1.0	1.85	1.40	1.1	1.15	0.85
Farmers, agricultural workers	≤1(0.9)	0.6-0.7	>0.45	0.5	0.55	0.3	0.50	0.3	<0.8	<0.9	<0.35

Note: It is difficult to match the socio-professional categories defined independently in the different surveys and in the 1966 census. Further, the basic categories of the census are obscure. In the first two columns, the school population percentages have been adjusted to the social categories of Table 9.11; independent allowance was made for private schools. Columns 2 and 3 are likely to underestimate inequality because again the definition of social groups and total population was not wholly consistent with the definition in the school surveys. Figures in columns 2 and 4 should be strictly comparable but are not so, because some pupils of category 2 were included in the category of blue-collar workers. In column 7, the figure 0.55 for the upper-class professional category looks suspiciously low, but that may be because upper-class children tend to go to the academic stream rather than the technical stream and therefore are not counted in column 7. In the "university" columns, the group of students of upper-class professional origin is underestimated, and farmers in the population were overestimated; hence the inequality signs in the table.

Sources: Recensement general de la population mai 1966, vol. 7 (Tunis: Secretariat d'etat au plan et a l'economie nationale, May 1966), 2nd section, Table 5.3; *Aspects de l'enseignement primaire en chiffres, 1969-70* (Tunis: Ministere de l'education nationale); L. Ben Salem, "Democratisation de l'enseignement en Tunisie: Essai d'analyse du milieu d'origine des etudiants tunisiens," *Revue tunisienne des sciences sociales*, no. 16 (March 1969); secondary school data 1967/68 from survey by A. Bsais and C. Morrisson of Centre d'etudes et de recherches economiques et sociales, Tunis.

258

TABLE 9.12

Tunisia: Selectivity Ratios by Income Group of Secondary School and University Populations

Income Per Head Per Year in Pupil's Family[a]	Secondary Teaching		University Level
	1969/70	1967/68	1963/64
200 dinars	1.5	1.7	3.3
160 dinars			
80-200 dinars	1.35	1.4	
80-160 dinars			1.7
30-80 dinars	0.85	0.9	0.6[b]
30 dinars	0.75	0.85	0.7[b]

[a]Population distribution per income group from figures per household, taking average size of household as 6 persons.

[b]One cannot explain the order of these two figures; it is probably due to some rough and unrealistic approximation of low-income ranges by L. Ben Salem.

Sources: La consommation et les depenses des menages en Tunisie 1965-68 (Tunis: Institut national de la statistique, December 1970); A. Bsais and C. Morrisson (full results of their survey not published), Centre d'Etudes et de Recherches Economiques et Sociales, Tunis; L. Ben Salem, "Democratisation de l'enseignement en Tunisie: Essai d'analyse du milieu d'origine des etudiants tunisiens," *Revue tunisienne des sciences sociales*, no. 16 (1969).

access, at the level of take-up, at the level of performance through various types of compensatory education, but above all it must release resources to compensate for the poverty that is one of the central causes of the biases we have illustrated.

We have found only one country where these conditions seem at least in part to have been fulfilled. As Table 9.11 shows, selectivity ratios in Tunisia are of a quite different order of magnitude than those we have inspected so far. Although, as the inequality signs indicate, there are some methodological difficulties with the table, that conclusion at least seems secure.

It might be argued that the occupational groups in Table 9.11 are so large that they disguise major inequalities with respect to income. Table 9.12 suggests that that is hardly true. In secondary teaching, the ratio of the selectivity indexes between the richest group and the poorest is only 2, and less than 5 at the university level. Inequality has survived. But what is striking in relation to the data we have already examined for other countries is that it has been reduced so far. How may this be explained?

First, it is important to remember that one of the traditions of Arabic teaching is that it is available to all, and that the poor man and the beggar have as much right to be taught the Koran as the rich man. This is a very much stronger tradition in Islam than an equal right to education has ever been in Christendom. Of course, it is difficult to say how far this cultural basis has, in fact, affected government policy towards education, particularly in the light of the French colonial interlude and the continuing dependence at the secondary level on expatriate teachers. But the strong streak of cultural identification in Tunisian nationalism has meant that both government and individual families have given a very high priority to education—and to ensuring that the Koranic insistence on the rights of the poor man are not ignored.

Second, the educational system as a whole has grown extremely rapidly since independence, achieving by 1970 an over-all enrolment rate of 73 percent. Within this expansion, there has been a strong determination, particularly at the primary level, to direct resources into the deprived areas of the country and to reduce as far as possible regional disparities inherited from the colonial regime. In the poorest regions, the lack of employment opportunities for young people encourages parents to enrol their children, because education is the one step they can take to improve a child's chance of finding a job. This is not to say that all regional disparities have been removed. That is not the case. But those discrepancies are much less marked than in any other country we have examined. Further, within the urban areas there seems to be very little social bias against low-income or low-occupation groups. The bidonvilles seem to be as well served as the residential suburbs at the primary level, and the demand for education is certainly high and powerfully expressed there.* Probably because of cultural factors, certainly because of the well-known economic advantages of education, demand for it is pervasive throughout the social structure.

Another level of explanation is the important financial intervention of the state into education. The state gives scholarships to encourage children from low-income groups to continue in school beyond the primary level. In 1965-66, three quarters of the secondary students in Tunis had scholarships (up to 1973, the scholarship was the same as a secondary school leaver, with two years' secondary education, would earn). Although there is not universally free education (so that there remains a residual financial advantage for the child of a rich family), the filter effect of poverty has been much reduced.

If Tunisia has any lesson to teach, it is surely that upward mobility comes neither automatically nor from a quantitative expansion of the educational

---

*But it is regrettably true that no data we have found adequately cover the very poorest groups and the nearly destitute. At that level, no doubt, all the mechanisms of exclusion operate as forcefully in Tunisia as elsewhere.

system. Direct intervention on behalf of the poor, and especially the rural poor, is required. Without such vigorous remedial activity, the educational system tends to act in two ways.

First, it is an access cone that allows upward mobility in proportion to social, and particularly economic, status. The richer one is, the more likely it is that one will stay and succeed in the educational system. But some of the poor do get through. It is important to emphasize this because, even when social differentiation becomes more rigid after a period of very rapid change triggered by independence, that rigidity is not absolute. To change the metaphor, the school system is a filter, not a dam. It is therefore possible to maintain belief in the myth that education is a social leveller. Confidence in the system is not often shaken, partly because some poor do succeed in it, and partly because it has the outward trappings of an open, but tough, competition. For the successful individual, education will bestow both upward mobility and, possibly after a delay, substantial increases in the level of living. For society as a whole, the numbers that pass through the filter from the bottom to the very top are so small that the very fact of their success bestows its own legitimacy both on such increases in rewards as they thereby acquire and on the system itself. Indeed, it is precisely its selectivity that gives the system its durability. Con-mech as it is, it has so far shown a remarkable ability to survive.

For the second way in which the educational system seems to operate, unless it is subjected to vigorous political control, is as a mechanism by which the privileges of the privileged are confirmed in both relative and absolute terms. Education acts as accumulated wealth that can be passed from generation to generation, bestowing on its way great advantages, in terms of both consumption and widening the choice of function for each successive generation of recipients. It is not an entirely closed system. Not only so some non-privileged groups break into the circle but, as we have seen with respect to Ghana, some of the privileged groups have to surrender at least a portion of their privileges. In these terms, then, there is both upward and downward mobility. But the chances of downward mobility are much greater for the lower-status and lower-income groups than they are for the top groups.

We begin to see the full implications of this when we relate it to the argument presented in Chapters 7 and 8. There were showed that the elite group tends to grow rather faster than non-elite occupations. If we assume that recruitment to the elite is going to depend increasingly upon education, then the advantages of those in the elite are double. As a group, they have a higher chance of being educated and therefore a higher chance of remaining within a social group that is growing rapidly. By contrast, those who are excluded from school (for example, before completing secondary school) are likely to find it increasingly difficult to get a job and a secure income. We have presented evidence to suggest that it is precisely the low-income groups that are excluded from the educational system and thus find themselves the victims of a self-reinforcing, self-feeding system.

But it is a system that is changing through time. So far we have laid emphasis on its expansion. But when we see education in the perspective of Chapters 7 and 8, we have to recognize that, in some African countries, expansion already is becoming a *relative* contraction. Only rarely has this taken the form of an absolute fall in the number of children enrolled at any one educational level, but as governments attempt to control the rate of expansion of education, so far rather unsuccessfully, the pressures within the educational system become even more intense. Under these conditions, the advantages of the rich are likely to increase both absolutely and relatively. Inversely, the disadvantages of the not-rich are likely to become more severe: Without determined counteraction, the likelihood of exclusion, and the penalty for exclusion, are both likely to increase for them. This suggests that the need for direct and far-reaching intervention in the educational system on behalf of the non-privileged has always been strong. It is likely to become much stronger.

NOTES

1. George A. Auger (co-ordinator), *Absenteeism in Primary Schools in Tanzania,* Studies in Tanzanian Education no. 2 (Dar es Salaam: Institute of Education, 1970). Cf. the report on the "Study of Opinion about Education and Society," which shows that overall enrolment is rather weakly but negatively related to distance from school. Broken down by race, the relationship is inverse for Chinese but direct for Malays—a result that may well be related to the report's finding of a much higher level of motivation among Malays than among Chinese. Murad bin Mohd. Noor, *Lapuran: Jawatankuasa di atas kajian pendapat mengenai pelajaran dan masyarakat (lapuran Keciciran)* (Report on the "Study of opinion about education and society") (Kuala Lumpur: Ministry of Education, 1973).

2. M. Epstein, "Primary School Provision in Kapwepwe and Matero Suburbs," mimeo. (Lusaka: Ministry of Education, 1970).

3. Mary R. Hollnsteiner, "Socio-Economic Themes and Variations in a Low Income Urban Neighbourhood," in "Workshop on Manpower and Human Resources," proceedings of a seminar held at the University of the Philippines at Los Banos, Laguna, October 1972 (mimeo.), Table 6.

4. S. Heyneman, "Socio-Economic Status and Academic Achievement in Uganda: How Fair Is the Primary Leaving Examination to the Less Privileged?" and "Some Correlates of Primary School Achievement in Uganda," mimeo. (Chicago: Comparative Education Center, University of Chicago, 1973).

5. *Education Survey Report: Education for National Development*, Presidential Commission to Survey Philippine Education (Manila, 1970), p. 133.

6. L.F.B. Dubbeldam, *The Primary School and the Community in Mwanza District, Tanzania* (Gronigen: CESO, 1970), p. 24.

7. *Report of the Committee on Non-School Going Children*, Sessional Paper no. 3 (Colombo, 1960), p. 9.

8. Sessional Paper no. 5 (Colombo, 1972).

9. A. Bsais and C. Morrisson, unpublished research at Centre d'Etudes et de recherches cconomiques et sociales, Tunis, 1972.

10. H.H. Tias, M. Carnoy, and R. Sack, "Middle Level Manpower in Tunisia: The Link Between Socio-Economic Origin, Schooling and Job History," mimeo. (Washington, D.C.: International Bank for Reconstruction and Development, October 1972).

11. Heyneman, op. cit.

12. The data for this and the following paragraph are from D.A. Shiman, "The Relationship of Socio-Economic and School Factors to the Achievement of Male Secondary School Students in Ghana," doctoral dissertation, University of California at Los Angeles, 1970.

13. Cf. A. Somerset (unattributed), "The Examination and Selection System and the Certificate of Primary Education," in *Employment, Incomes and Equality: A Strategy for Increasing Productive Employment in Kenya*, report of an inter-agency team financed by the United National Development Programme and organized by the International Labour Organization (Geneva: ILO, 1972).

14. J. Silvey, "Preliminary Thoughts on Aptitude Testing and Educational Selection in E. Africa," East African Universities Social Science Council, Kampala, 1962, pp. 8-9.

15. Heyneman, op. cit.

16. ILO, *Matching Employment Opportunities and Expectations: A Programme of Action for Ceylon*, report of an inter-agency team organized by the ILO (Geneva: ILO, 1971); Noor, op. cit.; I.K. Chinebuah, "Candidates' Performance in the 'O' Level English Examination," *Ghana Journal of Education* 1, no. 4 (September 1970).

17. See, for example, S.H. Irvine, "Factor Analysis of African Abilities: Constraints Across Cultures," *Psychological Bulletin* 71 (1969): 22-32; E.L. Klingelhofer, "Performance of Tanzanian Secondary School Pupils on the Raven's Standard Matrices Test," *Journal of Social Psychology* 72, p. 204.

18. P. Foster, "Secondary Schooling and Educational Opportunity: Ghana and the Ivory Coast," in *Social Sciences and the Comparative Study of Educational Systems* (Berkeley: University of California, 1969).

19. *Les rendements de l'enseignement du premier degre en Afrique francophone* (Paris: Institut d'Etude de developpement economique et social, 1967).

20. Shiman, op. cit.

21. J.E. Goldthorpe, *An African Elite: Makerere College Students 1922-60* (London: Oxford University Press for East African Institute of Social Research, 1965).

22. See J.-P. Arles, "Ethic and Socio-Economic Structures in Malaysia," *International Labour Review* (Geneva) 10A, no. 6 (December 1971); U.A. Aziz, "Access to the University of Malaya," report submitted to UNESCO, mimeo. (Kuala Lumpur, 1972).

23. *Education Survey Report*, op. cit.

24. E. Miao, "The Structure and Performance of the Proprietary Institutions of Higher Education in the Philippines," doctoral dissertation, University of Wisconsin, 1971; E. Tan and E. Miao, "The Structure and Performance of Philippine Educational Institutions" (Institute of Economic Development and Research, University of the Philippines, 1971); F. Lynch, S.J., "Socio-Economic Status of Ateneo Students" (Manila: Institute of Philippine Culture, 1970).

THE ORIGINS OF THE PROBLEM

Let us now turn to other forms of selection apart from formal education. At the point at which a child is excluded from further education, he might be expected to start to look for a job. As we emphasized in Chapter 8, one of the determinants of success in that search is the degree of competition for jobs at a given skill level. We argued there that, the higher the education a young man or woman has received, the less competitive the search for a job is likely to be. Those with primary education alone are now so numerous in every country, in relation to employment opportunities in the formal sector, that competition for jobs is inevitably intense. Indeed there are countries, such as Sri Lanka and the Philippines, where there is already such a surplus of university graduates that possession of a high academic qualification is no guarantee of employment. But in general, the higher the qualification, the less competitive the market and the quicker an acceptable job may be found.

Some examples will illustrate the point. We have already seen that in Ghana employment in the middle and lower white-collar group is growing at about 10,000 posts a year. It is possible that this is an underestimate as it is based on official labour enumerations, with the well-known problems of under-counting. But they are high estimates and could credibly be increased by only 10 to 15 percent.

Yet the output of secondary schools at form V level in 1971 (i.e., excluding those who go on to upper secondary) was about 8,000. (This includes a 10 percent drop-out rate.) From this it would be a mistake to conclude that the market was under-supplied or approaching equilibrium, because simultaneously over 40,000 middle school leavers were released onto the job market. Many of these would aspire to employment in at least the lower ranks of the middle-level skill group. Thus while, at least in the early 1970s, secondary school graduates in Ghana would not generally find it difficult to get a job at this level, competition among middle school leavers was intense. (In 1965, a total of 45 percent of a sample of middle school leavers was still unemployed—in the sense of seeking work and not absorbed in regular employment on the family farm or business—18 months after leaving school.[1])

This situation seems likely to continue. For whereas secondary school enrolments grew relatively slowly in Ghana in the late 1960s (indeed they fell after 1965 and did not recover to the same level until 1970) the disequilibrium at the level of middle schools is fundamental. Chronic over-supply is therefore likely to continue for many years yet (over-supply, that, is, to the formal, enumerated sector). This underlines the importance of selection at the secondary school level, for it transfers a youth from a market in chronic and serious disequilibrium to a market that is roughly in equilibrium. For that very reason, it is politically difficult to resist expansion of secondary schools.

In Ivory Coast, the disequilibrium already seems to involve the secondary schools. In 1972, the likely output of secondary students with the BEPC (roughly equivalent to "O" Level) was 9,000, of whom about 6,500 were seeking jobs at this level.* Since only 5,000 such jobs were created, it is clear that competition for middle-level jobs among secondary school leavers is already intense, and that the less able and the less fortunate of them, and all the drop-outs, will have to compete with primary school leavers for blue-collar jobs.

In Cameroon in 1970-71, one estimates suggests that there was a surplus of 3,800 secondary school drop-outs over the number of vacancies for untrained labour in the modern sector. (This assumes that the secondary school drop-outs will in fact accept work as untrained labourers.[2]) This implies not only a high penalty for those who fail to secure a secondary school place, but no less a penalty for those who fall by the wayside thereafter.

Two more surprising examples are Zambia and Tanzania. In the former, by 1972 nearly 60,000 children were leaving primary school and unable to continue at secondary school. By 1978, that figure is expected to reach 100,000 or almost 75 percent of the entire 14-year-old age group. As one commentator has put it:

---

*This is a minimum estimate of the disequilibrium because it ignores secondary school drop-outs, and it assumes that lower-grade white-collar workers all have secondary education.

These young people are puzzled and discouraged by the lack of opportunities for them at secondary school, in pre-vocational training programmes, and in urban employment. The Zambian public is perplexed at the shortage of employment and educational opportunities in one of independent Africa's most industrialised countries, a country whose rate of educational expansion since Independence has been remarkable even by African standards. They tend to be incredulous that a country so lacking in educationally qualified personnel at independence should suddenly be faced by an acute school leaver problem.[3]

The scale of the problem is indicated by the fact that between June 1971 and June 1972 African employment in Zambia increased by 5,000.* Now it is true that the figure is an underestimate, since it is based on the official employment enquiry, which does not cover small firms, family businesses, and the whole of the informal sector. It would therefore be misleading to conclude that a primary school leaver had one chance in twelve of finding employment, but it is quite clear that competition for a preferred job would be intense.

It would be made the more intense by the fact that in 1972 more than 10,000 secondary school leavers entered the job market. Whereas in Zambia in the 1960s a secondary education was an infallible guarantee of formal employment, by 1972 it was clear that only half of the secondary school leavers would be able to find jobs in the formal sector. A proportion, and possibly a large proportion, of those jobs would be unskilled manual jobs hitherto undertaken by the uneducated or (reluctantly) by the primary school leavers.

In Tanzania, the same problem has already emerged despite the official policy of expanding secondary and higher education only as fast as manpower demand expands. Partly this is a technical problem: Tanzania has had little more success than other African countries in successfully projecting the demand for manpower sufficiently far ahead to take account of the lags in the educational system. More interesting, it is a political problem in that attempts to hold down the expansion of secondary education have been continuously challenged at every level of the party structure. The loudest complaints have come from areas presently ill served by secondary schools—despite the fact that selection is national and most secondary schools have boarding facilities. But that is probably no more than a peg on which to hang the argument that a severe squeeze on secondary school places deprives a larger number of families of the chance of competing for the small number of prizes. If you do not have a lottery ticket, you *cannot* win a prize; if you do have one, you *may* not.

---

*This is net of retirements. With a young employed labour force, retirements are likely to be low for some years. At the *secondary* level, a high estimate would add fewer than 1,000 jobs to the annual net increase.

The result has been that competition among post-primary entrants to the labour market has roughly doubled (in terms of jobs per entrant in the formal sector) between 1964 and 1970. While in 1964 the total numbers of jobs and school leavers were roughly in balance, by 1970 there were four school leavers for each job in the formal sector.[4]

If this is a new problem in Africa, its scale is still trivial by comparison with that in Sri Lanka. Table 10.1 shows that as educational achievement increases, so unemployment rates increase up to "A" level, where (except for young women in the rural areas) unemployment rates fall sharply. Here the structure of the labour market and the structure of the educational system are so out of kilter that the majority of those who pass "O" level are still unemployed at the age of 25. For our purposes, the contrast lies not with those who are unschooled or had only primary school—who show quite low levels of unemployment, by Sri Lankan standards, after the age of 20—but with the "A" level group. For the decreased difficulty that those with "A" level have in finding employment readily explains the intense competition in Sri Lanka to stay in school to take this exam and indeed to go on to a university.*

The point does not need labouring. Although the "floor" may be higher in countries with a very developed educational system, educational achievement has the effect of transferring people from over-supplied labour markets to under-supplied labour markets. Only in countries like the Philippines—and India— which have a surplus of university graduates does this floor effectively cease to exist; elsewhere, the penalty for exclusion from the educational system is to be placed in the highly competitive market. There employment brings little job security, although it may bring increases in real income for those who are able to find employment in the formal sector.

THE JOB HUNT

This brings into focus the importance of selection and exclusion mechanisms in the actual search for employment at any given level of education. This is

---

*But interestingly, the rate at which "A" level holders find employment in the early years after graduation is less rapid than that of "O" level holders. In other words, the "A" level candidate who is unsuccessful in finding work soon after graduation seems to have more difficulty in his late twenties and early thirties than does the "O" level candidate. The most likely explanation is that the "A level candidate is slower to revise his aspirations than is the "O" level candidate—a reluctance that could be partly explained by the *higher* rate of employment of "A" level candidates.

TABLE 10.1

Sri Lanka: Job Seekers by Education, Age, and Sector, 1969/70
(both sexes; percentages)

	Aged 15-19				Aged 20-24			
	Urban	Rural	Estate	Total	Urban	Rural	Estate	Total
No schooling	13	(11)*	31	23	29	8	5	8
Primary	44	34	27	34	16	17	12	15
Middle	57	41	71	46	44	38	25	39
Passed "O" level	87	93	–	92	45	69	(33)*	63
Passed "A" level	–	–	–	–	(22)*	(83)*	–	69
Total	51	41	32	41	37	39	11	34

*Parentheses indicate fewer than ten observations.

Source: International Labour Organization, Matching Employment Opportunities and Expectations: A Programme of Action for Ceylon, report of an inter-agency team organized by the ILO (Geneva: ILC, 1971), p. 28, as corrected by subsequent corrigendum sheet. Ron Dore tells us the figures in the table were based on the first round of the Socio-Economic Survey 1969/70. The second round raised the aggregate values significantly, but the sector breakdown is not available.

269

another under-researched area in which only a very few general propositions seem to be supported by adequate field work. One area that is almost wholly under-researched is the way in which the elite and white-collar groups, which tend to secure a disproportionate share of educational opportunity, use their own networks to secure employment for their own children. For, as we have seen, the days in which secondary education guaranteed employment have already passed in many countries and are passing in the rest. Is it the case, then, that a secondary school leaver from a relatively advantaged home has greater opportunity of securing employment than a fellow school leaver with precisely the same academic qualifications but from a poorer home background?

In most countries of Africa and Asia, ethnic and kin relationships are important, perhaps the most important, means of securing employment. A kinsman will accept his obligation to help in the search for a job. But other relationships also may be helpful—e.g., political dependence, religious affiliation, or friendship.

Helga Jacobson has well described how this system works in Cebu City, Philippines:

> A characteristic feature of social relationships in this local context is that people obtain positions, privileges, and social advantages through the manipulation of contacts and connections and through the use of intermediaries. In the urban area almost any service or item that is required can be made more readily accessible by the strategic manipulation of such contacts and connections. Whether one is buying a boat ticket to Manila, applying for a position as a bank clerk, or obtaining a licence to operate a stall on the market makes no difference, all transactions are carried out more efficiently if there is a social connection between the participants. Where aid is given a return is expected—either an equivalent service or the provision of another contact, or sometimes participation in the formation of a clientele. These alternatives failing, the service must be bought.
>
> In order to operate this system it is necessary to maintain a wide range of differentiated contacts which can be activated when needed. There are various ways in which this can be accomplished and *the higher one stands in the social hierarchy, the greater the range of possible contacts*. The basic network of "human resources" centres on relatives and it is through them extended to non-kin. This latter circle can then be extended further. The important point is to attain as differentiated a network of connections as possible in terms of relationship to the members and their occupations. *The school and university situation are ideal for they provide a setting in which people can make the right kind of friends*. The maintenance of this kind of a

network of social relationships can be regarded as an investment. However, *it can only be an investment for those with resources.* At the lowest level almost the only opening is that of becoming in some sense a client.[5] [Emphasis added.]

As Jacobson points out, those who can establish a reciprocal or potentially reciprocal relationship are at a great advantage over those who can never be more than dependent clients. But a client with access to, and a claim on, a powerful or influential patron is at a great advantage over whose who have no patron.

How, then, does one acquire a patron? There is no general answer to that question; it varies from society to society, and from group to group. In Sri Lanka, for example, one of the occupations of all politicians is the writing of letters of recommendation for constituents. In Africa, partly as a result of very rapid social change over the last quarter of a century and partly as a result of the traditional concepts of social obligations, a patron's obligation to a client is no less real if the client comes from very humble rural origins than if he comes from an elevated urban family. That, at least, is the theory. But there are reasons for doubting its validity in practice.

David Jacobson made a careful study of elite/non-elite friendship patterns in Mbale, Uganda, and concluded that it is in practice difficult and perhaps impossible for a low-income father to discharge his family obligations *and* maintain a relationship of friendship with the high-income elite. If he does not discharge his family obligations, he will certainly be condemned by his kinsmen and peers, and probably by his would be elite friends. If he does not maintain friendship with the elite (principally by common drinking), his claim upon them is far less valid.[6] It may generally be true that a patron's determination to discharge his obligation varies according to the possibilities of reciprocity, the political, social, and economic *need* to oblige a client of his kin, and the very volume of requests from clients. We simply do not know. Both Helga and David Jacobson, however, give empirical evidence that job-seekers from families with a low social and economic status usually are at a disadvantage. Given the very small size of the elite-patron groups and the intensity of the competition for jobs, it is probable that, while some job-seekers from poor families and all elite job-seekers have such access to patrons, a large number of job-seekers from poor families do not have such access. (It should be noted that the openness, in this sense, of patron-client relationships may be enhanced by the employment of "brokers"—e.g., foremen charged to find reliable workers. If a broker is used, he becomes a quasi-patron and those who can claim a client relationship with him are, all things being equal, more likely to find employment than those who cannot.[7])

An alternative hypothesis is that the patronage system stays wide open but becomes relatively ineffectual. This seems to be what has happened in Sri Lanka, where a chit from a Member of Parliament is easily obtained but is not very effective in securing employment (although it may be true that, without a chit, one has no chance of getting a job at all). Here the very volume of requests has devalued the efficiency of the relationship in rather the same way as prolonged recourse to the relationship seems to make its discharge decreasingly generous.

A third variable that may act differentially in the job hunt is the length of time that a job-seeker can remain in town looking for work. This depends on the means of support (particularly the provision of food and accommodation) that he can mobilize during his search for a job.* A job-seeker typically passes from house to house of close kin, staying as long as he can with each and moving on when his welcome is exhausted or the demand for reciprocal labour jeopardizes the effectiveness of his search for employment. A job-seeker without supportive kin or with a family (since a kin group will support a single man but less willingly his family[8]) is driven to settle in a peri-urban village. There he (or his wife) can grow subsistence food while his wife (or he) takes paid employment in the informal sector or runs a small business—such as a market stall or beer shop or making simple artifacts. Clearly, the period for and efficiency with which a man can look for work depends upon the success of these attempts at securing a subsistence, and inversely upon the time such activities take. For the search for a job is a demanding and almost professional occupation in which the man who adopts a casual in-and-out approach is unlikely to be as successful as the man who keeps his contacts "warm," hears of new businesses starting or new factories opening, and generally widens his networks.

It is again very dangerous to relate these variables directly to social background. Except perhaps among the elite, there is no one-to-one relationship between social origin and the ability to survive. A more crucial variable is the location of residence. If the nuclear family and immediate kin group has its home in town or within easy access of town, then the young job-seeker is unlikely to be under the same pressure to move as is the rural migrant staying with kinsmen who have settled in town. Particularly if the nuclear family has a small piece of land or simple business to which the job-seeker can make a token contribution of labour, he is likely to be able to continue his search for satisfactory employment much longer.

This raises an important distinction, because it suggests that those who have adequate urban "life support" systems are able to hold out for longer before

---

*The level of living of job seekers is considered in Chapter 11. But neither there nor in this chapter is the role of ethnic and other associations discussed. Despite their possible importance, we know too little about the way the lowest-income families use these associations in the job hunt to include an adequate consideration here.

being obliged to trade down to more menial jobs than those to which their educational qualifications would in theory give access. In this context, subsidized
food or free food as in Sri Lanka and, to a much lesser extent, Egypt, may be a
very important cushion that allows the young job-seeker to continue to look
for employment at an appropriate level. Certainly the data in Table 10.1 suggest that in Sri Lanka young educated and semi-educated job-seekers do not
hurry to revise their aspirations or to accept any job they can get—a suggestion
confirmed by the reported inability of employers to recruit workers for manual
jobs, even quite well-paid manual jobs, at a time when unemployment among
young "O" level holders is, as we have seen, extremely high.[9] Sooner or later
some such adjustment does take place, and it may well be that marriage and
child-rearing are important catalysts in this adjustment—in much the same way
that the need to raise a bride price seems to have been in an earlier period in
East Africa.

THE JOB HUNT AND VOCATIONAL TRAINING

Competition for any job is likely to be intense; the search for it hard,
exhausting, and (in some cases) demeaning. It is made a great deal easier for the
man who has a specific, recognized skill to offer. But in every country we have
reviewed, we have been struck by the inadequacy of technical training—in
terms of both quantity and quality. Virtually every manpower survey we have
seen has revealed serious and prolonged shortages at this level. Yet the scale of
resources devoted to technical training at this level remains pitifully small. In
Uganda, the most recent critique of manpower policies speaks of technical
training as "an unmitigated disaster."[10] In Ghana, the foundation of the University of Science and Technology at Kumasi was a bold attempt to break the
bottleneck at the higher white-collar technical level. But at the blue-collar level
the latest manpower survey shows that in 1970 there were likely to be vacancies for 1,590 fitters, mechanics, and electricians. And yet the total formal
training capacity can produce only 350 a year. In another important occupation, that of blacksmiths and toolmakers, less than 16 percent of likely demand
was filled by formal training capacity. In Tunisia, the ISEA (Institut des
sciences economiques appliquees) model for 1966-80 foresees a short-fall of
nearly 30 percent in training capacity at the high-skill level and of nearly 40
percent at the middle technical level.[11] In 1968 in Ivory Coast, 400 young
people graduated from technical training centres—to meet a demand for 6,000
additional skilled technicians.[12]

In Zambia, government investment in training facilities is particularly
interesting. In 1968, for instance, government was training roughly 2,300

employees in professional and technical grades, compared with only 375 in the clerical grades. At a time when training facilities of all sorts were extremely scarce and when the returns of such training were very high, the greatest share of public resources went into expanding the top end of the white-collar occupational category. This inevitably accelerated the process of social and economic differentiation in the industrial economy at a time when political leadership was trying to develop a philosophy that laid emphasis on traditional virtues of the Zambian society—of which *economic* differentiation was not generally one.

Even in cases where highly trained workers were in extremely short supply, governments and industry have been show to expand training facilities, with the inevitable result that they have become yet more dependent upon alien skills. This is supremely true in Ivory Coast and can be illustrated in some sectors and some skill groups in Cameroon, Zambia and Kenya (see above, pp. 208-9).

The effect of the inadequacy of technical training and the large number of expatriates employed is, of course, to give to those who do secure technical training a particular market advantage that, whatever may happen to registered wage rates, the more footloose can exploit. (This assumes that those with technical training have no difficulty in finding employment. This is not always so. A survey in 1971 in Cameroon showed that 35 percent of graduates of technical schools took 6 to 9 months to find a job and 25 percent of surveyed graduates were still without employment. This is partly an indictment of the quality of the schools and partly a reflection of employers' preference for untrained manpower that can be trained for highly specific functions and thus rendered much less mobile. In Tunisia, Christian Morrisson has shown that many of the technically trained young men go to France; of those who stay in Tunisia, only 49 percent actually work in the industrial sector. Thirty-five percent work in the public sector in jobs that bear no relation to their technical training.[13])

These difficulties of adjustment notwithstanding, we would like to know more about selection for technical training. Of this we know little. But two common characteristics are the urban (and metropolitan) bias of the location of training institutes, which presumably gives a particular advantage to urban dwellers,[14] and the tendency for training establishments to adapt their educational qualifications to the supply of educated applicants. In times of acute shortage, as in Zambia from 1964 to 1967, both employers and training institutions adjust their requirements downwards, recognizing that that is the only way they will be able to fill their quota. Conversely, when more educated manpower becomes available, they tend to increase their educational requirements, in some cases to levels that are above what is objectively required to complete the course.

This common under-investment in training for skilled blue-collar workers is excused on the grounds that such skills can only be learned on the job.* Even if this is true, it is important to emphasize that on-the-job training requires two features of employment at this level. The first is stability: An employee must have an incentive, and indeed an opportunity, to remain on a given job, with an adequate level of supervision, for long enough to learn the trade thoroughly and systematically. Conversely, he must have the opportunity to progress up the skill ladder, so that his skill inventory is continually expanded and his experience is accumulated in mutually reinforcing packages. Only so is on-the-job training likely to be as successful from the trainee's point of view as a full "formal" course.

This requires not only that the employer take a sufficiently long-run and enlightened view of his own self-interest to provide such a training programme, but also that the individual take a long-term view of his economic prospects. Particularly if the market for his skill or semi-skill is tight, there is every incentive to sell his skill to the highest bidder, irrespective of the long-term training opportunities the employment offers. The greater the economic pressure on the individual, then, the less likely he is to be able to meet the preconditions of skill accumulation. In this sense, skill accumulation tends to be biased in favour of the more economically buoyant members (e.g., those with fewer dependents) of this group. It has become well recognized in rich countries that, even when earnings are not forfeited during training, the economically precarious are less likely to acquire skills.[15] The same mechanisms of deterrence seem to operate in the poor countries; indeed, the pressure of poverty is likely to be more intense.

The high blue-collar skill group, then, is not open in any fundamental sense. Like the bureaucratic elite, it has a set of selective biases. It is biased against those who cannot, or will not, stay on a particular job long enough to acquire necessary skills. It is biased against those who do not find an appropriate progression of skills. And it is biased against those who cannot compete educationally with the requirements of the employer.

---

*This is a particularly common explanation from employers. But it is usually in the employer's interest to employ cheap, untrained labour and equip the employee with only one highly specific skill. He is then much less mobile than a fully trained worker and can be paid at a lower rate.

CONCLUSION

In the last two chapters, we have seen some of the systemic biases against poor families in the competitive search for education and a job. Those who are excluded from school and those who are excluded from a job market in rough balance are the victims of the processes we have described in this chapter. In the next chapter, we examine in more detail the effect of those processes on the level of living of the urban excluded.

But there is another sense in which they are victims—a sense that is significant also in the context of the next chapter. There we shall present much evidence to show that one of the effects of education in rural areas is to encourage young school leavers to migrate to the towns in search of non-agricultural (not necessarily white-collar) employment. Some find it quickly. Some find it eventually. Many eke out a precarious and vulnerable living, caught in a ravel of relationships in which they are always the weaker partner.

But some, and perhaps a growing number, never establish themselves in town and return to the rural areas, perhaps temporarily, perhaps permanently.* Their frustration, disappointment, and sense of defeat is not only psychologically damaging; it is a paradigm of relative impoverishment. Having "failed" at school and in town, the returned migrant is doubly impoverished—precisely by the institution that serves to enrich others. For him, at least, the nature of education and the biases in the search for a job as currently conceived are nothing short of cruel oppression. But it is to his peers who stay in town, unable to break into (or stay in) the formal sector, that we turn in the next chapter.

NOTES

1. C. Scott and T. Subrahmanyo, *Survey of Ghana Middle Schools*, Technical Publication Series no. 4 (Legon: Institute of Statistical, Social and Economic Research, 1957), p. 50. Cf. Kenneth Blakemore, "Resistance to Formal Education in Ghana: Its Implications for the Status of School Leavers," *Comparative Education Review*, forthcoming; we are grateful to the author for allowing us to see a draft of this article.

---

*The volume of research on returned "failures," except in so far as they feature in general rural surveys, is negligble by comparison with that on urban immigrants. For that reason, we have not been able to treat them adequately in Chapter 5. Hopefully, increasing interest in income distribution and equity will lead to more work in this field.

2. Computed from data in Ministere du plan et de l'amenagement du territoire, *Troisieme plan quinquennal de developpement economique et social, 1971-76* (Yaounde, 1971); Ministere d l'education nationale, *La formation technique et professionale en Republique Federale du Cameroun en 1970-71* (Yaounde: Service de la planification, 1971).

3. C. Angi and T. Coombe, "Training Programmes and Employment Opportunities for Primary School Leavers in Zambia," *Manpower and Unemployment Research in Africa* 2, no. 2 (November 1961): 1.

4. R.H. Sabot, "Education, Income Distribution, and Rates of Urban Migration in Tanzania (Economic Research Bureau, University of Dar es Salaam, and Institute of Economics and Statistics, Oxford University, March 1972).

5. Helga E. Jacobson, "Some Indirect Effects of Poverty and Lack of Educational Opportunity in a Philippine Provincial City," *Manpower and Unemployment Research* 2, no. 2 (1969).

6. David Jacobson, "Culture and Stratification among Urban Africans," *Journal of African and Asian Studies* 5 (1970).

7. See International Labour Organization, *Employment, Incomes and Equality: A Strategy for Increasing Productive Employment in Kenya*, report of an inter-agency team financed by the United Nations Development Programme and organized by the ILO (Geneva: ILO, 1972), pp. 509-10.

8. Peter W.C. Gutkind, "The Energy of Despair: Social Organization of the Unemployed in Two African Cities: Lagos and Nairobi," *Civilisations* 17, no. 3 (1967): 199.

9. ILO, *Matching Employment Opportunities and Expectations: A Programme of Action for Ceylon*, report of an inter-agency team organized by the ILO (Geneva: ILO, 1971).

10. E.O. Ochieng, "High Level Manpower Planning in Uganda," master's thesis, Makerere University, 1973.

11. *Perspectives Sectorelles et globales au niveau de l'emploi en 1980* (Tunis: Direction du plan and Institut de licence economique appliquee, 1970).

12. A. Achio, *Physiognomonie de l'emploi, Cote d'Ivoire, 1968-75* (Abidjan: Ministere du Plan, 1969).

13. Ministere de l'education nationale, *Le devenir des eleves de l'enseignement technique* (Yaounde, 1971). See also C. Morrisson, "Emploi et formation en Tunisie," *Cahiers du Centre d'Etudes et de Recherches Economiques et Sociales* (serie economique) no. 4 (Tunis, 1973).

14. Angi and Coombe, op. cit.; *Matching Employment Opportunities*, op. cit., pp. 180-82.

15. See, for instance, the detailed study of low-income groups in Sweden, *Svenska folkets inkomster* (Stockholm: Soll., 1970).

11

THE URBAN EXCLUDED IN AFRICA

The process of economic growth is accompanied by occupational differentiation and, over the longer term, social stratification. In most African countries, opportunities for those adequately qualified have been greater at high-skill levels than at the manual level. This means that those who cannot compete in the middle- and high-level skill groups are at a relative disadvantage in finding a job. But for those who succeed in finding a full-time job in larger firms, political and institutional pressures have ensured at least the protection of existing levels of real income in most countries for most of the time. In this they, the lucky few, stand in marked contrast to those who cannot find jobs in the formal or enumerated sector. It is with these, the relatively under-educated and unskilled who are squeezed out of the formal sector, that we are concerned in this chapter.

They are excluded from full-time employment in the formal sector by the interaction of two processes—the slow growth of employment and the rapid increase in the numbers of those seeking employment at this level. It is to an analysis of these two forces that we must turn first.

Table 11.1 presents data on the rate of growth of formal employment as enumerated in labour surveys and the rate of growth of the urban population. It is important to understand the significance of the former. Most of the countries conduct yearly (in some cases half-yearly) labour enumerations. These are designed to cover all government departments and all private enterprises above a certain minimum size—usually five or ten employees. Because smaller firms

TABLE 11.1

Selected African Countries: Annual Rates of Growth of Enumerated Employment, GDP, and Urban Population (percentages)

Country	Non-Agricultural Employment in Formal Sector		GDP Growth 1960-71	Urban Population	
	Year	Growth		Year	Growth
Kenya	1965-70	2.0	6.1	1962-69	7.2
Tanzania	1964-71	9.4	4.3	1957-70	7.8
Uganda	1961-70	3.9	3.8	1961-70	8.8
Zambia	1961-73	4.9	1.2	1963-69	8.3
Ghana	1953-69	2.7	2.8	1960-70	7.2
Upper Volta	1963-69	5.8	3.0	1960-70	6.1
Ivory Coast	1963-70	4.1	7.4	1965-70	8.7
Cameroon	1964-70	2.4	6.1	1965-70	6.4
Tunisia	1960-69	7.5*	4.5	1956-66	3.9

*Private sector 1960-69; public sector extrapolated from 1968-72 data.

Sources: Annual statistical reports of each country; urban population from Decennial Census data.

come and go and because smaller entrepreneurs are not always punctilious with their paper work, the coverage of these surveys of the smaller firms is often very incomplete. The figures are therefore not usually a good guide to the total level of employment. In nearly every country that has an employees' provident fund, the number of employees contributing usually far exceeds the number of employees enumerated in the labour surveys. Similarly, labour statistics from censuses usually much exceed those from labour enumerations. Nonetheless, unless there has been a marked shift in the structure of industry and commerce from large firms towards smaller firms, the labour enumerations give a reasonable indication of the rate of growth of employment. This is the more true the greater the proportion of public employees in the total. Thus the labour enumerations in Ghana, with nearly three-quarters of the labour force employed directly or indirectly by the state, may be less imperfect than those of Ivory Coast. This means that the figures in Table 11.1 should be taken as orders of magnitude of a trend around which there are of course major short-term variations.

For periods of falling employment or of no growth at all are not uncommon. There was no recorded employment growth in Ghana between 1965 and 1968; in Uganda from 1961 to 1964; and in Zambia from 1960 to 1963. During these periods, the supply of jobs came only from replacement of the existing labour force--usually rather a low figure as there are few old men in employment. But those who did find jobs within the limits of the modest growth rates in the table secured substantial advantages thereby. For the workers covered by the enumeration are those employed by the larger firms in the modern sector and in the public sector. They are therefore those who are likely to have whatever protection the law provides in terms of conditions of employment, minimum wages, security of tenure, the right to organize, fringe benefits, sick pay, paid holidays, and overtime. (Obviously, not all employees have all these benefits; all have some of them, and public sector employees and employees in the largest private firms have most of them.)

Table 11.1 shows that, with the exception of Tanzania and Tunisia, the rate of growth of employment in all our countries has been between 2 percent and 6 percent a year. Rates of growth of GDP have usually been higher—testimony to the fact that much of this growth has been achieved by rising labour productivity rather than by increased employment. The exceptions are Tanzania and Tunisia (both marked by rather modest rates of growth in GDP but high rates of growth of employment*) and Upper Volta (where the GDP figures are particularly suspect).

It is not part of this chapter to investigate the reasons that explain this slow rate of growth of employment. The most significant reason—rising labour productivity associated with capital-intensive technologies—is analysed in Chapter 13 in terms of the bias towards capital intensity introduced by a range of government policies. Of more immediate interest to us is the contrast between the rate of growth of employment and the rate of growth of urban population.

We use the latter as a proxy for the rate of growth of demand for jobs in the formal sector in the towns.† It is not a very accurate proxy, partly because the data themselves are not very accurate and partly because it does not follow

---

*The figures in the table may well exaggerate the rate of growth of employment in Tanzania, since there is some evidence that the coverage of the labour enumerations improved markedly in the middle 1960s. Certainly urban employment increased by only 7.6 percent a year between 1966 and 1970. Further, between 1964 and 1968 total employment was static as a result of a very rapid rundown of the labour force in agriculture (particularly on the sisal estates). This was balanced by an increase in non-agricultural employment. Improved coverage of statistics may explain some of the Tunisian figures, too.

†Thus, estate agriculture is excluded. The operational definition of "formal" is those firms covered by labour enumerations. Its practical significance is those firms that feel obliged to obey most labour legislation most of the time. We assume that these are in fact identical, since firms that know they are on an official list are likely to feel under pressure to conform.

that because a man does not migrate to the towns, he would not like a job in the formal sector. He may well have a realistic view of his chances of finding such employment, or he may be working as a migrant labourer in the rural areas between bouts of job seeking in the urban areas. To that extent, the figures of urban population growth are an underestimate (and perhaps a very substantial underestimate) of the rate of growth of those who seek, or who are only prevented from seeking by a rational pessimism, employment in the formal sector. If we are primarily concerned, as we are in this chapter, with those who actively seek urban employment by migrating to the towns, then the figures may give a reasonable suggestion of the order of magnitude of the group.

But there is a further sense in which the figures may be misleading. We know very little about the age structure of this increase in the urban population. Naturally, it is comprised of two elements: the natural rate of increase of the urban population and migrants to the towns. We know too little about the age and sex structure of migrants to be sure what proportion of all migrants are genuine job seekers. From the 1960 Post-Enumeration Survey in Ghana, for instance, it seems that a significant proportion of migrants bring with them their wives and children (thus, 32.3 percent of female migrants above the age of 15 were classified as homemakers; for urban non-migrant females, the equivalent percentage was only 17.3[1]). The trend for migrants increasingly to bring their families with them to town before they have found a job is also reported in Kenya, Tanzania, Zambia, and Ivory Coast. If there is indeed a structural change in the sex and age composition of migrants, this would suggest that the rate of growth of the urban population overstates the rate of growth of job seekers. But it also suggests, as we shall emphasize more pointedly later, that the implications for a migrant who does not find a job are much more severe.

Allowing, then, that the right-hand column of Table 11.1 is a very imperfect proxy for the rate of growth of those who are seeking employment in the formal sector, the fact that demand for employment is growing faster than supply in every country except Tunisia and possibly Tanzania suggests that the probability of finding employment in the formal sector has been getting progressively smaller over the last decade. This implies that the number of those who are excluded from employment in the formal sector has been increasing.

But when we try to estimate the number in this category, we run into serious methodological problems. A guesstimate for the rate of exclusion* in Kampala

_____

*By rate of exclusion we mean the proportion of the labour force available for (and assumed to be ready to take) jobs in the formal sector. It is therefore parallel to what economists used to call the unemployment rate when they equated all employment with employment in the formal sector. We use the term exclusion rate in this sense and reserve the term "unemployed" for those who have no source of income but who are available for work.[2]

suggested 35 percent, and for the smaller towns of Uganda show rather lower rates: Jinja 17 percent, Masaka 17 percent, Entebbe 14 percent, and Mbale 8 percent. In Tanzania, a 1965 survey gave a figure of over 31 percent (the figures in the 1967 census are much lower—a maximum of 7 percent for any individual town—but that follows from the very restrictive definition of unemployment used).[3] In Yaounde, in 1969 the rate of exclusion was over 30 percent (or 37 percent if domestic servants are excluded from the formal sector).[4] For Cameroon as a whole, labour demand is expected to grow at 5.8 percent per annum, but the supply of untrained labour from secondary schools alone (i.e., ignoring altogether the 121,000 primary school leavers in 1971) is expected to grow at 8.4 percent per annum. In Abidjan, in 1965 the rate seems to have been somewhat higher—around 62 percent as a result of the extraordinary rate of migration into Abidjan in the early 1960s.[5] Rather less reliable data for the whole gouvernorat of Tunis (of which 8 percent is rural) suggest a figure of 28 percent.[6]

None of these figures should be taken as more than an order of magnitude. Nonetheless, their implication is clear. It is that, in most of our countries, between a quarter and a half of the urban labour force is excluded from employment in the modern sector. This gives an indication of the size of the so-called informal sector—the detailed working of which we know very little.

But before we turn to that, it is worth inspecting rather more closely the composition of this excluded group and the process of recruitment and selection within it. As we have already seen, the urban excluded are comprised of two quite separate elements, both engaged in intra-group competition for formal employment. These are (1) those who were born in the urban areas or who have resided there for some time and (2) new migrants coming from rural areas or from the smaller towns in the hinterland. In Ivory Coast, Cameroon, and (at least until the Aliens Compliance Order) in Ghana, an additional flow was from the Sahelian countries to the north. It is not part of our purpose to review in detail the extensive literature on migration in Africa. But it is relevant to highlight one or two features of this stream of entrants to the urban job market. The first is that it is now well established that the migrants tend to be better educated than the non-migrants in the urban areas. (Except for alien migrants: In West Africa, the alien migrants tend to be least educated of all; in Abidjan, only 2 percent of Mossi heads of household [from Upper Volta] had finished primary school in 1963—a far lower percentage than any Ivorien ethnic group.[7])

The generally higher education of migrants does not necessarily mean they are sufficiently well educated to compete effectively for the middle-level and high-level jobs in the urban areas. In Ghana, for instance, a significant proportion of the migrants are middle school leavers who have neither the form education to qualify readily for white-collar jobs nor the technical skills to compete effectively for blue-collar jobs (see above, 206, 266).

A second feature of the migrants is that they tend to be younger—more than half fall within the age group 15-24. This is, of course, consistent with the educational characteristics of the migrants. The school leaver who cannot get a formal sector job in the rural areas or in the small towns in the hinterland goes to the larger towns in search of formal employment.

A disproportionate number are male, although, as we have already seen, in Ghana and elsewhere there are signs that the rate of female migration is increasing. This may be because more male migrants are bringing their wives with them rather than leaving them in the rural areas, or it may be the direct result of increasing education for girls.

A further characteristic is that a large proportion of migrants have not had formal employment or even any semi-permanent employment before. They thus have no work experience to offset their lack of technical skills and their unexceptional educational background.

We might assume that the urban migrants are those who are being squeezed out of the rural areas. We saw in Chapters 2 to 4 that the process of rural development, particularly when it is accompanied by rapid population growth, tends to create a group of hired labourers, some of whom may be landless or have access to so poor or so little land that they cannot earn a subsistence. One might therefore assume that a significant proportion of migrants to the towns comprises those who have thus been squeezed out of the rural sector. But there is in fact little empirical justification for such a view. Although the data are exiguous, they point in the opposite direction.[8] Few of the migrants are the victims of the process of rural differentiation. If they also are not those who profit most from that process, the very fact that they are not uneducated suggests that they are the sons and daughters of at least moderately prosperous peasants. (For example, for the 464 peasant migrants studied in Tanzania, the median value of cash crops solid in the year before migration was Shs.150. This is the average per capita cash income of farm households in the rural areas; to it must be added the value of subsistence production.[9])

There is a good reason for this. The real victims of the process of rural differentiation are in such a precarious position financially and socially that they are the least likely to take the risk of searching for a job in town. Further, there is probably a process of natural selection. Those who can go to town believing that they have access to a job go before they are reduced to the status of permanent hired rural labourer. Those who are left as hired labourers are those who rate their chances of finding a job in town as poor.

If these are the major characteristics of the urban migrants, they have to be compared with those of the existing urban population with whom they compete for jobs in the formal sector. The existing urban population has one great advantage. Although perhaps less well educated than many of the migrants, the job seeker of urban origin is likely to have a wider network of contacts, friends, and brokers than are the majority of rural migrants. This is not to deny that most migrants depend upon kinsmen in town; we saw in the last chapter that this is an essential part of the life support system of the unemployed. The migrant may turn to his kinsmen for contacts, but the urban job seeker is likely to have his own already. And Sabot reports that in Tanzania only a minority of migrants get help from relations in finding a job—although 90 percent get material support.[10] The longer the urban job seeker has been at school, the more likely it is that former school friends have acquired jobs and influence and the more valuable contacts they will prove to be.

The educated migrant is less likely to have this type of contact. But there is some evidence that the younger age and higher education of a migrant offsets this lack of contacts. In Tanzania, a survey of over 5,500 urban dwellers found that non-migrant men were more likely to be employed than migrant men. (This was not true of women, where the proportions were very similar.) Furthermore, the migrants, both men and women, were less likely than the non-migrants to take no action to find work.[11] In Ghana, migrant men in the urban areas are much more likely to be employed than non-migrants, but the reverse is true for women. (The low employment ratio for women may reflect the lower age of female migrants and/or greater difficulty in establishing themselves in the informal sector.[12]) In the Tunis area, migrants are not much to be found working in agriculture—the great majority are in the modern sector. It is the local excluded who have to take jobs in agriculture and in the "chantiers du chomage"; it is also true that a somewhat higher proportion work in services.[13]

Migrants, then, seem able to compete effectively with the urban residents for jobs in the formal sector. There is little evidence of the bias that is a hallmark of the con-mech. Whether they are as adept at establishing themselves in self-employment in the informal sector is a more difficult question. In countries such as Ghana and Cameroon, market trading is a highly established form of economic activity, particularly for women. As it depends upon specialized knowledge, a wide range of contacts, and market experience, it is at least probable that immigrants will find it more difficult to compete effectively. For example, in Ivory Coast traders have their own language—"dioula." Without it, an immigrant cannot compete. It is no coincidence, then, that market trading tends to be dominated by one tribe—in Accra by the Ga, and in Cameroon by the Bamilike. In East Africa, where market trading is less highly developed, it may be easier for migrants to compete. But, in so far as many of them are young and have not had previous employment, even the modest capital requirements of the street hawker may be beyond them.

Of the structure of the informal sector as a whole we know remarkably little. Nothing so well reveals the obsession of governments and researchers with the "modern" sector as the almost unrelieved lack of information about the ways in which a large proportion of the population actually earns a living.

However, on the basis of the slender information available, we can make one or two important distinctions. First, it is almost certainly a mistake to conceive of employment in terms of mutually exclusive categories—of either the formal sector or the informal sector. It is not unusual for employees in the formal sector to have business interests in the informal sector that they supervise either through their wives or other kinsmen or in their spare time. Those who are able to do this see their formal employment as bestowing security and a regular reliable income and their informal interests as offering the possibility of establishing a viable business of their own that will, at some future time, give them no less security and income with the additional benefit of independence. They also, of course, see it as a means of increasing their current income. Keith Hart has argued that formal sector employees in Ghana are obliged to try to make money in the informal sector by the low level of wages in the formal sector.[14]

From our point of view it is highly significant that there is this cross-relationship, because it suggests that a proportion, and perhaps a substantial proportion, of the profits generated in the informal sector accrue to those who already have jobs in the formal sector. In other words, those who are already privileged receive profits from the labour of those who are excluded from those privileges. It is quite impossible to say how common this is (there is indirect evidence of this for Uganda[15]). But, if one includes as part of the informal sector the provision of low-income housing (e.g., by subletting one or two rooms), it is highly probable that it is widespread and that this inter-relationship extends far up the income scale of the urban privileged—for it is the urban privileged who at least have the possibility of accumulating sufficient capital from their earnings to enter the informal sector at a level above the most desperate attempts to scrape together a subsistence.

More particularly, where the informal sector provides services or goods used by the formal sector—e.g., transport, construction, painting, sign writing, even (usually at a very modest level) school equipment—the opportunities and incentives for those in the formal sector to organize or control these activities in the informal sector are clearly very substantial. Such a relationship is not necessarily corrupt; although it could lead to a conflict of interests on behalf of, for instance, a school manager or a parastatal purchasing officer, in essence the relationships stem from the fortunate congruence of ability to identify a market and organize the means to supply that market.

This implies a second important distinction. The informal sector is sometimes seen in purely self-employment terms. This is mistaken. Indeed, the term "informal sector" derives from the relationship between the employer and the employee. The fact that that relationship is informal—i.e., not registered with the labour office and not conditioned by labour law—does not disguise the fact that it is a hire-and-fire relationship. Although much of the informal sector is organized within the nuclear or extended family, the use of hired labour is common:

Our estimate, admittedly crude, suggests that about 12,000 persons are employed directly in the informal sector in the urban areas of Tanzania, or about one fifth of those earning their living in the informal sector.*

Employees in the informal sector are engaged in a wide variety of occupations, principally retailing, vehicle repair and maintenance, other service occupations, and transport. Their status and security is not dissimilar to that of hired labourers in the rural areas, the major difference being that they have, or think they have, greater opportunity for improving their position. Like their rural counterparts, they have little, if any, bargaining power with their employers. Even if they know of the existence of minimum wage legislation, they have no way of ensuring that they are paid the minimum wage. They can be fired without notice. They are not usually provided with either lodging or food. There is no limit to the hours they work: In Tanzania, traders, hawkers, and the self-employed were found to work the longest hours of all surveyed occupational groups; more of these worked over 49 hours a week than any other occupation.[16] In the Philippines, 57 percent of women in the service sector worked more than 49 hours, compared to 18 percent of male clerical workers.[17]

We have a hierarchy of competition. There is first the competition between the informal sector and the formal sector. To that we turn in the last section of this chapter. Next we have just seen the inter-group competition between the entrepreneurs (the owners of the assets of the informal sector) and the employees for the "surplus value" of the informal sector. We have suggested—and will later try to illustrate—that in this competition the employees inevitably lose. Finally in this competitive hierarchy there is the intra-group competition between the self-employed.†

For a much larger group of the excluded are self-employed rather than "informal" employees. Within this group the important distinction is between those who regard their self-employment as a stop-gap, a means of earning a living (albeit an inadequate one) while they continue their search for employment whether in the formal sector or in the informal sector; and, on the other hand, those who have established themselves in the informal sector sufficiently well to regard it as a long-term source of employment and income. This distinction is closely related to that of income level. If a self-employed worker is

---

*This figure is derived by subtracting from those enumerated in the 1967 Population Census as urban employees the number of urban employees enumerated in the annual survey of employment and earnings; as such, it should be taken as an order of magnitude.

†Analytically, there is also the intra-group competition between the informal "firms" and the self-employed—e.g., in services or woodwork. We can say nothing of this.

earning very little, he is unlikely to regard it as a long-run proposition. Conversely, if his business is prospering, he may not give a high priority to securing employment in the formal sector.

Equally, there may well be an occupational distinction. Such occupations as portering, street hawking, car washing, car minding, beer selling, and touting are, as we shall see, unlikely to be very profitable and therefore provide a long-term living. By contrast, occupation as a driver or a motor mechanic, or as any of a wide range of craftsmen from metal worker to carpenter, from glazier to weaver, or as a specialist retailer, is more likely to yield a satisfactory income and therefore be a long-term proposition.

Family Incomes in the Informal Sector: East Africa

The very small spread of data we have suggests that some informal occupations can yield incomes that compare favourably with middle-level manpower in the formal sector. For instance, some Ghanaian market mammies and transport contractors are, by the standards of all but the top elite, very wealthy.[18] In Zambia, some of the more successful pub and beer shop owners are among the wealthiest Zambians. In Uganda, coffee trading and, more latterly, trading in food crops have long been recognized as ways of accumulating capital.

But these are the wealthy extremes. Table 11.2 presents data from Tanzania on the monthly incomes of twelve groups of self-employed in seven towns. This shows that for all groups the median income is about Shs.200 a month, but that there is great variation between occupations. The median income for street traders, for instance, is Shs.125 a month, while that for craftsmen and those engaged in manufacture is over Shs.200. Thirty percent of those whose incomes are stated earned under Shs.100 at a time when the minimum wage in Dar es Salaam was between Shs.200 and Shs.170 (depending on the employer and the grade of worker).

There is no means of telling how far the pattern revealed in Table 11.2 is typical of the urban areas in other East and Central African countries. A survey in Nairobi showed that 4 percent of all employed men and 20 percent of women were earning in 1970 less than Shs.100 a month; 13.6 percent of all employed men and 32.8 percent of all employed women were earning less than the real minimum wage (by real minimum wage, we mean the minimum wage as enacted in 1965 in constant real terms[19]). The great majority of these were employed in the informal sector.

So far we have couched this discussion in terms of individual income earners. From the point of view of urban poverty, more significant is household income. It is sometimes said, for instance, that low-income earners are unmarried and

TABLE 11.2

Tanzania: Numbers of Income Recipients in the Informal Sector by Income Group, 1970/71

| Occupation | Income (shillings per month) | | | | | | Median Income |
	0-24	75-149	150-249	250-349	350-499˙	500+	(shillings)
Crafts/manufacture	12	15	18	9	8	9	200
Transport	2	0	0	1	1	5	(750)
Porter	1	1	5	0	0	0	(158)
Contractor/fundi	4	6	7	5	4	2	228
Street trading	30	24	22	11	4	10	124
Shopkeeping	12	3	9	3	3	25	350
Hotel bar keeping	4	4	4	1	2	5	212
House rental	25	23	20	3	2	8	116
Farming	11	1	4	1	1	1	49
Fishing	1	1	0	1	1	2	(350)
Professional	0	0	0	0	0	2	(1,000+)
Other	1	3	1	1	1	0	(124)
Urban non-farm households							1,241

Sources: Unpublished data from M.A. Bienefeld and R.H. Sabot, *The National Urban Mobility Employment and Income Survey of Tanzania* (Dar es Salaam: Economic Research Bureau, University of Dar es Salaam, September 1972); and (last row) *Household Budget Survey, 1969* (Dar es Salaam: Bureau of Statistics, Ministry of Economic Affairs and Development Planning, 1972), Appendix 7.

therefore low incomes do not impose on them the same privations as they would on a married man with a family to support. It is also sometimes said that low-income households are characterized by having more than one income earner in the household and that individual low incomes do not, therefore, impose privation on whole households. (The most recent restatements of these positions can be found in the submissions of British companies paying below the poverty datum line in South Africa.[20])

Despite the importance of this question, we have for East Africa little data that help us answer it. (West African data are presented on pp. 293-99.) In Tanzania, only 17 percent of women above 15 are employed or self-employed. Of these, about a third are employed in the formal sector. This suggests a very low female participation in the informal sector. Although we cannot analyse this according to whether income is earned in the formal or informal sector, it is clear from Table 11.3 that per capita income falls as household size increases in the urban areas. But there is a little evidence that very large households (9 or more members) are more likely to have more than one wage earner, with the result that income per head begins to increase.

Given the exiguous level of earnings in the informal sector, the difficulty of maintaining a family is acute. It is significant that, in an intensive survey of unemployed migrants in Kampala, Caroline Hutton found that there is a sharp difference between new immigrants from the rural areas who have not yet been employed on the one hand, and on the other formers employees who for one reasons or another have lost their jobs. The latter are far more likely to have dependents than the former, and the welfare effect of their unemployment is thus more widespread. Hutton found that all the unemployed who had children in town with them were men who had recently lost their jobs. All the other job seekers who had children were recent migrants, and all had left their children in the village.* Only 10 percent of all the unemployed whom she interviewed had wives in town. In all such cases, either the wife was earning a wage in paid

TABLE 11.3

Tanzania: Annual Cash Income in Urban Non-Farm Households by Household Size, 1969

Household Size	Annual Cash Income (shillings per person)
1 member	2,741
2 members	1,935
3-4 members	1,434
5-6 members	1,175
7-8 members	964
9 members or more	1,153
All households	1,241

Source: Household Budget Survey, 1969 (Dar es Salaam: Bureau of Statistics, Ministry of Economic Affairs and Development Planning, 1972), Appendix 7.

---

*The contrast with Ghana is striking (see above, p. 282) and we cannot explain it. The most promising hypothesis is that Ghanaian women are expected to contribute to the family income by trading; Ugandan women are expected to be more dependent.

employment or else she was cultivating a shamba in one of the many peri-urban villages to feed herself and her husband while he looked for work. If the wife could not provide her own maintenance (and at least minimal food for her husband), whe was sent back to the village. If this is generally true, it suggests that family incomes (for recent migrants) exceed individual incomes.[21]

There is evidence, from both Uganda and Kenya, that income level increases with family size. This is partly a matter of age, partly a reflection of the fact that more experienced men can earn higher wages and are more likely to have taken a wife in town or have brought their wife from their home village, and partly a matter of economic necessity. The very lowly paid cannot afford to maintain a family in town.

If the relationship between level of income and family size is generally true (and not just confined to recent migrants), then two things follow. The first is that the distribution of income per head in the informal sector is less skewed than suggested by Table 11.2. But it is also true, secondly, that the average and median incomes per family member are much lower than appears in the table. This raises one important implication: It suggests a difference in the welfare effect of different kinds of unemployment. When employment is contracting and relatively well-established people are losing their jobs, it may be that a larger number of dependents are affected than when employment is growing slowly and new migrants and young urban dwellers are not being absorbed into either the formal or the informal sector. The absolute level of unemployment— in the sense of those having no income— may be similar, but the social structure of those unemployed may be very different. This suggests that periods in which there have been falls in employment in East Africa, such as the late 1950s in Uganda, the early 1960s in Zambia and Tanzania, may have presented more people with real problems of survival than the later period when a larger proportion of the unemployed may well have been younger, unmarried or childless job seekers.

How severe is unemployment in the informal sector, i.e., how many people earn no cash income at all? What proportion of those who are excluded from the formal sector are also excluded from the informal sector? Or is it that some hover between the two sectors, unable to secure formal employment and yet reluctant to accept a job in the informal sector because to do so is to abandon the search for security? Certainly there is some evidence that this is so.

Caroline Hutton found that most of the job seekers whom she interviewed regarded looking for a job in the formal sector as a full-time occupation. Self-employment among those who were actively looking for paid employment in Kampala and Junja was extremely rare. Slightly less than half of Hutton's sample had taken casual (i.e., short-term) jobs to meet their necessities while they were looking for more permanent jobs. Only school leavers from Kampala gave "consideration to casual urban opportunities for making a living and attributed success to them. Casual jobs such as washing cars, toasting maize, selling news-papers, collecting empty bottles, brewing warigi, hairdressing under a tree, weav-weaving mats, or painting pictures for sale on the streets, were all mentioned as well as several ingenious methods of earning cash through deception."[22] This suggests that, in Kampala at least, knowledge of the possibilities offered by self-employment at the lower end of the informal sector is fairly widespread. But that knowledge of the opportunities is balanced by the realistic assessment of their limitations—the competition in the sector, the inevitable limitations on earnings, and the high opportunity cost of time spent earning money through casual labour rather than searching for paid employment. For many, the strug-gle to find paid employment is a full-time occupation rendered the more urgent by demands from home for cash to meet siblings' education costs or to pay taxes. To view this period of unemployment in the no-man's-land between the security of a job in the formal sector and the questionable living offered by the informal sector as a jolly modern initiation rite—a moment of anguish manfully endured on the threshold of blissful maturity—is romantic. All those in Hutton's sample of unemployed in Kampala and Jinja expressed concern about food. Many showed obvious signs of malnourishment. Twenty percent in the sample were not getting food regularly. Only 7 percent were living at home while they were looking for work. Forty percent of the Kampala sample were living in the squatments of Mengo in minimal circumstances. Many were sleeping rough. The fact that one in four had endured this for over a year is eloquent testimony to the valuation of the alternatives—self-employment in the informal sector or re-turn to the rural areas.*

How many, then, are in this wretched situation? It seems that the rate of unemployment (in the sense of those with no source of cash income) tends to be higher for women than for men and may be higher in the capital than in other towns. As we have already seen, it tends to be higher for non-migrants (i.e., those born or long resident in the towns) than for migrants. In Tanzania, the unemployment rate varies from 4 percent for migrant males in Dar es Salaam to 40 percent for non-migrant females in Dar (see Table 11.4). For Kenya, the International Labour Organization (ILO) report has brought to-gether what few data exist. These show rates as high as 53 percent for young women but very moderate levels, 3 to 5 percent, for men between the ages of 25 and 50. As one would expect in the context of East Africa, the more

---

*In urban Tanzania, migrant men seemed to be absorbed more quickly. Ac-cording to the national mobility survey, 80 percent of migrant men find employ-ment of some sort within six months. The difference between Uganda and Tanzania in this respect may be more more than a reflection of the different rates of growth of urban employment in the formal sector.

TABLE 11.4

Tanzania: Adult Population in the Labour Force by Sex and Migrant Status and by Earning Status, Dar es Salaam, 1971
(percentages)

	Total Population		Males		Females	
	Migrants	Non-Migrants	Migrants	Non-Migrants	Migrants	Non-Migrants
Employees	74	57	82	68	42	31
Self-employed	16	26	14	25	23	28
Unemployed	10	16	4	7	35	40

Source: M.A. Bienefeld and R.H. Sabot, *National Urban Mobility Employment and Income Survey of Tanzania*, vol. III: *The Wage Employed* (Dar es Salaam: Ministry of Economic Affairs and Development Planning, 1972).

educated men (but in general not women) find it easier to secure employment. Men with no education are nearly twice as likely to be unemployed as those who have completed secondary schooling. As the ILO report concludes, "The worst of all possible circumstances from the point of view of seeking work is to be young, uneducated, and female."[23]

It may be said that, while unemployment is severe and for a substantial minority prolonged, the privation associated with it is illusory. Social systems of redistribution, support of kinsmen, and (in the case of migrants) the well-attested "chain" all ensure that the unemployed are cushioned against the worst privations. Indeed, the fact that they choose to stay in town rather than return to the rural areas whence they came is evidence that life in town, even a jobless life, is endurable. But while true, such a judgment cannot leave one complacent or romantically attached to the view that social redistribution removes the sting from urban poverty—witness the evidence we have already presented from Caroline Hutton's survey of unemployed in Uganda. While it is true that migrants derive help and subsistence from their kinsmen in town and that the long-term unemployed do in fact survive, it betrays gross insensitivity to the realities of joblessness to imagine that social redistribution solves all the problem.

Kin hospitality, for instance, is not infinite. If the host thinks the guest is imposing upon him or is not taking the job hunt with sufficient seriousness, subtle means are found for ensuring his departure. The law of reciprocity demands that the guest eventually does household chores if he cannot earn his keep. The demands on the host's family are likely to be extensive—witness Guy Pfefferman's now famous finding that in Dakar in 1965 the average wage earner supported 9.6 dependents[24]—and if income and/or house space is scarce, monopoly of either by one unemployed kinsman will not be tolerated forever. If he cannot get a job and if he cannot make his way in the informal sector as self-employed, the unemployed is required to move on—to other and perhaps more distant kin, to school friends, or just out.

Again it is important to make the distinction between the single migrant and the urban family. The single migrant will almost certainly have kinsmen with whom to stay. Indeed, that is often a condition of his leaving the rural areas at all. The established man with a family who loses his job and faces a prolonged spell of unemployment is in a much more exposed position. If he is living in rented accommodation (as is most probable unless he has been able to build himself a house in a shanty town or peri-urban village), he faces eviction. With a family, lodging with kinsmen or friends is difficult and the family is likely to split up—the wife and children possibly to be sent back to the rural areas, the head of the household shifting as best he can while he continues the search for a job in town. When and whether the family is reunited is then an open question. If the household head finds a reasonably well-paid job quickly, he may be able to bring his family back and pick up life where it was broken. If the job search is long or the new employment ill paid, he may keep his family in the rural area. How they fare then depends upon their relationships with their rural kin, which are influenced by the gifts they have been able to send in the past (see above, pp. 99-100).

Life as an unemployed job seeker, then, is such that many do in fact return to the rural areas. But they may not return to agriculture. They may well seek employment or establish themselves in employment in the informal sector in the rural areas. There the earnings may be low, even lower than in town, but the possibility of combining jobs, changing jobs as new opportunities open up, and combining employment in the informal sector with agriculture may be adequate compensation. (In a study of youths in rural Buganda, Christine Wallace has shown the remarkable instability of employment as well as the frequency of shifts between rural and urban employment and formal and informal employment.[25])

Family Incomes in the Informal Sector: West Africa

The material we have presented thus far on family incomes in the informal sector has been drawn exclusively from East Africa. Is there evidence of the same general pattern from West Africa? A study of the urban areas of the Eastern Region of Ghana certainly revealed a close relationship between income and family size. But there are interesting differences between the occupations.

TABLE 11.5

Ghana: Unemployment by Sex, Residence, and Migrant Status, 1960
(percentages)

Sex and Length of Stay	All*		Non-Migrants		Migrants from Other Towns		Migrants from Rural Areas	
	Urban	Rural	Urban	Rural	Urban	Rural	Urban	Rural
Males								
All periods of stay	4.3	1.7	5.2	2.0	4.8	2.3	3.9	1.4
From birth or 5+ years	3.7	1.5	5.2	1.9	2.9	0.8	2.4	0.9
2 years but less than 5 years	2.5	1.3	5.7	3.0	2.8	2.3	2.2	0.9
6 months but less than 2 years	4.1	1.6	7.8	6.1	5.8	2.2	3.6	1.4
Less than 6 months	10.2	3.6	2.6	4.6	11.5	5.3	10.5	3.4
Females								
All periods of stay	2.4	0.6	3.2	0.9	2.3	1.0	1.9	0.4
From birth or 5+ years	2.4	0.6	3.1	0.8	2.0	1.0	1.6	0.3
2 years but less than 5 years	1.5	0.5	4.3	1.6	1.6	0.9	1.3	0.4
6 months but less than 2 years	2.1	0.7	4.2	2.3	2.4	0.2	2.2	0.7
Less than 6 months	3.6	1.3	3.4	1.6	3.7	1.7	3.7	1.3

*Including aliens.

Source: N.O. Addo, "Some Aspects of the Relation between Migration and Socio-Economic Development in Ghana," in Symposium on Population and Socio-Economic Development in Ghana, eds. N.O. Addo, S.K. Gaisie, G. Benneh, G.M.K. Kpedekpo (Legon: Department of Sociology, University of Ghana, 1968).

Children seem to make little contribution to income (either directly through earning income or indirectly by acting as an incentive to their parents) for urban farmers, traders, unskilled workers. But for service workers and skilled workers, there is such a relationship. As service workers are largely employed in the informal sector and skilled workers include a large number of craftsmen working at home, it is evident that children are soon put to work. But, perhaps surprisingly, the presence of more adults in the families of service workers does not add much to income. In all the other occupations there is a strong relationship, particularly for unskilled labourers. This may be a reflection of the fact that wages for unskilled labourers are low and there is greater pressure on other adults in the household to earn supplementary incomes. Certainly per capita expenditure in the households of unskilled labourers is above that of farmers and only fractionally below that of skilled labourers.

More extensive data for Yaounde and Abidjan show a less subtle relationship. As the head of the household rises in the occupational scale and as family expenditures increase, so the household size rises. For the unemployed in Yaounde, the average household is only 2.1 persons and expenditure per head 1,515 F CFA. Among fully employed artisans, family size is 5.0 and expenditure 5,213 F CFA per head. In the public sector as a whole (i.e., all formally and full-time employed but with a range of occupational skills), the family size is nearly the same but expenditure rises to over 7,000 F CFA per head.[26] In Abidjan, the same picture is repeated, but household size is much larger (possibly because of a difference in definition). Household size doubles from 4.2 for blue-collar workers to 8.0 for "cadres superieurs"; expenditure per head more than doubles from 4,100 F CFA to 8,500 F CFA.[27]

As to the rate of unemployment in West Africa (in the sense of receiving no income, Table 11.5 shows that rates of unemployment in towns are higher than in the rural areas and significantly higher for men than for women—in stark contrast to East Africa. Note the contrast between the ease with which newly arrived locals find employment and the long wait of those from other villages or other towns. Whether the situation has changed fundamentally since 1960 we shall not know until the 1970 census data are processed further. But, from an initial analysis of the unemployed as revealed in the census, it appears that urban unemployment rates may well have risen. In Accra itself, unemployment seems to have been over 10 percent for both men and women in 1970; the rate in Tema was even higher, reaching over 14 percent for women.* It may well have been higher in smaller towns.[28]

---

*The census defines the unemployed as "all persons who did not work at a fixed job during the four weeks preceding census night who were actively looking for work within the past three months. . . . Also included in the unemployed category was any person who was not looking for work because he had despaired

For Ivory Coast, a census of unemployment[29] was requested by the President with the promise that registration through the census would bring unemployment benefit—a promise that subsequently was not fulfilled. How far the census was biased by this promise and how far it was successful in covering the unemployed is open to question. Certainly the figures look suspiciously low—less than 2 percent in every case except 7 percent in Abidjan. More reliable figures suggest anything between 8 percent and 10 percent in the mid-1960s, growing by about 1 percent a year.[30]

The usual relationship between education and unemployment is clear in the 1970 survey. The bulk of the surveyed unemployed had completed primary education and the unemployment rate for primary graduates is three times as high as that for the uneducated (but 32 percent of immigrant Mossi men, nearly all uneducated, were unemployed). It then falls sharply for higher levels of education. But a much higher of uneducated men are unemployed than uneducated women. This may reflect the ability of uneducated women to find self-employment in the informal sector as in Ghana. This is tentative evidence that in Ivory Coast primary education gives both men and women an appetite for formal employment without giving them ability to compete successfully.

The other familiar feature that recurs is that three quarters of the unemployed are under 25. The figure is even higher for women—over 90 percent. Most of these are looking for work for the first time and can offer no special qualification. This is evidence of the inadequacy of technical training and, since most of those who have already been employed can offer some kind of specialization, of the speed with which at least the rudiments of a skill are acquired on the job. This is a point much emphasized by Christine Wallace in her study of rural youth in Buganda. But is this a function of the formal sector alone? Can people acquire a skill—e.g., in brick-laying, carpentry, motor mechanics, driving, tailoring—in the informal sector and then acquire jobs in the formal sector that pay them more highly? The training function of the informal sector has never been systematically researched, but is perhaps at least as important, from the point of view of both equity and growth, as its employment function.

---

of finding any. The unemployed category is distinct from the voluntary unemployed category; the latter includes all those who were not employed during the reference period but who, although able to work, were not interested in seeking work." How this definition was interpreted in practice in the administration of the census, particularly in the informal sector, it is impossible to say. Many informal jobs are not "fixed." But the definition of "home-maker" makes it clear that anybody working part time in the informal sector would be excluded from the homemaker category. We cannot be sure that the same is true of the unemployed. To that extent there is a risk that the census overstates those who were not in receipt of an income.

We know very little about the ways in which those without any kind of a job in West Africa survive. And, despite the considerable quantity of research on migration in West Africa, we know little about short-term migration to the rural areas to acquire a skill or a temporary income and then return to the urban areas.

No doubt there are mechanisms of social redistribution at work in roughly analogous ways to what we have described in East Africa. But again we think it a mistake to overestimate them—despite Pfefferman. Even the Abidjan survey already cited does not suggest very large households for the higher-income groups, with three dependants apart from children as a likely maximum average figure. If it is argued that gifts rather than inclusion in the household are offered to dependants, we have data from Cameroon that again lead us to qualify the value of these mechanisms. For, while in the rural areas the value of gifts rises strongly with total family income (reaching 29 percent when income exceeds 16,000 F CFA), there is no such relationship in Yaounde. The average value of gifts is 9 percent of income, and for the whole public sector (with a high concentration of relatively well-paid full-time employees) it was less than that.[31]

The major element that differentiates West Africa from East Africa in this respect is, of course, the greater readiness with which women enter the informal sector. In this respect, the married man who loses a job in town is unlikely to be as vulnerable as his equivalent in East Africa. A woman's earnings may be small: According to one study of the Eastern Region of Ghana, women traders made between ₵25 and ₵29 per month; men made more than ₵34.[32] And in Upper Volta, female beer sellers ("les dolotieres") earn an average of 1,000 F CFA per month which, little as it is, may be as much as 15 percent of household income.[33] Thus, the unemployed man's wife may be able to stave off the worst disasters by her own efforts.* As clear in West Africa as in East is the fact that, for most low-income earners, obligations to kinsmen impose a major strain on a budget that is already likely to be in serious and permanent deficit. Keith Hart has shown for one low-income area of Accra that an individual, much less a family, can hardly survive on the urban minimum wage in the middle 1960s.[34] Under these conditions, kin obligations—whether to distant villagers or urban neighbours—present a real financial difficulty. This is not to say that they are reneged on; it is further indirect evidence, amply documented

---

*This is one possibility. The other is that small-scale traders and hawkers use at least a proportion of their husbands' earnings to invest in their stock-in-trade. If the husband is paid by the week, three or four days' trading can be financed from his wage. If the wife is thus dependent upon the husband's wage for her own activities, then she may be forced to stop trading when he loses his job.

for Nigeria by Peter C.W. Gutkind,[35] that they are not infinite. To put it another way, the wholly unemployed who have kinsmen in the middle- and upper-income brackets are likely to be able to survive in unemployment less traumatically than those who have kin only in the low-income groups, but they cannot survive in this fashion indefinitely.

So far we have ignored both official and voluntary welfare and relief agencies, as well as formal insurance schemes. In nearly all African countries, the last can safely be ignored for the excluded. If unemployment benefit is payable at all, it depends upon continuous employment in the formal sector for a fairly long period. Benefits are usually small and of limited duration. They may ease a change of job or transition from the privileged to the excluded, but they do not constitute "social security" in its literal sense. Of welfare and relief agencies, we have been able to find out little, especially of the extent to which they do in fact reach the very poor. One systematic study in Kampala had this to say:

> The field areas chosen by both the local and governmental institutions and by the voluntary agencies show a concentration on sections in town which have an appearance of stability and respectability. Through their programmes they tend to reach or attract mostly those youths who are in school or regularly employed, that is those who are already one step up on the ladder. Very little is done for those who are unable to go to school or who fail to complete their studies. These children who form a very large section of the population are those who are most in need of help yet they get least. This is a serious shortcoming of the whole social welfare service.[36]

There is little reason to believe that this state of affairs is confined either to "youth work" or to Kampala.[37]

Two other approaches by government to urban poverty relief are worth brief mention, less because they were markedly successful than because they were unusual and, within limits, innovative. Egypt is the only country in our group, other than Sri Lanka, to have used food subsidies as a method of relieving the poor. A wide range of commodities such as wheat, maize, sugar, kerosene, and cooking oil are subsidized. Further, the prices of bread and flour are fixed at a level below import parity. The major beneficiaries of these subsidies throughout the 1950s and 1960s were the urban rather than the rural population, for, particularly with respect to wheat and flour, the major proportion of government expenditure on subsidies goes to items that are consumed almost exclusively by the urban population. Between 1959 and 1969, the retail price of wheat was constant; in real terms, therefore, the price of wheat to the urban consumer fell by nearly a quarter. Over the same period, government expenditure on all price subsidies rose nearly sixfold. By 1962-63, price subsidies amounted to more than half the total receipts from commodity taxes other than customs duties.

It is, however, extremely difficult to evaluate the impact of these subsidies on the level of living of the poorest urban consumers. It may be that one of the effects of the subsidy is to encourage substitution of wheat bread for maize bread. Further, none of the items subsidized are exclusively used by the poor, although it is, of course, the case that the poor spend a higher proportion of their income on these commodities than do the rich. Without a more careful study of the patterns of expenditure of the poor than the statistics allow, we cannot evaluate the efficacy of this approach.

A quite different approach to the same problem was tried in Tunisia. In 1970, one estimate of open unemployment in Tunis was 12 percent of the labour force, with rates as high as 20 percent in some of the peri-urban "gourbivilles." It was to tackle urban unemployment on this scale, as well as widespread under-employment (estimated at 60 percent of heads of family in the country as a whole) that the government instituted the "chantiers de chomage." At their peak in 1963, the chantiers were employing as much as 15 to 20 percent of the male population of working age throughout the country. But work in the chantiers tended to be of limited duration, with an average of under 100 days per year. According to one survey, the average earnings of workers in the chantiers did not exceed 53 dinars a year. They can only be regarded, then, even at their peak, as a way of giving the most meagre income for a limited period to a large proportion of the unemployed and under-employed.

After 1963, the resources that government was willing to put into the chantiers declined. This was the result partly of dissatisfaction with the effectiveness of the chantiers (in terms of both the work achieved and the actual benefit derived by the poor) and partly of a change in the structure of the unemployed. As the bulk of these became younger, more urbanized, and more educated, so they were less willing to undertake work on the chantiers—and indeed were less available to do so.

This is not to belittle the role of either food subsidies in Egypt or the chantiers in Tunisia. But neither was successful in reaching the poorest. In Egypt, it is highly arguable that it is the formally employed worker who benefits most from the food subsidies. In Tunisia, the wage rates were so low on the chantiers that they may even have contributed to urban poverty by discouraging workers from looking for alternative sources of income in agriculture and/or the informal sector.

THE URBAN EXCLUDED IN ASIA

Is the situation in the three Asian countries we have studied much different? Or do the great differences in economic structure and rural development modify both the numbers and problems of the urban excluded?

We have already commented on the fact that the rate of growth of aggregate employment in the urban formal sector has been unspectacular in two of the three Asian countries with which we are concerned. But in Sri Lanka, to distinguish between urban and rural unemployment is less meaningful than elsewhere. Over the island as a whole, unemployment seems to have risen from about 10 percent at the beginning of the 1960s to 15 percent by 1971.[38] The Socio-Economic Survey of 1968 found a rate of open unemployment of 20 percent in the towns. But this is a gross underestimate of the rate of exclusion. If we add in only self-employed workers in sales, crafts, and manufacturing, the figure rises to 32.2 percent. The total rate of exclusion is likely to exceed 40 percent. The great majority of those excluded were young middle and primary school leavers, although one in three girls with "O" level passes was without any kind of job.

By contrast, in Malaysia total employment in the formal sector seems to have kept pace with the rate of growth of the labour force at least since 1957. But this disguises rising rates of exclusion in the towns resulting from rapid migration of Malays from the rural areas to the larger towns, the peri-urban areas of Kuala Lumpur and Johore Baru, and states that have in the past given a high priority to increasing the employment of Malays in the state administration. Although many of the employment opportunities in the private sector are in the control of Chinese, and to a lesser extent Indian, entrepreneurs, government steps to increase employment for Malays, especially in the public sector, were bearing fruit.

According to a 1967/68 sample survey, in relative terms* Chinese and Indians were nearly three times as likely to be unemployed as Malays in the towns. But at the same time, as a proportion of the total labour force, more Malays were unemployed than Chinese. For in 1965 Malay males constituted less than 22 percent of the total urban labour force but over 30 percent of those without a regular job in either the formal or informal sector. By 1968, one in six Malays in the towns was without a job. Less than one in ten Chinese was in the same position. But in the private sector, and especially small-scale

---

*That is, the ratio of the racial group as a percentage of all unemployed to the racial group as a percentage of all urban population. This assumes that urban participation rates are similar; but in fact Indian rates are slightly higher.

businesses, Chinese find it easier to get employment in Chinese-owned firms, which tend to dominate these activities. One reason for this has been the traditional reluctance of Chinese craftsmen and smaller businessmen to take Malays as apprentices. Part of this is cultural: An apprentice is regarded almost as a member of the craftsman's family. Part of it is linguistic: Much business is transacted in Chinese. Partly it is tradition, a hangover from colonial patterns, that Chinese provide the capital and the skill, and Malays the labour. To this extent, aggregate figures of unemployment in Malaysia mean little. The reality is that, in some of the larger squatments round Kuala Lumpur, 70 percent of the squatters are excluded from employment in the formal sector.[39]

Apart from its racial character, unemployment in West Malaysia is of the same general kind as in many African countries—particularly heavy among women and the 15-24 age group.*

More unusually, the over-representation of lower/middle secondary school leavers is more marked than that of primary leavers. Primary education is no greater disadvantage than none (by contrast with Sri Lanka). It is only when upper secondary level is reached that employment chances begin to improve again.

In the Philippines, urban exclusion seems to have fallen slightly, at least since the middle of the 1960s. Nonetheless, by the end of 1972 it was still nearly 10 percent, with a predictably heavy incidence among the less skilled, young males.[40] (Female unemployment seems to have fallen faster than male unemployment; in 1950, for example, females accounted for over 50 percent of urban unemployed.) But there is a contrast between the structure of unemployment in the Philippines and Malaysia on the one side and most African countries and Sri Lanka on the other. In Malaysia, 66 percent of excluded men had worked before; in the Philippines 55 percent. In the Philippines, nearly half of the unemployed fell within the age group 25-44, a group most likely to have dependants. Furthermore, nearly one in five of these experienced workers took over ten weeks to find work again. In Malaysia, three quarters were in the age group 25-64, but reabsorption was surprisingly much slower and 70 percent took more than three months to find another job. The "welfare effect" of this exclusion is wholly different from that of the exclusion of large numbers of independent youngsters in Sri Lanka or many African countries.

It is important to establish whether the somewhat lower rates of exclusion in Asia are accompanied by a smaller gap in incomes between the formal and

---

*Unemployment rates decline steeply with age: 14 percent at age 15-19
12 percent at age 20-24
5 percent at age 25-29
<3 percent thereafter.

informal sectors. Is it the case that the lack of minimum wage legislation in
Malaysia and its sporadic enforcement in the Philippines has ensured that wages
in the formal sector are as low as earnings in the informal sector? Or, an alternative hypothesis, have low wages in the formal sector depressed earnings in
the informal sector so that the gap remains?

Inevitably, the evidence is unsatisfactory. According to the Malaysian Post-
Enumeration survey, nearly one in three urban households of "own account
workers" (nearly all presumably in the informal sector) had incomes of under
$M33 per month; one in five less than $M25. But suggestive is the fact that
these proportions exceed those of employees by only 8 percent. In other words,
own account workers are, to be sure, worse off than those in employment, but
not by much. In the Philippines, two independent surveys of incomes in Barrio
Magsaysay, one of the largest squatments in Manila, both reveal a median income of about P150 a month compared with the minimum wage of P176.[41]
Another survey in an area in which employment in the formal sector is particularly low found that the median income was slightly above the minimum wage.
It is dangerous to build much on data as limited as these. They may be evidence
of no more than the unsurprising fact that, in the absence of rigorous legislative
protection, the wages of the unskilled in the formal sector drift down to the
subsistence level of the informal sector. It would be more interesting if we
could show whether lower wages in the formal sector affect earnings in the
informal sector. Do people buy handmade rather than mass-produced articles
when their real incomes fall? We do not know. All we can say is that in
Malaysia and the Philippines there is much less evidence than in Tanzania of a
major gap between the informal and formal sectors.

This should not be allowed to disguise the fact that the poorest in the informal sector are poor indeed. According to one survey, 30 percent of those
receiving incomes in a low-income area of Manila received less than P50 per
week per household—or less than P9 per family member. In Magsaysay, in
1968 one family head in three had a monthly income of less than P100—
suggesting an income per head in the family of less than P20. In physical
terms, one pound of rice and four ounces of the cheapest meat each day would
take more than 85 percent of income—which explains why even this diet exceeds that of most low-income families.

It could be argued that this poverty is relieved by additional income earners
in the family, and low wages are tolerable because all adults in the family earn
a little. This is false. It is rebutted by falling per capita incomes as family size
increases. In the urban areas in 1971, the average per capita income of a two-
person family was P2,189. This fell sharply with the third member, more
slowly with the next two, sharply again with the sixth, and then more slowly
again until we reach the biggest families. In them, there may be additional
earners and average per capita income begins to turn up slightly.[42]

More interesting evidence comes from a detailed study of the second largest city in the Philippines, Davao in Mindanao. This showed that the dependency rate in low-income families is higher than in upper-income families. If we divide numbers of families between the non-productive (aged 0-14) and the productive (over 14), then in low-income families the proportions split 46:34 and in upper-income families 34:46. That this is explained by the tendency of girls in low-income families to marry young is suggested by the fact that the crude birth rate for the low-income groups is 4.1 percent, while for the upper-income class it is only 2 percent. This means that for the low-income families there is much less likelihood of supplementary income from other family members. As a proportion of total family income, supplementary earnings were nearly twice as high in upper-income groups as in low-income groups. In this way, family structure of low-income group *reinforces* differences in standards of living arising from differences in occupation. Indeed, in the Davao study the difference in family size and structure explains more of the difference of income per head than the amount of individual earnings.[43]

For Malaysia our data are less explicit; but it is quite clear that urban poverty is closely associated with increasing household size, number of children, and inability of additional members of the household to find work. A household of eight persons is three times as likely to have less than $M25 per family member as a household of only two. A household with four children is three times as likely to be poor in this sense as one with only a single child. The problem is that we cannot separate these data between the formally and informally employed. But it is clear that multiple income-earners are not common (55 percent of households have none or one; less than 20 percent have more than two), and household and family size are obviously critical variables in the struggle against poverty.

Family size, then, is probably more important than the nature of employment (formal or informal) in determining the incidence of urban poverty in the Philippines and Malaysia. But are there other ways in which those in the informal sector are at a disadvantage by comparison with those in the formal sector? The evidence suggests that there are biases against the informally employed but that they work indirectly. They result from social and economic characteristics that relate to the probability of finding employment in the formal sector. Formal employment as such does not much affect the level of living of low-income families.

A good illustration can be drawn from Malaysia. There a distinct pattern of settlement between the Chinese and Malays can be discerned in the squatments of Kuala Lumpur. While 37 percent of the population of Kuala Lumpur lives in squatter areas, there is a much higher concentration of Malays on public land and of Chinese on private land. This follows directly from the fear of the Chinese that they will be ejected from state land while the Malays believe (and events so far justify that belief) that the government would find it politically embarrassing to eject them. It may also be the case that Chinese owners of unused land are more tolerant of Chinese squatters than they would be of Malays. Whereas the Chinese squatters pay a higher rent than the Malays and enjoy a higher standard of service, the Malay squatters are the victims of government's concern that provision of services to the squatters would constitute recognition of their rights of settlement. Thus, while two out of three Chinese squatter families that settle on private land have pipe-borne water either in the house or close to it, the same is true of only one family in twelve of the Malay squatters on state land. Most Chinese families have some system of waste disposal; barely half of Malay families do. Most Chinese squatters on private land have electricity; this is almost unknown among Malay squatters on state land.[44]

These patterns are related to employment in the formal and informal sector because Malays in the informal sector are more reluctant to move into public housing when it is available. This is partly because they are heavily dependent upon growing at least some food for themselves, often keeping some small stock; partly because they fear that rehousing will destroy the social and economic networks upon which employment in the informal sector depends; and partly because they cannot afford the rents charged. For 70 percent of the Malay squatters, the home is a place of work. Not only would many of the activities thus pursued be banned in public housing, but the flow of customers, information, and passers-by would be much reduced. This has meant that at least until 1968 Chinese squatters have benefitted disproportionately from the limited rehousing programmes (for a more detailed analysis of housing policies see Chapter 12).

Let us now turn to the wholly unemployed, those receiving no income at all. In the Philippines and less certainly in Malaysia, these tend to be rather small in number in the urban areas—about 6 to 7 percent in urban Malaysia and 6 percent in Tondo.* The obvious contrast is between these rather low levels and the extremely high levels found in Sri Lanka. The socio-economic survey of 1969-70 found unemployment rates of 19 percent in the urban areas.† How can this be explained? The first point to emphasize is that the bulk of the open unemployment problem in urban Sri Lanka is a problem of imbalance between educational output and the labour market. This means that a very large proportion of those unemployed have finished primary and even secondary education.

---

*But the under-employed constitute, of course, a much higher proportion—over 20 percent in Tondo.

†It seems fairly sure that the great bulk of workers in the informal sector were excluded from those counted as unemployed since anyone who had done ten days or more of casual temporary work during the previous month was counted as employed.

Although the unemployment of educated people in Malaysia and the Philippines is giving rise to concern, a major structural imbalance on the scale of Sri Lanka has not yet appeared there.

The second point is that, more than in the Philippines or in Malaysia, the unemployed in Sri Lanka are young, first-time job seekers. They are educated migrants from the rural areas, in particular from the Wet Zone, who go to the towns seeking jobs appropriate to their training. Thus, the situation is not dissimilar to that we have already described in Africa. For instance, it is significant that unemployment among illiterates and those who did not complete primary school is much lower than among the more educated. In other words, it is not the situation that jobs are not available—indeed there are serious labour shortages in some manual occupations, particularly in the rural areas. The problem is one of adjustment of aspirations to the realities of an economy locked into a productive structure that is unlikely to create an abundance of white-collar and high-prestige blue-collar jobs. But why does the process of adjustment, whereby aspirations revised in the light of prevailing labour market realities, take so long?

The slow rate of adaptation is explained partly by the fact that most of the unemployed are young. Being unmarried and without dependants, they remain at home or with relatives. Second, because of the food subsidies these unproductive members of the household are less of a burden even on low-income families than they would be if free rice were not available. Third, it is clear that to accept a low-level job—i.e., to adjust to the realities—is to abandon all hope of finding employment at the appropriate level. "Once a toddy tapper, always a toddy tapper" may be an exaggeration, but it is too near the truth to encourage any "O" level graduate to take temporary employment at a level below his aspirations. There is, it is true, the same fear in some African countries. But there the social pressures on job seekers to contribute to the education of siblings and support rural kin tend to be directed more against joblessness than against inability to secure an appropriate job.

There is little need to describe again the precarious existence of those excluded from the formal sector and either eking out a subsistence in the informal sector or else wholly without income. As we have already suggested, in Sri Lanka the age structure of the unemployed and the availability of at least some free food does much to cushion the poorest families. In the Philippines, where the extended family is much less effective as a form of social redistribution in the towns—in low-income areas in Davao nuclear family structures predominate; the extended family is common only in higher-income groups—recourse is inevitably had to the short-term shifts of the familiar cycle of buying on credit, borrowing from friends, and seeking immediate help from the welfare agencies of government or private institutions.* Over the longer term, those without

---

*In the Philippines, employees who have served six months are obliged to

income try to establish themselves in the sections of the informal sector characterized by ease of entry, minimal capital requirements, low productivity, and
low earnings. It is significant that, despite the fact that the majority of low-
income families in Manila are migrants from the rural areas, return to their
place of origin is never seen as a way of solving their economic problems.[45]
However hopelessly trapped they may be by the cycles of poverty, the urban
poor see the city as offering a possibility of escape in a way that the rural areas
never can.

THE INFORMAL SECTOR: COMPLEMENT OR COMPETITOR?

We have described, in as much detail as the fragmentary data allow, means
by which the urban excluded survive their exclusion. They do so by supplying
goods and services to each other and to the privileged (whether local or foreign). Taken as a group, their sales of goods and services to the privileged must
at least yield a sufficient income to pay for food purchased from the rural sector and other essentials that must be bought from the formal urban sector,
such as kerosene for cooking and lighting, transport to work, and the financial
costs of education and health care. The more goods and services the informal
sector can sell to the formal sector, the more food and other goods and services
it can buy from the formal and rural sectors.

We can distinguish between inter-group and intra-group competition—i.e.,
those activities in the informal sector in competition with activities in the formal sector and activities in the informal sector that have a monopoly or near-
monopoly within that sector but nonetheless compete with each other (the
analogy is obviously between exportables and non-exportables). Water selling
and night-soil removal are different examples of activities that are confined to
the informal sector, whereas many types of craft and manufactures, plus street
hawking and vending, are examples of activities that compete with the formal
sector. The question that is relevant to our purpose, then, is the form of competition between the informal sector and the formal sector and the ways in which
the "exports" of the former are restricted or discriminated against.

---

join a social security system and contribute 2.5 percent of gross pay as premiums.
It is difficult to establish how effective this is. There are reports of widespread
default and of taking workers on the books for successive periods of six months
in order to avoid the employer's contribution. From the 1971 family income
survey, it seems that "gifts, support assistance and relief" form a significant
(greater than 10 percent) source of income only for families with a yearly
income of less than ₱500—less than 2 percent of all urban families.

It might be objected that the two sectors are not effectively in competition because there is a marked quality difference between products. Although both sectors may produce shoes, for example, those of the formal sector are so "superior" in quality that they do not compete with those cobbled together on the street corner from old tyres. At one level that is true. A banker or a cabinet minister does not wear shoes made of old tyres. But there is a group of customers—and the size of that group is determined by the distribution of income—that has to predetermined loyalty to either sector. The unskilled labourer may alternate his custom between the sectors in much the same way as we have already seen he may alternate his employment between them. So it is for a large range of both goods and services—furniture, transport services, vehicle repair, tailoring, even short-term credit. In all these cases, the two sectors are in competition—for a given band of income receivers.

In what ways, then, is that competition biased in favour of the formal sector? The most obvious set of biases are those relating to direct discrimination by large corporate purchasers from companies through parastatals to central government. In general, neither enterprises nor ministries place orders in the informal sector. The reasons usually given are inferior quality, inferior reliability, poor accounts and record keeping, and inability to produce in bulk. None of these need represent a permanent barrier: All can be overcome by breaking orders into manageable packages and redefining specifications realistically in terms both of final use and technical feasibility. It is significant that one of the first of the famous Mulungushi economic reforms in Zambia was precisely to require that the copper companies place all their property maintenance, painting, decorating, cleaning, and waste disposal contracts with small (and often informal) Zambian businesses. That this led to difficulties and frustrations for the purchasing officers of the companies concerned is not in dispute. Nor is the questionable quality of some of the work subsequently performed. But the real criticism is that this admirable start was not followed through by fixing and enforcing a ceiling on the size of the Zambian business that was thus to be patronized. For this new stream of lucrative contracts brought into being a rather small number of very profitable Zambian-owned businesses that were soon transferred out of the informal sector into the formal sector. (In the Zambian context, this was perhaps inevitable; the point of the reform was not to transfer income to the informal sector but to transfer income from European-owned enterprises to Zambian-owned enterprises.)

The second set of biases is also institutional. Credit for the informal sector is either not available or available at very high cost by comparison with the formal sector. In the Philippines, a domestic enterprise can borrow from the banks at 6 to 12 percent per annum. The going rate in the squatments is 20 percent—a week. This has a number of important ramifications. It means that the craftsman or handworker can buy only small parcels of materials at a time and therefore has to pay retail or near-retail prices for his raw materials. Retailers and services that depend upon stocks (e.g., motor repair shops) can carry only small stocks and thus offer an inferior service at a lower gross margin. Further, all trades are more vulnerable since they are unable to borrow for their business needs during a slack period. The lack of credit thus reinforces the natural disadvantages of the informal sector. It raises prices, reduces the quality of the product and the service, and makes informal "enterprises" more vulnerable and therefore more short-lived.

Another form of bias in favour of the formal sector arises from the financial strength of the larger enterprises. They are able to advertise and attract brand loyalty in a way that most small manufacturers are unable to do except in purely personal terms. This not only applies to individual brands; it applies to a whole conception of what is respectable and desirable. In creating this conception, the elite perhaps plays an even greater role than the advertisements. Doctors, politicians, senior civil servants, university professors do not patronize the informal sector. Their clothes, their homes, their diets, even their haircuts are incarnate reminders of the "superiority" of the products and services of the formal sector—and thereby no less reminders of the "inferiority" of handwoven cloth, handmade shoes, imperfectly finished furniture, and foodstuffs prepared and processed in a thousand back kitchens.

But all these biases pale into inconsequence beside the defining difference between the informal and formal sectors. For the formal sector has access to cost-reducing technologies. Depending on the structure of competition in the formal sector and/or government regulation of prices, these cost reductions appear to a greater or lesser extent in the form of price reductions. This form of competition is not confined to manufactures. The supermarket is a good example of modern technology applied to retailing in direct competition with one of the main activities of the informal sector. By consistently seeking to adopt cost-reducing technology—and indeed being subsidized by government to do so—the formal sector is able to lower the income band for which it represents a competitive alternative to the informal sector.

In this situation, the informal sector is not necessarily static. New products are developed; new materials are used; new markets (e.g., tourists) are exploited; even new techniques of manufacture are invented. These are defensive moves designed with questionable success to protect a living standard already precariously low. Furthermore, entry into many of these occupations is relatively easy. As exclusion rates increase in Africa, there are more people trying to generate a living in a sector that is already struggling for survival against the formal sector. Under these conditions, the maintenance of an adequate level of earnings from outside the informal sector to pay for food and other necessities becomes increasingly difficult. It is hard to see how levels of living in the informal sector can fail to deteriorate further unless the flow of migrants from the rural areas is arrested.

Governments tend to reinforce the competitive pressures against the informal sector by a range of economic policies, some of the most important of which we shall discuss in Chapter 13. Non-economic policies often work in the same way, and some of the most obvious are well known. They include public health codes and regulations regarding the production and sale of foodstuffs (which are usually based on Western standards and concepts and are thus unsuitable for application to very small-scale "home" food factories or restaurants);* the distribution and pricing of water (see Chapter 13); the distribution, pricing structure, and licensing of urban transport (see above, p. 157); and most important, but more subtle, the reinforcement of "specification bias" against the informal sector by a conscious or unconscious "malinchismo" or lust for what is foreign, "modern," "up to date." A brief perusal of the files of any ministry of information or of the information department of any ministry of trade will establish the point beyond dispute. "News" is exclusively concerned with the opening of this (foreign-owned?) plant or that (state-owned?) factory making locally a "superior" product. The achievements of the informal sector, the technical progress it makes, the ingenuity displayed in finding new materials, new markets, new products—all these go unnoticed.

There is a sense, then, in which the production of goods and services at the interface between the formal and informal sectors is a con-mech. It is a competitive process of enrichment systematically biased against the informal sector. Some informal sector entrepreneurs survive, prosper, and become substantial capitalists. Many more do not.

It is the openness of entry (usually) and the visible success of a few that retains confidence in the "mechanism" (i.e., the inter-group competitive activities) and gives both those who succeed and the formal sector itself a legitimacy in the eyes of the urban poor. But the major beneficiaries are clear. They are first the privileged groups that benefit from the formal sector as consumers, wage earners, or profit receivers; and second those who, receiving an income from a job in the privileged sector, also draw a profit from the activities of the informal sector.

---

*The argument is not that the informal sector should be allowed to spread disease freely, but that public health measures should not imply a scale of production above that of the very small-scale producer in the informal sector.

NOTES

1. N.O. Addo, "Some Aspects of the Relation between Migration and Socio-Economic Development in Ghana," in *Symposium on Population and Socio-Economic Development in Ghana,* eds. N.O. Addo, S.K. Gaisie, G. Benneh, and G.M.K. Kpedekpo, Ghana Population Studies no. 2 (Legon: Demographic Unit, University of Ghana, 1968), p. 108.

2. The Uganda figures are from C.M. Elliott, *Employment and Income Distribution in Uganda*, Discussion Paper (Norwich: University of East Anglia, 1973), p. 14.

3. Robert S. Ray, "Labour Force Survey of Tanzania," mimeo. (Dar es Salaam: 1966), p. 42.

4. *La population de Yaounde, 1969.* (Yaounde: Direction de la statistique et de la comptabilite nationale, June 1970), p. 49.

5. Employment figures from *Emploi etudes regionales 1962-65: Synthese,* (Abidjan: Ministere du plan, 1968), p. 97; population figures from Societe d'etudes techniques et financieres (SETEF), *L'image base 1970: Rapport de synthese situation en 1970* (Paris, 1973).

6. *L'emploi en Tunisie 1961 et 1971* (Tunis: Secretaire d'etat au plan et aux finances, 1964).

7. Societe d'Etudes et des Mathematiques Appliquees, *Etude socio-economique de la zone urbaine d'Abidjan* (Paris, 1963). For this point and further elaboration of experience in Ghana, see N.O. Addo, "Some Aspects of the Relation," op. cit.

8. See, for instance, J.C. Caldwell, "Determinants of Rural Urban Migration in Ghana," *Population Studies*, November 1968; and his *African Rural-Urban Migration: The Movement to Ghana's Towns* (New York: Columbia University Press, 1968).

9. M.A. Bienefeld and R.H. Sabot, *The National Urban Mobility Employment and Income Survey of Tanzania,* vol. I (Dar es Salaam: Economic Research Bureau, University of Dar es Salaam, 1972), p. 144.

10. Ibid., p. 157.

11. R.H. Sabot, *Urban Migration in Tanzania*, vol. II of *The National Urban Mobility Survey*, op. cit.

12. Addo, "Some Aspects of the Relation," op. cit., p. 108.

13. Centre d'Etudes et de Recherches Economiques et Sociales, *Migrations interieures en Tunisie*, no. 23 (Tunis), p. 87.

14. K. Hart, "Informal Income Opportunities and the Structure of Urban Employment in Ghana," paper presented to Conference on Urban Unemployment in Africa held at the Institute of Development Studies, University of Sussex, September 1971.

15. See Elliott, op. cit.

16. Ray, op. cit.

17. *Labor Force*, the Bureau of Census and Statistics Survey of Households Bulletin (Manila: BCS, May 1969).

18. Peter C. Garlick, *African Traders and Economic Development in Ghana* (London: Oxford University Press, 1971). Cf. Astrid Nypan, "Market Trade: A Sample Survey of Market Traders in Accra," mimeo. (Economic Research Division, University College of Ghana, 1960).

19. See International Labour Organization, *Employment, Incomes and Equality: A Strategy for Increasing Productive Employment in Kenya*, report of an inter-agency team financed by the United Nations Development Programme and organized by the ILO (Geneva: ILO, 1972), pp. 60, 63.

20. *The Wages and Conditions of African Workers Employed by British Firms in South Africa*, fifth report from the Expenditure Committee, Sessional Paper for 1973/74 (London: Her Majesty's Stationery Office, 1974).

21. Caroline Hutton, "Reluctant Farmers," doctoral dissertation, Makerere University, Kampala, 1968.

22. Ibid.

23. *Employment, Incomes and Equality*, op. cit.

24. Guy Pfefferman, *Industrial Labor in the Republic of Senegal* (New York: Praeger Publishers, 1968), p. 160.

25. Christine Wallace, "Abavubuka bonna balezewa? Where have all the youth gone? A study of the occupational activities of youth in rural Buganda," (mimeo). (Department of Sociology, University of Makerere, 1972).

26. Societe d'etude et de developpement economique et social (SEDES), *Enquete sur le niveau de vie a Yaounde* (Paris, 1965), p. 32.

27. *Etude socio-economique*, op. cit., p. 26.

28. See S.M. Ntim, "Urban Unemployment in Ghana," M.Sc. thesis, University of Ghana, who argues that both 1960 and 1970 censuses under-record unemployment.

29. A. Achio, "Le probleme du chomage en Cote d'Ivoire," mimeo. (Abidjan: Ministere du plan, 1970).

30. *L'image base 1970*, op. cit.

31. *Enquete sur le niveau de vie*, op. cit.; Institut national de statistique et d'etude economique (INSEE) and Office de recherche scientifique et technique outre-mer (ORSTOM), *Le niveau de vie des populations de l'Adamaoua* (Paris, 1966); SEDES, *Le niveau de vie des populations de la zone cacaoyere du Cameroun* (Paris, 1966).

32. Christine Greenhalgh, "Income Differentials in the Eastern Region of Ghana," *Economic Bulletin of Ghana* (2nd series) 2, no. 3 (1972).

33. G. Planes, *Les Dolotieres* (Ougadougou: Direction des statistiques, 1970).

34. Hart, op. cit.

35. Peter C.W. Gutkind, "The Energy of Despair: Social Organization of the Unemployed in Two African Cities: Lagos and Nairobi," *Civilizations* 17, no. 3 (1967).

36. M.R. Farrant et al., "Kampala's Children," a report to UNICEF (Kampala, 1972), p. 57.

37. Cf. A.W. Southall and P.W.C. Gutkind, *Townsmen in the Making: Kampala and Its Suburbs* (Kampala: East African Institute of Social Research, 1957).

38. P.J. Richards, *Employment and Unemployment in Ceylon* (Paris: Development Centre of Organization for Economic Cooperation and Development, 1971).

39. Tunku Shamsul Bahrin, "Rural/Urban Migration in West Malaysia" (University of Malaya, 1972).

40. *Labour Force*, the Bureau of Census and Statistics Survey of Households Bulletin Series no. 36 (Manila: BCS, November 1972).

41. "Slums are for People," Barrio Magsaysay Pilot Project Report 1968, mimeo.; B.A. Aquino and R.S. Juan, "Income and Expenditure Patterns in Barrio Magsaysay 1967" (Manila: Institute of Philippine Culture, 1968).

42. Data from the Philippine National Census and Statistics Office as published in "Handbook of Labor Statistics for Wage Determination" (mimeo.) 1, no. 1 (January 1974).

43. R. Hackenberg, "Economic and Demographic Trends in Davao City, The Philippines, in 1972," mimeo. (Manila: Institute of Philippine Culture, 1973).

44. Tunku Shamsul Bahrin, op. cit.

45. Mary R. Hollnsteiner, "Socio-Economic Themes and Variations in a Low-Income Urban Neighbourhood," Workshop on Manpower and Human Resources, Los Banos, Laguna, 1972.

We have now completed a rapid survey of the processes of differentiation in the urban and rural areas in a number of very different settings. The main theme of the exposition has been that, within those processes, the privileged groups owe their privileges to their ability to secure superior access to productive assets—land, credit, education—or employment in the formal sector. This superior access is not randomly distributed: It depends upon the interplay of political, social, economic, and ecological forces that combine not only to give specific groups preferential opportunities but also to reinforce that pattern and, all things being equal, make it decreasingly open and malleable.

In this chapter and the next, we examine the effects of these processes on some aspects of the level of living of the excluded. In Chapter 13, we shall focus primarily on economic mechanisms that tend to enrich the privileged and impoverish the excluded. But in this chapter we shall show how the influence, direct and indirect, of the privileged works to deprive the excluded of three of the basic elements of social consumption—health care, pure water, and housing—in much the same way as it does in education. We have chosen these three areas partly because, after education, these are social services that take the lion's share of government expenditure in the social sector and partly because there is widely scattered evidence (from household budget surveys to attitudinal surveys) that these are the main areas of social consumption in which the poor feel most deprived.

We would expect these forces of distortion to be most marked in countries in which the processes of enrichment and differentiation have gone furthest, particularly if (as is usually the case) those processes have produced high rates of urbanization and the centralization of political and administrative power in the urban centres. In less differentiated countries, or countries in which strong political leadership is committed (or wants to be thought committed) to correcting some of the imbalances that have followed from past processes of differentiation, we might expect inequities in social consumption to be relatively small. We would thus expect to find greater inequities in countries like the Phillipines, Ivory Coast, and Kenya than in Tanzania, Sri Lanka, and possibly Tunisia and Egypt. Obviously we would not expect a perfect correspondence, since some distortions are easier to correct than others and since, as we shall argue, shortage of resources itself imposes certain patterns of distortion or at least makes their appearance more, and their removal less, probable.

By analogy with income differentials, we would expect colonial patterns of distortion to have been modified at paces dictated by the scarcity of resources and the political priority given to such modification. But particularly in the first group of countries we would also expect to be able to detect the emergence of new forms of distortion designed to serve the interests of the newly emerging elites and privileged groups. One way in which we might expect that to manifest itself in a particularly sharp form would be the highly ambivalent attitude to the urban poor in general and the poor living in peri-urban townships, bidonvilles, shanty towns, and squatments in particular. For politically and administratively it is these groups that often present an acute problem to the urban elite for reasons that range from pure lust for urban prestige (to maintain the flow of tourists) to fear of mob violence.* But, however unsightly and politically embarrassing the squatters may be, it is common, in the less differentiated societies at least, for members of the privileged groups to have kinsmen and members of the extended family living in the squatments. This vertical relationship is most important. Indeed, in both East and West Africa it is not unknown for senior public employees, living in high-quality housing themselves, to own or rent shacks in peri-urban villages and shanty towns precisely to accommodate migrant kinsmen who would otherwise jeopardize the suburban respectability of their favoured relatives.

But squatments are not exclusively inhabited by unemployed rural migrants. On the contrary, there is much evidence, from both the African and Asian countries in our sample, that blue-collar and white-collar workers employed in the formal sector live there. They are not therefore in any sense an urban dustbin. If their political clout is severely limited, it can be used on individual issues

---

*The attitude of President Hophouet-Boigny of Ivory Coast to the bidonvilles round Abidjan would be a good example of the former; the attitude of President Marcos of the Philippines to forms of squatter organization in Tondo in Manila would be a good example of the latter.

at the municipal level with some effect.* For these reasons, then, the urban poor, and particularly the ill-housed urban poor, present both a greater administrative problem and a less easily contained (and perhaps less easily defined) political threat to the urban privileged. For our purposes, then, relations between the urban privileged and the squatment dwellers present a particularly illuminating insight into patterns of distortion.

In the pages that follow, we shall adopt a similar approach to that of Chapter 9. We shall first examine some spatial aspects of distribution of each of the three sectors; we shall then look at financial constraints on take-up. This is followed by an elaboration of a point touched upon in Chapter 8—that higher salaries for middle-level white-collar workers (e.g., teachers and nurses) tend to limit the availability of the service to the disadvantage of the poor. Finally, we return to a further consideration of mis-specification and con-mechs.

SPATIAL DISTRIBUTION

Health Care

The factors that determine the spatial distribution of health care are not very different from those that determine the distribution of education. Local initiative, missionary activity, duration and vigour of colonial rule did not necessarily reinforce each other but did tend to ensure that the most remote and the poorest parts of each country were relatively deprived. In Ghana, for example, only twelve mission doctors serve the whole hinterland of Ashanti, a highly populated area in which there were in 1972 no government doctors at all. Similarly, missions provided half the doctors in the two poorest regions. But it is no less true that the heavy concentration of doctors in the Eastern Region owes much to mission influence.[1]

Since independence, steps have been taken to make good some of the worst of these deficiencies but, as Table 12.1 shows, they persist to a very marked extent in countries that have been independent for relatively long, such as Ghana and Sri Lanka. That this is not only a matter of shortage of resources—an explanation that certainly has some force in extreme cases such as Upper Volta—is suggested by the first column in Table 12.1, which shows that it is common for

---

*Zoto in Manila, Mathare Valley in Kenya, and Kapwepwe in Lusaka are three (very different) examples of where that clout has been used. But note that it was used on specific local infrastructural issues, not on a generalized political platform committed to a specific ideology. Further, in the first two cases it was to some extent "ventriloquized" by outsiders.

TABLE 12.1

Regional Disparities in Health Facilities—Beds Per 10,000 Population, and Lowest Region as Percentage of Highest, 1970 or Nearest Available Date

Country	Beds Per 10,000 in Lowest	Lowest as Percentage of Highest
Tanzania	5	23.6
Kenya	8	11.5
Uganda	7	20.9
Zambia	27	50.0
Ivory Coast	5	20.0
Ghana	7	19.1
Upper Volta	2	4.2
Cameroon	16	43.0
Egypt*	3	7.9
Sri Lanka	17	19.7
Malaysia	12	31.7

*Free beds only; excludes frontier gouvernorats.

Sources: Compiled from data supplied by ministries of health in annual reports and unpublished documents; for Tanzania, kindly made available by Oscar Gish, Institute of Development Studies, University of Sussex.

the best provided areas (usually the capital and its immediate vicinity) to have at least three or four times the number of beds per ten thousand people as the remotest rural areas. While this does not mean that even the metropolitan areas are adequately served in all cases, it does strongly suggest that the urban areas in general, and the capital in particular, are able to commandeer an undue proportion of the available resources.

There is a powerful structural reason why spatial variations are to be expected. The health delivery system in all the countries under study depends upon the process by which serious cases are referred up a pyramid of diagnostic and therapeutic skills so that, in theory, the very small proportion of complex and serious cases end up in the metropolitan teaching hospitals. But, as has long been recognized, this referral system looks better in theory than it works in practice. The major constraint on its proper functioning, apart from poor diagnosis at the lower levels (which simply fails to pick up the difficult or serious cases) is the lack of communication between the lower-level units and the centres of skill. The most obvious form of that lack of communication is the lack of transport. Even if a referrable case is diagnosed, the chances of its being referred in time depend upon proximity to a larger hospital and the availability of transport. In this way the urban/peri-urban areas tend to have a higher quality of care than the remote rural areas. One very typical finding is that in Uganda 93 percent of cases admitted to Mulago Hospital, accounting for over 50 percent of current expenditures, came from Mengo District alone. M.J. Sharpston found a very similar pattern in Korle Bu, Accra.[2]

A more direct analogy between education and health is the effect of distance on usage. Since Maurice King's work in Uganda,[3] subsequently confirmed by many other researchers, it has become well known that in the rural areas the effective radius of a health facility is small—probably no more than five miles.* Given the much lower population densities of the rural areas, this implies that the inequalities as between the more remote rural areas and the urban areas are much understated in Table 12.1.

The mirror image of this problem is the problem of health care for the urban poor, particularly the urban poor in the squatments. For some, there is a real problem of access. Urban bus services sometimes do not serve the squatment areas,[4] and private transport—mammy wagons, jeepneys, taxis—is expensive, especially for the peri-urban village population. While it is doubtless true that many of the squatters live within five miles of clinics and even general hospitals, it does not follow that there is equity of consumption for the urban poor and the urban "bourgeoisie." As we shall see in later sections, there is a wide variety of inhibiting factors that reduce the level of take-up by the urban poor, even though in spatial terms there may be no marked discrimination against them. M.R. Farrant and colleagues, in studying squatments and low-income areas in Kampala, found a high level of usage of the central hospital and local clinics. But, as Farrant et al. point out, the areas in the study were all close to these facilities; only 10 percent of the 200 interviewees complained of lack of medical facilities.[5]

It could be argued that, by focusing the discussion on curative medicine, we are biasing the evidence in favour of the urban areas because hospitals are necessarily found in urban areas (since they demand a wide range of ancillary and supportive services) and particularly in the metropolis (since a wide range of specialist services is most conveniently situated there). To check how far this is

---

*In the Ankole Pre-School Protection Programme, 1967-69, Malcolm Moffatt found that the number of cases per square kilometre treated at the clinic in Ankole dropped very sharply at distances exceeding two kilometres. In a rather larger survey of personal characteristics of users of maternal care services in West Malaysia, a World Health Organization team found that three quarters of attenders at various categories of clinics usually came distances of less than three miles. For reasons that are not clear, this pattern was broken only by midwife clinics, where 43 percent of observed attenders came from distances exceeding three miles.

true, we would like to be able to present data on spatial distribution of such preventive services as immunization, health education, and improved water supplies. Unfortunately, such data are both rare and unreliable; where they do exist, they tend to be distorted by the temporary adoption of areas of concentration. An outbreak of smallpox, even in a remote area, can be followed by an intensive immunization campaign; this cannot be interpreted as evidence of a high priority to the rural areas in the distribution of preventive medicine. We shall argue in a later section that the marked imbalance between the proportion of resources devoted to preventive medicine compared with those devoted to curative medicine is itself the major form of discrimination against the poor, both rural and urban. It is indeed the best evidence of the imposition of the needs and priorities of the privileged upon the community as a whole.

One of the features of preventive medicine is that it tends to be carried out by low-grade personnel. This implies that, when one inspects the spatial distribution of medical skill, one finds the same urban concentration as for curative medicine. Indeed, since in most countries health centres are not staffed by doctors, the concentration of fully qualified skills is even more marked than in the case of hospital beds. But the more interesting question about the distribution of doctors is whether those in private practice themselves increase or diminish the distortion of distribution. How far is it true that private doctors serve in areas where government services are not available? Even though they may charge for their services and thus introduce financial constraints on take-up, is there any evidence that they improve the spatial distribution? The data are slender but suggest that the normal assumption that private practice accentuates distortions needs at least some modification. In countries with an excess of doctors—for example, Sri Lanka, the Philippines, and prospectively some African countries—the force of competition within the private sector obliges some doctors to practice in areas and among people under-served by the government services. Ankole in the late 1960s was a good early example. The effective rate of coverage by government doctors was 1:250,000 population, for the great majority of the district. There were, however, five private practitioners in the district.[6] Furthermore, where the government service is of a particularly low quality, private practitioners are often successful in attracting patients from the free services (see below, p. 325).

We thus sometimes find in practice the inverse of the theory. The rural, and to some extent the urban, poor are either not served at all or are offered low-quality services. In order to make good these deficiencies, fee-charging practitioners (whose quality may or may not be superior but whose efficacy may be made the more credible by the fact that they do charge a fee) sell their services to those least able to pay for them.

But even these practitioners in countries with an excessive supply of fully qualified doctors do not reach the mass of the rural poor. For the rural poor rely in part or entirely on traditional healers, and for deliveries on traditional midwives; as Robert Cook observed, "It seems unlikely that more than something between 10 percent and 20 percent of children ever receive in their last and fatal illness any treatment other than native medicine."[7] The efficacy of the healers is much debated; evaluations vary from the mildly optimistic to the wholly negative. But from the viewpoint of thes poor they offer a number of important advantages. They are accessible; virtually every village has its midwife, and most villages of any size have a healer. The service is quick. The healer is not beseiged by hundreds of supplicants and the patient is not obliged to wait in great discomfort for prolonged periods. The service is offered by someone who is known to the patient and/or his kinsmen. The patient does not come face to face with an incomprehensible expatriate or a white man in a black or yellow skin. The service follows a well-known and regular routine and produces prescriptions or potions that are familiar. Complicated self-medication over a prolonged period is not usually required. The consultation is not hurried and it offers supporting roles to a wide range of kinsmen. It may take place over two or three days so that instant recall is not necessary. It often depends upon or results in the creation of some kind of social bond between the healer and the patient. This may be symbolized by gift giving, or attendance at rites of passage.

For all these reasons, the traditional healer may be preferred by the rural poor even if a free government service is available. To that extent, from the point of view of many of the rural poor, the maldistribution of medical services as revealed in Table 12.1 is less relevant. At best they would regard the service as an occasional supplement to the traditional healer—to be consulted when the traditional medicine has not proved effective. But this is precisely the difference between the rural poor who are dependent almost exclusively upon traditional healers and the urban poor who can choose which system they patronize. For evidence from Ghana, Zambia, Sri Lanka, and the Philippines all shows that the urban poor (and indeed often the urban not-so-poor) hedge their bets by patronizing both systems simultaneously.

Housing

The major issues in the distribution of housing are not spatial. Although quality of housing may vary in the rural areas—e.g., as between estate workers and peasant farmers or as between differents tribes—the only questions relevant to our theme concern urban housing. These questions will be raised in later sections.

Water Supply

There can be little doubt that, for both the urban and rural poor, access to water is one of the major concerns of everyday life. It is revealing that a study of Barrio Magsaysay, a large squatter settlemen in Manila, found that the very poor do not rate employment and food as their most serious problem. They see their most serious problem as getting access to water and toilet facilities. It is only when these problems are solved that food and employment become the main anxiety.[8] We can infer the same priority accorded to water in an African environment from the amount of time and effort rural families devote to fetching water—and more particularly to the very limited effect of distance that it has to be carried on the quantity of water consumed.[9] The question to be asked in this section is whether there are obvious spatial distortions in the provision of access to water that are related directly or indirectly to the political, social, and economic power of the privileged.

Figure 4 gives a very neat answer to that question in broad terms for East Africa. For it shows that a major difference in consumption is related to access to piped water. There is relatively little difference between consumption in the rural and urban areas when water has to be carried or bought from water sellers. But for a piped supply there are predictably large differences between low-density housing (with large gardens to be watered, cars to be washed, servants to use quantities of water in washing and cleaning the house, and a rate structure that makes water relatively cheap for the large consumer* and high-density housing areas where the household size may be larger but where there is no garden and where acculturation to water on tap may not have gone very far.

The first spatial question, then, is about the distribution of pipe-borne water. That this is more common in urban areas than in rural areas does not need emphasis. The size of investment, the indivisibility of that investment, and the common convention that expenditures on water must be self-financing (which implies charging for water) means that piped supplies to dispersed rural communities are very rare. This is illustrated in Table 12.2, calculated from the 1970 Population Census of Ghana. This shows that, as the size of settlement increases, so the proportion of population having access to pipe-borne water increases and the usage of high-risk sources diminishes. As better educated people with more highly skilled (and paid) jobs are to be found in the larger settlements, there is an obvious bias in the availability of clean water towards such people. In a general sense, that is obvious. But we were surprised to find the same relationship persisting, at statistically significant levels, even in a

---

*See below, pp. 330-33.

FIGURE 4

Mean Daily Consumption of Water by Housing Type

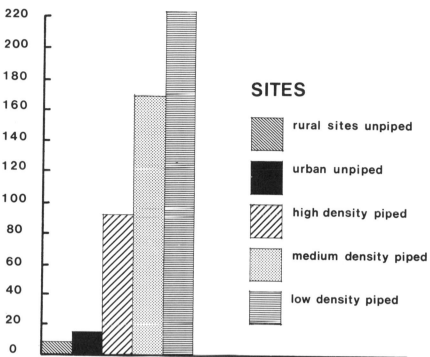

Source: Gilbert White, David Bradley, and Ann White, *Drawers of Water: Domestic Water Use in East Africa* (Chicago: University of Chicago Press, 1971).

TABLE 12.2

Ghana: Water Supply by Size of Settlement in Selected Regions, 1970
(percentage distribution)

Water Supply	Settlement Size (number of persons)								
	0-199			200-999			1,000+		
	Accra	Eastern Region	Volta	Accra	Eastern Region	Volta	Accra	Eastern Region	Volta
Pipe-borne	11.6	0.8	0.8	29.1	—	0.1	57.1	11.1	19.5
Borehole	0.7	0.2	0.8	1.9	1.2	—	—	5.5	7.3
Well	9.2	7.3	2.8	4.9	5.7	3.6	—	5.5	—
Spring	0.7	1.5	3.1	1.0	1.2	4.3	—	—	9.8
Rainwater	0.7	0.4	0.4	—	—	—	—	—	2.4
River	22.5	87.5	68.8	19.4	88.5	64.0	10.7	75.0	41.5
Lake/pond	0.2	—	12.4	—	—	8.6	—	—	—
Dam or pond	27.1	0.6	8.2	25.2	3.4	7.2	10.7	2.8	2.4
Dug-out	27.5	1.7	2.7	18.4	—	2.2	21.4	—	17.1

Source: Computed from data in *Special Report D of 1970 Population Census of Ghana* (Accra: Census Office, December 1971).

relatively remote area in Volta Region. There a small survey of 150 households showed no relationship between size of settlement and education or occupation of the head of the household, but it did show that the better educated, better paid villagers were more likely to have adopted non-traditional water sources. In this case, then, education and occupation act directly on people's readiness to secure clean water supply—and a better house and a more hygienic latrine, both important factors that affect the purity of water stored in the house.[10]

But note that Table 12.2 shows that, even in the immediate vicinity of the capital, a large proportion of the population of the peri-urban settlements is dependent upon high-risk sources.

A more interesting question is what determines the quality of supply in the urban areas. We need to distinguish between at least three levels of water supply in the urban areas: individual connections with at least one tap per dwelling; a communal tap or standpipe that provides clean water but leaves the individual to fetch it (sometimes from an unhygienic site); and high-risk sources of water such as a spring or stream, the site of which may be the breeding ground of parasites and the water of which is unlikely to be pure. The main forces determining the distribution and use of these three types of water supply are economic and will be discussed later, but there is a spatial aspect that can be mentioned briefly here.

As with most other services, density of settlement is usually regarded as a necessary precondition of supply. This means that the densely settled squatments within the municipal boundary are more likely to be supplied with at least a standpipe than are the less densely settled peri-urban villages outside the municipal boundary. This is evident from Table 12.3. But density of settlement is not the only—or even a very important—explanation of distribution of urban water facilities. Contrast the low-density but high-income areas of settlement, which have high quality of service at low unit cost, and the low-density, low-income areas of settlement which have no service (and therefore higher incidence of water-borne diseases) for which they may nonetheless have to pay directly or indirectly more per unit of water than the high-income areas. We shall return to this below.

For the moment, the major general point to be emphasized is that the major proportion of investment goes to the largest urban areas and particularly the capital. Thus in Ivory Coast, despite a very high rate of growth of population in Abidjan, the number of people "per rate" has declined from 46 in 1960 to 25 in 1971. By contrast, in Bouake, the second city of Ivory Coast, the number per rate has risen from 57 in 1960 to 63 in 1971.*

---

*A rate is a rateable water outlet. It may be a ten-storey building or a little house. In Abidjan, the population living in one unit tends to be higher than elsewhere. This implies that the number of people served per rate in Abidjan is higher than elsewhere.

TABLE 12.3

Tunisia: Water Supply and Urbanization, 1966/67

Gouvernorat	Rate of Water Access	Level of Urbanization[a] (1966)	Percentage of Urban[b] Population with Access to Water
Tunis	90	92	98
Sousse	69	66	69
Sfax	54	57	92
Bizerte	49	49	90
Nabeul	47	45	91
Gabes	38	45	65
Medenine	20	22	85
Kasserine	18	14	77
Le Kef	18	20	74
Jendouba	13	16	60
National average	47	47	88

Note: Figures include standpipe as well as pipeborne water.

[a]Proportion of population in settlements of more than 2,000 inhabitants.

[b]In this column, urban is defined as settlements of more than 5,000 inhabitants.

Source: Unpublished data from Secretariat d'Etat aux Travaux Publics et a l'Habitat and the Societe Nationale de l'Eau et de l'Electricite, Tunis.

The same point is well illustrated in Tunis. Table 12.3 shows the proportion of total population in each gouvernorat with water access. In most rural regions, more than 60 percent of the population having pipe-borne water lives in settlements with more than 5,000 inhabitants. On the average, less than 11 percent of the rural population has tap or stand-pipe water. Thus, if we divide the population into those living in settlements with more and those with less than 5,000, we get the following distribution of water access: only 2 percent of the rural population on this definition have water from the tap; 57 percent have water from unprotected sources.

One might expect that a country that sets a high priority on rural development, and in which a real attempt is made to be responsive to the demands of rural people, would not show the same pattern. An obvious example is Tanzania. There rural water supply is given an unusually high priority—witness the abolition of all charges for water in 1966, and repeated calls at national conferences of the ruling party and of the National Trade Union for more expenditure on water supply. Government responded to these calls in 1965 by changing the arrangements by which water supply is financed, so the wealthier areas would not continue to pre-empt natural and technical resources; and again in 1970 after continual pressure from TANU, by producing a priority list according to the existing stock of water facilities, total population, and numbers and distribution of livestock. But neither of these administrative changes has yet had much effect. Those areas in which the Ministry has concentrations of trained men and equipment continue to benefit. There are, of course, the richer areas—Coast, Kilimanjaro, Arusha, and West Lake—and the areas in which the Ujamaa programme is making the most rapid progress, most notably Dodoma. Meanwhile the least developed regions—Shinyanga, Mwanza, Mbwara—continue to receive less than their theoretical allocation. Regional inequalities thus persist.[11]

FINANCIAL CONSTRAINTS TO TAKE-UP

Health

We have already seen that in the rural areas, and to a lesser extent in the urban areas, the lowest-income groups are likely to find access to free health facilities difficult. They therefore use traditional healers and pay for their services. How far this acts as a disincentive we do not know. In a bidonville near Abidjan, a survey found that one family in three did not use formal services because of the cost involved—a cost increased by the fact that poor and uneducated families are often charged for medicine that is supposed to be issued free. There is some indirect evidence that the poorest find the overt and covert charges burdensome. In Tanzania, for instance, the lowest-income group spends nearly four times as much on health care as it does on education—a discrepancy that may be explained at least in part by family structure. In Sri Lanka, expenditures on health care as a whole (indigenous and Western) are between a half and two thirds of expenditure on clothing for all those with incomes of less than Rs2,400 (38 percent of the sampled population).

But there is some evidence that, at the margin, financial charges may influence or even determine the type of care a patient receives. For example, a small survey of rural out-patients in Kenya discovered that 50 percent would have gone to private practitioners if they had been able to afford the fees. In the same way, in the squatter areas of Manila, the lowest-income groups go to free government clinics in or near the squatments. But as incomes rise, so the tendency to patronize private practitioners increases. The survey of Tongu District in Ghana showed that education, occupation, and wealth were all highly correlated with preference for Western medical care over traditional healers and for government midwives over village midwives.

There may well be a hierarchy of medical care—the poorest in the isolated areas use traditional healers nearly exclusively. Thus, in the Tongu survey only 10 percent of household heads, all uneducated, used traditional healers only; 55 percent, most of them uneducated, used both modern and traditional. In a small sample, none with more than primary education used traditional healers.[12]

As incomes rise and/or density of settlement increases, there is readier access to free government services. But there is a twilight zone where the social (and even psychological) advantages of the traditional healer are matched, in the patients' eyes, by the advantages of the (free) government service. As incomes rise further and outlooks and attitudes are "modernized," so the traditional healer is abandoned for the "Western" practitioner. But now the limitations of the government service become increasingly resented, and patients who can afford it transfer to the private practitioners. We do not know in detail how closely this progression relates to income levels; we have already seen that, in some areas, even quite poor people may go to private practitioners because government services are simply not available.

The opportunity cost of the long waits at clinics and out-patient departments can be high for the self-employed or for those employed and paid by the day. One in three of the patients at a Kenyan clinic who wanted a speedier service was anxious about his job or his earnings. Only one in twenty thought his employer would understand that the service is slow and the wait long. But, as with education, so with health—there is no unambiguous evidence that these costs deter the poor from using health facilities. It is, however, clear that they are a disproportionately heavy burden on the poor. When the margin between subsistence and deprivation is so narrow, the loss of half a day's work at any wage rate is a financial blow.*

Housing

In housing, the evidence is much less ambiguous. In nearly every country that we have examined, government does not provide housing for lower-income groups. Even though the funds for housing are subsidized directly or indirectly from public revenues, they are devoted to housing the urban privileged. We shall return to this in a later section; for the moment we need only emphasize that the rents for the lowest public housing in most of the countries that we have examined far exceed the total income of the poorest urban families.

In Tunisia, for example, the very policy of financing public housing militates immediately against the urban poor. Public housings is sold to the occupier on a prolonged mortgage, but the occupier is obliged to put down a deposit of 30 percent of the value of the house on occupation. The same policy is followed in

---

*It is also the case that regular full-time employees paid by the week or month do not have "sick time" deducted from their pay if they are absent less than a full day. For the daily paid, there is usually a pro rata deduction.

Upper Volta, with more explicit discrimination in favour of public officials. For the state housing agency will lend only to public servants; in general, only they can find the 30 percent deposit. In Cameroon, 80 percent of the publicly financed housing is occupied by state employees who pay a rent equivalent to one tenth of an economic rent. On average, expatriates spend the same absolute sum on rent as does a Cameroonian unskilled labourer. The former is subsidized by the state and lives in high-quality modern housing; the latter is not subsidized and lives in the shanty towns.

In Ivory Coast, where government priorities are well revealed in the plans to develop Abidjan as the Riviera of West Africa, the minimum rent for public housing is 6,000 F CFA a month—60 percent of the average monthly wage of an unskilled labourer. Inevitably, then, the number of slum dwellers in Abidjan doubled in only five years (1965-70). In the Philippines, the major agency for subsidized housing finance demands as security a quality of house that is beyond the reach of those earning less than P-7,000—more than three quarters of the total population. In Sri Lanka, where one might expect very different policies, public housing was not given a high priority in the 1960s, but in 1971 the Ministry of Housing and Construction adopted as its first priority "to accelerate the building of low-cost houses for the lower income groups in the urban and rural areas by the State, housing co-operatives, private individuals and organizations; to clear slums as a long term measure; and to ameliorate the conditions of slum dwellers by providing amenities such as water and light to them and rehousing them as short term measures."[13]

Accordingly, the government introduced a rent act that covered all residential premises and offered substantial rent reductions to some tenants. But for the promotion of low-cost housing the government was able to do little despite the rhetoric quoted above. In 1972, incentives to the building of smaller houses were introduced. Loans were limited to a maximum of Rs25,000 but were "restricted to those whose family incomes are less than Rs1,500 per month."[14] Although this limit was supposed to operate as a "disincentive to the affluent classes who would like to build luxury dwellings," the fact is that less than 7 percent of the urban population was disqualified by this income ceiling. Although no doubt the most affluent were thereby excluded, it is highly improbable that the urban poor and slum dwellers have gained anything material from these incentives.

Nor is the experience of the other leftist country, Tanzania, much different. The object of the colonial power in housing finance was to encourage the building of improved houses for a stable house-owning class in the urban areas. The coming of independence and of the Arusha Declaration have not fundamentally changed this. The Permanent Housing Finance Company of Tanzania, one of the two major state-owned housing finance companies, offers finance to potential house owners—but on terms that reduced *potential* borrowers to fewer than 4,000 persons in 1968/69.[15] The other major institution, the National Housing

Corporation (NHC), which had as one of its terms of reference slum clearance and rehousing the urban poor, has done hardly better. The average cost of houses built by the NHC during the period of the First Five Year Plan was Shs.15,400—a sum that implies a monthly income for tenants of over Shs.700. Even the lowest-cost house offered by the NHC in 1968 cost Shs.7,700—implying a monthly income of around Shs.340. This might be a reasonable target for those in full-time white-collar or highly skilled occupations in the urban areas; it is quite beyond the means of the families whose housing needs constitute the bulk of the "housing problem."

Experience, then, is almost universal. Remarkably little experimentation has been undertaken in the supply and financing of improved housing and living environment for the very poor. Such experiments as have been tried have not been wholly successful. The roof loan scheme in Tanzania, initiated by the colonial authorities, but continued by the independent government, was badly mismanaged and perhaps internally inconsistent. For it may have encouraged at least some families to put relatively expensive and permanent roofs on inexpensive and impermanent houses. The result was that the houses collapsed before the roof loans had been repaid.

In Zambia, the site and service scheme, whereby government provided a concrete slab with one tap and in some cases one electric point, leaving the owner/tenant to build the structure, was financially viable only because very substantial costs of supervision were hidden in the Ministry's budget. This by itself would not be an objection. But a common experience of successful site and service schemes is that allottees sell the site to wealthier claimants. Leaving aside the temptations to corruption and manipulation that this windfall profit breeds (temptations that have not been much resisted in Manila and Nairobi), the effect is that a significant proportion of such schemes is taken over by the less poor—and the really poor revert to the squatments.

This problem is not, of course, confined to site and service schemes. In West Malaysia, state governments subsidize low-cost housing by providing land and infrastructure. In allocation of these houses, there is an income ceiling of M$300 per month per household, but preference is given to prospective purchasers rather than permanent tenants. Such purchasers can resell their houses at the full market price, thus making a substantial profit. But as 65 percent of squatters in Kuala Lumpur earned in 1966 less than M$200 per month per household, it is clear that this profit does not accrue to the lowest-income groups.[16]

An alternative approach, usually stoutly resisted by a range of lobbies from the environmental to the tourist trade, is to provide basic services to existing squatments so that water, drainage, minimal lighting and firefighting equipment are provided. But even this approach is not unambivalent in its welfare effects. For if a large proportion of the land and/or buildings of the squatment is owned by landlords, the effect of such improvements is to enhance the value of the land and, in the long term, raise rents. Land at Mathare Valley, for instance, increased tenfold in price within two years of the City Council's change of policy—a change itself not unrelated to the ownership of much of the property in the valley.

To avoid high land costs, sometimes maintained by subsidized credit through state institutions, resettlement areas may have to be a long way from the city centre. A leading example is Carmona, outside Manila. As rehousing policy is not coordinated with regional policy, local employment is not available. Unemployment in these resettlement areas is therefore much higher than in the central squatments. Fierce resistance to "resettlement" among existing squatters and the return of resettled squatters to their old habitats are the inevitable result. Over five years, 50 percent of families resettled in Carmona returned to the metropolitan area.[17]

Given the prevalence of the problem and the inadequacy of solutions, or even searches for solutions, is there anything that explains why housing policy seems to be systemically biased against the poor? It is not enough to say that the urban middle classes have deliberately structured the distribution of housing finance in their own interest. This may be true, but we have to ask why they have been allowed to do so. For we have seen already that in some countries the urban poor are, or are thought to be, if not politically powerful at least potentially embarrassing.

A number of reasons can be advanced. The first, which we shall postpone to a later section, is the mis-specification of the problem. The problem is not to provide scaled-down versions of middle-class houses; it is to provide a less hazardous and exploitive environment for the homes of the urban poor. To this we shall return. Second, it is perhaps true that the urban poor give better housing a fairly low priority. Certainly there is much evidence that slums and squatments have a social, political, and economic life of their own into which at least many slum dwellers are wholly integrated. The periodic flattening of squatments by the administrative agents of the privileged destroys not only physical houses but the networks of relationships that form a significant part of the survival system of the excluded. While many slum dwellers are not unaware of the inadequacy of water supply, drainage, and ventilation, they are also fearful that a higher standard of housing is incompatible with the preservation of these crucially important networks. This is not to argue that the poor like living in slums. But it is to suggest that one reason why improved housing (and particularly "official" housing) seems to have a lower priority is that the social and economic costs of of improving their housing (which usually means another and often more distant neighbourhood) are simply too high for the urban poor.[18] Apart from the advantages for those employed in the informal sector, low rents, low transport costs, and low property taxes mean that the cost of living in the squatments is lower than that in improved locations.

This is consistent with what we have found with respect to both health care and education. In all three sectors, the poor are squeezed out by the fact of their poverty. They cannot send their children to school because they cannot afford the fees, because they are continually on the move, because they are at a remote distance from the school, or because they cannot afford to live in the right administrative area. They cannot use free medicine because they cannot reach the clinic, they cannot afford the transport, they cannot afford to wait. They cannot agitate for better housing because to do so will involve the destruction not only of the inadequate housing they may already have but also because it will involve the abolition of a series of social networks on which they are dependent for their livelihood, for economic and social support, for information and social integration. A housing policy that does not protect these is no service to the poor; it is a further exploitation of them.

Water Supply

We have already seen that a major determinant of the amount of water that households use is whether or not they are connected to the water mains. In this section, basing the analysis almost entirely on Gilbert White, David Bradley, and Anne White's data from East Africa, we ask three questions. First, is there any evidence that the poor pay more for their water than the rich? Second, is there any evidence that price affects the amount of water that people use? Third, does price affect the source of water, and therefore its purity? The first is fundamentally a question about the effect of pricing policies on real incomes of the poor (for a further discussion of this whole theme related to goods other than water, see Chapter 13). The second and third questions are fundamentally about the relationship between the economic distribution of a social good (water) and the level of health. For there is much evidence that, although the relationship is not simple, both the quantity and quality of water that a family uses are related to the incidence of a number of diseases.[19]

We begin, then, with an analysis of the cost of water. Immediately we must distinguish between those having connections to a main and those using water carried from a source—be it stream, spring, well, or standpipe. Let us take this latter case first. It might be thought that those who fetch their own water from a spring have their water free. In a crude sense, they do. They do not pay for their water from their cash income, but that does not mean that their water is costless. It costs them the effort of walking to the source and carrying water home, sometimes over considerable distances, and it costs them the time that might otherwise be devoted to productive work or to leisure. Putting costs on either of these concepts is extremely difficult: we shall use the technique developed by White, Bradley, and White by which money cost is placed on the energy required to fetch water.

Considering first water from a free source that is carried home, White, Bradley, and White found that, allowing only for the energy cost, water for most rural dwellers was more expensive than for urban dwellers by a factor of around 1:6. If we were to include the opportunity cost of the time involved, there are two reasons for thinking that this difference would be increased. First, at busy times of the agricultural year, the cost of fetching water is leaving the fields early. It is therefore more likely that there is a real cost involved (in this sense) for rural families than there is for urban families. Second, rural families tend to have further to go than urban families.

Not all urban families, even in high-density areas, carry their water from a free source. A common form of low-cost provision is the erection of a limited number of standpipes; users pay for water they draw from the standpipe. The water is likely to be pure, but the environment around the standpipe may be less hygienic. This source of water, however, is expensive since there are two sets of costs involved: payment for the water itself plus the carriage. (And sometimes water is bought from private houses having a tap connection; this is common in Manila and Kuala Lumpur.) If the carriage is undertaken by water sellers, then the cost is likely to be the most expensive of all. There is little evidence that the lowest-income families in the urban areas buy their water from water sellers rather than carrying it themselves. The only case where this is likely to happen is in a single-member household where the person concerned is too old or too weak to carry water for himself. More frequently, those who buy from water sellers are the rather wealthier households, those with no one at home during the daytime to fetch water because everyone is at work.

How do these costs—ranging in White, Bradley, and White's sample from U.S.$0.03 per 1,000 litres for free water carried to the home in the rural areas to $1.40 per 1,000 litres for water bought from water sellers in the urban areas— compare with the costs borne by households enjoying connection to the water main? The cost of piped water depends upon the volume of water used. Since most authorities charge a relatively high fixed overhead and a rather low unit cost (either for all units consumed or for units in excess of the basic free allocation), it follows that the unit cost of water falls with the total volume consumed. White, Bradley, and White thus found that the unit cost of piped water for low-density housing in three East African cities is 20 percent cheaper than in the high-density areas of two of those cities. On average, piped supply is less than half the cost of unpiped water in the urban areas, but great discrepancies can arise even within one city. Thus those in Mathare Valley, the squatment in Nairobi, who do not have piped water pay ten times as much for their water as those in the lush low-density suburbs of that city.

But does it follow from this that the poor are inhibited from using water by its price? The evidence suggests that, for most people for most of the time, the cost of water is not a constraint on its use—whether that cost is a direct cash cost or the cost of time and effort in carrying it. For unpiped water, White, Bradley, and White found "no association . . . between cost per litre and the total or per capita volume withdrawn."[20] For piped water, there is a statistical relationship between cost per litre and use, suggesting that unit cost of water does constrain its use. But this statistical relationship needs careful interpretation. It may be that the relatively wealthy inhabitants of low-density housing use more water and pay lower prices. It does not follow from this that they use more water because the cost is lower. Similarly, the relatively poor inhabitants of high-density housing pay a higher unit cost and use less. This may not be a causal connection; we have already seen that the use of water on gardens and cultural habit explain much of the difference in use of water. The association of price with this pattern of usage may be coincidental. At the margin, it may well be the case that heavy consumption of water—e.g., for watering a garden— is constrained by price. There is no evidence that the use of water in essential functions is constrained by price.

A potentially more important welfare effect of price, however, may be to encourage households to use impure, but free, water in preference to pure, but expensive, water. Is there evidence of this? There is little direct evidence in either direction: There are few reports of poor households using standpipes or buying water from tap connections because they fear local water is polluted; nor is there evidence of householders refusing to pay for water but eliberately using impure water in order to save money. That no such evidence exists merely shows how little research has been done. White, Bradley, and White do, however, quote one revealing example. In 1966 Tanzania abolished all charges for standpipe water, and delivery of standpipe water doubled in the following year. Even allowing for increases in wastage, rising urban population, increases in consumption by households previously using standpipes, and imprecise data, it is hard to resist the conclusion that there was a rather considerable diversion of water use from impure sources to standpipes. It is hard to believe that water charges encourage the use of pure water by the poor; and this is at least superficial evidence that they actually discourage it.

This raises a more fundamental point. Why do municipalities charge for water at all? Or, given that there is evidence that charges reduce wastage, why do they use a price system that discriminates against the low-volume user? It is hard to resist the conclusion that two factors provide much of the explanation. The first is international or, more properly, rich country practice. There the origins and financing of water undertakings made a relatively high standing charge desirable, irrespective of its impact on low-income groups. The second is an administrative disinclination to threaten the interests of those who profit by the existing system. The relatively small sums directly involved do not raise issues of principle. It is safer and less trouble to maintain the status quo than to upset the majority of piped water users—and the staff of one's own department. We see no evidence here of a political plot. We see much evidence of the rational selection of the line of least resistance. For the poor offer no resistance.

SALARIES AND THE COST OF SERVICE

We have seen so far that, in terms of both the spatial distribution and the financing of social consumption, there are major biases against the low-income groups. With respect to both of these it could be argued that a major reason for such biases is the shortage of provision. If there were more schools, more children would have easy physical access. If there were more clinics, people would have to spend less on transport to reach them. If the cost of the service was lower, the fees could be lower and one form of discrimination thus reduced.

By definition, these services are provided by the privileged—teachers, doctors, medical assistants, bureaucrats. Education and health are both highly skill-intensive. In both, salaries are the greatest direct component of cost. In the Philippines, 90 percent of primary education costs are teachers' salaries, and in Uganda it is scarcely less; such high proportions in themselves are indicative of the low quality and quantity of buildings and other material inputs. In health care, the proportion of costs directly attributable to salaries and wages depends on the level of the facilities. It can be as high as 80 percent at a clinic or simple district hospital with few beds and a rather low level of medication. At a major hospital, it is less because amortization, feeding costs, equipment, and drugs form a higher proportion of the total cost. Overall, wages and salaries typically take 50 to 60 percent of the total health budget.

The best example of the effect of rising salaries of these skill groups on the cost, and therefore availability, of a particular service is given by Richard Jolly in his case study of education in Uganda.[21] He shows that in the whole period from 1938 to 1958—a period in which primary teachers' starting salaries increased nearly sixfold—the rise in teachers' salaries has added more to the educational bill in Uganda than the near sevenfold increase in primary school enrolments. The net effect of this is best demonstrated by dividing the period in two—1938-49 and 1949-58. In the first period, enrolments increased by nearly twice as much as salaries and, in the second, salaries by over twice as much as enrolments. Thus, although expenditure on primary education rose much faster in the 1950s than it had in the 1940s, the increase in enrolments was much less. The difference is almost entirely accounted for by the increase in salaries. Jolly comments: "However justified in keeping teachers abreast of others in employment, these increases greatly increased the cost of education and thus limited the amount which could be done with the money at the disposal of the Ministry. Nor did the trend of salary increases stop after 1958. Further revisions followed in 1960 and 1964."[22]

There is no reason to believe that this experience has been confined to Uganda. The economies that can be made by increasing student/teacher ratios is limited, particularly when political concern begins to develop over high drop-out rates, high repeater rates, and generally low quality of education. In nine years, teachers' salaries in Tanzania increased in money terms by 31 percent. (This refers to starting salaries for grade A teachers; the top of the scale for this grade and both starting and top salaries in other grades were increased slightly less, with the lowest increase 24 percent.) Over the same period, primary school enrolments increased by over 65 percent, but the pupil/teacher ratio rose very little; indeed, it began to fall. The cost per student place is therefore likely to have risen by all, or nearly all, of the rise in teachers' salaries. Although data on health services are less precise, the same mechanism is at work. Indeed, there may well be less scope for economizing by reducing unit costs. What scanty evidence there is suggests that patient/practitioner contact is already near (or even below) an effective minimum. To this extent, rising wage and salary costs are likely to have a direct and immediate effect on the rate of expansion of the service. This is made all the more probable by the fact that at cabinet or planning office level, the ministry of health is usually able to muster less political support than the ministry of education. But this is not to argue that greater cost effectiveness cannot be achieved. There are usually great economies to be made by changing both strategy and tactics of health care—e.g., diversion of resources from large central hospitals to rural health clinics (see below, pp. 336-37) and a better use of skilled time at all levels of service. In Malaysia, for example, a study of facilities in districts found that staff nurses in district hospitals spent less than half of their time with patients; the rest was taken up by administration. Doctors, on the other hand, spent more than 80 percent of their time in contact with patients. Average doctor/patient contact time was less than four minutes at the general and district hospital levels; less than that at lower levels.[23] The structural changes required to improve cost effectiveness imply new patterns of manpower deployment that would be resisted by professionals and patients.

There is no need to labour the basic point; it could be illustrated from Ghana, Sri Lanka, or many other countries. There is a direct conflict of interest between the privileged groups that provide such services and seek to increase, or at least protect, their standard of living on the one hand, and on the other the consumers of these services.

It is not part of this argument that primary teachers in Tanzania or "assistant medical practitioners" in Sri Lanka are overpaid. The argument is, rather, that partly because their skills have been in short supply, partly because they are relatively well organized, but principally because they have administrative and political leverage, in nearly every case these skill groups have ensured that, in the inter-group conflict between users and practitioners, the interests of the latter are protected. The cost has been a deceleration in the provision of these services to those who do not already have them.

MIS-SPECIFICATION

In Chapter 9, we saw that one of the biases against the poor is the type of education that is offered. Even rather timid steps to adapt the system to remove this bias—e.g., provision of vocational schools—tend in fact to reinforce this bias. Before passing to a more detailed consideration, a general point on specification is worth making. It applies no less to education than to the other services we are considering here.

Very often the whole "package" in which the service is presented is wholly out of keeping with the social environment of the poor, especially the rural poor. In Cameroon, for example, children who start primary school two years after the minimum age and then repeat a year are barred as too old from secondary school. Further, children must present a birth certificate in order to register for secondary schol—an administrative detail that many poor rural families overlook. Apart from these bureaucratic snares, more generally education and health systems are modern, impersonal, and individualized. They minimize the value of personal relationships; they deal with the child, parent, or patient as an individual rather than as a member of a wider supportive group. To a "recipient" unintegrated into modern (essentially bureaucratic) structures, these characteristics make the services threatening and even frightening.

F.J. Bennett, for instance, has shown the role played by language in constraining the take-up of medical care;[24] we may legitimately extend his remarks to education. A would-be client in a village or peri-urban squatment may not speak the language of the dominant tribe that has monopolized middle-level medical or educational jobs. He is afraid to lose face, to be ridiculed by Westernized bureaucrats. He therefore limits his contact with them. A similar deterrent is illiteracy. The patient or parent fears he may have to read a notice or write his name; he will lose face if he reveals he is unable to do so. All these fears bear more heavily on the less integrated, less educated, less aggressive members of the community. The "modern" structure of the service, so flattering to the self-importance of the administrators, is a specification problem that biases take-up against the poorest.

Health

Mis-specification is perhaps nowhere as well demonstrated as in health care. The issue can be presented very simply. If there is a limited health budget, should it be spent on a highly sophisticated level of curative service for the relatively few, or on a very much simpler level of service aimed primarily at eradicating the major preventible diseases for the whole community? Between these extremes lies a whole spectrum of policy possibilities; for given the fact that on average £1.75 (or $1.75) is available for health care from every £100 (or $100) of GNP per head, a sophisticated level of service for the whole population is simply impossible.[25]

There are a number of pressures on government health departments (and even on missions in those countries in which a non-government health care is still important) to opt for the curative and sophisticated end of the spectrum reather than the preventive and democratic end. The first of these is historical. During the colonial period, the major focus of medical effort was on curative services, particularly in the urban areas. While it is true that in some countries— e.g., Malaysia, Sri Lanka, and West Africa—death rates fell sharply as a result of control of some of the major preventible diseases, most particularly malaria and yellow fever, the emphasis of health services came to be on the provision of a curative service primarily for the expatriates, secondarily for the fee-paying indigenous population, and finally a free service for a tiny minority of the local population. The colonial government had little incentive to provide curative services for the rural population. The missions had neither the resources nor the motivation to provide the preventive services, and it was more in keeping with both their tradition and their missionary strategy to have a hospital in the mission compound staffed by expatriate professionals.

The second set of factors that prejudices the decision in favour of the curative end of the spectrum is the professional interest of doctors. The political power of the medical profession is hard to exaggerate. In most of the countries with which we are concerned, they are a sufficiently small group to be well organized, even personally known to each other. They come from the same background as, and are often direct contemporaries with, the political leaders. Indeed, a caucus of doctors in parliament or its equivalent is common. Doctors also have great status in the community at large. Like their colleagues worldwide they are able to surround themselves with a professional mystique that discounts criticism or suggestions of alternative approaches from non-medical sources. They are therefore able to influence and even control political decisions about health services. It is a rash minister of health or permanent secretary who falls afoul of the profession—as at least one permanent secretary found during the writing of this book.

Doctors are not interested and are not trained to be interested in taps, sewers, latrines, and the ventilation of houses. Indeed, they are not much interested in vaccinations, immunizations, health education, nutrition, personal hygiene. To highly educated professionals, who judge their professional merit by their diagnostic or surgical skill or by their ability to contribute to the abstruse professional literature of the West, these nuts and bolts of a healthful environment are matters of derision. It is no surprise to find that in every university that we have visited the department of social medicine is treated as an aristocrat treats the plumbing—as a regrettable admission of the earthiness of nature.

Under these circumstances, there is intense professional and political pressure to devote resources to tasks that are medically interesting. The results are bizarre. In the Philippines, a country in which much of the population has no health care beyond that of the helot, is to be found one of the most sophisticated cardiology units in the world. In the Ivory Coast, the Centre Hopital Universitaire has facilities that few hospitals in France can rival. The fact that such facilities are used at half capacity, but pre-empt the lion's share of the recurrent budget of the ministry of health (over 50 percent in both cases) are only two of the absurdities that necessarily follow.

The third set of forces is what we may call the grass-roots political. Principally because it is the only thing they know, most people in the rural areas and in the squatments call for more hospitals to serve their particular communities. In this way, the present system can justify itself by wide political appeal. People do want hospitals.[26] They do not want a preventive service. They also may not want to be badgered into improving their sanitary environment. Further, the evaluation of a preventive service is a much more subtle exercise than the evaluation of a curative hospital. Just as education reform is blocked from below, because people fear change means deterioration, so medical reform is blocked because a more appropriate service can easily give the external appearance of being an inferior service.

Finally, and again by analogy with education, external pressures on the health service are towards the curative end of the spectrum. The hospital contractors, the drug companies, the equipment manufacturers, and perhaps more important than any of those, the aid donors have much greater interest in a sophisticated hospital-based service than a preventive rural clinic-based service. In the case of the aid donors, this is partly the desire to build monuments to themselves. It is much more a direct result of the tying of aid to external costs. For the external costs of a rural health clinic are next to zero. The external costs of a large teaching hospital are very considerable. From the health planners' point of view, this means it is easier to find resources for a wholly inappropriate medical technology, as incorporated in the Centre Hopital Universitaire in Abidjan or the Central (Teaching) Hospital in Lusaka than it is to find resources (necessarily domestic) for a service that will reach the poor.

(There are at last signs that some donor agencies, both official and non-governmental, are beginning to appreciate this. The danger is that this conversion comes too late.)

As a result of these four sets of forces and the consequent mis-specification of the nature of health carē, the specification bias against the poor is very striking. We have already noted examples from Ivory Coast and the Philippines. In the former, only 8 percent of the total health budget is spent on preventive medicine;* in the latter, the base of the health pyramid is the municipal health unit staffed by a doctor and three paramedicals, serving an area of 15,000 to 20,000 persons with a curative service. In both countries, the traditional healers are wholly ignored by the medical profession, who regard them as irritating competitors whose principal effect is to delay treatment and complicate diagnosis.

But it should not be assumed the countries that are less dominated by the urban elites have succeeded in breaking the power of the forces we have sketched above. The only area in which they have been more successful is in coming to terms with traditional forms of healing. In Tanzania, traditional healers are now registered—a first step towards control and training. In Sri Lanka, ayurvedic hospitals now receive public funds and serious research is conducted on the healing properties of traditional ayurvedic prescriptions. Other countries have not progressed as far. In Ghana, there is gradually developing an interest in the services of village midwives, and there are sporadic discussions in Zambia of taking steps to regulate at least some traditional healers.

But in other respects these countries reflect the appeal of curative medicine. Although Zambia, for instance, made a fine start in the First National Development Plan towards covering the country with a system of rural health centres and indeed built 150 such centres within the first five years of independence, there is evidence that professional interests of the doctors, not unconnected with the establishment of a school of medicine at the university and a teaching hospital in Lusaka, have begun to subvert the whole of the rural health centre system. In 1972, estimates indicate the total allocation to health centres (both rural and urban) was only 18 percent of the allocation to central, general, and

---

*In general, preventive/curative allocations are an inaccurate guide since there is no certainty that the functional division is the same as the allocative division. In the case of Ivory Coast, however, we were able to break down the expenditures in some detail. While, according to the budget estimates, over 20 percent was allocated for preventive medicine, we found that in fact over half this allocation was used to finance additional curative services. A detailed analysis did nor prove possible in Cameroon, but there too, the stated figure of 20 percent on average for 1964-74 is certainly an overestimate.

district hospitals. In 1972, on a per capita basis more than twice as much was spent on urban health centres as on rural health centres.

The most striking example in indubitably Tanzania. As in Zambia, the most important element of the rural health service is the rural health centre. Although this centre is designed to offer simple curative services, the main emphasis of its work is supposed to be preventive. It was not designed to be staffed by a fully qualified doctor but to be supervised by the district medical officer from the district hospital. Such was the intention. Reality has been quite otherwise. During the First Five-Year Plan, 80 rural health centres were planned; 5 were built. Under the Second Plan, 80 rural health centres were again projected; less than 30 were built.   During the same period, two large hospitals were built in regional capitals. (At least this was a net gain. In Kenya, between 1965 and 1967 the number of health centres actually declined, despite the fact that the target ratio of one health centre per 20,000 population was only one third fulfilled; in 1965, less than one health centre in four was fully staffed.[27])

The Zambian example alone reveals the political priorities at work since the official explanation of the failure of the rural health centre programme was lack of money. But money that was devoted to the regional hospitals would have given the country its entire basic complement of rural health centres. Furthermore, the Ministry of Health flirted with the idea of increasing the curative emphasis of rural health centres by enlarging them and upgrading the health personnel (in 1971, preventive services spent Shs.6.8 million; curative services, Shs. 111.8 million[28])—a route already taken by Sri Lanka, with dismal results. (An interesting hypothesis that we have been unable to test is that the curative emphasis in rural clinics is related to the availability of locally trained (or perhaps any) doctors. As there are more doctors available for employment, indeed demanding employment, so pressure builds up to "upgrade" clinics and man them with fully trained doctors. Given the curative bias of doctors' training (and the local pressure on their curative skills), the clinics are quickly subverted into mainly or even exclusively (poorly equipped) curative centres.[29])

Although there is some evidence that Tanzanian health planning was drastically re-overhauled between 1972 and 1974,* it must remain an open question whether any change in priorities will be permanent until the training of health

---

*Following much criticism of the failure to improve rural health care voiced at the 1971 TANU Conference, the government committed itself to constructing 20 to 25 rural health centres and 100 rural dispensaries every year to 1980. Hospital bed growth was to be limited to the rate of growth of population, and much greater emphasis was to be placed on preventive medicine. It is too early to assess how far these plans have been implemented.

personnel from dressers to surgeons is fundamentally re-examined. As long as there is a medical elite being trained in a sophisticated urban teaching hospital, having only sufficient contact with rural services to innoculate them against rural service for life, it must remain a very real danger that democratization will be a short-lived experiment.

Housing

We saw above that housing authorities are unable to provide houses for low-income groups? How far is that a result of mis-specification?

There are a number of sources of mis-specification. For any housing scheme to be financially viable, a number of preconditions must be met. Rent or repayments must be paid regularly with a low rate of default. Maintenance costs, turnover of tenants, land and construction costs must all be kept low. The best solution is, or is thought to be, the sub- or peri-urban high-density development, using well-tried building techniques incorporating low-maintenance finished and let to settled urban dwellers in regular formal sector employment at wages above the minimum. Since that is the ideal clientele (or the politically imposed clientele since ministries demand an allocation of houses for their employees), there is no incentive to innovate in design. Already incorporated in the ranks of the privileged, such clients demand houses that may be neither imposing nor spacious but are recognizably houses.

We have here four separate pressures making for a commitment of public funds to a type of housing that is inappropriate for the great mass of the excluded. There is a financial pressure, to ensure that costs are minimized and revenues are maximized.* There is an administrative pressure, stronger in Africa than in Asia, to ensure that such public housing as is available is allocated to civil servants. There is a popular pressure that public housing should be "proper." There is additionally a professional pressure, from architects and housing administrators, that public housing must have a theoretical asset value not less than the book value. Hence, low-quality housing that depreciates rapidly does not commend itself to those most intimately concerned with housing policy—especially if there is a prospective shift of policy to tenant purchase.

These pressures are strong but not insuperable. They have been overcome in

---

*In Malaysia, cost minimization led to the construction of large apartment blocks in Kuala Lumpur. As the flats have no garden, Malays are most reluctant to accept them—in marked contrast to the Chinese. But, as we have already seen (p. 304), Chinese housing problems are not as severe as those of Malays.

most of the countries we have studied by one counter-pressure alone—the sheer size of the urban (and particularly metropolitan) housing problem. In the Philippines, a minimum estimate of the urban housing gap in 1973 was over 600,000 houses in metro-Manila and Rizal alone.[30] At least 100,000 new houses are needed in these cities each year—with no improvement in the present situation of over one family in three living in squatments. That is not necessarily an extreme example. In Kuala Lumpur, an even higher proportion of the population is ill housed and migration rates show no signs of falling. In Africa, the picture is not fundamentally different—high rates of migration to towns where the housing stock is already inadequate.

Under these circumstances, even the most inert bureaucracy has had to recognize that to build a few hundred middle-class houses is a wholly insufficient response. Site and service schemes offer a cheap, face-saving, and politically accommodating way out. Blessed by the United Nations and characterized by a low level of continuing involvement, such schemes allow politicians to advertise their efforts to house the homeless. The fact that such schemes do little to help the really poor is, to them, hardly relevant. For by presenting some with windfall profits and others with release from the worst effects of landlordism, the schemes will never attract political hostility.

Water Supply

We have already seen that slum dwellers may use impure water because pure water in standpipes is expensive. There are three reasons why it is expensive. The first is that it is not easily accessible to slum dwellers; it has to be carried from the from the nearest access point and someone has to be paid to carry it. Second, it is charged at a flat rate like most other consumer goods so that the privileged suburban dwellers pay the same rate as slum dwellers. Third, it is refined to a high degree of purity; particularly in arid areas, this involves the use of advanced hydrological engineering dependent upon imported capital equipment, imported technology, and frequently imported skill; most important of all, it depends upon imported standards.

Purity is a relative concept depending upon the uses to which water is put, the density of the ambient population, the number of people using the particular water outlet, the drainage available, and the health environment. What is regarded as a minimum standard of purity in New York or London may not coincide with an objective definition of a minimum standard of purity in Lusaka, Kandy, or Quezon—i.e., the health hazards associated with a given level of purity may be very different in each environment. Standards are very seldom established locally. Water engineers' handbooks give Western standards, and expatriate consultants will automatically use those standards and encourage their local counterparts to do so, too. This is reinforced by political pressure from elite and privileged urban dwellers who resist any attempt to modify standards on the grounds that departures from international standards are inevitably inferior.

It is also reinforced by administrative systems that give no encouragement to local adaptation of existing (international) norms and procedures. Precisely because funds are short, risks have to be minimized. A civil servant who fights the treasury or the planning office for every cent in his budget is unlikely to underwrite radical departures from conventional wisdom—even though slavish adherence to conventional wisdom is both distributionally unjust and technically inefficient.

For Western standards and the associated technologies bring one more major bias: the mal- or non-functioning of new systems. The technology required for their maintenance and repair is too demanding for local organization and skills, and the result is that some modern systems are abandoned in favour of traditional methods and sources. The same is not true of urban or even of improved peri-urban systems. The administrative and political pressures from a large community threatened with a cut-off of its water supply ensure that whatever meagre resources are available are put to work to keep the system running. The cost is borne by those who cannot mount such pressures.

It is, then, an open question how far the adjustment of standards of purity to local needs would make possible an increase in the number of people having access to pipe-borne water. The relationship between purity and cost varies from locality to locality depending upon the source of the water and the environment in which the water is to be used. That is a technical issue that is not open to generalization. But there is also a political issue. Even if the cost of providing people with adequately pure water could be reduced by 30 percent, it does not necessarily follow that the total number of people served would be increased. That is a political and administrative decision that depends upon the nature of competing claims upon scarce resources. In very few countries we have studied is there any evidence to suppose that an increase in resources available for water supply would certainly increase the availability to the urban and rural poor. It is much more probable that it would increase supply in the "official" urban areas and perhaps in the showplace rural projects.*

---

*One example of this is the Gal Oya Development Scheme in Sri Lanka. There has been much criticism of the standard of workers' houses and facilities, and at least one evaluation has held over-specification of these to be one of the main reasons why the scheme has not been economically viable.

CONCLUSION

The central argument of this chapter has been that there is a set of political, administrative, economic, and cultural forces that bias social consumption against the excluded. As a sub-theme, we have emphasized the international transmission of these biases through technology, through training, through specification, through a misplaced desire to emulate, and through the commercial interests of Western manufacturers, agents, and distributors. The major beneficiaries of the services we have reviewed, together with secondary and higher education, are the urban privileged and, to a much lesser extent, those in the rural areas who participate in particular government development schemes— from "organismes regionals de developpement" in Upper Volta to Ujamaa villages in Tanzania to colonization schemes in Sri Lanka and Malaysia.

How far can this pattern of distribution be explained in terms of the con-mech? It meets the criteria almost perfectly. Social consumption as a whole is a competitive mechanism of enrichment that is biased against the excluded. But the biases are not so obvious that confidence in social consumption as a form of redistribution is widely shaken. Some of the urban excluded do benefit from health services, site and service schemes, and free water from a nearby standpipe. Some of the rural excluded are near a clinic or a new well. Indeed, it is part of any government or ruling party's propaganda function to convince both rural and urban excluded that the social environment, in this sense, is improving. The evident poverty of the country, it is argued, inevitably means that the pace of progress must be slow; but the progress is no less real. Faith in the con-mech is thus relatively easily maintained.[31]

The most striking feature, as we have already emphasized, however, is that those who control the con-mech—politicians, the bureaucratic elite, middle-level white-collar workers—are able to appropriate the major gains. Interestingly, we have been unable to detect any clear principle of division along ideological or political lines between countries. This may well be because our analysis, dependent upon very limited and unreliable data, has had to be couched in rather general terms. But the examples of housing policy in Sri Lanka, and of health planning and water provision in Tanzania, militate against the easy assumption that leftist rhetoric from the political leadership will readily transform the inhibiting structures. At the very best, they may put some pressure on those structures. Housing policy did change in Sri Lanka. New guidelines on water investment were adopted in Tanzania. That these new policies function imperfectly is not to be wondered at. The real issue is to make them work—and then improve them further. The con-mech may never be entirely smashed, even in these countries. But the biases can be reduced, and the benefits can be more (but not perfectly) equitably shared.

NOTES

1. See M.J. Sharpston, "Uneven Distribution of Medical Care: A Ghanaian Case Study," *Journal of Development Studies* 8, no. 2 (1972): 205-22.

2. See Oscar Gish, "Health, Manpower and the Medical Auxiliary," in *Towards an Appropriate Health Care Technology* (London: Intermediate Technology Development Group, 1971). Cf. Sharpston, op. cit.

3. Maurice King, ed., *Medical Care in Developing Countries* (London: Oxford University Press, 1965).

4. Mary R. Hollnsteiner, "Socio-Economic Themes and Variations in a Low-Income Urban Neighbourhood," Workshop on Manpower and Human Resources, Los Banos, Laguna, 1972.

5. M.R. Farrant et al., "Kampala's Children," a report to UNICEF, mimeo. (Kampala, 1972).

6. Robert Cook, "The Ankole Pre-School Protection Programme, 1964-7," mimeo. (Kampala: Department of Preventive Medicine, Makerere University, 1968).

7. Ibid., p. 23.

8. "Slums Are for People," Barrio Magsaysay Pilot Project Report 1968, mimeo. (Manila: Institute of Philippine Culture).

9. Gilbert White, David Bradley, and Anne White, *Drawers of Water: Domestic Water Use in East Africa* (Chicago: University of Chicago Press, 1972), pp. 101-7.

10. Unpublished data from a commissioned survey of Tongu District, Volta Region, by Ellen Sondermeijer, University of Leiden.

11. See Bo Westman and Fred Hedkvist, "The Impact of Rural Water Program in Tanzania," mimeo. (Stockholm: Swedish International Development Authority Research Division, 1972).

12. Marie Duponchel, "Enquete socio-sanitaire sur un quartier d'Adjame" (Abidjan: Institut national de sante publique, 1971).

13. *A Review of Government Activities, 1972*, supplement to the Budget Speech presented to the National State Assembly by the Minister of Finance (Colombo: Government Printer, 1972).

14. Ibid.

15. F. Binhammer, "Financing Housing in Tanzania," mimeo., no. 5 (Dar es Salaam: Economic Research Bureau, 1969).

16. See *The Low Cost Housing Proposals of the Commissioner of the Federal Capital of Kuala Lumpur* (Kuala Lumpur, 1969).

17. F.D. Abesam, "Squatter/Slum Clearance and Resettlement Programs in the Philippines," in "Housing in the Philippines," preparatory material for the National Economic Development Agency Conference on Housing, mimeo. (Manila, 1973).

18. See, for instance, M. Peil, "Reactions to Estate Housing: A Survey of Tema," *Ghana Journal of Sociology* 4, no. 1 (1968). Cf. P. Marris, *Family and Social Change in an African City: A Study of Rehousing in Lagos* (London: Routledge and Kegan Paul, 1961).

19. This is not pursued here; see White, Bradley, and White, op. cit., Chapter 6.

20. Ibid., p. 133.

21. Richard Jolly, *Planning Education for African Development: Economic and Manpower Perspectives* (Nairobi: East African Publishing House, 1969), pp. 84-88.

22. Ibid., p. 88.

23. Unpublished data from combined World Health Organization/Ministry of Health sample survey of local health services in eight non-metropolitan areas of West Malaysia, 1972.

24. F.J. Bennett, "Evaluation de l'education sanitaire au Centre de sante de Ka angati," *L'Enfant en milieu tropical* 52 (1968): 32-33.

25. C. Elliott, "Financial Resources, Now and in the Future," in *Human Rights in Health*, eds. K. Elliott and J. Knight (Amsterdam: Elsevier-New Holland, 1974).

26. See, for instance, F.T. Sai, F.K. Wurapa, and E.K. Quartey-Papafo, "The Danfa, Ghana, Comprehensive Rural Health and Family Planning Project—A Community Approach," *Ghana Medical Journal* 1, no. 1 (1972): pp. 13 ff.

27. See F.J. Bennett, "Priorities in Medical Development in Developing Countries," mimeo. (Kampala: Department of Preventive Medicine, Makerere University, 1968).

28. This paragraph draws heavily from Malcolm Segall, "The Politics of Health in Tanzania," in *Towards Socialist Planning*, Uchumi Editorial Board (Dar es Salaam: Tanzania Publishing House, 1972).

29. See David Morley, *Paediatric Priorities in the Developing World* (London: Butterworths, 1973); J.H. Bryant, *Health and the Developing World* (Ithaca, N.Y.: Cornell University Press, 1969).

30. J. Ramos, "Housing Policies of the National Government," mimeo. (Manila, 1973).

31. For a most interesting detailed micro-investigation of satisfaction and dissatisfaction with the status quo at the village level, see Anthony Oberschall, "Communications, Information and Aspirations in Rural Uganda," *Journal of Asian and African Studies* 4 (1969).

13

THE ECONOMIC MECHANISMS OF PRIVILEGE: SOME EXAMPLES OF REINFORCEMENT

In Chapters 9 and 10, we saw that the processes of selection and exclusion are biased in favour of those who are already privileged. To that extent, the process of selection acts as an agent of reinforcement of the privileges of the minority and conversely an agent of exclusion of those who are already excluded. In this chapter, we examine economic mechanisms that have the same effect of reinforcing certain patterns of privilege. We do not wish to argue that these are the only forces at work or that the effects that we shall outline are the only effects of given economic changes. Our intention is more limited. It is to clarify some of the major processes by which the distribution of the social product to the privileged is maintained and the deprivation of the poor is perpetuated.

Two of the mechanisms we examine are ways in which welfare might be transferred from the excluded to the privileged. In terms of our original analogy, they might be parts of the upward circulatory system, delivering a net flow of "nutrients" from the lower "bowls" to the higher. These mechanisms are the tax system and food pricing.

The remaining two mechanisms both centre on the process of industrialization. We shall argue that industrialization itself is a vehicle of comparable transfers—through the pricing mechanism (in the context of import substitution) and from unskilled to skilled workers and profit receivers (in the context of biases towards capital intensification). This latter point extends further an argument already advanced in outline in the last section of Chapter 11.

TAXATION

The first and most obvious method by which welfare might be transferred is through the tax system. We have already seen that direct (income) taxes on most low-income groups tend to be low and that tax rates are usually designed to rise as income increases. From this, of course, it does not follow that the total tax burden is progressive. For the poor pay a number of other taxes of which the most important are such indirect taxes as sales tax, import tariffs, and excise duties on alcoholic drink and tobacco.

It is a general principle of taxation that necessities are either untaxed or taxed at a very low rate while "luxury" goods are taxed severely.* Thus fresh and lo-cally manufactured foods are typically taxed at very low rates while imported foods, tobacco, and alcohol are taxed severely. This ensures that the poor pay less tax in proportion to their income than the rich if, but only if, their expend-itures conform to the pattern implied by this distribution of indirect taxation. But, as Table 13.1 shows, the proportion of total expenditure devoted to alco-hol and tobacco can vary between 4 percent and over 10 percent. In nearly every case, clothing, alcohol, and tobacco represent the main non-food expend-itures of the very poor. In so far as these are taxed therefore (and alcohol and tobacco are taxed at high rates in almost every country), taxes are paid by the poor. Clothing does not usually carry a high sales tax, but if it is imported there is usually a protective tariff, a theme to which we return (see pp. 369-70).

When we look at the very limited number of tax studies that have been done in the countries under study, we find that indirect taxation bears heavily on the poor. The taxation of tobacco and alcohol are the main sources of indirect taxation.

As Table 13.2 shows, the two poorest groups in Sri Lanka (comprising over 90 percent of the total population†) pay slightly under 14 percent of their in-come as taxes—a higher proportion of total income than the two wealthiest groups (income of Rs1,000 and above) pay as *direct* tax. This is revealing be-cause we may assume that legislators regard the incidence of direct tax as progressive and relatively high for the highest-income groups. But if low-income groups pay (indirect) tax at the same rate as the rich pay direct tax, this implies that, by the legislators' own standards, the poor are highly taxed.

---

*Ideally, goods that are both non-essential and price-inelastic are taxed. It is assumed, wrongly as we show below, that such goods are not, and even should not be, bought by the poor.

†One of the problems of this study is that the bottom income groups are so large.

TABLE 13.1

Expenditure on Selected Items by Two Poorest Groups in a Number of Countries
(percentages of total expenditure)

Country	Expenditure/Income Group[a]	Percentage of Households	Food	Clothing	Alcohol	Tobacco	Transport	Total
Uganda	229[a]	89.0[a]	53.4	7.2	7.7	2.5	2.0	72.8
Tanzania	Shs.999	66.0[a]	62.5	8.8	4.2	1.1	0.7	77.3
	Shs.1000-1999	18.6[a]	57.3	10.0	4.1	1.1	1.1	73.6
Ghana	N₵15	7.6	55.9	2.4	4.5		0.9	63.7
	N₵15-25	26.0	59.5	5.5	4.1		1.5	70.6
Tunisia	30 dinar	17.7	66.3	13.6	5.1[b]	3.5	1.4	89.9
	30-42 dinar	25.1	63.8	13.6	4.6[b]	3.6	1.6	87.2
Malaysia	$150[a]	48.5[a]	67.3	4.7	6.8		2.4	81.2
	$151-300[a]	35.0[a]	59.8	4.8	6.6		3.2	74.4
Philippines	₱500	11.6[a]	67.3	5.5	2.1	3.4	1.2	79.5
	₱500-999	17.7[a]	64.6	6.1	2.4	3.1	1.3	77.5
Sri Lanka	Rs50[a]	9.5[a]	65.9	4.4	6.2	2.0	0.5	79.0
	Rs51-100[a]	17.7[a]	66.1	6.1	3.2	2.0	1.4	78.8

[a]Income group as opposed to expenditure group.
[b]Includes non-alcoholic drinks.

Sources: Uganda   *The Patterns of Income, Expenditure and Consumption of African Unskilled Workers in Mbale, 1967* (Entebbe: Government Printer, 1967).

Tanzania   *Income and Consumption, 1969 Household Budget Survey,* vol. I (Dar es Salaam: Bureau of Statistics, Ministry of Economic Affairs and Development Planning, 1972).

Ghana   D.K. Dutta Roy, *Eastern Region Household Budget Survey, 1969,* Technical Publication Series no. 6 (Legon: Institute for Statistical, Social and Economic Research, University of Ghana, 1969).

Tunisia   *La consommation et les dépenses des ménages en Tunisie, 1965-8* (Tunis: Institut national de la statistique, 1970).

Malaysia   *Household Budget Survey, 1957-58* (Kuala Lumpur: Department of Statistics), p. 5, Table 1.

Philippines *Family Income and Expenditures 1965,* the Bureau of the Census and Statistics Survey of Households Bulletin (Manila: BCS).

Sri Lanka   "Consumer Finances 1963," *Survey of Ceylon's Consumer Finances, 1963* (Colombo: Department of Economic Research, Central Bank of Ceylon, 1964).

TABLE 13.2

Sri Lanka: Incidence of Taxes by Income Group, 1962/63

(rupees)

	0-200	200-400	400-800	800-1,000	1,000-1,500	Over 1,500	All Income
Indirect taxes							
Import duties, excise duties, and licence fees	(12.26)	(27.49)	(45.42)	(101.43)	(128.94)	(204.42)	(20.11)
Food	1.21	1.95	2.22	2.64	2.85	3.20	1.45
Clothing	1.06	2.18	3.01	3.96	4.49	4.61	1.47
Transport	1.48	5.46	12.35	42.07	54.44	112.34	4.35
Tobacco	3.58	7.59	11.98	18.67	25.02	29.02	5.34
Alcohol	3.72	7.52	10.88	27.82	34.57	40.35	5.56
Other	1.21	2.79	4.98	6.27	7.57	14.90	1.94
Profit on the sale of flour and sugar	6.24	10.16	11.89	11.49	11.86	15.34	7.51
Total indirect taxes	18.50	37.65	57.31	112.92	140.80	219.76	27.61
Direct taxes:							
Income tax	—	—	30.81	81.34	141.33	468.35	6.62
Personal tax	—	—	—	—	19.70	87.48	0.67
Total direct taxes	—	—	30.81	81.34	161.34	555.83	7.29
Total all taxes	18.50	37.65	88.12	194.26	301.83	775.59	34.90
Average income	135.36	272.13	534.15	875.58	1231.24	2430.40	216.08
Taxes as percentage of income	13.67	13.84	16.50	22.19	24.51	31.91	16.15

Income Group (rupees)

Source: Report of the Taxation Inquiry Commission, Sessional Paper X (1968), Appendix VII(A).

The same result was established by a similar study in the Philippines. This showed that the two poorest groups, representing about 30 percent of the total population, paid as sales tax between 4.6 percent and 6.2 percent of their total income, whereas the wealthiest group paid only 1.3 percent. Taking all indirect taxes, the poor paid half as much again, in relation to income, as did the rich— 18 percent against 12 percent of income.[1]

It might be said that the rich pay high rates of direct taxation while the poor do not. Of some groups of poor, that is true. Agricultural labourers and low-paid urban workers do not pay direct tax unless a capitation tax or personal levy is made, as is the case in many African countries. In North Cameroon, for example, the personal levy is the third highest expenditure for the poorest group and accounts for 15 percent of total cash expenditure. Also, employers provident fund contributions may be paid by low-paid workers in the formal sector; these are not formally taxes, but naturally serve to reduce the level of present consumption.

Apart from capitation fees, there is a set of very important direct taxes that are paid by some of the poor. These are taxes on export crops.* It has been argued that export crop producers are, by definition, not among the poorest of the rural society and therefore should be taxed.[2] While it is true, by definition, that those who have an export crop to sell are not among the very poorest, we have already seen that in Ghana 38 percent of cocoa farmers had lower gross incomes than any workers recorded in the official labour statistics. Further it is a strange inversion of the normal principles of taxation to impose a regressive and unusually high tax on those who, although not among the very poorest, are certainly not wealthy.

In the case of Ghana, we have to distinguish between the export tax—which is paid by the Cocoa Marketing Board (CMB) out of the gross margin on the cash price it actually receives—and the difference between the price paid to the cocoa farmer and the price received by the CMB. The first is clearly and explicitly a tax; the second is formally a trading profit by the CMB but effectively a direct proportional tax on cocoa production. (It appears in the national accounts as the producer sales of cocoa plus the total tax made up of export and local duties plus the trading surpluses or deficits of the CMB and the transfers from the CMB to government.)

The export and local duties on cocoa are both proportional taxes, and they vary on a sliding scale basis according to fluctuations in the f.o.b. export price of

---

*We assume that all export crop producers face perfectly elastic demand and therefore that export taxes are unshiftable. This, it is true, is a maximum assumption; it therefore tends to overstate the argument, less in the case of rubber and cotton than cocoa.

the commodity. In the 1966/67 crop year the rate was increased to 50 percent of thes difference between the export price and N₡100. If the price exceeds N₡260, the whole of the excess is collected as duty. Table 13.3 shows that, as a result of these taxes, the cocoa farmers as a whole have received as income less than 60 percent of the full value of the cocoa crop.

Since all these taxes are proportional—i.e., they are fixed in terms of production and not related to total income—they bear more heavily on the poor cocoa farmers than on the rich. An average tax of 43 percent of cocoa income for the 20-year period 1947-66 must be one of the highest average tax rates for low-income groups in the world. Whereas the poorest cocoa farmer pays 43 percent of his "income" as tax, a wage and salary earner (married with two children) would have to earn over £8,000 a year before he paid the same proportion of his income as direct tax. Only a tiny handful earned such an income.

It is true that, over the whole period 1947-66, one third of the tax revenue was redistributed back to the cocoa industry as benefits. But there is no guarantee that this was distributed in a way that would benefit the poorest cocoa farmers; indeed, there is some evidence that it was not. Even if we accept that some benefits accrued to the poorest cocoa farmers, the rates of net taxation are still striking. Indeed, it would be hard to find a better example of differential social, economic, and political power in action.

It is no surprise, therefore, to find that this situation is not confined to Ghana. In Ivory Coast, Table 13.4 shows that direct and indirect taxes on agriculture account for between 20 and 25 percent of total tax revenue. Additionally, the surpluses of the Caisse de Stabilisation have typically added a further 10 percent except in those years—e.g., 1964/65—when the prices of the major export crops were particularly weak and had to be subsidized from the resources of the Caisse.

In Cameroon, the Caisse de Stabilisation is less important as a source of government revenue; greater reliance is placed on direct taxation. On coffee there is a fixed rate of 29 percent on the "nu-bascule" price to the producer at Douala and on cocoa a rate of 32 percent. However, these rates understate the actual rate charged to the producer since marketing and transport costs from the farm to Douala are excluded. If they were included, the rate would rise by 2 to 4 percent.

It might be assumed that such regressive taxes are confined to countries where rural development is subordinated to urban/industrial development. The case of Tanzania suggests not. There the average rate of direct taxation on cotton growers in 1953-68 was 30 percent, with only a slight reduction in the post-independence years.[3]

Nor is this highly regressive type of direct taxation confined to Africa. Chris Edwards has calculated that in Malaysia rubber smallholders have, since 1951, paid between 16 and 22 percent of their income as export duty or research and

TABLE 13.3

Ghana: Tax on Cocoa Income 1947/48 - 1965/66
(cumulative data)

	1947/48-1955/56 N₵		1956/57-1965/66 N₵		1947/48-1965/66 N₵	
	Millions	Percent	Millions	Percent	Millions	Percent
Potential producer income	1026.0	100.0	1338.3	100.0	2364.3	100.0
Gross monetary income of farmers	520.8	50.8	833.6	62.3	1354.4	57.3
Total tax on farmers' income	505.2	49.2	504.7	37.7	1009.9	42.7
Export and local duties	273.4	54.1	452.8	89.7	726.2	71.9
Cocoa Marketing Board trading surplus/deficit	184.2	36.5	-7.9	-1.6	176.3	17.5
Cocoa Marketing Board transfers to government	47.6	9.4	59.8	11.9	107.4	10.6

Source: Sam Nii Dodoo, "Redistributive Effects of the Taxation of Cocoa Farmers," unpublished report commissioned for this study.

TABLE 13.4

Ivory Coast: Agricultural Taxation
(F CFA million)

	1963	1964	1965	1966	1967	1968	1969	1970
Tax receipts								
Export tax	7,776	8,585	10,013	10,336	8,569	10,882	12,419	16,442
Taxes on forest products	74	206	632	463	592	1,057	1,143	1,267
Reafforestation levy	–	–	–	–	236	294	392	781
Total tax receipts	7,850	8,791	10,645	10,799	9,397	12,233	13,954	18,490
Surplus of Caisee de Stabilisation								
Coffee	6,800	- 1,100	2,600	4,300	1,600	- 1,100	5,900	7,700
Cocoa	1,400	- 1,100	- 3,500	500	4,900	9,600	11,900	2,100
Cotton and others	–	–	–	–	–	100	200	300
Total surplus	8,200	- 2,200	- 900	4,800	6,500	8,600	18,000	10,100
Total	16,050	6,591	9,745	15,599	15,897	20,833	31,954	28,590
Percentage of total revenue	47.5	15.5	20.8	31.3	31.5	33.7	45.9	34.5

Source: Essai d'estimation des revenus agricoles (Abidjan: Ministere du plan, May 1972).

353

replanting cesses.* Since 1970, there has been a significant change: Not only has the proportion of income paid by smallholders been raised from 18 percent to 22 percent but that paid by estates has been reduced from 18 percent to 15 percent.[4] The proportion of income paid as tax by the smallholder is, therefore, now half as much again as that paid by the estates—many of them foreign-owned.[5] In order to pay 22 percent of earned income as income tax in Malaysia in 1969, a wage or salary earner would have had to earn over M$30,000—a level of income reached by under 5,000 people.[6] It must be one of the most unambiguous denials of the principles of taxation that those in a group whose cash income is thought not to exceed that of estate labourers pay the same rate of tax as the 5,000 richest men in Malaysia.

It might be argued that the poor receive such disproportionate benefits from the expenditure of tax revenue that they recoup their tax payments in the form of social benefits. But we have already seen in Chapter 12 that there are reasons for believing that the poor are systematically excluded from the enjoyment of some of those major benefits. We saw how in education, in health, in housing there are structural factors that tend to minimize the benefit accruing to the poor from expenditures on these services. The only systematic study of social benefits (based on Sri Lankan data) fudges this issue. Although it shows benefits exceeding income for the poorest groups, there are a number of reasons why such a result was inevitable given the method used to apportion benefits.[7] Further, the very size of the two lowest-income groups biased the results in this direction. A finer screen would have revealed that, for a significant number of rural dwellers and even of urban dwellers, the benefits from education and health expenditures were near zero. For subsistence cultivators and rice farmers, the value of the rice subsidy is much reduced, especially in the Wet Zone areas.

Final empirical proof, then, is not available. But we have shown that benefits tend toward zero for significant groups, especially in the rural areas.† We also

---

*Edwards is obliged to make a number of assumptions about the relationship between f.o.b. price and income for estates and smallholders. It is possible he somewhat underestimates the income of smallholders and, therefore, overestimates the proportion of income paid as tax. Much depends on how depreciation and interest payments are handled. In any case, the proportion of income paid as tax is not highly sensitive since smallholder production costs are low in relation to the f.o.b. price.

†We are ignoring general "overhead" expenditures, such as defence and administration, and non-specific development expenditures. The rural poor may derive some benefit from these (most obviously from roads). But the scientific apportionment of benefits is impossible on the data available, and a rule-of-thumb of "equal benefits" implausible.

have shown that the burdens are positive and in some cases high for the poorest groups. This implies that, for at least some groups of the poorest, especially in the rural areas, burdens exceed benefits so that there is a direct transfer from these groups to net-beneficiary groups. A "weaker" form of the same argument is that the redistributive effect of the tax system is less than is immediately obvious, especially when subsidies to capitalists are considered—a theme to which we return later in this chapter.

THE PRICE OF FOOD

If the tax system seems to transfer welfare from the poor and excluded to the privileged, is it the case that food pricing has the same net effect? This is an important question since low-income groups spend a high proportion of their cash income on food, sometimes as much as 80 percent. Even those who produce much of their own food themselves may still spend a significant proportion of their cash income on manufactured foods or on staples during seasonal shortages. For instance, in Northern Cameroon the lowest-income group spend nearly 40 percent of monetary income on food. If there is evidence that the price of food is manipulated to the advantage of the food producers, this implies a transfer of welfare from the consumers (and particularly those consumers who spend a high proportion of their income on food, predominantly the urban poor) to the producers. Conversely, if there is evidence of food prices being kept low (for instance, by importing cheaper foodstuffs), welfare is transferred in the opposite direction—from farmers (or at least those who produce foodstuffs that are imported and their close substitutes) to all consumers and especially the poor. In either case, we would want to know more about the farmers involved: Are they themselves among the lowest-income families or are they rather large-scale producers with at least average levels of living?

If government acts as a monopoly buyer of locally produced food crops and is therefore able to determine food prices, we might expect that it would seek to keep food prices down in an attempt to hold wages down in the urban sector.* It would have many motives for doing so: to moderate the rate of growth of its

---

*Throughout this section, it is important to bear in mind that we use "urban" as a shorthand for those who do not produce their own food. It therefore includes wage earners living in the rural areas who are not provided with food or with land on which to grow at least some of their requirements of staples. In this sense, some urban dwellers (especially in Africa) may be excluded since many urban residents do in fact grow their own food.

own wage bill; to attract foreign and local investment; to increase the return to capital and encourage reinvestment of profits; to maintain (or increase) its own political acceptability among all urban groups, usually a much more powerful political force than the rural sector. In this case, then, we would expect to see an enforced transfer from the farmers (and indirectly hired labourers) to food consumers.

A government pledged to improve rural incomes (on the assumption that the bulk of the poverty problem is a rural problem*) may take exactly the opposite view. It would see as an important part of policy the attempt to raise rural incomes by raising product prices. If this reduced urban real incomes, it might check the rate of urban migration and probably also would reduce income differentials in the urban population. It might legitimately take the view that investment is not much affected by money wage rates since most urban investment is capital-intensive anyway, and/or it might be optimistic in its assessment of its own political ability to keep down urban wages despite rising food prices.

At its crudest, then, we would expect a very different set of policies in Tanzania to Ivory Coast, or in Sri Lanka to the Philippines. But whether any of these food price policies actual transfers welfare to the poor—both urban and rural—is a much more difficult question that will need careful consideration against a statistical background remarkable only for its inadequacy.

When we examine the barter terms of trade of food producers in countries for which we have data, we find no consistent pattern. In Zambia, Uganda, Philippines (for rice only), and Sri Lanka, there is fairly clear evidence that, at least for substantial periods, food prices failed to rise as fast as the prices of manufactures, so that the barter terms of trade of farmers fell. But this does not seem to be a consistent movement, having been sharply reversed in all three cases in the last five years. By contrast, in Tanzania, Ghana, and Ivory Coast, we can be fairly confident that food producers enjoyed relatively high prices, although for Tanzania at least that has been reversed since 1971/72.

There are sound theoretical reasons that explain, at least in part, both this division of experience and its inconstancy. But to understand those reasons it is well to approach each country individually, for very different circumstances operate in each.

In Zambia, F.J. Maimbo and J. Fry have shown that the barter terms of trade deteriorated by 22 percent between 1964 and 1969.[8] But between 1969 and 1973 agricultural pricing in Zambia, for both food and non-food crops, underwent a sea change. In the first five years after independence, there can be little doubt that maize price policy was dictated by two considerations: the need to

---

*In both senses: in that most of the poor are in the rural areas and that the urban poor can be persuaded to be productive in the rural areas if food prices are high.

keep down the urban cost of living and reluctance to present to European farmers, who in 1965 produced 76 percent of all formally marketed maize, a windfall profit. But by 1969 it was becoming clear that agriculture was the weakest point of the whole development strategy; that importing maize was disproportionately expensive and disruptive given the change in transport routes; and that political rhetoric on the evils of urban migration was unconvincing in the light of cash incomes achieved by most Zambian maize growers. The price of maize accordingly rose rapidly, by 30 percent to "village growers" between 1970 and 1972.

With other products, the story is slightly less clear but not fundamentally dissimilar. As long as milk production was exclusively a European monopoly, prices remained practically static and production declined; shortfalls were made up from imported powdered milk. Meat prices were raised somewhat earlier than maize prices but primarily for the same reason: the need to increase local production given the difficulty and cost of importing meat from non-traditional suppliers. Vegetable prices, important for a small number of co-operatives and individual producers near the main urban areas, rose rapidly from 1966, but at least some of that increase was due to inefficient and high-margin marketing and was not passed back to the producer.

Over-all, the pattern seems clear. As long as there was no pressing political need to do otherwise, the government was satisfied to allow urban consumers to benefit at the expense of rural producers, especially in products dominated by expatriates. Despite a vigorous, vocal, and highly organized pressure group of European farmers, government was able to maintain a high degree of urban bias—for a period. But it was not as rural counterweight that changed that situation. Rather, the rising cost of imports and the political threat posed by urban migration (and unemployment) combined to make a strong political and economic case for a wholly new approach to agricultural prices.

In Uganda, the evidence is slightly less sophisticated. In Tables 13.5 and 13.6 we have computed income and barter terms of trade during the period 1961-69 for the main food crops (see Appendix). Despite methodological imperfections, the main trend seems clear, namely, falling terms of trade throughout the decade. Uganda is a very different case to Zambia, however. For the Ugandan government did not have the same control over food prices and, apart from sporadic attempts to enforce minimum prices, usually successful,* its influence was negligible. Supply elasticities seem to have been rather high (or the marketing network very efficient at "commercializing" more distant producers, especially of plantain), with the result that, until 1969, food prices rose very much more slowly than the prices of imports

---

*Principally because the merchants simply refused to pay minimum prices and ceased trading until farmers would accept lower prices.

TABLE 13.5

Uganda: Index of Farmers' Income Terms of Trade

	January 1961	January 1965	December 1966	December 1967	December 1968	January 1969	December 1969	December 1970
Total production index	100.0	134.2	96.0	166.0	132.0	161.9	151.5	211.6
Index of real total production	100.0	126.7	84.4	146.5	82.5	96.1	83.9	130.8
Deflated total production index	100.0	119.2	80.4	135.0	104.2	127.8	116.1	157.4
"Per capita" income terms of trade index	100.0	112.6	70.7	119.2	65.0	75.8	64.3	97.3

Source: See Appendix.

TABLE 13.6

Uganda: Index of Farmers' Barter Terms of Trade

	January 1961	January 1965	December 1966	December 1967	December 1968	December 1969	December 1970
Chain Laspeyre agricultural price index	100.0	134.3	76.3	115.0	94.2	119.1	127.8
Barter terms of trade index	100.0	126.8	67.1	101.5	58.7	66.0	79.0

Source: See Appendix.

and manufactures. We do not have satisfactory data for the later, post-Obote period. Food prices rose very sharply, partly because of the breakdown of marketing facilities, and partly because of falling production. But whether that rise exceeded that of non-food items we do not know.

In the Philippines, it is important to make the distinction between rice and other foodstuffs. The barter terms of trade of the pure rice farmer declined unevenly from 1949 to 1962—as indicated by the ratio between the rice price and the consumer price index with rice excluded[9]—a period over which they fell by nearly 50 percent. They regained most but not all of that ground during 1962/67 and then, largely as a result of a political attempt to hold rice prices by increasing rice imports, they declined sharply during 1967/71. It is this tendency for the barter terms to decline that has given rise to the charge of urban bias in the Philippines. As one observer has put it:

> It seems clear . . . that the long run objective of the Philippines with
> respect to rice is a level of security and contentment for the rice
> *consumer*, especially the *urban* rice consumer. This holds for past and
> present leadership and in all likelihood will hold for future leadership—
> whatever political leaning may be the source—as well . . . . The welfare
> of rice farmers, landowners, millers and traders is of no real conse-
> quence except in so far as the actions and achievements of these per-
> sons affect the welfare of rice consumers.[10]

Certainly there is some evidence that imports have played a part in reducing the rate of rise of rice prices for limited periods over the last 25 years. The heavy imports in 1958 and 1963 seem to have been associated with falls in the price of rice (as well as with presidential elections) and it may be the case that the moderate imports in the late 1960s played a role, perhaps a minor role, in keeping the price more or less constant in that period.[11] But to ascribe a major role to import policy would be to ignore the activities of hoarders, the inconstancy of official policy, and above all the importance of money supply as a determinant of domestic prices. This accounts for the very rapid rise in all food prices, particularly rice from 1971 to 1973, when government was attempting to stimulate investment in manufacturing industry—an end to which an easy money policy was thought to be fundamental.

By contrast with rice prices, food prices in general have been strong: An index of food prices (including rice) in relation to the price of manufactures shows an increase of 52 percent from 1950 to 1972. Unfortunately, it has not been possible to extract rice from this index, but the deviation between the rice index and the food index strongly suggests that producers of non-rice foodstuffs have suffered little   if anything of the fall in real prices inflicted upon rice producers. Some disaggregated series for the period 1960-71 certainly support that view: maize prices tripled, banana prices doubled, poultry prices nearly tripled.

Interpreting the distributional impact of this is difficult. Poor urban consumers spend a very high proportion (over 90 percent) of their food expenditures on rice; to that extent, the decline in the real cost of rice over much of the 1950s and 1960s has indubitably increased their real incomes. To that extent, it has achieved a major political objective. But at whose cost? Under most sharecrop arrangements, a fall in price bears most heavily on the sharecroppers. We also have seen that real incomes of agricultural labourers fell sharply in the 1960s. The presumption is, then, that the major transfer has been from the rural poor to the urban poor.*

Of the other crops, it is not wholly true that only large-scale farmers produce "preferred foods"; indeed, small-scale vegetable growing is widespread. But milk, meat, sugar, and wheat are produced predominantly by larger-scale farmers and hardly at all by the poorest. In so far as they have benefitted from rising real prices, there has been a transfer from the urban middle- and upper-income groups to the rural middle- and upper-income groups. "Urban bias" therefore seems to be limited to rice prices.

In Sri Lanka, the details are different but the same feature of falling real rice prices tolerated for the sake of urban consumers (and, in this case, government revenue) emerges. Sri Lanka has for many years cross-subsidized food by charging taxes on consumption of wheat and sugar and using the proceeds, plus a subvention from general revenue, to subsidize a limited quantity of rice for low-income groups. This represents the most important single element of redistribution by central government and a significant portion of total income for low-income groups. The mechanism is in outline simple. The food commissioner buys rice from the producers at a guaranteed price or at the open market price, whichever is higher. As a monopoly importer, he can import rice and other grains to make good any deficiency in home production. A guaranteed price thus acts as a floor to the market but it is one to which prices have very infrequently descended within the last ten years.

There is no evidence that the guaranteed price or the state's monopoly on imports has been used to lower artificially the price of rice and other foods. Indeed, the guaranteed price was originally an incentive price, and the lack of diversification out of rice into other more profitable crops suggests that many farmers regarded the guaranteed price as a remunerative one.[12]

Although the guaranteed price has been stable (except for an increase in 1968 to account for devaluation) and remunerative, the key question is whether the farmers' barter and income terms of trade have improved or deteriorated. We have no adequate price index for the rural areas in Sri Lanka but, given the fact that between 1952 and 1971 the price of clothing in Colombo increased by 50 percent, the price of fuel and light increased by 40 percent, and the

*Not all rice is produced on small-scale, sharecropped farms; there has been a transfer from *all* rice producers. In income terms, moreover, increases in labour

whole Colombo consumer price index increased by 42 percent, it would be surprising indeed if, given the relative constancy of the guaranteed price (and the wholesale price, which has seldom moved far from the guaranteed price) the barter terms of trade have not in fact deteriorated.

More problematic are the income terms of trade. Productivity per acre has risen sharply, by nearly 25 percent from 1960 to 1969. Acreage also has increased, and total output of padi has increased by nearly 50 percent in the 1960s. We do not know how far this increase in production and yield has been achieved by the more efficient use of labour and how much has been achieved by the increased use of labour. The tripling of fertiliser use and the near doubling of transplanted acreage both suggest increasingly labour-intensive methods of production that the rather low stock of tractors is unlikely to have fully offset. On the income terms of trade, then, it would be foolish to try to draw a firm conclusion. But unless the numbers employed in padi production have grown much more slowly than the rural population as a whole (which seems highly unlikely), the data are most easily consistent with a fall in the income terms of trade as well as in the barter terms of trade.

It would be fallacious to conclude that this is an example of the rural producers, most of whom are very small-scale farmers, subsidizing the urban poor. For the urban poor do not pay the full cost for their rice. From 1952 to 1966, four pounds of rice per person per week were supplied at a subsidized price, the value of the subsidy being about Rs1.20 per person per week. To redeem an electoral promise, the government changed the system in 1966 and provided the first two pounds free and the second at a subsidized price. As a result of pressure from the World Bank and aid donors, the "free" measure was abolished in 1973 and the system reverted to its pre-1966 form. Under these circumstances, the urban poor are effectively insulated from changes in the price of rice in the short run. But, since a high proportion of public expenditure goes to subsidize rice, it is arguable that other government projects are made possible when rice prices fall in real terms. To the extent that the poor benefit thereby, they receive the benefit of falling rice prices indirectly. Conversely, when rice prices rose rapidly during 1973-74, the conventional wisdom was that it was impossible to increase government revenue by raising taxes. In this case, government was convinced that other projects could not be postponed and the subsidy was cut. The fact that the government had just postponed elections for two years was not, perhaps, coincidental.

Over the period 1952-74, however, there can be little doubt that the most immediate beneficiaries of the falling real price of rice (apart from the better-off urban consumer) have been those who have benefitted from general government expenditures and, to a much lesser estent, the taxpayer. We have already seen that, in general, the rural poor can be excluded from the former category (except for those who profited from the large-scale irrigation projects in the

_____

productivity of over 30 percent in the same period have been enough to raise aggregate incomes at least since 1962.

Dry Zone); it would be dangerous to make the same generalization for the urban poor.

Politically and ideologically, these four countries are a very mixed bag. In three—Zambia, Sri Lanka, and Philippines—the evidence suggests that there have been prolonged periods of deliberately manipulated urban bias in the pricing of the main staples. But this bias is unlikely to endure unless two unusual conditions are met. First, the price must be kept down by imports. This is an expensive procedure and involves a constant (and possibly increasing) drain on government revenue and foreign exchange. For urban bias to continue indefinitely, government must give it a sufficiently high priority to accept that drain. Second, urban bias will be acceptable to farmers if their labour productivity is rising at least as fast as the barter terms of trade are falling. In that case, real income will be constant. The implications of this condition are far-reaching. They include a wide adoption of improved techniques, subsidized inputs, and increasingly efficient marketing. At times of rapid inflation, the required rate of increase of productivity would be extremely high by the experience of any developing country—even if these conditions were met. Furthermore, they would most likely be met by the most privileged farmers, with serious long-run implications for land concentration and income distribution.

It is not coincidental that, in all three countries, the prices of staples have risen very sharply in the last four years, nor that in two of them there has been much talk of a "food crisis." This has engendered a pricing revolution with the gravest implications for the urban poor—and for those in the rural areas who cannot earn or grow their own food. Having been subsidized by producers, the most vulnerable and impoverished are now having to pay the price of an ill-founded policy, pursued for largely political motives. That they are the least able to pay that price might suggest the need for food subsidies to either the producer or consumer. But the one country that has tried to do this has been obliged to reduce the level of subsidies by development experts from the international agencies and donor countries.

A recent international report on Sri Lanka had this to say:

> While we are well aware of the social value of the rice subsidy, cutting it is the only way to finance a programme that would markedly reduce unemployment. It is a direct stimulus to consume one of Ceylon's leading imports. It is a form of government expenditure that provides no employment—indeed one could say that since much rice is still imported, it keeps foreigners busy, and since industries are working part time for lack of imports, it keeps Ceylonese out of work. To receive free rice must have some discouraging effect on production and employment in paddy farming. Finally, a free rice ration makes it possible for young people to wait for white-collar jobs.

Essentially, rice subsidies are a less effective form of welfare than a combination of more selective payments to those in need and measures to eliminate chronic unemployment. To switch money purposefully to these objects would increase welfare, not reduce it. And if general sacrifices have to be made to meet an emergency, such as the present payments crisis, it is surely better and more effective to sacrifice this than to cut back social services.[13]

Implementing at least some of these proposals was further urged upon the Sri Lankan government by the World Bank when it granted a major loan to Sri Lanka in 1974.

Is the hostility of the development establishment to food subsidy well deserved?

There is no doubt that the subsidization of food is extremely expensive. It is particularly expensive when the food is imported and, as the International Labour Organization Mission was at pains to point out, when employment-creating expansion is inhibited by foreign exchange constraints.* Leaving aside some of the more contentious comments from the ILO report—such as the alleged negative effects of free rice on production, a statement for which there is not one shred of hard evidence—the basic argument is that the general subsidization of food is an inefficient way of eradicating poverty. The very substantial sums involved (25 percent of government expenditures in 1970) can, it is argued, be redirected towards more productive uses that will ultimately create jobs and therefore make food subsidies unnecessary.†It is a policy that does nothing to *eradicate* poverty; it does much to *relieve* it. If resources are to be made available to eradicate poverty, they must (so it is argued) be withdrawn from those whose poverty they now alleviate. Employment for some is to be at the cost of the deprivation of others.‡ In the meantime, government subsidies

---

*The ILO Mission calculates that, if foreign exchange was valued at its equilibrium price, the cost of the net food subsidy was Rs1,114 million as opposed to the Rs459 million that appears in the national accounts.

†That this begs a huge bagful of problems, both of political commitment and of technical ability, must be ignored for the purposes of this argument. Whether the ILO report is justified in ignoring it is a moot point.

‡One way out of this dilemma that is theoretically available is to relate food subsidies to means or even relate the rate of subsidy to a sliding scale of incomes. In this way, the very poorest would be subsidized fully, whereas the less poor would pay a rising proportion of the cost of food. But, as the ILO report mentions, and as indeed has been the general experience in developing countries, means-related benefits are extremely difficult to administer in a developing country, particularly among groups whose income by definition is insecure,

are paid to international companies to open luxurious hotels in Colombo. These will perhaps contribute to "growth." They have already called into question the validity of the government's commitment to redistribute consumption to the poor.

Let us now turn to countries where the reverse seems to have happened— that is, where there has been no urban bias in food prices. They are all African countries where the statistical base is even more limited. The price data ignore changes in quality and sometimes composition of the index. Yearly figures disguise severe fluctuations over the year and opposite price movements for different products. Production data in most African countries are still extremely crude and even major censuses, such as the series of agricultural censuses at the turn of the last decade, still leave a great deal to be desired in terms of coverage, accuracy, and analysis. Only large, prolonged, and unambiguous changes can therefore be interpreted securely.

There is evidence of such a change in Ghana. If we take 1948 as a base year, the farmers' barter terms of trade improved to 162 in 1960, and further to 178 in 1964, and then fell back (largely as a result of the increases in the price of imports and some public utilities after the fall of Nkrumah) to 138 in 1969. (The effect of price control on farmers' terms of trade was almost certainly small, partly because it was not very effective and partly because control concentrated more on luxuries and semi-luxuries than on the necessities and quasi-necessities that enter the budgets of most food farmers in Ghana.[14]) The only periods, apart from the late 1960s, when the farmers' terms of trade deteriorated came in 1957 and briefly in 1960. Over the rest of the period, terms of trade were either constant or moving in the farmers' favour.

If that is substantial evidence of improvements in the barter terms of trade, what can be said of the income terms of trade? Since production and employment data in Ghana are rudimentary, it is extremely difficult to draw any firm conclusions. For what they are worth, production data are presented in Table 13.7. On these very rough figures, it looks as though there was a rapid expansion in agricultural output in the 1960s, certainly at a rate that far exceeds the rate of growth of agricultural population and the probable rate of growth of agricultural employment. This *suggests* that crude agricultural labour productivity (i.e., not corrected for any increase in hours worked) increased in the 1960s. Therefore the barter terms of trade and the income terms of trade may have

---

variable, and unpredictable. Further, the size of the "household" can vary greatly over time and therefore the number of people living off a given income can vary. There is also the more general experience that means-related benefits tend to discriminate against those who are reluctant to take up a benefit that they regard as charity.

TABLE 13.7

Ghana: Production of Selected Crops in Selected Years
(thousands of tons)

Crop	1950	1961	1963 (Seven-Year Plan)	1963 (Agricultural Census)	1972
Cereals	286	—	422	386	675
Maize	166	151	212	180	383
Millet and guinea corn	97*	130	185	174	246
Rice	23	—	25	32	46
Roots, etc.	2,744	3,770	2,255	3,789	5,979
Cassava	504	1,750	767	1,175	2,769
Cocoyams	510	500	309	334	929
Plantains	1,256	430	766	1,200	1,632
Yams	474	1,090	413	1,080	649

*Millet only.

Sources: Figures for 1950, 1961, and 1963 quoted from Walter Birmingham, I. Neustadt, and E.N. Omaboe, *A Study of Contemporary Ghana*, vol. I: *The Economy of Ghana*, p. 226. Figures for 1972: Sample Census of Agriculture— unpublished data kindly supplied by the Ministry of Agriculture, Accra.

moved in the same direction and thus secured to food producers substantial increases in income.

It is not easy to explain these changes, apart from rising urban (and rural) demand and supply inelasticities. The real question is why supply should be so sticky, by contrast, for example, with Uganda. Deceleration of new cocoa planting may be part of the answer, since food crops are often interplanted with young cocoa trees. The failure of the marketing system to pass incentive prices back to the farmer sufficiently quickly may be another part. Whatever the explanation, by 1971 the cost of food had become so burdensome to the urban poor that they were being urged to grow their own on any waste land in the towns and peri-urban villages and to patronize state-supported "food cooperatives" where basic foods were available at competitive (but unsubsidized) prices. The fall of the Busia government was not directly linked to the rising cost of urban foodstuffs: Rises in the cost of imports as a result of devaluation were a more proximate cause. But the widespread dissatisfaction in the towns had already begun to erode the popular base of the government before devaluation.

In Tanzania, we would expect to find a deliberate strategy to raise rural incomes by fixing incentive prices for staples. While the development of pricing policy has been neither strategic nor wholly deliberate, it is not insignificant that, when a formal consultative group was established in government to advise on pricing policy, consumers were not represented. Although data are not available for a sufficiently long period (1964-72) to establish any trend, it does seem that government was prepared to encourage high producer prices of both rice and maize until such huge surpluses accrued that production had to be cut back. Perhaps unfortunately, these surpluses coincided with Zambia's revision of price policy (and subsequent rapid increases in production), thus removing from Tanzania the one potentially profitable export market. Over the long run, therefore, Tanzania cannot produce more marketed maize than can be sold internally. This suggests a long-run price policy that will encourage only the most efficient producers. Whether these will be low-income, small-scale producers (whose monetary costs are low) depends, among other things, on what alternative sources of cash are available. It cannot be assumed to be axiomatically true that lower prices will force out of production the rural poor. But such prices will, of course, reduce the income of all producers except those who can raise productivity. It is highly improbable that these will include the poor, small-scale peasant producer; if he does continue to produce, his income will most probably fall.

To conclude this section, one generalization seems to emerge. Given that the approach of every country we have examined is a variant of free enterprise, it is inevitable that the realities of the market for food cannot be resisted indefinitely. Neither urban bias nor rural bias is a feasible long-term strategy except under bizarre conditions. From our perspective, this means that the urban and rural poor are exposed to all the imperfections of a market dominated by other groups with different and sometimes conflicting objectives. The poor producer is exposed to competition for markets and inputs from farmers and traders more powerful than he, economically and politically. When self-sufficiency is reached and prices begin to fall, this competition can be lethal (see above, p. 92). The poor consumer is exposed to two different sets of competition—to competition for food from wealthier consumers who can bid up the price of food in times of scarcity and to competition for resources when governments (or others) try to increase agricultural output (or increase food imports).

Short of a much more drastic, non-market-determined approach to agriculture (for which the auguries are not outstandingly good), a systematic and consistent policy designed to relieve competitive pressures on poor producers and consumers may be a second best. This involves discriminating in favour of poor producers in the distribution of productive assets and marketing facilities, and subsidizing either the small-scale producer or, if necessary, the poor consumer. That this is expensive of resources and skill is not contested. That such discrimination in favour of poor producers could be a highly productive use of funds (and efficient in that sense) is now universally recognized. That subsidization of producers and for consumers is less efficient (in the classical sense, with equal weights on all consumption streams) but highly equitable has earned it the undying hostility of the liberal establishment—hostility the more surprising in view of the fact that, in one form or another, it has been adopted in the United States, the European Economic Community, and Japan. The poor, it seems, are too poor to be allowed to be just to their poorest.

INDUSTRIALIZATION

We turn first to industrialization as a transfer mechanism that works in a way analogous to the tax system. Industrialization that is carried out as part of a policy of import substitution usually has the effect in the short run, and sometimes in the long, of transferring welfare from the lower-income groups to the privileged. Having established that and tried to quantify the effects for two countries and illustrated them for a third, we look at a final transfer mechanism—from unskilled labour to consumers, skilled labour, and profit receivers.

Redistribution Through Pricing of Manufactures

With the possible exceptions of Tanzania and Sri Lanka, every country we have examined has given a high priority (usually the highest priority) in its development strategy to industrialization through import substitution. The attractions of such a strategy are obvious. Under ideal conditions, it can save foreign exchange, increase employment and income, and set in train a self-reinforcing process of industrial development. Since it depends upon exploiting a mass market, it begins with the domestic production of consumption goods, usually quasi-necessities—soap, cooking oil, pharmaceuticals, manufactured foods, clothing, building materials, and cheap furniture. Almost by definition, these are goods that are consumed by low-income groups. Table 13.1 has already shown that even the poorest groups spend a significant proportion of their income on clothes.

In general, import substitution demands the exclusion of foreign manufactures that could threaten the market for the newly established domestic producers. Imports are thus excluded by quota or usually by a punitive tariff.

In many countries, the tariffs and/or quotas are specific to individual products; that is, they are imposed in order to protect the output of a single firm. As such, they are negotiated between the would-be producer and the government. In these negotiations, the government's hand is—or is thought to be—weak. It does not know what is the minimum profit level required to ensure that the producer will be prepared to invest. It cannot check the costings submitted by the producer, especially if these involve royalties or management fees. It is not usually able to hold the ring between two competing producers, encouraging each to undercut the other. Multinational companies are particularly wary of being caught in such a situation and, since any one operation is such a small part of total sales, they prefer to withdraw altogether rather than be put in such an exposed position. At the same time, the government is likely to be anxious to see the establishment of a new plant—for a variety of reasons from the hard-nosed economic to the political need to be seen to be achieving "success." It is therefore reluctant to overplay its hand, a reluctance much increased by informal pressures that run the gamut from indictable corruption to the normal exercise of political leverage. For the company, the stakes can be high. A high tariff or a limited quota can allow it to charge a high price in the domestic market—with obvious benefit to profits. Nor need taxation much prune those profits, especially if the firm is a subsidiary of an international company. Under such circumstances, the company has every inducement to use legitimate and illegitimate means to ensure that the tariff is high—and is maintained.

The net effect is that the locally manufactured article is available to the consumer at a price that exceeds the price of imports, since if the new producer could undercut imports he would not need a tariff. The payment of this higher price represents for the consumer a transfer to the producers of the local products. When the import substitute is a product much bought by the poor, the low-income consumer subsidizes the entrepreneur and his employees to the extent by which the price of the local product exceeds import parity.

That subsidy is then divided between the employees and the entrepreneur. In what ratio it is divided depends upon the wage policy of the government and the firm, the technology employed by the firm, the time horizon and risk tolerance of the entrepreneur. If the firm is using a highly productive technology, has negotiated a high tariff, and is making substantial profits, it is likely that wages and salaries will be above average—with prejudicial effects on wage policy as a whole and, perhaps more important, on the ability of more competitive firms to recruit able and efficient personnel. For us, more relevant is the transfer of welfare from the poorer groups to groups that are more privileged. It is, to repeat, a fundamental and inescapable concomitant of import substitution behind tariffs that such a transfer takes place.

In theory, such a transfer is temporary. As the new domestic industry becomes more efficient, so tariffs are supposedly lowered and in time both tariff and transfer disappear. If the new domestic industry can then sell at prices lower than the old import price, consumers are rewarded for their subsidy of the new industry during its "infant" phase. But, given the monopoly position of most import substitutive industries, the balance of bargaining power, and the distribution of pay-offs, it is no surprise to find that in practice that does not seem to be the case. In the Philippines, the country with the longest industrial history in our sample and therefore the one in which we might expect tariffs to have been reduced, they were in fact simplified and reinforced by the re-imposition of import controls in 1968/69. Devaluation in 1970 was managed in such a way that the peso is probably now under-valued in relation to other currencies, with the result that the very high effective rates of production for manufactured industries in the Philippines have been increased.[15]

Table 13.8 shows the excess of the protected price over the free trade price for goods that family budget surveys in the Philippines show are consumed by low-income groups.* Two estimates are given: the potential excess theoretically attainable and the realized excess derived from observed prices. This latter is a

---

*The table includes an additional form of non-tariff protection, namely, a differential sales tax. In extreme cases, this can afford more protection than the tariff itself. The data refer to 1965, but the structure of protection has not been substantially changed since.

TABLE 13.8

Philippines: Expenditures by the Poor on Selected Protected Goods, 1965

| Item | Consumption Group | Percent of Expenditures by Income Groups | | Nominal Protection | |
		<P500	P500-999	Potential	Realized
Cigarettes	Tobacco	3.6	3.2	191	19
Shoes, except rubber	Clothing and			71	7
Rubber shoes	other	5.5	6.1	164	10
Ready-made garments	wear			110	11
Cotton textiles				91	30
Candy, cocoa	Miscellaneous			149	66
Cocoa and chocolate	food	8.1	7.7	85	39
Electric lamps	Fuel, light, and water	4.0	4.2	2,320	125

Sources: J.H. Power, "The Structure of Protection in the Philippines," in B. Balassa et al., *The Structure of Protection in Developing Countries* (International Bank for Reconstruction and Development, 1971); *BCS Survey of Households,* Series no. 22 (Manila: Bureau of Census and Statistics, 1965).

minimum since only a small (10 percent) allowance was made for quality differences. In some goods that are bought by the poor, quality differences are substantially greater than this.

Even if we take the minimum figures in the last column of Table 13.8, it is clear that the two lowest expenditure groups in the Philippines (12 percent of all families) pay disguised taxes between 7 percent and 125 percent for goods that form a sizeable proportion of their total expenditures.* If we assume that cigarettes form 80 percent of consumption of tobacco by these groups, then those with annual expenditures of under P1,000 paid as a tax or subsidy to the producers P8.5 million in 1965 (16 percent of total expenditure on cigarettes). If we assume that the items in column 1 account for 75 percent of expenditures

---

*The fourth and fifth columns in the table cannot be used as weights since the consumption categories are not completely specified in the protection columns. A closer match is not possible since consumption data are not available on an ISIC four-digit classification.

on clothing, then the poor paid to the producers about ₱11.6 million as a subsidy (using 14.5 as nominal protection on clothes as a whole). On these two items alone, the poor paid to producers roughly a quarter of what they paid to government in total taxes. (This is a very crude estimate since the fiscal data are taken from the Tax Commission Report of 1964 and therefore refer to 1960. They also are based on income rather than expenditure groups. But adjustments to take account of these imperfections are not likely to change the order of magnitude involved.)

Given that the real incomes of minimum wage earners in the Philippines have declined, it is improbable that inflated prices* of these protected goods have resulted in entrepreneurs paying higher wages to their workers. One likelihood is, then, that the subsidies have enriched the investors in these industries directly. We do not know whether these subsidies—or the high prices on which they depend—are a necessary condition of investment in these industries. If that could be proved, it would be arguable that they are a necessary price for creating jobs for the unskilled. Such an argument would be specious. Cigarette manufacture, for instance, is highly automated and the number of jobs for the urban poor created thereby is tiny. The wider point remains: A system that depends upon the poor subsidizing the rich to create jobs for the poor is unlikely to do much to eradicate poverty. But that is precisely what the strategy of import substitution, especially in its early stages, implies.† When the rich thus subsidized are foreign investors, the inherent absurdity of the strategy is clear.

Very few governments (Taiwan and South Korea are examples) have been sufficiently impervious to the wide range of social, economic, and political pressures mounted by the beneficiaries of this system to reduce protection (by lowering tariffs and/or increasing quotas) and thus make domestic producers reduce their prices or go out of business. Indeed, the evidence from the Philippines is exactly the reverse, namely, that producer interests are able to persuade government to increase the level of protection. Interestingly, exactly the same seems to be true in Malaysia—a country where producer interests are hardly less strong. Tariffs have been applied to a range of intermediate industrial products as part of a third-stage import substitution strategy, with the result that the effective rate of protection on consumer goods has been increased—from an

---

*For the structure of protection is more widespread than indicated in the table: The *average* effective rate of protection of all manufacturing industry is 51 percent.

†At the early stages, mass-market quasi-necessities are the prime objects of import substitution. In later stages, when luxuries or semi-luxuries are included, the privileged subsidize the super-privileged. The unskilled may thereby gain employment, but at a very high social cost.

admittedly low level. But at even that low level, urban Malays earning less than
M$150 per month (one third of all urban Malays in 1958) may have been pay-
ing as much as 35 percent of their expenditures on tobacco and clothing to foreign, Singaporean, and local producers (see Table 13.9).

The same broad arguments can be applied to the African countries we have
studied. High rates of effective protection affect the prices of many items
bought by the poor. For instance, in Kenya, of 23 items enjoying above-average
protection, 9 are articles bought by the urban and/or rural poor. They include
some foodstuffs, cotton goods, blankets, and cycle tyres. These tariffs, rising in
the 1960s and extending to a wider range of goods, are reinforced by quotas
and import licences. M. Phelps has revealed a particularly interesting feature of
this latter.[16] In many cases, import licences are granted only for superior-
quality goods. This has the effect of keeping down the local cost of high-quality
items but allowing local manufacturers a monopoly of the low-quality market.
Nothing could better illustrate the distributional biases inherent in this system.

There is a further feature of Kenya's system of protection that calls for comment, especially as it is paralleled in some important aspects by that of Ivory
Coast. Some of the products that receive the most protection in Kenya are agricultural products—pork, sugar, cotton, cashew, canned fruit, and vegetables—

TABLE 13.9

Malaysia: The Cost of Protection to Poor Urban Malays

Item	Monthly Expenditure (M$)	Nominal Protection (percent)	Monthly Subsidy (M$)
Cigarettes and tobacco	4.30	107	2.22
Clothing	2.19	25	0.43
Textiles	1.15	24	0.22
Footwear	1.07	25	0.21
Total	8.71		3.08
			(= 35 percent)

Note: The expenditure data refer to 1957/58 and the protection data to
1965. This is unsatisfactory because it assumes that expenditures would not be
affected by rising prices. (Tariffs rose somewhat between 1957 and 1965.) To
that extent the table may overstate the effect of protection, but the proportionate effect is likely to be small.

Sources: Household Budget Survey, 1957/58; J.H. Power, "The Structure of
Protection in W. Malaysia," in B. Balassa et al., *The Structure of Protection in
Developing Countries* (Baltimore, 1971), p. 212.

originally produced by white settlers and now produced extensively, but not exclusively, by large-scale "capitalist" Kenyan farmers. It is not surprising that among the 20 industries most protected (ranked by the increase in the rate of return produced by protection), these agro-industries account for six.[17] The successors of the white farmers have been no less politically astute in ensuring that import substitution is used as a cover for increasing their income.

Capital- or Labour-Intensive Technologies?

So far we have been concerned with transfers from the poor and excluded to the privileged. We now look at a group of policies that have the effect of transferring welfare from unskilled labour to skilled labour profit receivers, and consumers.

We have already seen in Chapter 11 that the ability of economic growth to create jobs in the formal sector has been disappointing in every economy we have examined; we have seen some of the effects of rising unemployment in the urban economy. The causes of this slow growth of employment are complex. In this section, we wish to examine only two: the subsidization of capital and the output mix. We have chosen these because they are good examples of the ways in which liberal development strategy becomes simultaneously self-defeating and reactionary—self-defeating, because it triggers the wrong set of reactions at the interface between capitalists and government, and reactionary because those (wrong) reactions in fact make effective solutions less likely rather than more so.

We shall not treat the effect of rising real wages on the choice of technology, nor the fact that the technology most readily available is usually unsuitable to the economic circumstances of the poor countries. This latter point is now well known, even though action to counter it is still hard to design. The former point—high wages leading to lower employment growth—is exceedingly difficult to prove as a general case; we have quoted some specific examples, usually from the public sector, in earlier chapters. We do not wish to discount the importance of those factors; but we want to concentrate on two others that perfectly illustrate the main theme of this book that the cost of the enrichment of a few is the impoverishment of many.

But we cannot escape questions of technology entirely. For, in so far as our argument is that governments allow themselves to be persuaded to subsidize investors' capital and thereby make employment growth less likely, we are assuming that investors do in fact have a choice of technology—i.e., the technical processes are not fixed and investors (or their agents) choose from a range of technologies that which will produce at the lowest cost. It is sometimes said

that the techniques of production are given and invariant. Such an objection
can be dismissed immediately. The wide international and inter-firm variations
in labour productivity in identical industries in rich countries is good evidence
to the contrary. A very limited number of detailed studies of technology choice
in poor countries show that employment created per unit of capital invested is
highly variable and is dependent on the relative prices and productivities of
machinery and labour. If the technique decision is open and economically
motivated,* then it follows that any policy that has the effect of making capital
cheap in relation to labour is likely to prejudice the decision in favour of capital
intensity. There are three main groups of such policies.

First, the government may seek to encourage investment by giving particularly favourable tax treatment to the purchase of capital goods. Second, it may
subsidize credit either directly through a state bank or indirectly through the
tax system. Third, the government may deliberately maintain an under-valued
exchange rate or a system of tariffs in order to depress the price of capital in
relation to labour.

Before we briefly review each of these devices as they have operated in the
countries under study, it is worth tracing the inner lack of logic underlying all
these policies. All governments seek to expand production. Assuming that technologies are inflexible, they therefore assume that an expansion of production
implies an expansion in investment. Investment from domestic resources is, or
is thought to be, limited, and therefore it becomes necessary to attract foreign
capital in order to reach acceptable rates of growth of output.

But this process of encouraging domestic investment and attracting foreign
capital conflicts with another government objective, namely, that of ensuring
rapid increases in employment. For the means by which capital is attracted
biases decisions against labour-intensive processes and technologies. The process
feeds on itself. As capital intensity increases, so the second objective, the rapid
expansion of employment opportunities, is consistently under-fulfilled. This
leads to the search for fresh incentives to attract capital. These incentives have
the effect of further cheapening capital in relation to labour and making more
unlikely the adoption of labour-intensive techniques as a result. Therefore,
further incentives are offered and the price of capital falls further in relation to

---

*This is not to argue that only economic, or rather neo-classical economic,
motives apply. Perhaps as important are such criteria as internationally standardized methods of production in a multinational corporation; distrust of
organized labour; fears of future developments in labour legislation and wage
costs; and, again in the context of multinational corporations, the need to adopt
a particular technology in order to remit profits disguised as royalties on patents,
management fees, or other payments for head office expertise.

labour. The bizarre result is that an international auction for capital successively raises the price of labour in relation to capital in countries that are all facing chronic under-employment. Further, since there is seldom any attempt to monitor the effectiveness of the subsidies to capital, nor usually any attempt to negotiate the subsidies with individual firms, it is entirely possible that at least for many firms the existence of the subsidies constitutes pure gain. They do not affect the decision on whether or not to invest, although they may well affect the decision on what technique to employ or what labour intensity to aim at. (This is particularly true where investment in local manufacture or processing is defensive; that is, undertaken by a multinational firm primarily to protect an existing market.[18])

It may be the case that the Asian countries have gone particularly far in developing a range of tax and other incentives.[19] But even those with ambivalent or hostile attitudes to foreign investment, such as Tanzania, have not been slow to develop their own range of policies ostensibly designed to attract foreign capital or encourage the investment of domestic capital but implicitly raising the price of labour in relation to capital. The most wisespread of these incentives, often borrowed from metropolitan country legislation and unchanged since independence, is a system of capital allowances. These allowances permit a company to write off its capital against corporate tax at high rates in the early years of operation. In Ivory Coast, 40 percent of fixed capital, including buildings and housing, can be so written off. In Zambia the system is more flexible, with high rates (50 percent) for prime moving equipment and much lower rates for industrial buildings—20 percent for low-cost housing and 15 percent for other buildings. In Kenya, the rate is lower—20 percent for new fixed assets including buildings in the first year. (In all these cases, there are additionally normal depreciation allowances, the rates of which vary according to the type of asset.)

The effect of these accelerated depreciation allowances is to transfer income from government to entrepreneurs. The scale of that transfer obviously depends upon the rate of corporation tax and the accelerated depreciation allowance. In the Ivory Coast, it is equivalent to a grant by government to entrepreneurs of 12 percent of the value of their fixed assets. In Zambia, on prime moving equipment the grant is worth 16 percent of the value of that equipment. In Kenya, it is worth 8 percent of all fixed assets. There is no need to labour the point. In a seemingly capital-starved environment, governments feel that investors need some encouragement. But the form that that encouragement takes, borrowed as it is from the entirely different economic circumstances of rich countries, certainly deprives central government of revenue (this loss is incurred by long tax holidays, another widespread investment incentive), and probably the unemployed of jobs.

Apart from reduced taxation, two other techniques are used to encourage domestic and foreign investment, with much the same effect on employment. The first is the direct subsidization of capital by preferential lending arrangements for given types of investment. The Philippines again offers a good example of this type of arrangement. Throughout the 1950s and 1960s the Central Bank deliberately kept re-discount rates low so that commercial banks could keep lending rates low.* Further, favoured industries have had access to long-term finance at low interest rates through government lending institutions supported by the Central Bank. In Malaysia, low-interest capital has been provided by the Malaysian Industrial Development Finance Company; in Sri Lanka, commercial banks' lending rates have been kept unrealistically low—unrealistic, that is, both in terms of world interest rates and in terms of the social value of investment capital in Sri Lanka.[20]

Nor is this subsidization of capital confined to the private sector. In enterprises wholly owned or controlled by the state, the price of capital charged to the enterprise is not necessarily its social cost. In Zambia, the Industrial Development Corporation seems to have subsidized some of its undertakings from the profits of its holding in breweries. Certainly it has not led a major campaign to extend labour-intensive technology in secondary industry.[21] The way in which parastatal companies cost capital to individual projects is not clear. There is scattered evidence from Tanzania, and more solid evidence from Ghana, that the rate of interest (notionally or actually) charged to projects at the design state is the cost to government of borrowing, for example, from the Central Bank. Since this cost seldom reflects the social cost of capital, this internal accounting technique tends to disguise a subsidy on the capital deployed by parastatal organizations. To the extent that this is true, one objective of nationalization of existing corporations or the planned expansion of the public sector—to expand employment—can be seriously jeopardized.

The final structural distortion that can impinge upon capital/labour ratios is exchange rate and tariff policy that is designed to make all imports, particularly capital imports, relatively cheap. This happened throughout the 1950s and 1960s in the Philippines. Even after the introduction of a dual exchange rate system in Sri Lanka, the continued importation of capital goods at a preferential rate ensured the perpetuation of this bias. In Ghana, the distortions created by an unrealistic exchange rate were well revealed by the effect of devaluation in

---

*The cross holdings between commercial banks and manufacturing and trading companies, a common feature of industrial organization in developing countries, but one particularly marked in the Philippines, makes a thorough cost-effectiveness analysis of subsidies politically difficult and practically unfeasible.

1967. The price of capital equipment leaped nearly 50 percent and, despite pressure on wages, one of the major price biases against labour disappeared. (On the assumption that the capital investment is financed abroad over a period of ten years, the crude wage-rental index declined from 124 in 1966 to 99 in 1967. On other assumptions about the financing cost of capital, the decline in the index would be bigger.[22]

If a relatively simple operation like devaluation can make such a large difference to the relative price of capital, why is it so long delayed and so reluctantly implemented? One reason is that it raises the cost of living to urban consumers—a political fact that governments in Ghana and the Philippines have found to their cost. But another is that producers who import their machinery and raw materials have every incentive to resist devaluation, especially since they are already well protected in their home markets by tariffs and quotas. Given the administrative and political power of this lobby, it is no surprise that the social cost of employment opportunities forgone is readily met by attempts to protect an over-valued exchange rate. The unemployed, after all, have no voice in the planning ministry.

In sum, it is difficult to see how these subsidies can possibly benefit the poor, who contribute significantly to them. In the worst case, they are a straight hand-out to international and national capitalists and have no effect on decisions either to invest or to use a given technology. In the best case, they are essential to persuade capitalists to invest, but it is inconceivable that they will bias decisions in favour of the employment of unskilled labour. The only beneficiaries among the poor, then, are those unskilled who are employed even in a capital-intensive technology. That their numbers are small needs no emphasis. It would not be difficult to design a more cost-effective way of using the sums involved in these subsidies for the eradication of poverty. But that is not, of course, the purpose they are designed to fulfill.

This raises a much wider question. Even if labour-intensive techniques were used in manufacturing, the number of jobs created thereby would, for all our African countries and Sri Lanka, be small in relation to the number of job seekers. Even in Malaysia and the Philippines, countries with a much larger industrial base, a 50 percent increase in those employed in manufacture would provide jobs for less than three years of urban labour force growth. For the fact is that manufacturing industry is an exceedingly inefficient producer of jobs, even when full allowance is made for the indirect demand for labour created by expansion of manufacturing output.

Two examples can illustrate this. Both are based on analysis of input-output matrixes and both therefore include employment created through effects on sectors supplying inputs to manufacturing.

In Malaysia, Chris Edwards has shown that most industries in which foreign capital is involved—oil refining, beverages, tobacco, machinery, and transport

equipment—produce less than a third of the number of jobs per million dollars
spent, compared with agriculture and agro-industries, such as rubber processing,
sawmills, fishing, and food processing.[23] The only manufacturing industries
that compared with this group fall in a residual category of "other manufacturing," of which the most important components are clothing and textiles—
industries in which foreign capital is much less significant in Malaysia.*

Corroborative evidence comes from a similar (but methodologically less satisfactory) study of the Philippines.† The most labour-intensive industries are
agriculture, agro-industry (excluding fertilisers), food processing, and service
industries. Typical manufacturing industries, especially those that attract foreign investment, rank much lower: radio and TV manufacture, washing com-
pounds, tires, motor vehicles, pharmaceuticals, electrical and mechanical
machinery—all produce fewer jobs, directly and indirectly, per unit of output.

We therefore have to ask why substantial public resources are devoted to
attracting this kind of investment. For it has few economic virtues to offer.
Much of it is import-intensive‡ and skill-intensive as well as capital-intensive. It
uses disproportionately three of the scarcest resources. Its redeeming feature,
of course, is that it is highly productive, the more so since prices are distorted
in its favour.

But, as should by now be obvious, the productivity accrues to groups that
are already highly privileged: capitalists, domestic and foreign; skilled workers;
merchants, wholesalers and bankers; and, in so far as local manufacture either
lowers price or increases availability, consumers. It is surely not over-fanciful
nor over-cynical to seek an explanation for the high priority and generous subsidies given for foreign and local investment in these industries in the concurrence

---

*In terms of employment per M$1 million worth of final demand, "other
manufacturing" at 487 man-years was much less job-sensitive than rubber
growing (642), agriculture and livestock (629), and rubber processing (561).
But it compares well with chemical products (296), metal products and
machinery (229), beverages and tobacco (82) and basic metals (79).

†The analysis was based on the 1965 input/output accounts for the Philippines as published in the *Journal of Philippines Statistics*, 1971/72. The major
difficulty is that, in order to convert the labour coefficients computed from
the input-output accounts, average earnings in broad sectors (i.e., single-digit
ISIC sectors) had to be used. For this reason, the absolute values are not presented here but, since the dispersion of average earnings between some sectors
is in general (although not universally) thought to be quite small, the rankings
are thought to be sufficiently reliable to support the conclusion in the text.

‡In the Philippines 96-industry analysis, the rank correlation between job
intensity and import intensity was 0.49 (significant at 1 percent).

of interest between the major beneficiaries and the decision makers. Of the latter, the planners value production in both the short run and the long for its own sake and are little concerned with who benefits thereby; the politicians are so concerned, but are more responsive to the needs of the major beneficiary groups, the privileged, than to the needs of the excluded. If either the politicians or the planners accepted as a major (but not necessarily dominant) criterion for any investment of public funds its effect on the excluded, it is hard to see how the expenditures (or revenue losses) outlined in this section could continue.

CONCLUSION

We have reviewed a number of ways in which the privileged use their power to transfer welfare from the excluded to their own groups. None is formally a con-mech (except at the competitive interface between the formal and informal sectors), but we must conclude by asking how it is that confidence in the system as a whole is maintained when transfers of such magnitude—in both relative and absolute terms—are built in. This takes us beyond the bounds of this research and into the wider issues of conflict, resolution, and the control of political opposition. Nonetheless, in the most summary fashion, a few of the major points can be sketched in.

First, we have to recognize that confidence is not in fact unshaken. Although the most vivid demonstration of African opposition to export taxes in recent times took place outside our group of countries—the Agbekoya Rebellion in Nigeria in 1969[24]—the activities of the Cocoa Marketing Board in Ghana (and more particularly of its local agents) have long been a focus of political disaffection. Simiarly, economic nationalism in its many forms has brought into question the payment of disguised subsidies to foreign capitalists—witness the storm that surrounded state investments in the foreign-controlled tourist industry in Sri Lanka in the period 1970-73, and the continual criticisms of Philippine relations with foreign investors that reached a crescendo in the constitutional convention.

But these criticisms usually are confined to a small circle of urban-based intelligentsia or opposition politicians. They may be declaimed widely, but how far they are properly appreciated,expecially in the rural areas, is a more difficult question. To take one small but illuminating example: The receipt given by agricultural buying depots to farmers for their crops seldom (in our experience, never) makes clear the implicit and explicit taxes paid by the farmer. (Some are now computerized and give the farmer a detailed but wholly unintelligible account of his financial transactions.) So it is with prices. The excluded may well be aware that prices are rising; but unless they are exposed to (opposition) political propaganda (as are the urban poor in Sri Lanka and as were the urban poor in the Philippines), they are most unlikely to see the connection between rising prices and the activities of local and foreign capitalists.

Second, precisely because they do usually control the mass media, governments can not only suppress the facts and hostile comments on them but, no less important, can raise "distractor issues," which may be tangentially related to the transfer mechanisms but which diminish hostility to them. These include, for example, "What government is doing for the people" (i.e., highlighting the downward flow of resources); variations on the theme of economic nationalism; symbolic solidarity with the excluded (e.g., leaders living in a village for a week or helping with the harvest); and the undeniable poverty of the country as a whole.

Third, leaders of overt hostility can be eliminated before they have a chance to build large popular support. There is no country in our group in which this has not occurred. While it is true that the proximate cause has seldom been opposition to the particular mechanisms we have discussed here (or, much less, that the leaders of the hostile parties would themselves have changed those mechanisms very profoundly), the political exploitation of these mechanisms is always a threat and sometimes—e.g., in Kenya, the Philippines, Ghana, Ivory Coast, to mention four very different examples—a fact.

Fourth, and in terms of our frame more fundamental, these transfer mechanisms are themselves legitimized by the complementary processes of access and redistribution. It is the possibility of eventual benefit from these processes that bestows both legitimacy on and confidence in such parts of the transfer mechanisms as are detected. When that possibility is widely discounted, the transfer mechanisms are less likely to be directly rejected, because they are less intelligible. Criticism is more likely to centre on the other processes or, in the extreme case, on the system as a whole. It is to that point that we return in the last chapter.

NOTES

1. *A Study of Tax Burden by Income Class in the Philippines* (Manila: Joint Legislative-Executive Tax Commission, 1964).

2. International Bank for Reconstruction and Development, *The Economic Development of Nigeria* (Baltimore: Johns Hopkins University Press, 1955), pp. 85-89.

3. Calculated from data in G. Helleiner, "Agriculture Marketing in Tanzania—Policies and Problems," mimeo. (Dar es Salaam: Economic Research Bureau,

1968). The Lint and Seed Marketing Board does not pay its surpluses over to government in the way the Cocoa Marketing Board does in Ghana, but it undertakes development projects on its own account.

4. Cf. Charles McClure, "Incidence of Taxation in West Malaysia," *Malayan Economic Review* 17, no. 1 (March 1972), where he shows a clear "U" shape for the incidence of taxation by income group.

5. C.B. Edwards, "Protection, Profits and Policy: An Analysis of Industrialisation in Malaysia," doctoral dissertation, University of East Anglia, forthcoming.

6. Data from the Department of Inland Revenue, as published in *Statistical Handbook, West Malaysia, 1971* (Kuala Lumpur: Department of Statistics), p. 146.

7. *Report of the Taxation Inquiry Commission*, Sessional Paper X (Colombo, 1968), pp. 225-26.

8. F.J. Maimbo and J. Fry, "An Investigation into the Change in the Terms of Trade between the Rural and Urban Sectors of Zambia," *African Social Research*, no. 12 (December 1971): 109.

9. C. Crisostomo, W. Meyers, T. Paris, B. Duff, and R. Barber, "The New Rice Technology and Labor Absorption in Philippine Agriculture," *Malayan Economic Review* 16, no. 2 (October 1971): 143.

10. M. Mangahas, "Philippine Rice Policy Reconsidered in terms of Urban Bias," Discussion Paper no. 72/8, mimeo. (Institute of Economic Development and Research, University of the Philippines, May 1972).

11. M. Mangahas, "The Effect of Importation on the Price of Rice," *Philippine Review of Business and Economics 5, no. 2* (December 1968): 41.

12. For a detailed costing of rice production in three areas in Sri Lanka, see P. Richards and E. Stoutjestijk, *Agrilculture in Ceylon Until 1975* (Paris: Development Centre of Organization of Economic Cooperation and Development, 1970), pp. 91-92.

13. International Labour Organization, *Matching Employment Opportunities and Expectations: A Programme of Action for Ceylon*, report of an inter-agency team organized by the ILO (Geneva: ILO, 1971), pp. 205-6.

14. See A. Killick, "Price Controls, Inflation and Income Distribution: The Ghanaian Experience," Economic Development Report no. 223 (Cambridge, Mass.: Centre for International Affairs, Harvard University, September 1972).

15. International Labour Organization, *Sharing in Development: Programme of Employment, Equity and Growth for the Philippines* (Geneva: ILO, 1974).

16. M. Phelps, "Protection of Industry in Kenya," in "Developmental Trends in Kenya," mimeo., proceedings of a seminar held in the Centre of African Studies, University of Edinburgh, April 1972.

17. Ibid., p. 286.

18. For a detailed description of one such case, see Michael Faber, "The Development of the Manufacturing Sector," in *Constraints on the Economic*

Development of Zambia, ed. C. Elliott (London/Nairobi: Oxford University Press, 1971), pp. 299 ff.

19. Nilda D. Vasquez, *Review of Fiscal Incentives in Selected Asian Countries* (Manila: Republic of the Philippines Joint Legislative Executive Tax Commission, 1972). Cf. J.H. Power, G.P. Sicat, and Mo-Huan Hsing, *Philippines and Taiwan: Industrialization and Trade Policies* (London: Oxford University Press/ Development Centre of OECD, 1971).

20. *Matching Employment Opportunities and Expectations,* op. cit.

21. M. Williams, "State Participation in the Zambian Economy," *World Development* 1, no. 10 (October 1973): 47.

22. M. Roemer, "Relative Factor Prices in Ghanaian Manufacturing, 1960-70," *The Economic Bulletin of Ghana* 1, no. 4 (1971): 12.

23. Edwards, op. cit.

24. See G. Williams, "Political Consciousness among the Indian Poor," in *Sociology and Development.* eds. E. de Kadt and G. Williams (London: Tavistock, 1974).

14

THE MEDIUM-TERM OUTLOOK

In this chapter, we address two wider issues in an attempt to put the detailed analysis of preceding chapters into a broader perspective. First we sketch out some of the major trends that we expect to endure over the medium term—say, five to fifteen years—on the basis of the mechanisms we have tried to investigate so far. In a sense, this is a simple extrapolation of current experience and, as such, is in fact likely to prove an unreliable guide to future events. For, as we shall suggest in the second half of this chapter, there are a number of forces that feed back upon and modify these basic trends. It is these modifications that are at once most analytically interesting but also more difficult to predict. For, as we stressed in Chapter 1, we do not claim that the analytical frame that we have used in this book is a predictive model. All it may do is show some areas in which either endogenous or exogenous modifications may originate, the form they may take, and some likely reactions to them.

If this whole book should be read as a series of inadequately tested hypotheses, then it follows that this last chapter should be read as untestable hypotheses about untested hypotheses. That said, we do believe that some of the hypotheses about future developments are significant for those who are obliged to make decisions about the future and who presumably seek to minimize the inconsistency of the assumptions governing those decisions.

We start with a number of trends that seem to us fairly well established and that, subject to very major changes in the socio-political environment, are likely to endure. In the urban areas, it is hard to see how high and perhaps rising rates of exclusion can be quickly reversed—if they can be reversed at all. There seems little prospect of significantly staunching the flow of migrants to the towns as long as (1) formal employment in the rural areas is scarce; (2) farm cash incomes are low both in absolute terms and in relation to the inherent·risks and the work required; and (3) urban labour markets give a strong inducement to students to press ahead with their education until they are finally excluded from the system. Further, the age structure of the urban areas is such that the natural rate of increase of urban populations is unlikely to fall sharply in the medium term. Given the biases we examined in Chapters 11 and 13, it seems to us highly improbable that employment in the formal sector will grow at rates comparable to the rate of growth of the urban labour force, especially in the light of the current age structure of the urban population.

Under these conditions, it is hard to see how the numbers living in relative poverty in the towns can diminish. If we assume that the privileged (taken as a total group) are successful in maintaining their real income taking one year with another, and perhaps slowly increasing the real income of the lowest paid in the formal sector, we must be much less sanguine about those in the informal sector. We thus expect the pattern that we suggested in Chapters 7 and 8 to continue— whereby the concentration of income in the formal sector may diminish but the concentration of urban income as a whole may increase. This implies falling real incomes in the informal sector. Particularly for·families with a larger number of dependents, this implies a rising number of those in absolute poverty.

For the prerequisites for a rapid growth of real income per head in the informal sector look daunting. Put at its simplest, the net income of the informal sector will have to grow at a rate higher than the rate of growth of exclusion. Figures at this point are almost meaningless; the relevant order of magnitude is in the region of 4 to 8 percent a year. Growth of this order is exceedingly demanding in light of the structural obstacles, which we have sketched out, to an increase in net exports to the formal sector. For we have argued that the impact of technical change in the formal sector is to reduce the cost of competitive services and to expand the range of services offered by the formal sector that are in competition with the informal sector. Simultaneously, steps taken to "indigenize" industry and commerce almost inevitably have the impact of increasing the subsidization of individuals and firms at the interface between the formal and informal sectors and who, if successful, shift the locus of that interface against the informal sector.

This is not to say that an increase in the net exports of the informal sector must be ruled out as impossible. A deliberate policy among government purchasing departments to discriminate in favour of firms employing fewer than five persons in specific sectors—e.g., transport, printing, textiles, carpentry, building—may have this effect without endangering the survival of firms in the formal sector. Another possibility would be either technical or economic changes that encouraged vertical disintegration in manufacturing industry, with the resulting proliferation of small workshops as in Japan in the 1940s and 1950s.

But either of these possibilities raises the difficulty that major beneficiaries would not themselves be the excluded in the informal sector at all; they would be the owners of informal sector "firms" who are themselves neither excluded nor poor. We see no easy way round this objection within the socio-political constraints that operate in all the countries that we have had under study. But we return to the question in the next section of this chapter.

Although it would not necessarily solve that particular problem, it is probably the case that the most effective external stimulus to the informal sector would be the banning of imports and local formal-sector manufacture of a very limited range of goods that the informal sector does already, or could with rather minor technological development, make quite efficiently—furniture, shoes, simple forms of metal and wire work. Such a ban would be vigorously resisted by the privileged (as producers, importers, and consumers). But in Tanzania, Sri Lanka, possibly Zambia, conceivably Tunisia where these interest groups are at least partially controlled, it would be worth serious discussion.

Would any such attempts to raise the aggregate (and possibly the per capita) income of the informal sector delay the effects of feedback mechanisms that will anyway act upon the urban rate of exclusion? The neo-classical economist, for instance, might argue that such policies would raise the supply price of labour in the formal sector and therefore reduce the rate of growth of formal employment. The Harris-Todaro model of migration might suggest that rising incomes in the informal sector will merely increase the rate of migration and thus be self-defeating. We would argue that such conclusions stem from a misapprehension of the causes of urban exclusion, of which income in the informal sector is at best a very minor one. Urban exclusion is basically a rural problem—not in the sense that the poorest and the landless are driven out of the rural areas (since that is not the dominant theme suggested by the data), but rather in the sense that the retention of the more intelligent and the better educated, the younger, and, increasingly, the educated *women* is a problem of rural development that has been solved in none of these countries. Let us turn, then, to an examination of the rural areas.

There the detection of major enduring trends is much more difficult, if only because there is an even greater variety of economic and ecological conditions. Let us at least make the fundamental distinction between the rice economies (Sri Lanka, Malaysia, Philippines, and Egypt) and sub-Saharan Africa. The total impact of the Green Revolution on the rice economies cannot yet be assessed. However, what is beginning to emerge is the possibility of the same kind of differentiation in the rural areas as we find in the urban areas—namely, that among those benefitting from the new agricultural technologies there may have been a fall in the concentration of income, but the disparity between the technically progressive and the technically regressive and/or non-rice growers has increased. Where major structural changes—e.g., the enlargement of holdings, the more rapid adoption of cost-reducing techniques on larger farms—have occurred, concentration may have increased even in the technically progressive sector, but of that there is rather little evidence in our countries. Much clearer is the widening disparity between the technically progressive rice farmer and his dry land competitor.

Although the volume of research addressed to the problems faced by the latter, and even the poorest of the latter, has certainly increased in the last five years, it would be rash to assume that an equivalent technical "package" *can* be developed—a package that can be delivered to and adopted by the poorest cultivators under known institutional and managerial constraints. True, neither of these constraints is absolute. But it has been the institutional back-up to the original Green Revolution that has proved a nearly intractable problem—and that in areas that were already relatively highly developed. It is for that reason that we are not optimistic about the prospects of raising rural incomes—even if the technical and agronomic problems can be solved. Perhaps the best intermediate hope is that "areas of concentration" will be selected where special institutional support is given to reach at least those who seek to adopt new techniques. The political problem (already posed in some countries with respect to existing technologies) is then the choice of those areas of specialization. As we have emphasized in previous chapters, the pressures will be to choose areas in which the institutional constraints are already minimized and the "success" of the package most easily assured. These are unlikely to be the poorest areas—which may indeed find themselves further impoverished by competition from the new dry land technologies. This is a theme to which we shall return in a rather different context.

A more difficult, but more profound, issue is whether the existing new technologies increase the demand for labour. Although generalization is dangerous, our main conclusion is that the demand for labour at labour peaks has increased, but that this has been accompanied by shifts in the structure of the labour supply to the disadvantage of the long-term or permanent casual labourer. He may have benefitted from higher wages paid during the peaks but is likely to face increasing competition both from mechanization and from either greater use of family labour (if wages rise) or greater use of short-term casual employment of mostly resident women.

If that is right, we have to ask how in the long term a rising number of landless or quasi-landless labourers are to be supported. First, where the frontier of settlement is still open, that may, under a number of rather optimistic assumptions, provide a major part of the solution. But only in the outlying islands of the Philippines (and perhaps in parts of Mindanao) is this a real possibility. Progress of "official frontiersmen" like Federal Land Development Authority is inevitably too slow to make the kind of impression we are looking for. Second, future technological changes may increase the demand for labour among those so far unaffected by technological progress. This seems unlikely, not only for the reasons we have already outlined but also because, if a "poverty-focused" technology demands hired labour, its wide adoption is jeopardized by the implied problems of cash flow.

The third possibility is land reform. In Egypt, Sri Lanka, and the Philippines, land reform may make a contribution to the solution of this problem. But in all three countries, the major emphasis is, perhaps inevitably, on improving the conditions of tenants rather than on redistributing land to the landless. Only in Sri Lanka is this latter feature strongly emphasized, and there, as we pointed out, such redistribution as does take place may in fact have the result of making the lot of the non-citizen Tamils even worse.

The processes that we have described, then, do not suggest that either the relative or absolute poverty of one of the most vulnerable sections of rural population is likely to change much over the medium term. Indeed, the conditions under which we could foresee a major improvement for this group are even more demanding than for the urban excluded.

Let us now turn to sub-Saharan Africa. Leaving aside the possibility that current international changes in product prices, particularly that of oil, will open up major new markets for peasant agriculture (of which cotton is perhaps the most likely possible candidate), is the basic pattern likely to be much different from that of the rice economies? We have suggested that, particularly but not exclusively in East Africa, the emergence of a proto-capitalist agriculture is already well under way, almost irrespective of government policy towards it. Government may be successful in checking the emergence of large-scale farms dependent upon hired labour in Tanzania; it would be folly to try to predict the outcome of what is basically a political struggle between a rather small number of wealthy farmers and the leadership of the ruling party (Tanzania African National Union).

The wider question is whether the structural change associated with the further growth of proto-capitalist agriculture will bring with it a permanent impoverishment of significant sections of the rural poor. In the *longer* run, this seems improbable while the frontier of settlement is relatively open. In the short run, the annexation by a small group of land and agricultural services (in both senses of subsidized inputs and the ownership of the means of distribution) may certainly increase the concentration of income and thus the relative poverty of the poor. The huge social, psychic, and economic costs of resettlement for families forced out of a particular area, perhaps after a period as permanent labourers, may well bring a period of absolute impoverishment. Further, those who, for whatever reason, are unable or unwilling to move (or who are prevented from doing so by government regulations regarding the allocation of new land) are likely to see their real incomes fall on any reasonable expectation about the speed with which the necessary transfer of population is achieved.

That said, one qualification is necessary. Even in countries that have not in the past given a particularly high priority to considerations of equity in rural development, there is evidence of an increasing awareness of the tendency for subsidized inputs to be appropriated by a relatively small group. How far this rising political awareness impinges upon the administrative machine at the district level is still a very open question, but it would be surprising if, over the medium term, greater attempts were not made to remove at least some of the structural obstacles to take-up and adoption that we have described. To this extent, the "floor" at which improved technologies become operative may well be slowly forced downwards, but that is most likely to be achieved by spatial specialization that will inflict its own biases. For reasons that should by now be clear, those biases are again likely to be against the poorest in the most backward areas.

This leaves unanswered the question of whether the basic problem of raising rural incomes and levels of living is likely to be solved sufficiently far to react upon urban migration and therefore exclusion in the urban areas. It follows from the previous paragraphs that at least some farm incomes are likely to rise rather fast over the medium term—e.g., those who adopt double-cropping with imrice varieties, new proto-capitalist farmers of East and West Africa, those who by design or chance benefit from particular programmes designed to deliver existing or new packages of agro-technology to less progressive farmers. The question is whether this experience of some farm incomes rising rather rapidly will be enough significantly to reduce the rate of migration. On this we are almost wholly pessimistic.

Some rural incomes rose very rapidly in the 1950s and 1960s in nearly every country under discussion. This was a period during which intra-urban differentials fell; in which secondary education was not as widespread as it is now; and more particularly a period during which female education was still confined to a small minority. Two assumptions then become important. The first is that lower-skill groups in the formal sector of the urban areas are going to suffer sustained falls in real income (i.e., real differentials are going to widen again). The second is that potential migrants are going to be more deterred than they have been in the past by the difficulty of finding a job in the formal sector, either because they come to appreciate the existing difficulty more accurately or because formal employment does actually become more difficult to find and potential migrants learn of this increased difficulty. Without one or other (or both) of those assumptions, it follows that urban migration is more likely to increase than to diminish. Further, in so far as the existence of kinsmen in town is an important inducement to migrate, there is a built-in exponent that would have the same effect.

We do not believe that adjusting the price of agricultural products, particularly food, in favour of the rural areas would constitute the whole, or even major part of the solution of this problem. In those countries in which urban bias persists there is, no doubt, point in removing the bias—but the fact that the bias exists already is prima facie evidence that urban groups have sufficient political leverage to maintain it in the short run. They may be unable to do so in the long. Neither changes in prices nor changes in productivity, then, are likely to raise the cash incomes of enough farmers to reduce substantially the rate of migration. We therefore do not see any sign of an automatic check on the basic problem in the urban sector coming from the solution to the problems of the rural sector.

It might be argued that adjustments will come not from economic change but from a rising disinclination of rural parents to put their children through school in the light of the low chances of securing formal sector employment either in town or in the rural areas. This seems to us implausible. No doubt some of the initial enthusiasm for education as a guarantee of immediate social and economic promotion will begin, and indeed has already begun, to want. Some "marginal" parents will then withdraw children from school and aggregate enrolments may even fall in absolute terms, especially in areas where education came late. But to generalize from this seems unwarranted. It seems more likely that the net effect of such a "feedback" will be to increase the social selectivity of education (on the assumption that withdrawal is most common among the rural poor) and thus strengthen the biases we examined in Chapter 9.

So far we have couched this discussion purely in terms of real income. We now turn to a brief consideration of other forms of social consumption. We have argued in Chapters 9 and 12 that the expansion of social services does not automatically reduce the relative or even the absolute impoverishment of deprived groups. In so far as the provision of these services tends to be biased in the direction of the privileged, in spatial, social, or economic terms, the expansion of the services tends to reinforce the relative deprivation of the excluded. In absolute terms, we expect some (very slow) improvement in the social consumption of the excluded, but this would be consistent with widening relativities.

THE SURVIVAL OF THE SYSTEM

If the foregoing are some of the basic underlying trends that in our view are likely to endure over the medium term, we must ask under what circumstances or by what combination of policies a less gloomy picture could become a reality. At this point, we need to refer again to the basic model. An important element of that model was the hypothesis that access and resources are controlled by the

privileged groups (in the language of the analogy, the "topmost fish") in a way
that, as a minimum, will maintain confidence in the various mechanisms at work.
We suggested in the model that the privileged groups wished to protect the basic
delineation of the existing system but that, in terms of access and the net flow
of resources, there is in fact some flexibility. The degree of that flexibility depends upon the identification of the interest of the ruling groups by those in a
position to make or change policy; their perception of the trade-off between the
long term and the short term and their estimates of the minimum combination
of improved access and net resource flows that are necessary to maintain confidence in the system as a whole and in each individual con-mech.

Let us concentrate for the moment upon access from one group to another
and then return to a consideration of intra- and inter-group competition. The
basic question can be put this way: Under what conditions are ruling groups
likely to try to make the channels of access that we have reviewed in preceding
chapters either easier (in the sense that more individuals actually pass through
the particular access cone) or less selective (in the sense of less biased against
excluded groups)? They may make access easier to skill groups that they regard
as important and as in short supply—i.e., for which there is a clear economic
demand—or in response to overt political pressure from lower groups trying to
enter skill groups with obvious particular advantages. In most African countries,
skilled artisans are an obvious example of the former and the middle-level white-
collar group an example of the latter. In this latter case, we have seen that there
is already a conflict between what is economically justifiable (on the criteria of
the manpower planner) and what is politically demanded. There is little evidence
to suggest that in this conflict the economic arguments ultimately carry more
weight. Mutatis mutandis, the same is broadly true of the Asian countries.
Despite higher levels of unemployment at secondary level, the political difficulties of containing the expansion of secondary education or even of higher education are formidable, particularly, as in the case of Malaysia, where there are
glaring, deeply resented and politically exploitable imbalances to be corrected.
("Politically exploitable" because there is much less evidence in Malaysia and
Sri Lanka of the ethnic imbalances suffered by the Indians/Tamils being
corrected.)

We have here two very different examples. The political demand by the
excluded for access to the blue-collar skilled group is usually ventilated in
terms of hostility towards expatriates or non-citizens. For the group is, and is
in most countries likely to remain, if not in chronic scarcity, at least not characterized by the gross over-supply that is such a feature of the middle-level white-
collar market.

There are two questions of obvious relevance about this conflict. The first
is this: Is there reason to believe that these channels of access will become less
biased against the excluded? We have detected few grounds for optimism.

Ruling groups have little incentive to undertake the structural changes and the budgetary cost of the kind of direct intervention that is usually required to secure equity of access for the excluded, as long as confidence in this particular mechanism is maintained. When it breaks down, as it did in Malaysia in 1969, and as it may have done in part at the higher level in the Philippines in 1970-72, there is an incentive to set in train no more than sufficient change to restore confidence in the system.

The second question is whether, through market mechanisms or otherwise, the desire for access is reduced. The urgency with which students seek secondary or higher education as a way of improving their long-term earning potential poses the government with a quite different problem. It would seek to reduce the flow but consistently meets political opposition. We then have to ask under what conditions that particular opposition to an expanding secondary school system is moderated. Our hypothesis (based on virtually no case material) is that it comes only when employment probabilities and cash differentials actually favour the candidate with no secondary schooling over the candidate with a secondary qualification. In other words, we suspect that most parents, particularly perhaps urban parents, are sufficiently well advised of the non-cash benefits of employment at the higher skill levels—running the gamut from prestige to promotion prospects to superior pension schemes—that there has to be an immediate cash incentive against secondary education before this particular pressure is removed.

If this is right, it suggests that the Sri Lankan situation is likely to be generalized, and that with local variations this particular imbalance is likely to endure, perhaps for the rest of this century. For, as we have emphasized, differentials are on our evidence being reduced but slowly. Further, we would guess that as the grossest post-colonial differentials disappear, so it becomes progressively more difficult to reduce differentials further. In other words, it would be a mistake to argue that, because differentials have been halved in fifteen years since independence, another fifteen years will see their disappearance. It seems to us much more likely that, as a result of political pressure, secondary and even higher education will continue to be expanded with the result that the competitive position of those who are excluded from secondary school will continually be eroded. This makes the removal of inequities in selection for secondary schooling all the more urgent. But it also makes the ruling elite all the less ready to bring it about. For that would increase inter-generational mobility upwards for others, but downwards for them. Although it would be a mistake to dismiss this possibility— witness the case of Ghana—it is more likely to occur in a country with a currently rather under-developed secondary and higher educational system than in one in which there is a relatively high level of enrolment at these levels.

In the rural areas, the most important access mechanism is the access to highly productive technology. We have already discussed this in this chapter; little need be added here. There is little reason to suppose that the basic con-mechs at work will be seriously challenged. Those who are excluded from them—i.e., those who compete unsuccessfully for access to the productivity packages—are not usually those with sufficient political voice, even at the local level, to bring pressure to bear upon any ruling group to ensure an adjustment in the equity with which the packages are distributed.

Land may very well be a different case. We have seen much evidence from both Africa and Asia that intra-group and inter-group competition for land can be intense. Access to land may therefore be an "access cone" we would expect to be modified, either through land reform or through the commitment of public resources to the opening up of new land. The problem, as we have already emphasized, is that in these official programmes the efficiency algorithm tends to bias selectivity against the poorest. There are examples, for instance, in Egypt and less markedly in Sri Lanka, where the efficiency algorithm has been set aside, but in both cases it is arguable that the impact of the reform programmes on the very poorest has been small and is likely to continue to be rather small. But it is significant that in these two countries, both allegedly searching for a more equitable distribution of the agricultural product, there *has* been a real political challenge to the algorithm. This lies in marked contrast, for example, to Malaysia where, despite continual political pressures on the distribution of FLDA land, the administrative structures have shown a tenacious resistance to major modifications of existing regulations and practices which are biased against the poorest of the rural poor.

Let us now turn to the more difficult question of the distribution of benefits of the transfer mechanisms we reviewed in the last chapter. The most obvious example would be import substitution, by which some derive employment and others derive profits—but at a substantial cost to consumers in general and poor consumers in particular. We have suggested that there are rather powerful reasons for believing that there is no automatic mechanism that ensures that this is a temporary transfer. Rather, the evidence suggests that, in the countries that we have been considering, those transfers continue indefinitely and may even increase. The efficiency algorithm may be applied in other parts of the system: It is set aside either by political intent (in order to retain political support among the major beneficiary groups) or because governments are in a weak bargaining positition vis-a-vis subsidiaries of foreign companies or even national capital own owners.* The question is under what conditions can governments be persuaded to use such a bargaining power as they have or to take steps to increase that power.

---

*In fact, their bargaining position is often not as weak as governments suppose and can be strengthened if there is a determination to do so. For instance, by opening negotiations with a competing multinational or by threatening to demand an equity stake and membership on the board or changes in taxation, *some* negotiating leverage can be acquired at very little cost. None of these in fact may prove actionable, but they can be used as means by which concessions

The issues are technical; the mechanism's effects are often indirect and sometimes difficult to measure accurately and unambiguously. In other words, the
nature of the problem puts influence and power into the hands of the bureaucratic elite rather than in the hands either of politicians or other groups that may
represent "popular" feeling. The only recognizable group that seems to have
undertaken this function in any of the countries we have examined is made up of
dissident university students who have at least the analytical skill to ask embarrassing questions and sufficient organizational ability to ensure that the questions
have to be answered. Their role in the development of economic nationalism in
the Philippines, for instance, is very clear. Although inevitably an ideological
mixed bag (and therefore often in conflict with each other) they played a significant part even before the constitutional convention in challenging the role of
foreign capital in the economic development of the Philippines. In very broad
terms, the same picture emerges in Sri Lanka, in Ghana, and, in much more
muted form, Ivory Coast and Tunisia. We are not denying that the great bulk
of university students seek to come to terms with the existing system by incorporating themselves into it to their personal advantage.[1] Our point is that pressure upon politicians and administrators on the rather more abstract question of
the distribution of benefits of con-mechs and transfer mechanisms can only
come from those who have at least sufficient training to cut through the profes-
sionally argued objections and cautions of the administrators.

The problem with groups of "dissident" students is that in general they are
easily crushed—as leaders as different as Presidents Marcos, Bandaranaike,
Nyerere, Kaunda, Obote, and Nkrumah have all found. Perhaps precisely because
they are so highly selected a group, they have not usually been successful in
forming alliances with other groups, and perhaps least successful in forming
alliances with the urban and rural excluded. While they have an ideological orientation and professional training to raise pertinent questions, they have usually
proved soft meat in direct confrontation with established authority.

Is there any evidence that challenges to the enrichment mechanisms will
come from the rural areas? In our countries, there is very little evidence. For
instance, export taxes and other deductions from gross earnings of export crop
producers have not in general been a major focus of popular rural discontent.
Again, it is dangerous to generalize from our very limited number of countries.
The Agbekoya Rebellion in Nigeria shows clearly that under very specific conditions rural producers are not incapable of understanding the issues at stake
and organizing a sufficiently vigorous protest to ensure some redress.[2] It would
be erroneous, however, to suppose that this is a generalizable case.

We have seen even less evidence to suppose that the most vulnerable of the
rural excluded—the permanent labourers—are in a position to exert any more
than the most temporary and fragmentary direct pressure upon wages and
conditions. Even when proto-capitalist farmers become heavily dependent upon

---

can be extorted in a bargaining situation.

hired labour—as in the Kikuyu coffee case cited in Chapter 2—the resulting interdependence is not interdependence of equals. In other words, in these situations
there may, at the margin, be an area of negotiability. But the social and economic
structure of the labour force (with its very varying degrees of dependence upon
employment) and the fact that in the long term producers are not committed to
one crop together mean that the concessions that can be won are likely to be
modest rather than fundamental. Even in Malaysia, for instance, the National
Union of Plantation Workers has taken nearly fifteen years to achieve even a
minimal degree of protection for its workers—and that at the cost of an agreement that reduced real wages over a prolonged period.

This suggests a sober conclusion. It is more realistic to look for changes in the
nature and biases of a limited number of access cones rather than in a fundamental renegotiation of the distribution of the benefits accruing from the mechanism
of enrichment and impoverishment that we have analysed. It is not unrealistic to
look over the fifteen-year period for modest increases in equity of access to education, rural technical packages, and possibly artisan skills. But as long as the
fundamental dynamics of differentiation, and the distribution of political power
and influence associated with those dynamics, remain unchanged, it is in our
view over-optimistic to expect far-reaching changes in the pattern of distribution
of benefits.

But that should not be taken to imply that the situation is static, wholly
determined, or incapable of limited degrees of manipulation. Indeed, one of the
sub-themes that has recurred throughout this book is that, to a limited extent,
there is flexibility and plasticity, within the full political and ideological spectrum that we have examined from the Philippines to Tanzania. It is therefore
helpful to conclude by outlining some of the pressure points that seem open in
this sense.

We have chosen three: the administrative structure, technology, and the many
interfaces between the international community and the privileged in the poor
countries.

In Chapter 8, we argued that differentials have fallen (slowly) but that these
are differentials between groups of the already privileged. Nonetheless, the evidence is that differentials have fallen because the lowest paid and least privileged
of these groups have been able to use the political and administrative structures
set up for the specific purpose of examining wages, salaries, and standards of
living in the urban areas.

In Chapter 12, we saw that major changes in housing policy (still inadequate
though they may be) have been brought about both by the scale of the problem
and by the administrative difficulties presented by that problem. This suggests
that, while the bureaucratic elite and the other ruling groups have their own
interests (which they will always strive to protect), limited change or reform
can be brought about within existing structures by those who know how to use

them. But let us be clear about the limitations of the use of existing administrative structures. They have their own dynamic (as well demonstrated in the case of water supply in Tanzania); they have their own constraints; they have their own limits to adaptation. But it is to make the best the enemy of the good to assume that all the administrative structures serve only the interests of the privileged and that "mere reformism" can never achieve anything for the excluded. Manipulation of administrative structures is unlikely fundamentally to change the distribution of benefits accruing from the mechanisms we have reviewed; it can change biases in access and, more significant in the long run, it can convince those who achieve such change that change is possible.

The extension of formal sector-type protection to workers in the informal sector, as has been achieved to some extent in Sri Lanka, is a case in point. This is not going to achieve an unambiguous benefit. But it can meet some of the major problems about the expansion of the informal sector, which we have already outlined. If more and more people are going to be employed in the informal sector, there seems to be much to be said for ensuring they are at least given more effective (though inevitably imperfect) protection from subminimal wages, summary dismissal, over-long hours, and the other abuses that currently flourish in that sector. This is not to minimize the problem of enforcement. But if that enforcement is seen as a political service rendered by the grass-roots political organization in return for votes (as in Tanzania, Zambia, and Sri Lanka) rather than as an administrative problem solved by the ponderous machinery of the ministry of labor, it can be sufficiently effective to produce at least some benefits for the urban excluded.

In the same way a number of decisions about the distribution of water supply in the urban areas, the siting of official and voluntary clinics, urban and rural transport, even administered prices for foodstuffs are issues that have a degree of administrative flexibility that too often goes by default because the views of the excluded are simply not articulated. Local politicians are usually too compromised to express those views. It is only when the structure of local political power makes some political figures dependent upon the excluded that their priorities are given a serious hearing.

There are other potential groups—radical students, radical clergy, even the despised middle-class do-gooders—who can manipulate the structures on behalf of the excluded. This raises the wider question of the position of the privileged who do, at least in part, appreciate the nature of the system that secures for them an inequitable proportion of benefits. Throughout this volume, we have dealt, in rather gross terms, with "the interests of the ruling groups," without analysing the conflicts and different levels of both consciousness and power within those groups. We do not want to ignore the possibilities of a radicalized (ex-"liberal") bourgeoisie that welcomes reductions in its own standard of living in favour of the excluded and will put its political weight behind moves in that direction. Indeed, vestiges of such groups are discernible in most of the countries we have studied. But they are (perhaps inevitably) very small, socially and politically isolated, and highly vulnerable to counter-pressure from those who uphold the existing interests. We do not assume that a wider appreciation of the reality of the system among its (perhaps largely ignorant) beneficiaries would bring about a major redistribution of benefits or redesign of the total system.

A further problem with the potential allies is that they are proxies and are easily dismissed as such. Some at least are learning the value (and frustration) of the role of facilitating or enabling the fragile leadership that may exist, particularly among the urban excluded to use the structures. (Zoto and Mathare Valley are the outstanding examples here; in a rural context, the National Federation of Sugar Workers in Negros is a less proven case.) It may well be that the best hope, particularly in the urban areas, is for the rapid spread of this role and associated techniques to generate not (perhaps for a very long time) a real grass-roots political "class" of the excluded but rather spokesmen who can extract what flexibility there is within the existing structures and use that experience to demand and achieve yet more flexibility.

The second pressure point is the technological. Again, it is important to be clear that any technical change is likely to bring benefits that are easily subverted by existing privileged groups. But we have isolated a number of areas in which technical progress would either make the removal of biases easier or would, under optimum conditions, actually construct an equity dynamic in favour of the excluded. The most obvious example is in raising productivity in dry land farming by the development of technologies that are readily adoptable by "less progressive" farmers. Inter-cropping techniques, complementarities between small stock and labour-intensive crops, and a re-examination of famine or "inferior" crops (of which manioc is the obvious example) are three leading areas.

But perhaps more fundamental than anything else is the rupture of the dependence upon international standards and international approval of local technical developments. In many fields, from education to water supply, from industrial technology to social welfare, we have seen how, even in countries that have been relatively successful in breaking many patterns inherited from the colonial past, technological dependence remains unchallenged. It is beyond the immediate purview of this volume to examine in detail either the reasons for that dependence or the ways in which it may be broken. Our emphasis is upon the fact that some of the biases analysed can be much reduced by the development and application of technologies that in embryo probably exist already. They are neglected because there is no incentive to develop them. But it does not follow that, where they are developed, there is fundamental resistance to their adoption. As we emphasized in Chapter 12, administrators are necessarily (and in a sense rightly) risk averters. If they are not expected to underwrite technical risks, much of the resistance to the use of "poor-biased" technologies is likely to disappear.

We do not overestimate the technical flexibility of administrators. The political constraints within which they choose the technology they use are all too clear; so are the vested interests of those selling or otherwise profiting from existing technological packages. In other words, the development of "poor-biased" technology is seldom a sufficient condition of their application; but it is a necessary condition.

This raises the third pressure point—namely, the many interfaces between the privileged in the poor countries and the international community at large. To what extent can the international community legitimately remove some of the biases we have analysed? A logically prior question is why the international community should seek to do so. That is a question we do not propose to discuss exhaustively here. There has been a resurgence of interest in the distribution of income and consumption amongst "development experts." This is slowly being communicated at other interfaces e.g., the professional (doctors, teachers, agriculturists, agronomists) and the commercial (at least some multinationals are aware that equity-weighted policies do not necessarily imply the abolition of all profit-making opportunities, and may in fact create them). Our suggestion would be that, again within limits, this re-orientation of international interests could affect both access and the distribution of benefits profoundly.

To take one simple example: The efficiency algorithm we have identified as one of the major biases against the excluded, particularly in the rural areas, can be transformed by the very simple technique of differential weighting for the incomes of the poor. In the past, this has not been common, primarily because economists were so captivated by growth that they temporarily lost interest in equity in their own countries and elsewhere. Now that it is on the way to becoming a new orthodoxy, one can foresee a situation in which one of the most powerful tools of economic analysis not only acquires a bias towards the excluded but also a certainty of application. For foreign funding agencies, from the World Bank to non-governmental organizations, can increasingly put pressure upon planning bureaus at least to abandon the assumption that all income streams are equally important irrespective of who owns them.

There are wider implications. Once it is known that international finance is available for "poverty programmes," planning offices can be expected to generate a plethora of such programmes. Many of these will be bad. They will nonetheless be funded by international agencies anxious to refurbish their image. That is part of the politics of aid and should not be allowed to engender a total cynicism. Even international institutions are, within limits, elastic and can be stretched by the process of making mistakes and being criticized for them.

Of much more serious concern is the fact that the present fashion for "poverty planning" is foredoomed to failure, at least to unnecessary disappointment, because it assumes that the eradication of poverty can be planned from central planning offices. While much can be learned of the mechanisms of impoverishment by rational enquiry "from on top," the overthrow of those mechanisms is unlikely to be achieved by the central organs of government. Put another way, the fear is that "poverty planning" will be the international equivalent of the kind of policies that we have described in Malaysia—with emphasis not on the redistribution of existing assets and the restructuring of the relationships within which those assets are used but on "redistribution from growth," which leaves the mechanisms of inter-group competition fundamentally unchanged.[3] The biases in access and selection may be shifted, but the mechanisms of the distribution of the product at every level, from village to international, may be left intact. To put it at its simplest, it is easier for an international organization to increase the rate at which new land is brought into cultivation, and even to remove some of the most obvious biases against distribution of that land to the poorest, than it is to smash the structures of village monopoly/monopsony that are a major cause of impoverishment, even for those who own the new assets. To that extent, the impact of poverty planning, whether it is initiated at international or national level, must not be exaggerated. Despite all the difficulties and all the political and administrative resistance, the incorporation of the excluded themselves into the process of poverty planning is a necessary precondition of its success.

Finally, we have cast the discussion in this chapter in terms of the original frame without considering the future of the system as such. We do so deliberately for, as we emphasized at the end of Chapter 1, the nature of the system is survival. That is the fundamental raison d'etre of the access, transfers, and conmechs. It is our belief that, despite all the turbulence and political instability of the last fifteen years in the countries we have reviewed (there is scarcely one that has not seemed on the brink of breakdown at some time during that period), the basic self-interest of the privileged is to ensure that, whatever modifications have to be made, the system as such survives. Confidence in the various mechanisms of enrichment has to be restored. The legitimacy of the system as a whole, and the ruling groups in particular, has to be protected. The distribution of benefits has to be such as commands at least the passive acceptance of most of the privileged and some of the excluded for the majority of the time. For this reason, we see no likelihood that, short of massive breakdowns in confidence (as were certainly near in Sri Lanka in 1971 and the Philippines in 1971-72), the system itself will be in danger.

This implies, then, that in our view the revolutionary potential in these countries is small and that reform through the pressure points we have outlined represents the best, though meagre, chance of redistributing both product and mobility in favour of the poor. The strategic question is how the pressure at these points can be maximized.

It follows from all we have said that in our view the most creative way forward is not through "poverty planning," as urged by the World Bank on the central planning agencies of government, but rather through the enablement of the excluded (most immediately through their leadership and bourgeois allies) to see for themselves the nature of the system in which they are caught and the ways in which that system can be used for their ultimate advantage.

If the con-mech is one of the major structural devices that both holds the system together and distributes products and mobility to the rich, it is the erosion of confidence in the existing mechanisms that will bring about the most rapid redistribution of both. In our belief, it is to that erosion that local and international effort can most fruitfully be addressed.

NOTES

1. Jael D. Barkan, "African University Students and Social Change: An Analysis of Student Opinion in Ghana, Tanzania and Uganda," doctoral dissertation, University of California at Los Angeles, 1970.

2. G. Williams, "Political Consciousness among the Ibadan Poor," and Adrian Peace, "Industrial Protest in Nigeria," both in *Sociology and Development,* eds. E. de Kadt and G. Williams (London: Tavistock, 1974).

3. International Labour Organization, *Employment, Incomes and Equality: A Strategy for Increasing Productive Employment in Kenya,* report of an inter-agency team financed by the United Nations Development Programme and organized by the ILO (Geneva: ILO, 1972).

The index of total production was calculated using the following crops: plantains (matoke), maize, groundnuts, sweet potatoes, beans, and cassava.

For year t and i crops,

$$\text{the index} = \Sigma_i \, \text{Quantity}_t \times \text{Price}_t$$

where the quantity produced was calculated by using the acreages of food crops in the appropriate year and the estimated yields of major food crops in Uganda, 1963 (from V.F. Amann, D.G.R. Belshaw, and J.P. Stanfield, *Nutrition and Food in an African Economy,* Kampala: Makerere University, 1972, vol. I, Table 10, IV: "Esimated yields of major food crops in Uganda"). The 1963 yields had to be used for all years as more detailed information was not available.

The Chain Laspeyre Production Index for year t (1961 = 100.0) was calculated from the formula:

$$\frac{\Sigma_i q^i_{1961} p^i_{1965}}{\Sigma_i q^i_{1961} p^i_{1961}} \times \frac{\Sigma_i q^i_{1965} p^i_{1966}}{\Sigma_i q^i_{1965} p^i_{1965}} \times \frac{\Sigma_i q^i_{(t-1)} p^i_t}{\Sigma_i q^i_{(t-1)} p^i_{(t-1)}} \times 100.0$$

It should be noted that this is not the true Chain Laspeyre Price Index due to the four-year gap from 1961 to 1965 and the two-year gap from January 1965 to December 1966 necessitated by incomplete data.

The cost-of-loving index was calculated by using information from the Statistics Division on prices in Kampala.

The weights used for each commodity were taken from the government worksheet and were kept the same for all years. Each sub-section was weighted to give the cost-of-living index using constant weightings obtained from the *Survey of Buganda Coffee Growers 1962/63,* Appendix III. Statistics Division, Ministry of Planning and Economic Development, *The Patterns of Income and Expenditure of Coffee Growers in Buganda, 1962/63,* Kampala, 1967.

For a sensitivity test, the maximum and minimum weightings were taken and a non-food index calculated for both these. These indexes followed the same trend and were insensitive to any plausible change in weights.

Two income terms of trade were calculated, one from the total production index and the cost-of-living index, and the other from the production index deflated by a 3 percent per annum rural population growth rate and the cost-of-

living index. Those years with December data (1966/70) were deflated by the
3 percent growth figure relevant to the January of the following year.

CHARLES ELLIOTT is Senior Research Associate at the School of Development Studies, University of East Anglia, England. A distinguished economist, Dr. Elliott has been involved with development affairs in Zambia and has been active with international organizations in London and Geneva. He has contributed to numerous books and journals of economics and African issues, and is the author of *The Development Debate*. Dr. Elliott studied at Oxford University, and was ordained Priest of the Church of England.

FOOD, POPULATION, AND EMPLOYMENT: The Impact of
the Green Revolution

> edited by
> Thomas T. Poleman
> Donald K. Freebairn

LEGAL AID AND WORLD POVERTY: A Survey of Asia,
Africa, and Latin America

> Committee on Legal Services
> to the Poor in Developing
> Countries

WORLD POPULATION CRISIS: The United States Response

> Phyllis Tilson Piotrow

DEVELOPMENT IN RICH AND POOR COUNTRIES: A General
Theory with Statistical Analyses

> Thorkil Kristensen

EDUCATION AND DEVELOPMENT RECONSIDERED: The
Bellagio Conference Papers

> Ford Foundation/Rockefeller
> Foundation
> edited by F. Champion Ward

ECONOMIC GROWTH IN DEVELOPING COUNTRIES—MATERIAL
AND HUMAN RESOURCES: Proceedings of the Seventh Rehevot
Conference

> edited by
> Yohanan Ramati

THE PUBLIC ADMINISTRATION OF ECONOMIC DEVELOPMENT

> Irving Swerdlow